Living in the Shadow
of the Freud Family

Living in the Shadow of the Freud Family

WRITTEN AND EDITED BY
SOPHIE FREUD

With contributions from
ESTI FREUD, Walter Freud, George Loewenstein,
Andrea Freud Loewenstein, Caroline Freud Penney
and David Freud (obituary)

With letters from
Esti Freud, Sophie Freud, Charlotte Kronheim,
Sigmund Freud, Martha Freud, Martin Freud, Walter Freud,
Harry Freud, Ida Drucker, Lily Boyko, Marianne Zittau
and Amalia Seitz

PRAEGER

Westport, Connecticut
London

Library of Congress Cataloging-in-Publication Data

Freud, Sophie, 1924–
    Living in the shadow of the Freud family / Sophie Freud.
        p. cm.
    Includes bibliographical references and index.
    ISBN 0-275-99415-5 (alk. paper)
    1. Freud, Sophie, 1924–   2. Jews—Austria—Vienna—Biography.
3. Speech therapists—Biography.   4. Jews, Austrian—France—Biography.
5. Refugees, Jewish—France—Biography.   6. Holocaust, Jewish (1939–1945)—
Personal narratives.   7. Holocaust survivors—United States—Biography.
8. Vienna (Austria)—Biography.   9. Freud family. I. Title.
    DS135.A93F735   2007
    940.53′18092—dc22
    [B]   2006038815

British Library Cataloguing in Publication Data is available.

Library of Congress Catalog Card Number: 2006038815
ISBN-10: 0-275-99415-5
ISBN-13: 978-0-275-99415-0

First published in 2007

Praeger Publishers, 88 Post Road West, Westport, CT 06881
An imprint of Greenwood Publishing Group, Inc.
www.praeger.com

Printed in the United States of America

The paper used in this book complies with the
Permanent Paper Standard issued by the National
Information Standards Organization (Z39.48–1984).

10   9   8   7   6   5   4   3   2   1

Contents

Family Tree Legend

Sigmund Freud—patriarch of the Freud family; Esti's famous father-in-law; Sophie's famous grandfather

Martha (Bernays) Freud—Sigmund Freud's wife; Esti's mother-in-law; Sophie's paternal grandmother

Esti Drucker Freud—daughter-in-law to Sigmund Freud; wife to Martin, eldest son and second child of Sigmund and Martha

Martin Freud—Sigmund and Martha's second child and oldest son; Esti's husband and father to Sophie and Walter

Sophie Freud—author and granddaughter to Sigmund; daughter to Esti and Martin Freud

Paul Loewenstein—Sophie Freud's longtime husband

The following family members are listed alphabetically by first name:

Adolf Schrameck—Esti's maternal grandfather (the other famous grandfather)

Alexander Freud—Sigmund Freud's younger and only brother

Amalia Freud—Sigmund Freud's mother; Sophie's great-grandmother

Andrea Freud Loewenstein—great-grandchild to Sigmund; granddaughter to Esti and oldest child of Sophie and Paul Loewenstein

Anna Freud (Tante Anna)—Sigmund and Martha's youngest child and third daughter; Esti's sister-in-law and Sophie's aunt

Annette (Krarup) Freud—Walter Freud's Danish wife; Esti's daughter-in-law; Sophie's sister-in-law

Anton (Toni) Walter Freud—grandson to Sigmund; son to Esti and Martin; brother to Sophie

Bea(trice) Boyko—daughter of Lily and Rudy Boyko; Esti's niece; Sophie's cousin

Caroline Freud—Sigmund's great-granddaughter; Esti's granddaughter; Sophie's niece; daughter of Walter and Annette

Dania (Loewenstein) Jekel—great-grandchild to Sigmund; granddaughter to Esti; second daughter to Sophie and Paul Loewenstein ("the blond one")

David Freud—Sigmund's great-grandson; Esti's grandson; Sophie's nephew; son of Walter and Annette ("the sweetest baby")

Dorothy Burlingham—Anna Freud's partner

Edward Bernays—Sigmund's nephew; son of Eli Bernays and Anna Freud Bernays; benefactor to Sophie

Eli Bernays—Sigmund's brother-in-law; husband to Sigmund's oldest sister, Anna

Ernestine Ehrenzweig Schramek—Esti's grandmother; Ida's mother, who died shortly after giving birth to son Bernhardt

Ernst Freud—Sigmund and Martha's fourth child and third son; Martin's brother; Esti's brother-in-law

Eva Freud—granddaughter to Sigmund and Martha; only child of Oliver and Henny Freud

George Loewenstein ("Martin's ghost")—Sophie and Paul's third child, first son; Esti's grandson; Sigmund's great-grandson

Harry Freud—nephew to Sigmund; son of Alexander and Sophie Freud; (family caretaker)

Heinele Halberstadt—Sigmund's Freud's favorite grandchild; Sophie and Max Halberstadt's second son

Heinrich (Henry) Zittau—"honorable" brother-in-law to Esti; husband to Marianne Zittau

Henny Freud—Sigmund and Martha's daughter-in-law; Oliver Freud's wife

Herbert Zittau—son of Heinrich and Marianne Zittau; Esti's nephew; Sophie's cousin

Ida Freud—Sigmund's great-granddaughter; Esti's granddaughter; Sophie's niece; daughter of Walter and Annette Freud

Ida (Schramek) Drucker—mother of Esti; Sophie's maternal grandmother (killed in Auschwitz)

Jacob Freud—Sigmund Freud's father

Julius Drucker—uncle to Esti; brother to her father

Leopold Drucker—father of Esti; Sophie's maternal grandfather

Lily Drucker Boyko (Tante Lily)—Esti's sister; Sophie's aunt; second daughter of Leopold and Ida Drucker

Lucie (Lux) Freud—Sigmund and Martha's daughter-in-law; Ernst Freud's wife

Margaret Freud—Martin Freud's partner in England, while married to Esti; adopted by Martin Freud

Marianne Drucker Zittau (Tante Janne)—Esti's youngest sister

Mathilde Freud Hollitscher—Sigmund and Martha's daughter and oldest child; Esti's sister-in-law

Max Drucker and Sidonie—grandparents to Esti; parents to Leopold Drucker

Max Halberstadt—Sigmund and Martha's son-in-law; Sigmund's daughter Sophie's husband

Oliver Freud—Sigmund and Martha's third child and second son; Esti's brother-in-law; Sophie's uncle

Regine Morgenstern Schramek—Esti's step-grandmother; Adolf Drucker's second wife; Ida Drucker's stepmother

Robert Hollitscher—Sigmund and Martha's son-in-law; Mathilde Freud's husband

Rosa Graf, Mitzi Freud, Dolfie Freud, and Pauline Winternitz—Sigmund Freud's sisters; Sophie's great aunts ("the murdered old aunts")

Rudi Boyko—Esti's other "honorable" brother-in-law; husband of Lily Boyko

Sophie Freud—Sigmund Freud's sister-in-law; Alexander Freud's wife

Sophie Freud Halberstadt—Sigmund and Martha's fifth child and second daughter; Esti's sister-in-law; Sophie's aunt, whom she was named after

A Drucker-Freud Family Tree

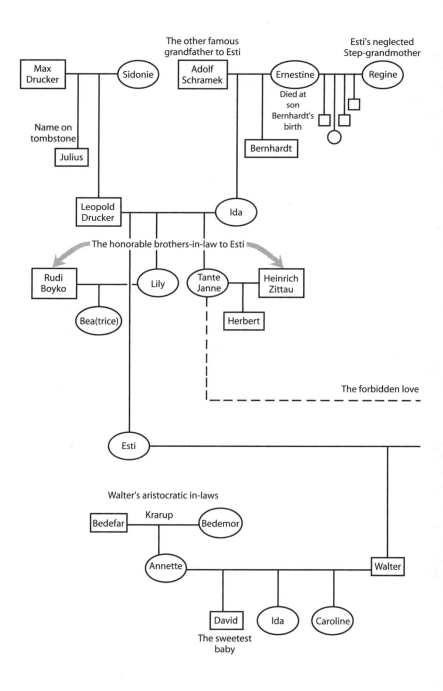

The other famous grandfather to Esti

Esti's neglected Step-grandmother

Max Drucker — Sidonie — Adolf Schramek — Ernestine — Regine

Died at son Bernhardt's birth

Name on tombstone

Julius

Bernhardt

Leopold Drucker — Ida

The honorable brothers-in-law to Esti

Rudi Boyko — Lily — Tante Janne — Heinrich Zittau

Bea(trice)

Herbert

The forbidden love

Esti

Walter's aristocratic in-laws

Bedefar — Krarup — Bedemor

Annette — Walter

David — Ida — Caroline

The sweetest baby

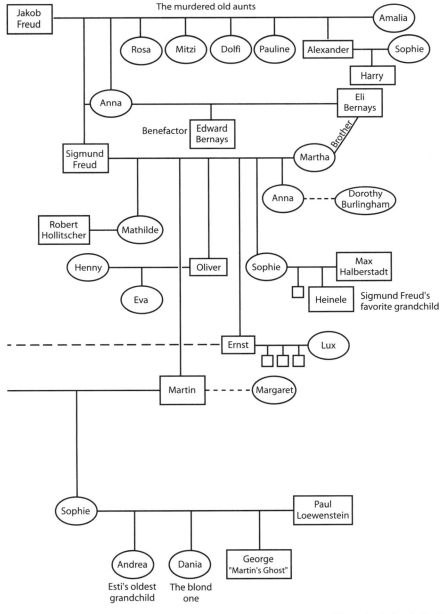

The murdered old aunts

Jakob Freud — Amalia

Rosa · Mitzi · Dolfi · Pauline · Alexander — Sophie

Harry

Anna — Eli Bernays

Benefactor Edward Bernays

Sigmund Freud — Martha *Brother*

Anna - - - Dorothy Burlingham

Robert Hollitscher — Mathilde

Henny — Oliver

Eva

Sophie — Max Halberstadt

☐ Heinele — Sigmund Freud's favorite grandchild

Ernst — Lux

☐ ☐ ☐

Martin - - - Margaret

Sophie — Paul Loewenstein

Andrea · Dania · George "Martin's Ghost"

Esti's oldest grandchild · The blond one

(Illustration by Brooks Hart)

A Long Voyage

With my 81 years, I am already two years older than my mother was when she wrote her autobiography at the age of 79. She did so at my urging. She found it to be an exciting and absorbing task. Eventually she sent her manuscript—*Vignettes of My Life*—to her two children and six grandchildren. Most of us were disappointed, or worse yet, dismissive, or worse yet, disapproving. My son, in his characteristic style, pronounced it "a depressing document of a life nearly devoid of love. The main sentiments expressed are envy, revenge, bitterness, bigotry, etc." My brother's opinion was even less charitable; we are a very critical family.

I was mostly overwhelmed and saddened by how much my mother's conviction acquired in childhood and confirmed by her marriage, that she was not lovable, dominated her life. I had known that for a long time, of course, but are there not new ways of understanding the same facts ever more deeply?

Mother's manuscript was put into the bookcase, next to a thousand other books, yet not quite forgotten. In 1997, thus 17 years after Mother's death, I received an honorable invitation from Professor Stein Bråten to spend a few months at the Institute for Higher Studies in Oslo, Norway, working on a project of my choice. I decided, or rather something in me decided to transcribe Mother's engagement letters into the computer. These letters were a package of about 40 letters that Mother had written over one year, to her fiancé, my future father, first to him at his army post and then to him while he was prisoner of war in Italy for nine months. I had already once read them in my youth in Nice and then found these letters in her estate. Mother had thus brought this package of her own letters from Vienna to Paris, to Nice, to Casablanca, and finally to New York City. After such a long trip, I wanted to rescue these letters for the future. My father's responses were not in the package and could not be found elsewhere.

This interesting endeavor lasted more than the two months in Oslo, even though I often worked into the night; the letters were written in gothic German and difficult to decipher.

I thus decided to write a chronicle of Mother's life, a life that extended almost over the whole twentieth century and that was shaped to a certain extent by its turbulent events. Yet I did not write this book in a few months, as Mother had done; instead it has accompanied me for the last eight years, at times in the background, but lately very much in the foreground. I retired from work during those years and became *a pensioner*. The book project helped me with this difficult transition. It gave meaning to my suddenly senseless life; it has become my closest friend in these somewhat solitary years. The endeavor lasted so long that toward the end I was worried that my age would defeat me before I could finish its conception—thus, it was a race between a piece of work and my aging brain, in which my drive to work, trained through many years, did win after all.

The more I delved into this endeavor, the more new fields opened up. I found documents in archives in Vienna about my mother's grandparents, especially about her rich grandfather, the coal merchant Adolf Schramek who had a synagogue built with his own money. Adolf Schramek, I learned, was married twice. The first time to Ernestine (Ehrenzweig) who gave birth to two children, my grandmother Ida and a son Bernhard after whose birth she died. A few months after his wife's death the 30-year-old widower then married 17-year-old Regine (Morgenstern) who in the next five years bore him three sons and one daughter. But my brother and I never had occasion, in my 14 years and his 18 years in Vienna, to meet these relatives.

Matters were different with mother's sisters whom we came to know quite well. My aunts' families did not live in Vienna, but they came quite frequently to visit their parents and thus our family next door, as well. Tante Lily was married to the coal merchant Rudi Boyko and lived in Prague; Tante "Janne" (Marianne) was married to the rich bank director Heinrich Zittau and lived first in Berlin and later in Paris. The first had a daughter Bea(trice), two years older than I, and Tante Janne's son Herbert was born one month before me, he in July and myself in August 1924. These aunts and cousins later played an important role in our lives, as the three sisters found themselves together, first in Paris and then again in New York City.

Relationships with my father's older relatives differed from those we had with the unknown Drucker/Schramek ancestors. I still knew

Grandfather's old mother, Amalia Freud. She also lived in the Leopoldstadt where my grandfather had grown up. Well, I did not "know" her, but we visited her once a year, perhaps for her birthday. All I remember is that we were told not to call her great-grandmother because that would make her feel too old. She died at age 95 when I was six years old. I regularly met four of Grandfather's five sisters, my great-aunts, and his brother Alexander, the last child born in that family, at the Sunday morning family gatherings at the Berggasse. My memories of "the old aunts" are blurred, perhaps because I never met them as individual people. They are now bound up, in my mind, with their desperate old years after Grandfather's departure from Vienna and their subsequent cruel deaths in concentration camps. Strangely, Freud's flat at Berggasse 19 was used by the Nazis as a transit station—called *Sammelwohnung*—for Jews expelled from their apartments and relocated there, before their final deportation to death camps. All four sisters had been cooped up in one room, along with other people, in such an apartment at the Biberstraße where one of them lived. They almost starved, since the money that their brother, my grandfather, had left them was confiscated—I mean robbed—by the authorities. Many people had come to Vienna to help my grandfather emigrate into safety, but the old aunts were not as important as their famous brother; they were only ordinary uninteresting women and were left behind.

Only Aunt Rosa stands out a bit because she was hard of hearing and one had to raise one's voice when talking to her. Poor Aunt Rosa Graf lost not only her son in World War I, but also her other child, her daughter Caecilia, who committed suicide when she found herself pregnant while unmarried. There were thus no children who might have looked after their old mother. Aunt Dolphi, I was told, could not get married because she had to take care of her old mother, but Aunt Mitzi and Aunt Paula had husbands and children whom I never met. Could it be that my aunts were widows by the time I saw them weekly? Uncle Alexander, his wife Sophie, and their son Harry—who would later become the caring family switchboard, also communicating with Mother during the war—are much more distinct in my memory.

Only one of Sigmund Freud's sisters escaped murder in a concentration camp: Anna, his oldest sister, the sister who was not allowed to practice the piano because it got on her brother's nerves. Anna married Eli Bernays, grandmother Martha Bernays's brother, and the young couple, viewed as unpromising, was shipped off to America. Eli became a rich man in America and was even in the position of helping the Freud family with food parcels

during World War I. Anna Bernays lived 97 years and died in honor and pros-
perity. The third of her five children and her only son Edward Bernays
became known as *the father of public relations* and a much honored and wealthy
man. He would come generously to my aid by paying my college tuition.

I have a vivid memory of Grandmother Freud's sister, Tante Minna,
who joined the Freud family after her fiancé had died of tuberculosis. She
did not belong to the "old aunts" but always sat at a little table and played
solitaire. But, in fact, she was viewed as a second mother in that household.

Part of the "family Freud" were of course also my father's five brothers
and sisters, although aside from my father only two out of the six children,
the oldest and the youngest (both daughters), had stayed in Vienna. Aunt
Mathilde, the oldest, born 1887, was married but could not have children for
health reasons. Her husband was Robert Hollitscher, a businessman 12 years
older, the family pessimist whose somber prophecies always came true.
Tante Mathilde had to be visited once a year for her birthday. I was warned,
unnecessarily so, to be well behaved and polite and there was much curtsey-
ing. Next in line was my father, the oldest son, who was born in 1889.

I had only fleeting contact with my father's two younger brothers, Uncle
Oli and Uncle Ernst, during their visits to their parents. Both brothers lived
first in Berlin and had married German women, respectively, Hennie Fuchs
and Lucie Brasch. Uncle Ernst met my Tante Janne in Berlin, an encounter
that led to a forbidden love affair. Uncle Ernst's family emigrated to England
after Hitler's ascent to power from where they could helpfully welcome their
parents, my grandparents, in London in June 1938. One of Ernst's sons,
Lucian, has become one of the most famous painters of our time. I had very
little contact with these cousins.

Uncle Oli had one daughter, Eva, who was exactly my age. He emigrated with his family from Berlin to Nice where he opened a photography
shop. I only came to know my cousin Eva when we took refuge in Nice during the war, maybe precisely because we had relatives there, although
Mother naturally disliked Aunt Henny. Eva survived the war by herself, in
France, under a false identity but died of toxemia after an (illegal) abortion,
very soon after the war had ended.

Finally, we come to Aunt Sophie, the fifth child, who had the reputation
of being the loveliest-looking daughter of the family. At age 20, in 1913, she
married the photographer Max Halberstadt who lived in Hamburg and one
year later had her son Ernst, Freud's first grandchild. Sophie became a victim
of the European postwar influenza epidemic and died in 1920. I was named
after her. Her second son, Heinele, Grandfather's favorite grandchild, died

three years later, in 1923, from a form of tuberculosis. Ernst Halberstadt—who later called himself Ernest Freud—came to live with his grandparents in Vienna after his mother's death, but I had little contact even with this paternal cousin, and only came to know him much later during my one-year sabbatical stay in London.

My father's only sister who continued to live with the family was my Aunt Anna, the youngest child in the family (born in 1895). My grandmother thus had six children in eight years. I had hardly any contact with Tante Anna in Vienna, but when I sought her out in London, in 1979, only a few years before her death in 1982, I grew to love her passionately and came to call her *my third mother*, in my mind and in writing about her. I met her this second time soon after her companion of more than 40 years, Dorothy Burlingham, had died, and she was thus perhaps more open to my great love for her.

Mother and Tante Anna and Uncle Oli were friends while Father was a prisoner of war in Italy, but the friendships did not last later on. It strikes me that in spite of a quite large extended family I had, during my first 14 years in Vienna, few close relations to any of these relatives apart from my adoring love for my grandfather.

The next step in the development of this book were the digging up of Mother's letters, journal articles, and other documents that I had found in her estate and preserved quite carefully. Most of those were of course in German. I was delighted when three of my diaries, which I had kept during the war years, also in German, appeared among my old papers. Although I wanted to keep Mother in the center of this book, it inevitably became the story of that part of my own life that I spent alone with her, in the early years of the war, as described in my diaries. Mother had even kept the letters I had sent her from my first difficult semester at Radcliffe College. They could almost be viewed as an extension of my diaries for which I had, by then, either no time or no interest.

After a long search, I found what I regard as my most important documents, the four French letters that Charlotte Kronheim had sent to me from Nizza to Casablanca, which suggest in her low-key voice the murder of the Jews of Southern France. She had hoped that we would safely reach America so that I could inform the world, one day, of the nature of these devastating times. I am happy that I can keep, with this book, almost at the last moment, my promise to her.

Two of my children, George Loewenstein and Andrea Freud Loewenstein, were ready to contribute to this book. They are both university professors and have written books of their own. My third child, Dania Jekel, the blond one in the story, detests to reveal private matters to the whole world.

I bear special gratitude to my brother, from whom I had been sadly estranged again and again through our lives, but who sent me his memories of our mother as a token of our last-minute reconciliation. I used his *Ernestine* in pieces, wherever they fit, as I have done with all my material.

The most surprising event of this book journey relates to him. My brother, Anton Walter Freud, lived in an unusually happy marriage with Annette Krarup, a Danish, naturally non-Jewish woman whom he had met at the end of the war. Each of their three children, David Freud, Ida Fairbairn, and Caroline Penney, gave their parents all their lives more joy than worry, which I also regard as an unusually happy circumstance. My brother was born in April 1921 and died February 2004, with 83 years, being one year younger than Mother was at her death. He had kept all his correspondence and his children found in his estate the many letters that Mother had sent him. They generously put these letters at my disposal for this book. Moreover, Caroline remembered Mother's fatal visit at her son's aristocratic parents-in-law and gifted me with her recollections, allowing me to finally understand the circumstances of those events. The book, by then three-quarters finished, suddenly had to undergo massive revisions. At this point, I can no longer imagine the book without this last contribution. The scaffold of the book, Mother's own manuscript, has remained the same, but these letters written from 1938 until her death, apart from the 10 years in which her son punished her with silence, are almost a second testimony of her life, a more honest and less polished account, albeit still a public self-representation. It is my hope that these different self-representations, as well as my brother's voice, and sometimes my father's writings and my own diaries, raise the question of our memories—how the same experiences are remembered, interpreted, and passed on by the heroes of their own lives.

I knew nothing of these many letters; the active correspondence between Mother and Walter was almost a secret. I had thought that I had been, to my chagrin, Mother's most important human relationship, maybe even her only significant connection. The discovery of these letters changed this picture. Mother was after all connected to both of her children, in her own way, with one, myself, through the telephone, with the other, my brother, through letters.

Naturally, I had to make a selection among so many documents. I used tedium and repetition as criteria but never omitted unpleasant truths. I wrote, for example, thoughts in my diaries and letters that I now experience as silly and embarrassing, but in my eyes, embellishments and dishonesties would make this whole enterprise meaningless.

I did intersperse Mother's manuscript with different voices, but I tried most of the time not to change the sequence of her writing. She divided her manuscript into nine chapters, which I have called parts, while dividing each part into my own new chapters.

Our lives were lived in three different languages and we often used a mixtures of languages and none necessarily correctly. Translation into one language unfortunately distorts the important experiences and events that dealt with the changing languages. My mother's autobiography had been written in English, as had Walter's *Ernestine*, but many of her letters, and my wartime diary and other letters and documents, had been written in German. As a bilingual person I felt in the best position to do all the translation into English for this book. I have indicated the original language of each letter and tried to reproduce the style and even punctuation of all the German material to the best of my ability.

Apologia

During my stay at the Institute of Higher Studies in Oslo I once read to my colleagues of different disciplines and from different countries one of Mother's engagement letters, specifically the one in which she solemnly accepts Martin's marriage proposal. One of my colleagues, a taciturn Norwegian, said he would now go home and burn all his saved-up letters. Another (woman) colleague who was exceptionally close to her mother opined that I did not have the ethical right to write about the life of a woman whom I had dreaded and kept at a distance during her life. I have thought much about these reactions.

This is already the second book that I have written about mothers. I wrote my first book soon after Mother's death, but at that time I wrote about my three mothers and my own first mother was not necessarily the most loved one. That role belonged, at the time, to my Tante Anna, my "third mother." One chapter in this first book was also an indirect indictment of my father, who, so I thought at the time, perhaps unjustly, had not done his best to assist me in my studies.

This second book now gives me the opportunity to take leave, leave from people whom I finally, with my stony heart, had not loved well enough, like my mother, my father, my brother and my Tante Janne. I now see all these people in a new light, especially my desperate parents, not only Mother, but also Father, and Tante Janne the depth of whose despair I grasped only after writing this book. The latter had been my beloved "second mother," whom I abandoned in her hour of greatest need.

Mother, dying of cancer, complained that there was no one in her life who would make her a cup of tea. "You should have made friends when you were younger," I said. "I had no time for friendships," she responded. "You always wanted to be left in peace (*in Ruhe gelassen*)," I reproached her, "and now you are paying the price of such a choice." I almost quoted the response of the ant in LaFontaine's fable who tells the starving grasshopper in the winter that he had wasted his time singing all summer and now he could dance alone. It is a perspective that I share with the ant, and one not easily divulged, being unbecoming to a professor of social work, but having such a bold and uniquely honest exchange with my mother carried me away. "You are right, I did want to be left in peace, and I am still glad that it worked out that way. All I really want is for someone to make me an occasional cup of tea," she then answered, apparently not offended by my harsh view of life, because it matched her own.

In the 20 years since my first book, in this time of my own aging, I have come closer to Mother. She no longer appears so alien to me; I too want to be left in peace. I chose to divorce a courteous reliable man after 40 years of marriage partly because I could not imagine becoming old with a man at my side. None of my three mothers, Mother, Tante Janne, and Tante Anna, had aged with a man at their side, and I could not contemplate a fate so radically different from theirs. There were different reasons for the divorce as well, but this was one of them. "If you leave me," my husband had said, "you will end up having a lonely old age similar to your mother's." He was right. I live alone and now and then I also feel alone. Others see me as an eccentric old lady. Many cadavers of cutoff relationships litter my life. I also might not have anyone preparing me a cup of tea when I am sick. Well, there are always electric teapots one can rely on.

Mother bequeathed me her energy and self-discipline, along with other less admirable qualities. I am, of course, not exactly like my unhappy mother, because fate has treated me with astonishing kindness, sparing me the harsh struggles that led my mother to draw her own hostile conclusions about the world. But in my new kinship of old age and life review, her thoughts no longer seem so utterly misguided and offensive. Her decision to survive, frequently against formidable obstacles and in many ways successfully so, is truly admirable. Since I have stepped into her shoes to a certain extent, I have come to feel entitled to present her autobiography in my own way. She would have allowed me to do so. This book is the magic bastion Mother has bequeathed me to combat futility in my old age.

Lincoln, Massachusetts
Summer 2005

AUSTRIA

Part I

Childhood

CHAPTER 1

Childhood Memories

Memories of my earliest childhood consist of single unconnected pictures of separate episodes, which for some reason unknown to me survive in my memory. I will try to arrange these memories according to their happenings in time and place.

I must have been just three years old, my sister Lily was still breast-fed, it was summertime, and my father had rented a cottage in Neuwaldegg, a village in the outskirts of Vienna. This was done so that my father could join his family every evening when he left his lawyer's office. I believe the still horse-drawn trolley had its final stop not too far away from where we lived and Father could walk from there to the house. The house and garden are very vague in my memory; however, I remember the garden gate on which I used to stand and rock it open and closed; in doing this I felt very brave and enterprising.

I know that we already had our Iglauer Nanny who stayed 12 years with us. I think she came to our house when I was just two. With her and my baby sister, I went for walks in the beautiful *Schwarzenbergpark,* which was open to the public, and walked in the meadows to look for some special herb (*Tausendguldenkraut*) that when infused made a very bitter drink, which Nanny thought had healing powers for stomach aches. I had to look all over the meadow for this tiny pink blossom, which later on I never found again in my life. I put the plants in the pram, and Nanny took them to be dried. One day, I don't know why, I took all the already-collected plants out of the pram when Nanny wasn't looking and carried them around with me while looking for other plants. I don't remember if I found any, but after a while I went back to the pram with my handful of herbs. Nanny thought that I had

Esti as a toddler in Vienna

just collected all of them and told me that I was really very good. She became quite angry with me when she found out that these were the plants already collected before, and she accused me of having lost some of them by carrying them around.

The other episode from this summer, still very vivid before me, is when I was bitten by a donkey. The donkey delivered the milk for the household and my grandfather, the father of my father, must have been visiting with us because he showed me how to give sugar to the donkey so that he won't bite. You had to hold the hand out quite flat and put the sugar lump on the palm. I did, but my hand was too small and my fingers came in between the teeth of the donkey.

This is the only time I remember my grandfather Drucker. Grandfather Drucker had a nice white beard; but I do not have a picture of him, nor of my grandmother whom I remember, however, very well. I don't know when my grandfather died; my grandmother passed away when I was 10 or 11 years old. Grandfather and Grandmother were unhappily married. As I could piece it together, the reasons were manifold. My grandfather was a ladies' man, he wrote poetry in the style of Heinrich Heine and my father used to show me a little volume of poems written by my grandfather. I believe I read them, but they were not as good as Heine's. The other reasons for the marital discord of my grandparents seemed to have been financial. My grandfather who lived in Brünn—at this time the still German-speaking capital of the province of Moravia (in the old Austrian Empire)—had beet-sugar factories. He refused to join the sugar cartel and consequently was ruined in this economic warfare. I believe that my grandmother lost her property too—they probably were married under common property laws—their oldest son, my uncle Julius, was drawn to rack and ruin, and the family could never recover from that financial disaster.

My personal recollection does not place my paternal grandparents in Brünn, but as living in a small rural town in Eastern Slovakia (Trenzcin) at this time still part of Hungary. There they lived, at least I remember my grandmother living there, in a big old house without plumbing in what seemed to me large dark rooms with old-fashioned furniture, surrounded by what seemed to me many uncles and aunts. When we were a little older, we used to spend a few weeks every fall in my grandmother's house. Trenzcin is an important place in my childhood memories.

Summer 1900 is the next childhood episode I can think off. It was the year of the Paris world fair, my parents went to Paris and we two children were left with my maternal grandparents in Vöslau, a small summer resort place near Vienna. I had a maternal grandfather, but a step-grandmother, my real grandmother having died in childbirth of her second child, when my mother was three years old. [*She had actually been five years old.*]

The scene I remember: I was walking with my Nanny and little sister in the pram holding on the skirts of my Nanny in order not to get lost. There was no room on the sidewalk for some time and I walked in the gutter. There came a place, where a drain was built into the gutter, which was protected by metal spikes protruding like dragon teeth. I ran into one of these spikes and injured my knee. Although it hurt, I did not say anything to Nanny because she used to say when I complained about something, "don't make a fuss." I bravely walked on, but soon passers-by were looking astonished. "The child is bleeding all over the place," one of them told Nanny. I don't know what happened from then on. Since the prongs were part of the sewer system, I could have died of tetanus. I couldn't walk for a time and limped around, although they wanted to make me walk when my parents returned from Paris. There I suffered another great disappointment; my mother had brought to my sister, who was then one year old, a beautiful bonnet with embroidered frills, whereas I received a rubber ball. I was too grown up for a bonnet, I was told.

During this summer, I also remember having started to learn how to swim. Vöslau is famous for its warm springs and a number of swimming pools with spring water of a very pleasant temperature were installed for the entertainment and pleasure of the summer guests and local people. At this time, mixed bathing was taboo and the sexes had different hours. However, there was a small pool reserved for only children and ladies where one could bathe at any hour of the day. This is the pool I remember. High wooden fences were built around the pools so that any curious people were prevented from looking inside, especially during ladies' hours.

Once I was hanging at the rope of the swimming instructor when a ball of knitting yarn of one of the ladies sitting near the pool rolled into the water. I dashed after it and appeared not to come back. The instructor was having a chat with an attractive young woman when several people rushed up to him to tell him about my disappearance. Eventually they pulled me up on shore. It was my first experience diving.

My third memory is less life-threatening. My father went mountain-climbing up to Mittagskogel, a mountain bordering on the Wörtersee. The exciting thing for me was his promise to make a big fire on the top of the mountain when he got there so we could see it below. Lo and behold, in the evening there was a shiny little star on the top of the Mittagskogel. When my father returned, he received a hero's welcome from me. Curious, that my most vivid memories were of summer vacations in these early years.

Mother remembers being bitten by a donkey, scolded and neglected by her unsympathetic Nanny, almost allowed to drown by yet another inattentive adult. Do happy memories disappear in a generalized glow, while unhappy memories remain much sharper? Let me add my own earliest bad memory also from about the age of three:

My mother had started going to work every day when I was two years old and I often sat on the windowsill of her bedroom—the only window from which one could see the door of the building—to watch her leave the house. But that special morning of my memory, I had trouble seeing her through my tears. I had wet the bed during the night, and I almost remember waking up and being too lazy to get up to use the potty. In the morning I was happy to put on a brand new dress. But when my mother heard from my Fräulein that I had wet the bed that night, she ordered me to strip off my new dress, and wear an old dress that I no longer liked. Bedwetters do not wear new dresses.

It is peculiar how these things come back to you when one thinks of it. A subject I don't have to remember but which is after all these years perfectly present in my mind, is the singing and the beautiful voice of my mother. It permeated my entire childhood and youth, as long as I stayed home, which is until I got married. Next door to the children's room was the room with the piano in it and my mother sang. She had a dramatic soprano of unusual brilliance. In the morning, she practiced scales and solfeggios and in the afternoon somebody came to accompany her to songs and arias from operas.

Whatever I know of singing and music in general I learned from my mother. Her fate was a tragic one. She was caught by the Nazis in southwest France and died in one of Germany's concentration camps, a fate my daughter and I escaped by a hairs breadth. She sang so much that her voice must have been all the time in shape for an immediate professional career. Why this was not the case is a rather sad story, which I will tell now as well as it was told to me. Already as a child, the other children with whom my mother went to school complained, that "they could not sing because the Schramek yells so loud." My mother's stepmother was advised by the school teacher that the child had an extraordinarily beautiful voice. My mother sang all the time as a young and adolescent girl, until eventually her stepmother could obtain permission from my grandfather to take singing lessons with the best singing teacher in Vienna, Mrs. Nichlas-Kemptner.

We get here the shortest glimpse of a caring stepmother who prevails upon her traditional dogmatic husband, no doubt a despot, to allow his daughter to nurture her talents.

This woman was an opera singer of renown and, since she was not young enough to sing on the stage, continued her career as a vocal teacher. In Vienna not only gifted singers learned to sing but knowing how to sing and understand music was part of the curriculum of the entire population, and especially of a well-brought-up girl from a good family. Madame Kemptner taught the upper crust of the Viennese population. It seems that my mother soon occupied a special position among the teacher's pupils. My mother also seemed to have greatly enjoyed her instruction and met a number of interesting people who courted her. My mother was not only a good singer with a great voice, but also a very beautiful woman and an excellent musician, gifts that do not often meet in one person. I fear that this was the only good time my mother had in her life. Madame Kemptner was called to become professor at the Berlin Academy for Music and Arts and left Vienna. Before she left she arranged a good-bye concert in which my mother as her best and outstanding pupil participated. As my mother frequently told, she had a sensational success, the critics raved about her and she was offered through her teacher to go to the *Berlin Staatsopera*. This was prevented by my grandfather who hid or intercepted the contract she received. To understand the action of my grandfather, one has to know that he was a religious Jewish man coming from a small ghetto town in Moravia. He was at this period already a very rich man and letting one's daughter go to the stage would probably have been regarded as a disgrace for him and the family. Mother never recovered from this disappointment. It was the whole world she held accountable for her not becoming a world-famous performer. Even as far back as the 1880s a 24-year-old girl could leave her family and strike out to try her luck, but my grandfather apparently was a conservative awe-inspiring Pater Familias. It was he who introduced her shortly afterward to the man who became my father.

My father once made some remarks about how he met my mother. He was a young lawyer and defended an opponent of my grandfather in court. After the trial, which my father won, grandfather invited him to his house. My father thought, why not? and so he went.

I do not wonder that my father fell in love with my mother. But why my mother took him, I really don't know. My father was rather small, stout with a little paunch developed already at the age of 35 and a struggling lawyer, without personal means, and an outsider. He did not belong to the wealthy well-established Jews of Vienna. He was intelligent, but far from brilliant and during a certain period of his life a gambler. It is difficult for a daughter who loved her father dearly to evaluate him objectively, as other people saw him; neither can I find out anything about him. Everybody is dead who knew him. I live now on a different continent. He seemed to have had great personal charm, and to have been very affable in manners and extremely correct and honest in his professional life. Maybe he won my mother with his charm. During his courtship, he passed every day on horseback before his bride's window, who had to step out on the balcony. My mother mentioned this casually on one occasion.

My mother practiced singing with a professional accompanist all her life and she could really have started a career after her marriage, but my father did not want my mother to sing professionally. She could sing at concerts that were arranged for welfare, and was frequently asked to sing at big dinner parties in the house of friends or clients of father. She never accepted any fee; one was a society lady and thus not supposed to receive a fee. Nevertheless, when she had to sing on such an occasion she was very nervous and behaved like a celebrated diva, as if her entire future career depended on her success on this special evening. The entire household trembled and was hushed.

Great scenes were made because of my not practicing for my piano lessons. I was not very gifted at the piano, since I would otherwise have learned more during the many years I took piano lessons, in spite of my not practicing well. That the constant nagging and scenes of my mother did not contribute to make me like my piano lessons more is evident.

Ours was a big household. Father, who was a lawyer, had his office attached to our private apartment. The second maid exclusively served his law office. We must have moved to Wollzeile 1, quite a formidable address, when I was two or three years old. On the other side of the street, the archbishop of Vienna had his palace and one block away was the famous gothic cathedral, *die Stephanskirche,* which was surrounded by the *Stephansplatz,* still the very center of the city of Vienna.

Our days in the Wollzeile apartment were terminated around 1906. Both of my sisters were still born there. During this period, wealthier women did not go to a hospital for childbirth, but had their children at home. I remember vaguely the birth of my third sister [1901]. I was called into the bedroom of my parents to look at her, I was five years old and I know that I tended her as an infant. Now our Nanny had three little girls to watch, one of whom was very frail, my second sister, and one a newborn baby. All of a sudden I was the oldest, who had to know how to behave, and not to make any fuss—*mach' keine G'schichten*—our Nanny told me and little ailments I happened to catch were hidden from my mother as long as possible. Even when I caught the mumps I went to school with it, although I felt rather miserable; that I had the mumps was discovered much later, when it was over, because the entire family caught the mumps, too. This "not to make any fuss about my health" became a character trait of mine and so far, except as old age is closing on me rather rapidly, I have not suffered or perhaps not taken notice of the thousand "ailments" the flesh is heir to.

My mother was born less than one year after her parents' 1895 marriage, as Ernestine Drucker, May 21, 1896. As I write about the important dates in her life, I need to keep rechecking her birth certificate, because Mother kept changing her age, as circumstances required. I had thought her death in October 1980 meant that she had died at age 86, but later, looking at her papers, I realized that in truth she was only 84 years old. And now that I am rapidly approaching this age myself, I can understand better why she had absolutely not been ready to die. Her sister Lily was born in 1899 and her youngest sister Marianne, whom we knew as Tante Janne, was born in 1901. The three sisters would have a lifelong relationship of mutual help—Tante Janne welcomed us in Paris, Tante Lily worked indefatigably and successfully to procure us American Visas—punctuated by bitter resentment and envy, at least on Mother's part. They grew up together in Vienna, they lived within a short distance from each other in Paris, and they died at a short but frequently unbreachable distance from each other, in New York City.

The next summer also provides vivid pictures. By this time, the family consisted of three girls. We had a cottage for the summer in Velden am Wörtersee, nearly a day's train ride from Vienna. Mother, who had just given birth and was breast-feeding, had the habit of taking a nap every afternoon. I was supposed to do the same but seemed to have resented this order. One day, playing with my mother's purse, I took out the train tickets and asked if I could have them. Half asleep, she said it was all right. I knew exactly how naughty I was. I took all the return tickets, including those for the nurse, the cook, and the maid, tore them into the tiniest bits imaginable, sure that I would not be punished for the act. My father tried to have the train company replace the tickets, but they refused.

Another episode that I took very much to heart must have happened around this same time. My mother's sister got married. I was to be the *Kranzeljungfer* (bridesmaid) at the wedding. I remember mother bought me a very pretty pink dress at Braun's, a very exclusive store, and a pink rose wreath for my hair. I went to the beauty parlor the day before and my hair was put up in curlers, to be opened only at the day of the wedding. I could not sleep all night because the curlers hurt me, and then my parents were told that the children of the sister of the groom had the measles and I was not permitted to go. It seems to have been the first great disappointment in my life and I still remember it more than 60 years later.

I remember many slaps and scenes of my mother, received and made because of my being supposedly fresh or unruly. If I was fresh and unruly, I don't think it was on purpose. I took these punishments of my mother, deserved or undeserved, very much to heart. One of the first slaps I remember having received by my mother happened as follows: my mother was dressing for a party or concert and put some powder on her face—I must have been eight or nine years old—and I said, "mother your nose it too white." She turned around and gave me a hard slap.

I did not have a happy childhood at all; most of the time I was terrified by my mother, who probably did not know what she was doing. I was convinced that my mother hated me and suffered very much from her unjust treatment. I was an easy and friendly little girl, but because of what I thought loveless treatment, became a difficult, morose teenager, made even more unhappy by constant nagging and scenes verging on the hysterical made for trifles by my mother.

END OF THE UNCENSORED PART OF THE AUTOBIOGRAPHY

There are two versions of the first 10 pages of Mother's manuscript, The first version is "dedicated to my granddaughter Andrea Löwenstein for her eighteenth birthday." It is this first version that I have used for the book since it has a much sharper voice, as contrasted to the blander voice used in the manuscript that she had sent to all of us. She had mostly censored the bitter words against her own mother. One does not accuse a woman who was killed "in one of the German concentration camps." Andrea focuses on the censoring of Mother's original version.

ANDREA'S VOICE

In omitting "the nasty details," the later version also obliterates the strong, highly individual narrative voice, which is what makes this text striking, worth reading, at least for me. As a teacher, it's what I urge my students to do, to allow their real "voice" to emerge, nastiness and all. This is, of course, especially an issue for women students, most of whom have spent much of their life learning to tame their own angry "unreasonable" voices, in order to get along, to be loved and accepted.

Of course this *nastiness* (which, as a word, is a diminishing one; what I really mean is the quality of rage and hurt which is the subtext here) is also what made my grandmother the "impossible" woman I recall—a woman who did not *get along* in terms of interpersonal relationships. I believe it is what made her such an isolated person, as no one cared to be in the presence of such consuming bitterness, such egotism. And yet, she chose her own rage over the possibility of connection. Perhaps not a conscious choice, but still, admirable in some way.

She was not a woman, like my other grandmother, who allowed her anger to be obliterated, smoothed over, by a veneer of niceness, of false smiles and feminine wiles. Instead her entire stance, even her body language, expressed her rage. So did her way of living—her refusal to be beholden to anyone, her pride in her work and insistence on continuing until the last.

This is why I find a censored version so upsetting. All this woman had was her accusatory rage, and it cries out from every paragraph of these "uncensored" pages that screams again and again, "You betrayed me!"

One of the things we must think about in this book is how these patterns are passed on, even when the resolve is not to. My own mother did not make scenes, but she was the indubitable center of the household, the "diva" on whose love and approval both the children and my father depended, and which we all vied for, unable to turn to each other. She, in her own way was also "terrifying"; that is, I lived in fear of disappointing her and the knowledge that I constantly was.

CHAPTER 2

The (Grand)Parents Next Door

B esides my father and mother and the children, the household included a cook, two maids, and our Nanny. Father, who was a lawyer, had his office attached to our private apartment.

The following excerpt is from The Intellectual Elite of Austria: A Handbook for the Leaders in Culture and Commerce *(Marcel Klang, ed., Vienna, 1936). I thank Dr. Johannes Reichmeyr for making this article available to me.*

Dr. Leopold Drucker, lawyer, lives in Vienna I, Franz Josefs-Kai 65. Telephone A-12-9-85. He was born on July 31, 1860, as son of the industrialist Max Drucker who descends from one of the distinguished patrician families of the capital of Moravia, and his wife Sidonie, born Neubrunn, in Brünn where he attended high school (*Real-gymnasium*). He came to Vienna in the year 1878, attained a doctoral degree in law from the legal faculty of the University of Vienna and graduated at the same time from the technical school for agriculture. Dr. L.D. then dedicated himself to legal activities and after a year of internship he joined the office of the famous defendant *Regierungsrat* Dr. Heinrich Steger, where he stayed until 1890. At this point he established himself as lawyer for both civil and criminal matters. He also published scholarly articles such as "Hypnotism and Civil and Criminal Laws," "Suggestion and Its Forensic Implication," and "Criminals and Defendants." Dr. L.D. was one of the first who pointed to the significance of suggestions and hypnosis in the legal realm and who illuminated their connection to civil and criminal law. He recently published an article in which he draws attention to the legal consequences of artificial insemination among human beings.

During the world war he founded a committee to help refugees from the south and as chairman and pro bono lawyer of the association for blind veterans he helped hundreds of them to find homes. For this activity he was honored by Emperor Karl

Leopold Drucker

with the war medal for civil merits second class. In the postwar years as well, he devoted himself tirelessly to a variety of humanitarian causes and due to his impressive knowledge and professional competencies, as well as to his noble humanitarianism he enjoys in the largest circles the highest esteem. He belongs to the most distinguished members of the Vienna legal community.

In his younger years he was an enthusiastic mountaineer and also gave lectures on subjects connected to tourism. He is the founder of the Viennese Chess Club and was for 40 years a member of the Vienna *Residenzclub*. This artistic man has embellished his intimate home with a valuable collection of paintings,

On June 25, 1895, Dr. L.D. joined in marriage Frau Ida born Schramek, a daughter of the wholesale coal dealer Adolph Schramek, known as a generous philanthropist.

Ida Drucker

She is blessed with a magnificent voice and became well known as a concert singer. The marriage has produced 3 daughters of whom Ernestine is married to Dr. Martin Freud, son of Sigmund Freud, the founder of psychoanalysis and also well known as lecturer at the University of Vienna and as a performance artist; then Lily, who is married to the wholesale coal-dealer Rudolph Boyko and lives in Prague; and Marianne who is married to Heinrich Zittau, one-time Director of the *Depositenbank,* and lives in Paris.

The main meal in Vienna was in the middle of the day, around one o'clock. My father who worked in the stock market building, an easy 15 minutes walk away, always came about half an hour late for this family meal. He came late because he made a small detour from the office to greet his parents in the Berggasse, on the way home. My mother would sit and fret during this half hour, and she would choose to do so in her parents' flat, and since I sat and fretted with her, I saw my grandparents sometimes almost daily over years. I only remember them as heavy-set and sedentary but paintings of them at an earlier age show my grandfather to have been quite attractive and my grandmother as a grande dame.

I do not remember any pleasurable interchanges with either my maternal grandfather or grandmother. The problems with my other set of grandparents were of quite a different nature, but I sometimes think I have not succeeded in my role as grandmother because I had no warm relations with any of my grandparents. Naturally that is one of those foul excuses that I like to use. My son will later, in these pages, state that my use of the somewhat formal appellation of grandmother for either my mother, or perhaps for myself, is a distancing device, but it is the only name that I associate with being a grandparent.

Still, there were some pleasant memories. Well, at least one, the goose liver pâté my grandmother (or her cook) prepared, which was truly delicious. Lucky that I had not known, then, that it was a cruel stuffing of the goose that caused such an enlarged liver. I remember celebrating occasional Passover meals with these grandparents, but even these festivities remain dim and joyless in my mind. I suspect, however, that my memory deceives me. I was a cheerful child who knew how to extract pleasure, whenever possible, from the happenings around me and I can't imagine not having enjoyed those Jewish festivities, given that only birthdays but no holidays were ever celebrated in my own family,

The reason for the coldness next door might also be due to my grandmother who, in this presumably respected and prosperous household, suffered from a profound disappointment with her life. "I hated growing up in our household," Tante Janne would tell me, "and spent as little time at home as possible." The reasons for grandmother Drucker's bitterness might have been the early loss of her mother and her cutoff career as a singer. Later I would learn—first from Tante Janne, and now in mother's memoir—that Ida's husband, this honorable upstanding man, was an addicted gambler, sometimes bringing his family to the edge of ruin.

My maternal grandmother was born in Leipnik, Moravia, in 1870 as Ida Schramek. As stated above, her father remarried quickly after the death of her mother, Ernestine. The family, with four more children born in the next five years, then moved to Vienna in 1880 to settle in the Leopoldstadt. Grandmother Drucker thus lost her mother at age five and acquired a stepmother who was later never talked about; burdened with four new siblings, she lost her home at age 10.

My mother thus had a step-grandmother, as well as numerous uncles and aunts who flow through the narrative of the years of her youth. She was, for example,

Elegant, successful Esti Drucker Freud before leaving Vienna

invited by relatives in Prague during World War I; they attend her recitals, or they criticize her in various ways.

As mentioned above, I learned these matters through a cursory look at the archives at the Vienna City Hall, not expecting that such ancestry research would be more than a conventional introduction to my mother's life. I was all the more stunned to realize that my mother, known as Esti, but whose full name was Ernestine was named after her mother's deceased own mother, who, although never talked about, was thus not forgotten. Even more amazing, almost outrageous, was the fact that

Ida's stepmother had lived across the Augartenbrücke, 21 Novaragasse, in the same house in which my grandmother Ida had grown up. I thus had a nearby step-great-grandmother within easy walking distance of our house, who was never mentioned, never did we go to see her, nor did we meet grandmother Drucker's full brother or any of her half siblings. Her being a stepmother, step-grandmother, or step-great-grandmother clearly disqualified her from true kinship status. In my mother's words above, "I had a grandfather but a step-grandmother" [emphasis mine]. Neither my brother nor my maternal cousins were aware of the nearby existence of Regine Schramek. She died in November 1939, at age 81. I am grateful that this unknown step-great-grandmother could still die in her own bed, as I am grateful that my grandfather Drucker died of prostate cancer a few months after our emigration in 1938, without being submitted to the agonies of deportation.

The marriage between my maternal grandparents was solid enough, but perhaps not very happy.

My four-years-older brother Walter also declares to have no pleasant memories.

WALTER'S ERNESTINE

I am afraid that the whole family Drucker was much below par. I cannot recall a single meaningful conversation with these grandparents, although they lived next door. I once borrowed 10 schillings from Grandfather to buy a transformer after I had run out of pocket money. He made an incredible fuss about getting his money back. ("When do you get your pocket money? How much is it? Don't forget, etc. etc.") You would not believe it.

When our grandmother quarreled with her husband, which was a frequent occurrence, she would shout at him: "If I had not married you, I would now be a famous opera diva," Her husband was very much under the influence of his much more forceful wife.

Still, my brother called his first daughter after his maternal grandmother Ida, no doubt out of respect for her grim death. My brother does not know that my mother used to refer to him as a Drucker, a curious apparent mark of contempt in her eyes, given her love for her father. I, in contrast, was designated as a Freud, a distinction which carried its own problems.

Regardless of all those difficulties, bitter tears were shed as we parted from Vienna in May of 1938. My brother received a very intricate watch as a good-bye gift—intricate for that time—the kind that told not only the date of the week but also the movements of sun and moon. It was the kind that men wore in the pocket of their waistcoats with a gold chain attached to it. It survived emigration and war years but has not functioned for many years. I received my first piece of jewelry, a coral necklace with three strands. The necklace has survived my travels and I gave it to my oldest daughter Andrea who seldom wears jewelry. These things are all that is left of my grandparents' beautiful belongings.

CHAPTER 3

Early School Years

When I was in first grade it was decided that I would have a tutor, the reason being that I might infect my sisters with any childhood diseases I brought home from public school. It must be remembered that in the early part of the century such diseases as diphtheria and scarlet fever could be fatal. A desk was given to me and a teacher came once or twice a week to initiate me in the four R's. I don't know where my parents found Frau Nagel, but she did not seem to have much knowledge of modern pedagogy. I received a primer, a slate with a pencil, and a sponge. The first word in the primer was *apfel* (apple) because it started with the first letter of the alphabet. Neither my parents nor I knew that writing on a slate and beginning with one-word reading was outdated at least by a quarter of a century. I had two years of this type of instruction. I learned how to read and read everything I could put my hands on, but I never learned to spell even unto my ripe old age.

At the end of each school year, I had to pass an examination given by the public school board. Big changes in my life began to happen in the fall of 1904 when I entered third grade. Again, we have a summer story....

My parents rented a cottage at *Klamm am Semmering*, eight or nine hundred meters above sea level, surrounded by farms and woods. The upper stories of this cottage were occupied by another family. They had four children, a big girl of 13 or 14, a boy of 12, a girl as old as I was, and a boy the age of my sister Lily. It was the first time in my life that I had intimate daily contact with other children. Nanny had kept us pretty isolated and, to my amazement, the Beyer children made fun of me.

The custom of assuring playmates for one's children at an early age was already in place when I raised my own children, not to mention my grandchildren whose playdates started at age one. It is true that, unlike my mother, I had an older brother, but I was still raised, like my mother, with no same-aged friends as companions, except occasional encounters when my Fräulein talked to other Fräuleins with "their" children, on park benches. I was not even sent to kindergarten, an unnecessary expense, because there was a Fräulein around to take care of us. No wonder I could not wait to start school with its intensely absorbing social life.

I just did not have the experience I was supposed to have had at my age: I did not know how to jump from the back of a bench, I could not run down a forest path full of roots, gravel, and pine needles without spraining my ankle or falling, I did not know the best places where to find strawberries. I did not recognize which mushrooms were edible or poisonous and I did not have nails at the soles of my shoes so as not to slip. My sisters were still too young to have learned these skills. Lily was soon taught all that was needed by the boy who was a year older. But I, being compared to the girl who was only a few months older, was just despised as being backward and awkward. I practiced jumping benches, falling on my right arm and seriously injuring it. I tried to run down slippery forest paths, but never achieved real smoothness at it. The girl who had all the skills, Anny Beyer, later became the woman ski champion of Austria! It was with her that I had to compete that summer.

It was Mrs. Beyer who recommended the grammar school that I attended in the fall, the *Schwarzwald Schule*, which was the best and most progressive school in Vienna for educating girls. Apart from going to school, I had little contact with the real world, except for dinner discussions where there was talk of the Russo-Japanese War, the fall of Port Arthur, and the defeat of the Russian fleet.

I was lucky to have Fräulein Elsa Reisz, one of the outstanding grammar school teachers of all time, as my teacher. She must have recognized my deficiencies of school learning, although I am certain I was a good reader. I must mention here an incident in third grade I took very much to heart. Father said to me that if I brought home a good *Ausweis* (report card) I could go with him to visit my grandmother who lived in a part of Hungary that is now Czechoslovakia.

We had just learned that qualifying adjectives in German were spelled with a small letter while nouns began with a capital letter. We had to write after dictation. The subject was the names of Babenbergers, the royal family who governed Austria before the advent of the Habsburg family. They had names like Frederic the Pugnacious or Leopold the Illustrious. I, who had just learned that qualifying words had to begin with a small letter overlooking the articles preceding "pugnacious" and "illustrious," spelled them with a small letter. The result was a C and my crying my heart out because now my father surely would not take me with him on his visit. On my imploring, Fräulein Reisz took pity on me and changed the grade to B-. As I view the situation now I realize that Father would have taken me anyway as he wanted his mother to see me.

One of my nightmares as a six year old who knew no Hebrew was that I had to recite the *Mah nishtanah* at my grandparents' house at Passover. For a six year old who knew no Hebrew, it was a hard task to memorize those questions. I think I did fairly well, however, in reality.

I was exposed to the Jewish religion through the mandatory Jewish religious instructions at my gymnasium, the same Schwarzwaldschule *that Mother attended (except I attended, as a matter of course, the more academic track of the school). We even learned to read elementary Hebrew. Our teacher was Bernhard Taglicht, a dearly loved teacher, who gave each of us a nickname that would endure for years. Mine was Zapferl. What an immense relief to know that Taglicht was not among those murdered by the Nazis. I had a chance to visit him in New York City, an old and shriveled man living in obvious poverty, but alive. It was this teacher whom I asked, after Hitler had entered Vienna, why God allowed Hitler. "When your grandfather makes a decision, you do not ask for the reasons—the same is true for God," he had explained.*

I got used to C's during my first three years in high school (called lyceum there) where I was a very average student. I had not learned how to study and, while most of the other girls had French governesses and learned much of the language with them, we had our Nanny until I was 12 years old.

One incident about Nanny is worth relating. She was a very pious woman and went with us children every day to mass at St. Stephan's Cathedral. Nanny wanted us, especially me as the oldest, to convert to Catholicism. One of her arguments was that we would never ascend to heaven unless we converted. I remember telling her that if my father didn't go to heaven, I didn't want to.

I remember asking my parents if there were two kinds of *lieber Gott*, one for the rich and one for the poor, because Nanny and all the servants in our household and all the other Nannies I knew went to pray at the Cathedral, whereas my mother whom I considered to be upper class went to the synagogue on holidays.

Just as upper-class white children were raised by black mammies in the racist American South, Jewish children of even modest middle-class families were raised by Catholic nannies in Austria. In our family the nanny stories started with grandfather Freud who had had a Catholic nursemaid until he was two and a half years old and still lived in Freiberg (Príbor). All the historians, starting with Ernest Jones (1953), report that she "used to take the boy to church services [and] . . . implanted in him the ideas of Heaven and Hell" (p. 6). The nursemaid later was caught stealing by a family member, denounced to the police, and jailed. Some historians (Krüll 1979; Breger 2000) have ascribed much importance to the traumatic disappearance of this beloved Catholic nursemaid. Krüll (1979, p. 148) mentions that the little Sigmund had given his nanny pennies he had received, and that some injustice may have taken place. My chest tightens every time I come upon the incarceration of that poor nursemaid in yet another Freud biography. There is never any evidence that my grandfather, later in life, perhaps in his famous self-analysis, worried about the just treatment of that once-beloved nursemaid.

It does not seem at all strange to me that my grandfather gave pennies to his nanny. For years, while I still shared a room with my Fräulein, I pulled out and prepared her foldaway bed before going to bed myself. It was my private act of love that no one else in the household, except of course my Fräulein, needed to know. My Fräulein did not take me to church, but one year, when I was perhaps 11 years old, our cook Rosa and my Fräulein could no longer bear to see me deprived of a Christmas tree. They secretly decorated a tree in Rosa's own room and the lovely little tree with colored glass balls and silver chains highlighted the drabness of that airless cubicle. Both Fräulein and Rosa seem to have anticipated great joy on my part when they enthusiastically showed me the tree on Christmas morning. Torn between appreciating their good intentions while feeling a sense of treason my reaction must have deeply disappointed them.

CHAPTER 4

Growing Up

When I was 13 and becoming developed in various ways I suddenly became an excellent student, one of the best in my class. This was the point at which one had to decide about remaining at the lyceum. The alternative was to go to the gymnasium, where one learned Latin and prepared for an academic career at the university. Because I was such a good student, I opted for the latter. My mother offered stiff resistance. She became hysterical when I announced my decision, saying that I would become blind and hunchbacked, making veiled allusions to my nearsightedness and poor posture. No doubt the unconscious reason for this behavior was my mother's begrudging me a career because she had forfeited one.

I discovered at this point that I had a talent. I loved to recite poetry and memorized passages from famous German classical plays. Always when we read one of these plays in class, the entire student body yelled *Die Drucker soll lesen* (the Drucker should read). Although I never went on stage, I developed the art of recitation to the best of my ability. It was an easy thing to do and I was entirely happy at the time I was doing it. The gift stayed with me for life and was indirectly responsible for the way in which I earned my living. I made my parents promise to allow me to study to become an actress since they would not permit me to go to the gymnasium.

I did not get along with my mother very well. I began to resent her fits of hysterics and making big scenes all the time. Mother's behavior did not contribute to improve our relationship.

In 1911, when I was 15, I accompanied my mother to the famous spa Marienbad where one drank the spring waters to become thin. My mother was obese and so was my father. I had a large-brimmed Florentine straw hat, which I was told to put a lining in one day while my mother took her afternoon nap. She showed me how to do it by reversing the lining. The method was cumbersome for me and I decided to use a less professional one. The whole matter seemed to me of minor importance, but when my mother awoke and saw what I had done, she was provoked to such an attack of hysteria, that today, after nearly 70 years have passed, I can hardly comprehend it.

When my father arrived there, things became easier for me. We met a distant relative of my mother's, five or six years older than I, and I was permitted to hike and wander about in her company.

During my last years at the school, I developed an odd illness. I became nauseous in class and it often became so bad, I had to leave the room. Sometimes I would fall into a dead faint in the corridor. After this had happened several times, my family was informed and I was taken to the doctor who diagnosed the condition as an allergy to breakfast coffee. From then on I received a different breakfast drink and became careful to always be around the bathroom before I fainted. I remember once stretching out on the floor because I felt so sick. In retrospect I see the disorder as the effect of emotional stress.

Not only did my mother make scenes, but we had the most obnoxious French governess who did things like tell me I had elephant feet when I went to my dancing class. Between the two of them, my psychological capacities were taxed.

At the end of the year, we had our final exams (*Matura*), which I passed *mit Auszeichnung* (cum laude). The same year, we went to a very fashionable hotel at a Swiss spa where I discovered people thought of me as a very pretty girl.

Part II

Young Womanhood

CHAPTER 5

Climbing Mountains

At the afterdinner dances at the spa, I was constantly asked to dance. Some young men went to my father, introduced themselves, and asked permission to be in my company. All this astonished me because I had never thought of myself as attractive, thanks to my governess et al.

The most rewarding days for me were during the summer when we went to resorts in the Austrian Alps and I could accompany my father on hikes to Alpine huts. The tours were too strenuous for my mother so there was no one there to nag me. Father was a member of the *Alpen Verein* and had certain privileges of which he was very proud. These huts were built within the 3,000 meter boundary and served as a rest camp to enable people to prepare for the next day's climb to surrounding peaks. Father was always very careful and very much aware of the dangers one could confront in the mountains, such as sudden changes in the weather, falling rocks, and the precariousness of flower picking on steep mountain meadows. Many accidents occur on such meadows because they looked perfectly harmless. When there was a possibility of danger, he hired an Alpine mountain guide.

In spite of all my father's forethought I nearly had a serious accident. We crossed the pass from Madonna di Campiglio to Molveno where we stayed for the summer; my father had hired a guide for this tour. We went through a patch of snow. It looked so easy but suddenly I slipped on the snow and began to glide downward. Fortunately, I could stop the glide before it gained momentum. My father's face, pale as death, was a testimony to the danger I had been in, of which I had been completely unaware. When my father was in his mid-fifties he began to suffer from arthritis in his knee and had to stop the more strenuous hiking, but I was allowed to continue with an Alpine guide as a companion.

Although I had the strength and skill, I could not go on really big climbs because I was not permitted to stay overnight in the huts, because this could have endangered my reputation. It was important to my parents that I maintained this reputation as a sexually inexperienced girl for fear it would interfere with my chances of making a good match if I lost it. This was an extremely important matter to an upper-middle-class family in the Viennese Jewish ghetto.

How sad that my parents, who were both ardent mountaineers, did not even share that one common pleasure except very early in their marriage. It was I, not my father, who accompanied my mother up mountains as soon as I was strong enough, during the summer vacations that we always spent together. There were arduous climbs, and my mother had to urge me on: "just a little longer and then we will be there . . . you can take a little rest, but not for too long." Up and up we went—I was such an obedient and willing child—until eventually, after many hours, we would arrive at some peak with a tremendous sense of triumph and relief and of course a splendid view of the valley below.

In the summer of 1916, when I was 20, we were in a resort called Ischl, where the emperor Franz Josef has his summer residence. I made plans to take a long hike with Egon, my cousin, who was 12, a girlfriend of mine, and a married man. On the morning of the hike, the girlfriend did not feel well and dropped out. The hike started out with very steep serpentine paths and the man suddenly said it was too much for his heart and returned to the resort. The reception, when I came back, was totally unexpected. "You were on a hike with a married man," my parents said, "what will people think of you?" When I assured them that the "married man" was not with us, they continued to carry on about being alone with my cousin, who was a child, that something could have happened to us, etc. I had the feeling my parents had simply made up their minds to make a scene.

My mother refers several times to customs of the "upper-middle-class Jewish ghetto," and her parents' constant anxiety to preserve their daughter's reputation for an optimal marriage. She does so each time with indignation and contempt, although we notice that she still remembers, 60 years later, the gossip stories of the time.

Moreover, she was ready to inflict upon me the same constraints. No doubt she would have considered herself an irresponsible mother, had she done otherwise. When I was 13 years old, shortly before the Anschluss, my brother's best friend whom I

Mother and Sophie on summer vacation

had secretly loved for years asked me to go to the theater with him. It was my very first semidate and stood for total happiness, but not for long. My mother insisted that my Fräulein would accompany us to the theater and fetch us after the performance because I was already at an age at which chaperons were required. Needless to say, it spoiled the whole outing. I can still remember my rage about this particular mortification. My vigorous protests were totally useless. Disobedience or rebellion against parents does not seem to have been in my mother's repertory, nor later in mine, at that time in Vienna.

Then there was the apparently related matter of ensuring that I would grow up to become a lady. I was an athletic girl, eager to excel in high jumping, dodge ball, and handstands, but my mother insisted on enrolling me in ballet and other such hateful dancing classes with the express purpose of transforming me into a more graceful young woman. Like her, I was called a little elephant by my dancing teacher. Vienna of those days must have been full of elephants.

A few months later, my mother and I were living alone in Paris. I was free to roam the streets by myself, no more chaperons, no more dancing classes, no more orthodentistry, no more upper-middle-class Jewish ghetto.

CHAPTER 6

Austria's War Soon Turned into Defeat

That year was the second year of the war that started in August 1914, that awful event that not only ruined Europe, but also brought disaster to our personal lives. On June 28 we were on our way to our summer vacation at Marienbad when newsboys called out *Extra-ausgabe* (a special edition of the newspaper). "Erzherzog (Archduke) Ferdinand and his wife assassinated in Bosnia" was the headline. When my father heard the news he said, "this means war." Although his prediction was correct, he didn't realize what the consequences would be, and thus did not draw the proper conclusions in accordance to the events.

Archduke Ferdinand was Austria's successor to the Habsburg throne after the suicide of Crown Prince Rudolf, Emperor Franz Josef's only son Ferdinand was not popular in Vienna because he was, supposedly, haughty and arrogant. Aside from that, he married below his rank. Instead of marrying into royal blood, he chose a Czech countess. He had to promise that his children would have no right to ascend the Habsburg throne. The rumors in Vienna were that he favored the Czechs and that, when he would become emperor, he would let himself be crowned the King of Bohemia as well.

Archduke Ferdinand was sent to Sarajevo to inspect the army, in spite of the fact that the commanding general of that southern frontier province (annexed in 1908) wrote to Vienna that he would be unable to ensure the Archduke's safety. Ferdinand was sent anyway. The assassination of him and his wife is an oft-told story, so I need not retell it here. It seems circumstance points to the fact that the Austrian establishment wanted the Archduke to be killed. The youth who shot him was of Serbian nationality and Austria requested of Serbia that he be extradited to face Austrian justice. The rest is history.

In August 1914, Europe was in a state of war. This war killed 5 million young European men. The Austrian Empire was dismembered by the Treaty of St. Germain; the German Hohenzollern Kaiser Wilhelm lost his German Reich and had to flee to Holland where he chopped wood. The Russian Czar and his family were murdered and Russia turned Communist. Hitler waited in the wings in order to conquer practically all of Europe 14 years later, beginning a new war and decimating the Jewish population under the most horrible conditions.

When the Austrian emperor was informed about the assassination of Ferdinand he supposedly said, "one has to believe in a higher justice." Franz Joseph died in 1915 and his grandnephew Archduke Karl became the last emperor of the Habsburg Reich. He married a princess of royal blood and no "higher justice" had to intervene.

What did the first world war mean to me personally? My father had no son to sacrifice on the altar of the Fatherland. He was a good Austrian patriot, so he suggested that I become a volunteer nurse. I had to give up studying with *Burgtheater* actor Gregory toward a career of acting. Anyway, nursing was more highly regarded in the Jewish middle-class ghetto than becoming an actress. There was some training involved in becoming a Red Cross nurse and I enrolled in a ward at the *Allgemeines Krankenhaus* (general hospital).

The nurses in the surgical ward were nuns and the training was rather rigorous: making 40 beds a day, night service every third night, carrying and washing bedpans, etc. I was full of enthusiasm and worked very conscientiously, which the nuns appreciated. I soon became a favorite in the ward. One day the "big" professor Büdinger visited the ward and he ordered that I should be trained as an assistant instrument nurse when the professor was doing surgery. This resulted in a lot of jealousy among my covolunteers who asked, "Why she and not I?" Being an instrument nurse was no bargain. At the beginning of the war, the sick and wounded came directly from the Russian front to Vienna. The volunteers were supposed to scrub them and prepare them for surgery. This was not an easy job as the men were full of lice. One day I discovered one covered with red spots. After this, the wounded were no longer sent directly to Vienna but instead hospitals were set up in small towns where the war casualties stayed until the convalescent stage, when there was no longer a danger of contamination that would bring an epidemic to the capital.

I must have told the story of the man with the red spots to my family doctor, because soon strings were pulled and I got transferred to the convalescent hospital in the Austrian Parliament building, one of the most magnificent buildings on the *Ringstraße* in Vienna. It was built in the neo-Grecian style. Prime Minister Graf Karl von Stürkh had dissolved Parliament for the duration of the war. He was shot when he went to lunch one day in the Hotel Meissl and Schaden, by Friedrich Adler, the son of Victor Adler. [Victor Adler was the founder and leader of the Austrian Social Democratic Party.] I did night service every third night at this hospital too, but this did not bother me too much. I was still able to follow the normal course of activities during the day, going skating and flirting with officers on leave from war zones.

Austria's war soon turned into defeat. One day the news in the paper was "Lemberg noch in unserem Besitz" ("We still hold the city of Lemberg"), which meant that the road to Vienna was open to the Russian armies and my parents began to pack their luggage for fleeing. The defeat of the Russian army fighting Germany saved the Austrian capital from this disaster. However, thousands of refugees from the northern provinces poured into Vienna, where they were not very well received.

The food situation in Vienna became worse and worse. One received coupons for the most essential foods, and if one had enough money, one bought on the black market. There was enough food in the rural areas, especially in Hungary, the breadbasket of the old Austrian Empire, but the farmers hoarded and did not want to sell for the prices determined by the government, and, from all I could see, the distribution of food supplies was mismanaged.

There were inspections on the trains on the border between Austria and Hungary, although it was still the same country. Once when I returned from a visit to a sister of my father's who lived in Hungary, I smuggled flour in a big camera case and had bags of flour attached to my legs (in this period women were wearing skirts to the ankles). Obtaining coal for heating also became more and more difficult, but we were privileged because my mother's brothers were in the coal business.

After having served for nearly a year as a volunteer nurse, the strenuous work seemed to take a toll on my health and I was under pressure to resign at the Parliament Red Cross Hospital. A decoration was bestowed on me, to my surprise.

HOSPITAL CERTIFICATE

Military Hospital at the Parliament.

Esti Drucker was active from Sept. 26, 1914 to January 15, 1915 as voluntary assistant nurse. She was untiring in her services and proved herself conscientious and competent and can be most warmly recommended.

Vienna, Feb. 4, 1915, Prof. XX
Inspected, Hofrat XX

I wanted to enroll at the Viennese University to take a master's degree in French, but father did not permit it. I think he was afraid I might meet too many young men. Fortunately, I was allowed to take speech instruction and oral poetry interpretation from a retired *Burgtheater* actress, Mrs. Olga Lewinsky. With her help, I put together a repertory for recitation in public. One day my parents were told that I might damage my chances of making a good marriage because I was reciting poems in public! That was all I needed. Mother took the occasion to make a big scene and father decided he would censor my repertory.

Aside from my elocution lessons, I learned to sing from my mother. I had quite a pleasant voice and was gifted musically, but the nature of my mother's temperament made my singing lessons always end in tears. However, the fact that I now understand so much about voice and am able to work so successfully with pathological voice production of all kinds is partly due to those singing lessons.

Although when the war began it was said that the fighting would be over by Christmas of 1914, the war went on and on. The German armies were at the gate of Paris, but by what the French called "the miracle of the Marne" they were thrown back. One heard of more and more fatalities of young men one knew. Once, before the war I had thrown a dance in my home to which 30 young men were invited. Ten were "never to return again." An additional two died shortly after the war of diseases connected with the war. One of them was a second cousin, Bruno Drucker, a gifted and charming youth, whom we three sisters regarded as an adopted brother. He caught tuberculosis and malaria at the Serbian front and died of it. Others caught what was in that time called the Lung Plague, a disease of epidemic proportion just after the war, which killed many and did not discriminate between the sexes. One brother of my mother's was seriously injured, and another died of his wounds. All these young men were Jewish. Nevertheless, Nazis in Austria later declared that the Jews had shrunk from the war (*Drückeberger*) or had had profitable jobs behind the lines. A sister of my future father-in-law lost her only son. As a reward, the Nazis gassed her in a concentration camp. [Mother is referring here to Grandfather's sister, Rosa Graf.]

CHAPTER 7

The Other Famous Grandfather

During the first year of the war, my grandfather Schramek died suddenly of a heart attack. He had been a very rich self-made man who had started in Vienna with nothing, getting up at four o'clock in the morning to buy a freight car of coal and selling it at six o'clock for a profit. From these beginnings, he became the largest coal merchant in Vienna. He was a very pious Jew and erected with his money the most beautiful synagogue in Vienna, the Pazmaniten Temple. His death resulted in much disappointment. His last testament left all his money to his grandchildren and to the Viennese *Kultusgemeinde*. [The office for Jewish affairs, in Vienna.] There had been some dispute with his children. My mother never told me the cause of it and the reason he disinherited his children. Suddenly I was a wealthy girl who had inherited 100,000 Kronen.

Although my mother never mentioned her step-grandmother—who had tried to help her mother get singing lessons—she frequently proudly referred to her grandfather Adolph Schramek, who had spoiled her mother's potential career and happiness. She never mentioned her relationship to him or anything about his character. No doubt his affluence overshadowed his other qualities in her eyes. He was her counterpoint to the claim to fame on the other side of the family. "I also had a famous grandfather," she would say to me. "He gave me tableware of pure gold when I got married. Imagine, pure gold. And he built a synagogue with his own money." She would add that my father lost the gold of the cutlery in the stock market. She did not know at the time that the temple was to have an equally dire fate, as it would be burnt by the Nazis. A tablet indicates its former location at Pazmanitengasse 6.

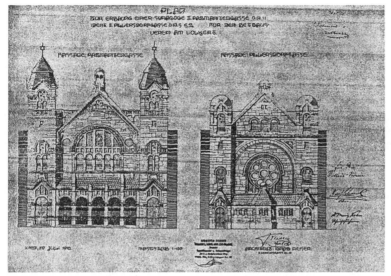

Entwurf für die Synagoge in der Pazmanitengasse, Westfront, nach einem Plan von Ignaz Reiser

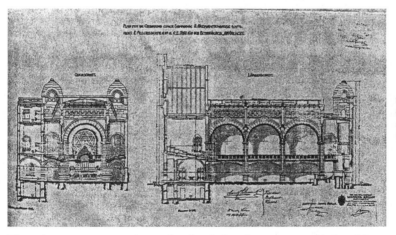

Baupläne für den Pazmanitentempel, Quer- und Längsschnitt, von Ignaz Reiser

Plans for a synagogue drawn by the "other famous grandfather," Ignaz Reiser

Perhaps we would have visited the Schramek family across the Donaukanal if Adolph had still been living, but he died during World War I, his life stretching from his birth in Leipnik Moravia in 1845 to his death in Vienna in 1915. The Vienna City Hall records list him as a homeowner, a wood and coal merchant, and a kaiserlicher Rat *(imperial counselor), no doubt a title of distinction in the Austrian monarchy. I could also verify my mother's boast regarding the temple. The*

Pazmaniten temple was built after a plan of Ignaz Reiser. It was not built by the Vienna Kultusgemeinde, but by a temple club Am Volkert Verein. *Adolph Schramek was the* Obman *(president) of the Verein and his name is the signature under the building contract in 1910. His obituary in a Jewish newspaper of the time praises his character, his kindness, and his generous philanthropy to the highest degree.*

Living off the interest was enough to maintain me. Since I was only 18, I had no say about investment of this money and my father bought a lot of *Kriegsanleihe* (war bonds), which became worthless when the Austrian empire dissolved. However, there were also stocks that had kept their value. I also inherited a gold flatware service for 12 and some jewelry. My mother started buying me clothing at the most fashionable Viennese dressmakers, the "Schwestern Flöge," one of whom was married to the famous painter Gustav Klimt. (It was said in Vienna that he designed clothes for the salon.)

I have to tell a little anecdote that I remember from this period. One of the customers of the Schwestern Flöge was Mrs. Piccaver (nee Johannie), the daughter of the Lutheran Pastor of Vienna. Before her marriage, she had been an actress. As Mrs. Piccaver became the official beauty of Vienna, she posed in the manner of the famous portraits of Mrs. Hamilton, Admiral Nelson's notorious mistress. Her husband, the leading lyric tenor of the Viennese opera, an American, supposedly earned fabulous sums for singing. One day we were both at the Flöge salon at the same time, admiring the collection being shown by a model. I overheard Mrs. Piccaver saying, "Send me the entire collection. I know everything will fit me." Such extravagance could not be supported, even by the highest fees her husband earned, and the Piccavers were divorced. A few years later, when I was already married, Viennese scandal-mongers had a heyday. The wife of a Hungarian landowner threw sulfuric acid (vitriol) at Mrs. Piccaver's face on the Kärtnerstraße (the Fifth Avenue of Vienna). Although her face was not injured, parts of her neck were. The story has a sad ending. Rumor had it she became a call girl and in 1936 there was a short item in one of the boulevard newspapers that the former Mrs. Piccaver had died at the age of 42 in a poorhouse in Czernowitz, a frontier town of the former Austrian Empire, near the Russian border.

My tastes became cultivated, but I became permanently spoiled.

While Mother takes responsibility here, for an apparently minor character weakness, she skips over it rather lightly. But her liberal spending habits offended the Freud family's scrupulous thrift, no doubt contributing to their rejection of her. They were also fatal to her marriage, scourging my father's constant anxiety about money, or perhaps his financial meanness, or both.

Adolf Schramek received a glowing obituary in the Jewish newspaper of the time. But my brother thought, perhaps unfairly, that Adolf Schramek's probably flawed character threw a curse on subsequent generations. He must have thought of the emotional problems of our grandmother, Mother, and maybe even those of her sisters.

WALTER'S *ERNESTINE*

I believe that the mental unbalance of Esti came from her mother's side, the Schrameks. By all accounts, Adolf Schramek, Esti's rich grandfather, was not a pleasant man. His villa in Baden was filled with soft and not-so-soft pornographic books. He died in the arms of a woman who was not his wife. He must have been a fairly ruthless operator to amass his large fortune.

Part III

Martin Freud

CHAPTER 8

Meeting Martin Freud

Looking back, it now seems odd that in the period I described I was not unhappy although I was surrounded by hunger and pestilence. We were invited to many parties where I was always a great success socially. The young men at the parties were officers on leave from the many battlefields of the Austrian army. There were three: the Russian, the Italian, and the Serbian fronts.

One of these parties was fateful for me. I met my future husband at the one given by Martha Brünner (now called Martha Ornstein who lives in Boston). Martin was first lieutenant of the artillery, then on leave. I was soon informed that he was the son of Sigmund Freud. In spite of my poor education I was very familiar with Freud's writings. I had sense enough to recognize these new and extraordinary concepts as being important and was fascinated with everything I read by him.

World War I had started, in steps, from the end of July to the beginning of August 1914, and my father-to-be had enrolled almost immediately, judging from the date of his father's letter. There are actually four letters that Sigmund Freud wrote to his son at the time. Three of them were published in my father's book about his relationship to his famous father, but the first of the letters was in my mother's possession and has never been published and, for the sake of Freud historians, I shall record all of Freud's letters in their original German version before presenting them in translation.

PROF. DR. FREUD (GERMAN LETTER)
    16.8.14 (August 16, 1914)
    WIEN, IX. BERGGASSE 19.
    Lieber Martin,
    Ich habe Deine Mitteilung daß Du als Kriegsfreiwilliger angenommen

worden bist, erhalten. Du kannst Dir denken daß ich es als eine Vermehrung der Sorgenlast empfinde welche dieser Krieg jedem auferlegt, aber ich will Dir das Zeugnis nicht versagen daß Du korrekt gehandelt hast. Wenn das Schicksal Dir nicht zu ungünstig ist, wirst Du wahrscheinlich später mit Befriedigung auf Deinen Entschluß zurückschauen. Laß mich bald wissen was Du von mir bedarfst, und welche Deine nächsten Schicksale sein werden. Schreib überhaupt soviel Du kannst. Zum Glück gibt es ja wieder eine Post-verbindung. Nach England allerdings nicht. Annerl bleibt abgeschnitten.

Ich wünsche Dir alles was Du in Deiner jetzigen Situation brauchen kannst u. Grüße Dich herzlich. Dein Vater

PROF. DR. FREUD (ENGLISH TRANSLATION)
　　16.8.14 (August 16, 1914)
　　WIEN, IX. BERGGASSE 19.
　　Dear Martin,
　　I received the news that you were accepted as a war volunteer. You can imagine that I view this as increasing the burden of worries that this war imposes on everyone, but I will not withhold the testimony that you have acted correctly. If fate is not too unfavorable toward you, you will probably later look back on your decision with satisfaction. Let me know soon what you need from me and what your next fates are going to be. Write in general as much as you can. Luckily there is once again a postal connection. How-ever not to England. Annerl remains cut off.
　　I wish you everything that you need in your current situation and greet you affectionately.
　　Your Father

Perhaps it was my unconscious at work, but I found myself putting on the charm and somehow convincing Martin, who was on his way to a second party, to accompany Lily and me home. As the fates had decided, I met Martin again a few days later at the Kärtnerstraße at midday promenade. Again he saw me home but was anxious to get to his own home, because the Freuds had their noontime meal, the main meal in Vienna, at the stroke of one, and war or no war, you had to be there on time or not eat. This gave me an inkling of the kind of discipline that ruled the Freud household. This was connected, as I discovered much later, with the "professor's" famous 50-minute hour. Martin told me that his leave had ended and that he had to rejoin his regiment at Linz. He asked whether he could write to me. My answer

Letter from Sigmund Freud to Martin, 8-16-14

was arrogant: "Don't write to me as long as you are in Linz. Write when you are back at the front."

A few weeks later I received the most charming poem on a *Feldpostkarte* (field postcard) requesting permission to call me up when he returned to Vienna. I remember only the end of the poem:

With rattling sword and boots a'creaking
I am longingly your answer seeking

The poem was so cute I could not restrain myself from showing it to my father, emphasizing that it came from the son of Sigmund Freud, a fact that did not impress my father very much. I usually did not show my father my war correspondence. On the contrary, I hid it and had arranged for a post office box to receive it. However, in this case, I seemed to sense from the very beginning that this would end up being more than a wartime flirtation, such as I had had with numerous men at the front in order to make them feel that they were not forgotten by the girls back home.

My correspondence with Martin was official from the very beginning. [The whole correspondence was of course conducted in German.]

FIELD POSTCARD
   Lieutenant Dr. Martin Freud
   February 6, 1918   (1)
Many thanks for your picturesque writing but for heavens sakes, dearest Doctor, have you really gone among the poets. This species of homo sapiens is said to appear in every Jewish family and overruns and seduces me with his love. Should I also include "Your" poems in my recitations! Please tell me, don't be embarrassed, I am quite used to it that poets want that from me. But if your feelings toward me should be quite selfless (although I doubt that there is such a thing) I shall bless you "into the thousandth generation." I admire your juridical sharpness which discovers humor in me, or do you actually possess graphological knowledge, should I perhaps, to exclude any errors, give you an exact character study of my personality? No, I would rather leave that to your personal face-to-face studies. That is a much better way and besides I don't want to embarrass myself in front of you; do you absolutely have to know that I like to sleep late, and that I can be bribed with chocolates? I expect that you won't make fun of me for just writing about myself, but about you I only know the actually quite important fact that you are a lieutenant in the artillery and have black hair but can one write anything about that? Are you interested in neutral things, like the calamities of the Vienna traffic system, worries about food provisions, prospects for peace and transmigration of souls? I assure you, I am gladly at your service; but do you think that it would be very fruitful and furthering the general welfare if I put my so highly qualified opinion on paper? Talk about oneself is after all more informative. So far I have not been defeated by a sense of grandiosity. Esti Drucker

About six months later when Martin's leave finally came and along with it the promised telephone call, my parents had arranged for a dinner party at

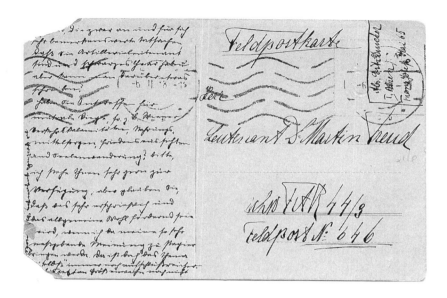

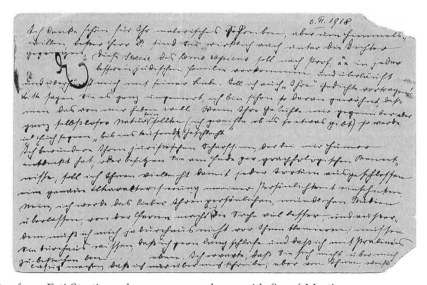

Letter from Esti Starting a long correspondence with fiancé Martin

the *Stadtpark* (the Viennese equivalent of Tavern on the Green in New York) and I invited Martin to join us. In this way, he was introduced to my family. Martin later told me that he had said to his parents that very same evening, "it seems this girl wants to marry me."

My parents were not very enthusiastic about my choice. I think they felt let down, having expected me to make what was then considered a brilliant marriage, into banking or industry. Father, as a lawyer, had made inquiries about the Freud family and discovered they were far from wealthy. Martin, who had a doctorate in law, would have to start looking for a job when he was out of the army. If he wanted to become a lawyer, he would have to be a *Konzipient* for six years in a lawyer's office, an apprentice so to speak, with a salary that could hardly support a single person. Neither of us really faced up to this reality.

Martin and I saw more and more of each other and after a time I was invited for dinner at the Freuds' house. I met Anna, the youngest of the Freud children, who was only a few months older than I and already a grammar school teacher in a private exclusive school. She was very different from the girls I had met so far. She did not care for fashionable clothes or for being invited to parties. She was very pretty but was obviously a bluestocking type according to the opinion of Vienna's society, a woman who put intellectual pursuits before looking chic.

I met *die Frau Professor*, who seemed rather frail to me and the formidable Tante Minna, her sister. If my memory serves me, I believe that Mathilde, Martin's older sister, was also there. They all looked me over. A few minutes before seven o'clock die Frau Professor said, "Papa will be out any minute. Let's go to the dining room." Sure enough, at the stroke of seven, the door opposite the end of the dining room opened, and out came the "Professor" wrapped like a god of antiquity in a cloud of smoke. I wish I could remember what he said to me. I do remember overhearing him say to Martin (my hearing faculties were always very acute), "Much too pretty for our family. . . ."

It is possible that grandfather recognized at a glance that my mother, who was probably beautifully dressed, came from a wealthy family and would be a threat to the thrifty lifestyle practiced by the women in the Freud family. But we shall hear that this meeting with the Freud family occurred only after Martin had returned from the war, a year and a half later.

The dinner conversation turned around the war and the difficulties of providing food for such a large family. They mentioned a certain visitor from Switzerland who had brought some cigars for Freud, the very brand he smoked, which were hard to obtain in Vienna. Anyway, I was impressed with Berggasse 19, especially by the professor's charisma, and I remember speaking to my father about it. He was not impressed as Freud was just another psychiatrist, and one who wrote pornographic books at that.

Esti, "too pretty" for the Freud family

Apparently Martin had come to Vienna, at this point, for a week's furlough.

Martin's leave was suddenly dramatically curtailed. He was ordered to return to his regiment as the Austrian army was starting its last big offensive in the south. The Austrian troops had progressed nearly to the gates of Venice in Italy, when their advance was stopped by English, Canadian, and Australian troops. When we parted at the *Südbahnhof* (South Station), Martin had his violet bouquet attached to his *Kepi* (cap) and I took a gold chain bracelet from my wrist and placed it around his. It was like a storybook romantic scene. That was the last I saw of Martin for a long time

MARIENBAD, ANGLER HAUS
    July 5, 1918   (2)
    Dear Dr. Freud,
    After a rather tiring trip we got here. It seems like a very nice place, good weather, and in spite of that I would so, so very much like to be in Vienna.
    Getting on the train, how disgusting, the way people behave. Ladies bicker like domestics, men push and shove, the culture of children. We fared quite well, we all had reserved seats, although I ceded mine later to more needy folks. I was annoyed because I was being vengefully bothered by a soldier whose advances I had rejected. Well, no more of that, I have become indifferent to all that.
    Now I will tell you something which I think will interest you and probably also surprise you. I think I was right to do this and to tell you right away about it. I told my parents about what you asked me yesterday. Mother was terribly nice, I think she has great compassion for us, and the parents said, for God's sake, what will you live on. Mother also said, and I think she is a very smart woman, that we are both too spoiled and used to a certain ease not to suffer in the long run from any freely undertaken deprivations. Otherwise she said she approved in every way.
    I hope that you are not angry at me that I did that without telling you ahead of time; but I did not know what to do and I was in such despair that I could not contain myself any longer. It could not get any worse, only better.
    I will start your book tomorrow, today I am already too tired. Did I properly thank you for it? Yesterday I was still together with you—why have I not become quite conscious that today there is nothing. Are you already hungry? Not I, not yet. I just keep looking at my yellow bracelet and caress my cheeks with it, and know that someone exists who has the second piece of the bracelet and loves it very much. . . .

AUGUST 4, 1918   (3)
    In Vienna the mood is supposed to be revolutionary—one talks about war against R. [*Russia?*]. The population, although miserably nourished (I find that outrageous), continues to be amiable toward the middle class which gets everything under the sky, albeit against suitable change (1 dkg. [half an ounce] ham 1.50 K 1 egg 1.70 K, 1 dkg. [half an ounce] butter 75 K) etc., it is uncanny, don't you think.

Today is Sunday, tomorrow I will send you, contrary to your permission, once again something to read, the book is this time without literary merit but very amusing.... Please do not worry about my pocket money, for one it is a lovely habit of mine never to make it last, I cannot manage money, it melts in my hands, and second I bought these books and since I liked them extremely I am curious as to your reaction....

Your Old Esti

August 12, 1918   **(4)**

My dearest best friend,

... I was naughty and did not write you for almost a week, why indeed? Not a minute during the day that I don't think of you, no action in which I don't ask your advice, everything I like I want to share with you, everything that is beautiful I want to give you. Life without you here is not reality for me, everything flows off me, barely touches me. I was infinitely happy with your letter before the last, I cannot hear it often enough from you that you love me, I want to hear it over and over, when people tell me here that I am beautiful, I am joyful because I am beautiful for you, when I am kind, it is to do you a favor.

You write to me in your last letter "my Dearest" am I truly that? "Your Dearest"??

My Dearest, I know a thousand beautiful soft words and tender stroking of hands, which I want to whisper to you in a very very low tone, ashamed to write them down. "Reunion" will that not be unthinkably wonderful, I can hardly believe that a human being can have such splendid experiences, I look forward to it so incredibly that I always worry something bad could intervene....

Martin, You ... We, meaning myself, have had a great deal of company. Some of them intensive admirers "with serious intentions" who never leave me in peace, today, on top of the Rübezahl I and my friend were alone with five gentlemen. We laughed so heartily and declared that we were losing our good reputation won with so much effort, because we were without chaperon, since my mother did not follow us up the mountain. Are you very shocked, my little one? ...

Embracing you, but unfortunately only in thoughts, is your Esti.

Martin must have come to Vienna at this point, for another week's furlough.

MILITARY LETTER

Saturday, September 14, 1918   **(5)**

My dearest friend and companion,

I hope you arrived safely at the goal of your trip, without being surprised by too many unpleasantnesses and annoyances. I assume a letter full of love and tenderness for me is on the way and I infinitely look forward to it. The sun shines today and although I just skimmed through your book *Poverty* I am in a happy and optimistic mood. This book is oppressively grey on grey, it is so well written that one could get depressed over it, but I have firmly decided not to let myself be defeated, what is the use of being sad and sorry? Life is beautiful after all because we love each other and I won't be deprived of my confidence that it will still bring us unending riches.

The week I spent with you, now seems like a dream, only now am I slowly starting to find my way back to reality, I really have a lot to catch up with, you know, in the middle of some activity it happens to me that I put my hands in my lap and I lapse into dreams, you know what about? I dream always only of the past, the present is too monotonous and when will I be able to dream of the future? Yesterday my sisters asked me how it is with us. My answer: In spite of father's statement that everyone has kept their freedom, we consider us engaged, I quoted you? They kissed me and congratulated me and are very approving of my choice. Everything is so strange, don't you think? Free but committed! My dearest Martin, yesterday I went out and I had to watch out and make a rejecting face if someone followed me, which was not necessary when you were here. Listen, I was so terribly happy to hear your telling me that I was your dear beautiful big girl. Childish, don't you think? ...

I am afraid I was not very nice to you in this letter, not as nice as I want to be, but I was very tired and harried so forgive

Your Esti

who loves you very very much.

MY ANSWER TO YOUR LETTER OF SEPTEMBER 9, 1918   **(6)**

My Martin,

On July 3, 1918, about 6:00 P.M. in the Seilergasse, opposite the entrance to the Kärtnergasse I gave you a little golden bracelet and said: Whatever may happen, when you look at the bracelet, remember that I will always love you very much.

This has happened more than three months ago, a short span of time. But we lived through infinitely much during that time, I mean not outer events, only things that concerned the two of us. The next day you asked me whether I wanted to become your wife, I did not give you an answer just then, that afternoon of the same day we kissed, in a way really for the first time, then I left on July 5. Something new had entered my life, something beautiful, but strange, unaccustomed that I experienced for the first time, against which I defended myself because it awoke wishes that I could not fulfill, it ignited thoughts that I did not want to think. Martin, it was much stronger than I and in a short time it took all my thoughts, captured all my wishes, my yearning and trying, my whole self, and my days are now illuminated by the blinding burning brilliance of strong love. We met again on September 5. You taught me to kiss, in those following eight days that we spent together, and to love you in a different way, novel for me, you awoke in me something physical that I had only obscurely guessed at. Since that time there is never a minute, day or night in which I am alone.

I can now write it black on white, which I have avoided so far (not thinking it very tasteful) taking it for granted that I am at any time ready with a thousand cheers to become your best and most faithful comrade for life.

Yet, I want to and may, in spite of everything I said so far, not become some obstacle for you, I am too proud for that. If the goal "Esti" ever shines for you in a less golden and rosy light then choose by all means and without another thought a different one. You may do this at any moment without any reproach from my side, I only demand the naked truth, without any consideration, it will never be too late for you, remember that Martin.

My answer may have become somewhat lengthy, but I think it is distinct and clear and I ask you to save this one among all my letters.

Perhaps it will never reach you, because I will not send it until I have received a letter from you, even if I should have to wait a whole lifetime.

In fidelity and love Esti Drucker

OCTOBER 10, 1918 **(7)**

My Martin,

We live in strange times, only at the outbreak of war did I have a similar feeling, waiting for the next day with the same tension without knowing what was about to happen. At home we have the following conversations: "Please father, pour us each a glass of wine."—"No, I am not raising my daughters to become drunkards."—"Come on, father, we shall be killed in any case." Many people consider already where they should flee if.... You know, I am absolutely staying in Vienna. As long as the population is halfway decently fed, there is nothing to fear. What will happen to the German emperor? I fear the worst (I mean for him).

Dearest Martin, it takes too long to give you my personal opinion about all the events, you will manage without it and to prove to you that women won't be defeated, I am getting a sweet new evening gown, albeit not sewn with new materials.

I am currently reading "the irrational knot" by Shaw, naturally in English, I could not get hold of *Candida*.

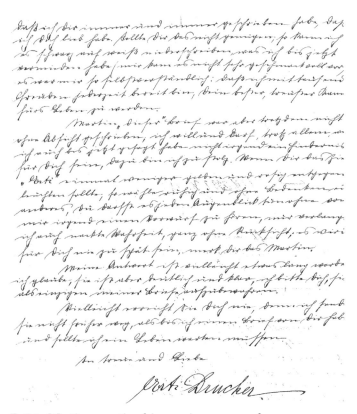

Letter from Esti to Martin accepting his marriage proposal

Martin, dearest, I am so happy and I love you. I have changed a lot since you left, I am no longer a little girl, but a developed mature woman, I think something quieter more goal oriented has gotten into me, and I am rich with love and kindness, which pleases me and it is right that I have changed that way.

Martin, tell me, I should not have written these words, but you will understand me, you know what I mean. . . .

Your Esti only wants to give you many warm sunkisses. May I?

The news from the Piave front, which was at first so optimistic, turned bad. What made it even worse, one heard of mutinies among the Hungarian soldiers. One heard of the disintegration of the German armies who were confronted by fresh American troops. The Czechs suddenly declared that they didn't want to be part of the Austrian Empire any longer.

My own world turned to chaos. There were no direct news from Martin. The paper informed us that the entire southern Austrian army had surrendered to the Italians. Life in Vienna went on as smoothly as ever. I do not remember any food riots. The opera performed every evening and one went to the Stadtpark in the afternoon to listen to the concert and eat a fruit sherbet at Hübner's Café.

My parents now had three daughters of marriageable age on their hands. On one afternoon, my mother came with us to the Stadtpark and made the seeming casual remark that a friend of my father's was joining us at our table and that we had better be friendly, and that was that. Another day father took a box for the opera, which was rather unusual (we girls always took cheap seats on the fourth gallery) and lo and behold—in the neighboring box was the lady from Brünn with her son in officer's uniform. We were distantly polite to each other. It became apparent to me that I had somehow passed the test in the eyes of the mother. My parents invited this young Mr. Bruckner to pay us a visit, which he did. He also attended an evening at the Urania where I gave a poetry reading. My parents told me that Erich Bruckner was a very wealthy man, an engineer, and part owner of a factory that produced wagons to transport coal and other freight materials. I was duly impressed.

One day my youngest sister came home with the news that one of the girls with whom she went to school bragged about the engagement of her older sister to Erich Bruckner who was considered the most eligible bachelor in town. It seems that Miss Kornfeld had known Mr. Bruckner for quite some time before those happy results came about. I wondered why old Mrs. Bruckner objected to the marriage of her son with the Kornfeld girl who was pretty and of a good family. The reason, I discovered, was that the Kornfelds were baptized and now Erich planned to be baptized as well. In time the wedding took place and four months later the young bride was dead of the Lung Plague, which was a raging epidemic all over the world. I heard that Erich did not get along with his partner who was a pious Jew. Bruckner sold his partnership and remained a widower with nothing to do until he made a foolish marriage to a Catholic, a "pure Aryan" 25 years his junior.

Mother leaves it open whether she would have responded to Erich Bruckner if he had been interested in her.

In the meantime Erich and I had become good friends. His is an odd and sad story. When I returned to Vienna for the first time after World War II, in

1954, I looked through the telephone book for names of people I had known. I found Erich Bruckner still at his old address in the Ferstelgasse. We met at a coffeehouse, as is the custom in Vienna. There was the former man-about-town, broken by misfortune, looking older than his age, with only one gold tooth left in front, his jacket full of spots. He looked so poor that I wanted to pay for his coffee. It seems that, as soon as the Nazis entered Vienna, his second wife had taken a lover into their home. Although she was urged to divorce Bruckner because he was Jewish, she permitted him to stay with her, which saved his life since otherwise he would have been deported to a concentration camp and exterminated. Bruckner had a daughter from this second marriage who was a teenager at that time. A few years after this visit I received a message from some friends we had in common that Bruckner was very ill (I believe he had a stroke), that his daughter was taking care of him, and that they were so poor that friends were taking up a collection for them. I contributed more than my share to it. How the fates shape our destinies!

In 1918, however, this was a different story. It was said that at the ripe age of 22 I had lost my last chance at a good match. Members of my family, including aunts and uncles who had married into it, were making remarks about my lack of sex appeal, my arrogance, and my stupidity in not recognizing my good fortune in that offer. Those remarks must have smarted because I remember them today, after all these years.

I had a cousin in Prague who wrote that she would arrange a poetry reading for me in one of the concert halls there. It was a good opportunity for me to escape the unpleasant gossip around me. Prague became a big success. The critics in leading German newspapers raved about my talent, praising the choice of recitations and calling me the "female Marcel Salzer" (he was the foremost elocutionist in German-speaking lands). It was easier to get food in Prague and I found myself staying with that cousin for a few weeks. I returned to Vienna on the last train one could travel on without a passport. The ancient Kingdom of Bohemia, for 800 years under the rulers of the Habsburgs, declared independence from the monarchy and became Czechoslovakia.

Observing this disintegration of the Habsburg Empire, I spoke to my father and asked him to exchange the money I had inherited from Grandfather to Swiss francs. In 1918, Austrian Kronen were worth half of what Swiss francs were, while before the war they had been approximately equal in value. Father was upset by this request and said he wouldn't do it because I would lose half of my fortune. He was blind to the reality of the situation and thus I nearly lost everything except for the money invested in good stocks.

Soon after I had returned from Prague, a Red Cross card arrived via Switzerland informing me that Martin had been made prisoner in a camp near Genoa. I immediately told the Freud family the good news.

Below is a warm greeting from Martin's no doubt greatly relieved mother with faithful news of the whole family, including "his friend Esti" whom, we hear, grandmother has not yet met.

VIENNA, FEBRUARY 18, 1919

My dearest Martin,

We received all your cards from January and are happy to know you are in good health. Hopefully you have meanwhile also heard that thank God, everything is in order with us. Papa luckily bears up quite well under the daily work of nine hours and, even if the nourishment situation is less than ideal, one has learned in all these difficult years to manage. This winter even surpassed its predecessor in terms of lack of light and warmth. The doors to houses get locked at 8:00 P.M., the houses darken, so do the streets, and the last trolley car runs at 8:30 P.M. You can thus imagine that our evening entertainments are not very varied. Oliver, who can naturally not find any work at the moment, spends his time with photographic games, hoping for the summer. Ernst is working very hard in Munich, will hopefully graduate after this summer. Annerl is always very engaged in her job, and much liked by mothers and children. Mathilde and Robert are also well, they play much music. Sopherl, as you already know has given birth to another little son; unfortunately I could not take care of her this time, since travel circumstances are impossible and she is still alone with the children in Schwerin while Max [Max Halberstadt, Sophie's husband] has reopened his photo studio. In March they will get again a flat in Hamburg.

Your friend Esti has returned from Prague and has invited Annerl, I have not yet met her. We are happy to approach spring and hope that a reunion with you is also in the wind. Good-bye my dearest Martin, stay healthy and see to it that time does not linger too long. With greeting and kiss, your Mama.

Chapter 9

Letters to a Prisoner of War

*M*y *mother then starts a long and one-sided correspondence with her prisoner-of-war fiancé. In her first letter, she must just have learned about his having been taken prisoner.*

ADDRESSEE: PRIGGIONERA DE GUERRA. OSPITALE DI CAMP 107. ZONA DI GUERRA.
FORWARDED TO CAGOLETTO

December 3, 1918   **(8)**

My dearest Martin,

Today I finally received two cards from you, they make me so glad and happy. Don't worry at all, everything is quiet in Vienna, the theaters are playing, concerts, etc. one can go safely alone in the streets at any time of day and does not get more than usually importunated. I tried last week to send you news but I think you must not have received them, maybe it works this time. Your people are well, I telephoned with your sister Anny today, your brothers are at home.

My deeply loved Martin, a huge load came off my chest today, since I received your news. I love you so, so much, think of you all the time and look forward to our reunion after which I will never let you leave me, that I know.

My most affectionate congratulations for your birthday, with all my heart, a soon-to-come fulfillment of all your wishes. The birthday kiss will be postponed, but I don't think we can restrict ourselves to a single one.

My dear boy, surely you are taking good care of yourself and don't let yourself in for foolishnesses, all I want is to get you back in good health.

There is little to tell about myself, I live very withdrawn, am said to look well, which surprises me, sleep a lot and take it as easy as the circumstances permit; I try to cancel my January lectures, have lost all motivation, without you, but I think it is too late, but I think the lecture room will be locked in any case due to shortage of coal. Besides it is very cold and much snow, if you were here I would ask you to give me ski lessons, to be postponed to later times. At the moment I have the irresistible wish to buy myself a lute and to learn to play it, are you "very glad" about that; I generally pass my time with similar useful occupations. I guess you are journeying through beautiful Italy at the cost of the government, do you know what I associate with that?

My Martin, I hope that it will be possible for you to write me soon again, your news are my life. I pray to God that he protects you, kiss you and remain forever your Esti who loves you with all her heart.

Addressee: Tenente Dr. Martin Freud. prigioniero deguerra in Italia, Clogoleta, Prov. de Genova.

Prague, January 27   (11)

Dearest Martin,

I am not letting any opportunity pass by to try and get some news of me to you. I have already been two months without a line from you. Sometimes a huge bleakness descends upon me, I don't really know whether you still love me. Perhaps you feel the same way, you need not worry, I so so long for you; I am a guest here at relatives and do everything to make the time pass more quickly. I shall bless the day that brings you to me.

My thoughts and wishes are ever with you, I kiss you, your Esti.

Addressee: Tenente Dr. Martin Freud. prigioniero deguerra in Italia, Clogoleta, Prov. de Genova. Do not write between the lines.

February 24, 1919   (13)

Dear Dr. Freud, thank God, I have now regular news from you and I conclude from them that you have not changed your sentiments toward me, I am so glad about that. I was just four weeks in Prague, danced a lot and gave a reading with very great success and excellent critical reviews. Now, only a short time in Vienna I was drawn against my will into a big social turmoil, if a certain gentleman were present, I would rest much much happier on my laurels and other successes. May God grant that the time is no longer so distant when the sun will shine again for us in Vienna.

March 10, 1919   (16)

My dear, dearest Martin,

I must try again to write you a letter. I would like for you to know approximately what I am about. My main occupation is to love you. You can't believe how time consuming that is, in the middle of some activity I sink my hands, look into the blue and dream after you; now it is already much much better compared to before, but in November, at a point when I knew nothing about you, for such a horribly long time, I sometimes started to cry for no reason (I mean for the others), I would not want to live through that time once again. From January 15 until February 15 I was staying with relatives in Prague, to help me not to get too downcast, it was quite nice, I gave a reading there with much success, went to big balls, etc. and all that time I felt limitless yearning for you. Now, In Vienna I am much invited, and we, meaning friends of mine, have founded a youth club with literary and musical purposes, I was twice, at mother's special wish, at exclusive dancing parties. How lovely it would be if you were here, I am being courted a lot, heavy, thick compliments, but you know, nobody can tell me with equally deeply felt conviction that I am beautiful, better than you, and nobody can kiss the hand in such a knightly fashion as you do and now I also want to make you a compliment from my innermost conviction. The more I get together with people, the more people I come to know, all the more clearly I see how much I love you and how nice you really are. Or, listen, tell me do I just imagine that because you are not here? Perhaps you will be interested that I refused two big proposals, and if you do not return soon, a third will have its turn. It is really too silly that people do not know yet that we belong together, meaning, I don't really know whether you still want to? I have to personally excuse myself with all my relatives, aunts, grandmothers, etc. that I dare to say no, and one Aunt said: "If a girl is halfway pretty she thinks right away that she has to get at least a prince;" it is a good thing that I already have my prince. Spring has started quite powerfully, I feel it in all my limbs and it hurts me, if possible, even more to be alone, when I am quite so sad, I take your old letters, I think I already know them all very well by heart, but that doesn't matter, tell me do you still love me the way you wrote to me back then, I would be so proud about it? I will of course keep my promises, but not because a decent person has to keep promises, but because I cannot do anything else. That should also be the only reason for you....

It is no wonder, given this almost one-sided correspondence, that my young mother struggles with her constant doubts whether her intense passion is answered in a similar vein—or whether the affection of her distant lover has perhaps cooled down. In spite of her strict upbringing, she dares to express the depth of her feelings, perhaps to hold onto him with her love and conquer him ever anew. She wants to win over this man, this prince she has chosen. It was a daring, independent enterprise for those times, quite against the usual conventions in which she was brought up.

MARCH 14, 1919   **(17)**

My Martin,

You know that I have had no news from you since January 31. Listen you, I have not yet turned completely ugly but I did get a lot of white hair. But now I do nurture already a very quiet little hope to have you soon here. A cousin of mine who is also a medical man and had been in Elba, came home last week and reported that all doctors, students, pharmacists etc. will be sent home and now an acquaintance came to Vienna who personally went to fetch her son who had been prisoner in Italy. How much I would like to fetch you; I so terribly much would like to be already nice and good and loving with you, to be allowed to spoil you, I can't do anything, anything for you except to try to write and think of you, but I make full use of that, namely the thinking. Listen you, I believe there is not an instance day or night, when you are not fully conscious in my mind, tell me, do you feel it, I sometimes imagine to feel your thoughts of me. But perhaps you no longer love me, and it is terribly intrusive of me to write you such letters. Listen you, then I would be so ashamed, because then it would be none of your business that I love you so tremendously. In fact, I am no longer totally sure whether I should look forward to a reunion, or not also be afraid of it. You will tell me, won't you, that I am a totally stupid girl. For one thing I beg you, Martin, do not worry about us, there is time until we are together, then I help you, that way things will become easier.

Yesterday my sister had a birthday, in two months and one week later I have a birthday, my wish is that you will already be here, and we then go on a common excursion. Imagine, last Sunday I made a excursion with your sister Anny, your brother and another man, we sent you a common Red Cross card, I must stop now, otherwise the poor man who censors letters has too much to read.

Martin, continue to love me, think of me, dream of me, stay healthy, come home soonest and be many many times greeted, kissed and embraced by your Esti.

VIENNA, MARCH 23, 1919   **(20)**

Dearest, dearest Martin,

I am so very glad, to finally get, after two long months, a sign of life, your card from March 2, from you. You have no idea how much I agonized about you, enough to get grey hair and become old and ugly, but I really did get grey hair. Whenever your parents or I do not get any news for so long, the days start to creep along like tired grey shadows without sun or life, in my head hammers the one thought, what is it with Martin! All that while I must go out into society, give recitations, allow them to court me, in sum all the stuff that makes up daily life but constantly the anxiety about you. Tell me, do you deserve that one lives through so many anxious hours for your sake, will you be rich enough to pay me back for them?

Enough of that, now I am happy, I have your card, know that you almost lack for nothing except freedom and myself, well, poor guy, also money and underwear, that you even received my letter and if we have a little luck, I might not have to wait again for your next card for two months, because you will come in person, hopefully even earlier, I want to get my birthday kiss from you personally, I assume you still know when.

Nothing much to tell about myself, I sometimes go dancing, give frequent recitations, am much invited, am much celebrated and courted, people even say *very* much so, am used to and can bear strong portions of that, as you probably know, have several lovely dresses that suit me very well and think every instant of you.

Continue to love me very very much and be tenderly embraced and kissed. Martin, you, my worry child, from your Esti.

MARCH 27, 1919   **(21)**

My dearest Martin,

Today I got your card from March 9, I am so happy that you are recuperating and that you feel well and are getting mail from me. You want to know, Dearest, how I live in Vienna, the same as before, perhaps I sleep a bit more, but eat less because there is nothing to buy. Given the circumstances I think I look quite well, I do quite a few recitations; on April 14 I have my own evening in the little concert hall, when I will recite only from the works of a very young and unknown poet Robert Neumann, courageous of me, don't you think? But since I know that you are quite well and that I will, perhaps, hopefully even surely, have you with me before all too long, will be able to kiss you, I have gained confidence. If all goes well, meaning if it is sold out, I might earn about 300 Kronen, because I have a 50 percent share in the profits, is that not great, but the very best is that I already know what I will do with the money and can use it fabulously well, which, it seems, is always the case with money. I frequently go out, am constantly invited to parties and sometimes I accept, but naturally only the very exclusive ones, am always surrounded and flirt at least with 6 men simultaneously, if you don't come home soon, I will bring it up to 10. Yesterday I was also invited, got home only at dawn, about 5:30 A.M. because could not get my sister to leave and for that I have now quite a hangover. In the course of a conversation with somebody, the talk came to the Cadima [a Jewish fraternity] and your name was mentioned and the man informed me of the big news that you are a very pleasant intelligent guy. And he also said that you are engaged, whereupon I said that I knew your sister and that you were in Italy as a prisoner of war. So I sort of disowned you, what a disgrace. . . .

Yesterday your sister Anna called, to tell me about your long letter, I am even a bit envious of it. I like to be together with her, she reminds me in some ways of you, the way of speaking, the eyes, and I simply like that. But she has a way of being severe, reserved and cool so that I still don't know whether she actually likes me. I also know your brother Olly [*sic*] who certainly likes me, with men I succeed most of the time quite easily, and oh yes, I have also met your favorite sister Tilde and your father, but only to say hello. . . . Please accept in any case for each word a long kiss, that much I will certainly still manage. Affectionately Your Esti.

PRIGIONERE DE GUERRA IN ITALIA
    April 7, 1919   **(25)**
    My Martin, my Dearest Darling,
    How sad for both of us that we have to be separated for so long. At times I think my heart will shatter from yearning and longing for you. I am writing this letter in a very somber mood, perhaps I should not write to you in such low

Martin in youth

spirits but to whom can I turn except to you, you my only true friend! I don't think that you can imagine how things look around here, how much the situation has worsened since our last get together, all the commercial and industrial enterprises are downsizing, the prices for food and articles of daily use are climbing into the immeasurable and what else will come, *dieu le sait* (god only knows). I am positive if only you were already here, it would all leave me indifferent, tell me, have I ever mentioned that before you entered my life I was practically finished with it, out of tiredness or boredom or meaninglessness I would not have given two pennies for it, I know I had hours in which only laziness or cowardice prevented me from saying good-bye. Martin, you, since you are here, I enjoy living, I want to sing a hymn to life in spite of all the worries, because I can love you, I have a goal in front of my eyes, I want to be happy with you, a purpose has come up, I want to make you happy. Listen, listen, I am royal with kindness and love and tenderness, I want to give it all to you, it should all belong to you. I like to imagine that you also need me, that I am also your best possibility, your longing, perhaps it is all only an empty delusion of mine, and once again I build up too much in my head? Martin, you, however it is or will be, dearest, do not worry about things as long as you are gone. Please, not you, once you are here it cannot be helped, but then I can at least run my hand through your hair ever so gently, stroke your hands and kiss away the folds on your forehead. . . .

Be sure to keep thinking about me, then please write me letters, that you will keep for me and give me to read upon our reunion.

There is little to tell about my life. I have told you already about my recital evening on the 14th, poetry of Robert Neumann, I think the piece is very effective, I do a wonderful job with the reading, the poet is always totally amazed. He is a very nice young man who has a lovely looking young blond bride who would surely greatly appeal to you, I read everything to him over two sessions, the bride is of course always present since she is most interested and practically collaborates, but I suffer greatly from this and feel double lonely when I have to watch how they sometimes hold hands or lean their shoulders together, quite naturally, not at all tastelessly, this open joyful mutually loving each other, to belong together and be able to be together, Martin, you, why can you not be present as well! Quite soon I am to give a Jewish recital evening in the Reading and Discussion Hall for Jewish University students, I am not yet sure when, I am able to perform once again, for a time in November, December and January I was not able to do so, it is the only thing that gives me pleasure and a sort of narcotic for me, I also think to have made much progress, everything has become very mature, my voice also sounds very good and soft, all of which are opinions of my mother, who, as you well know is a very severe critic, you have never heard me really perform.

Sundays I sometimes go on excursions with your sister Annerl and your brother Oliver, he is exactly as you have described him to me, but also a kind dear fellow, but you are, thank God, quite different from him, meaning if you were like him, I would hardly love you or you love me. I sometimes have some peculiar conflicts, my sisters also want to go on excursions with young people and I will naturally go along, but then they want to take along some young man but it does not seem right to me to allow someone to court me a whole day who may then perhaps fall in love with me, if that is not already the case, and I also don't think that you would like that, now the weather is beginning to be lovely and warmer, until a short time ago it was bitterly cold, spring is arriving with its colorful sweet-smelling blossoms and sun and green, if it brings you to me, it should be welcome.

So many kisses as is room in your heart for me

Your Esti

PRIGIONIERE DI GUERRA IN ITALIA

April 14, 1919   (26)

My dearest Martin,

This evening was my Robert Neumann reading, I am just after dinner and my first activity is of course to write to you to tell you everything exactly. So, let us start, nicely in sequence, I wore a white and black low cut dress—had gotten it in January—light stockings, black low shoes, hair as usual, but for once not all entangled, I think it suits me very well. I mean the dress. The hall accommodates 200 persons, it was almost sold out, among the audience were your two sisters. I got quite a few flowers, but unfortunately only from very uninteresting personages, all of them women, a big pot with flowers from an aunt, a huge lilac tree from an elderly cousin, and a smaller plant of roses with Easter eggs and candy inside from the wife of Dr. Moser, a friend of my mother's and an azalea plant from a colleague of my father. Among the audience there were partly acquaintances of R. Neumann and of mine, some girlfriends, dance companions, relatives etc. It's being Passover evening interfered a bit. Now, about the recital. The poems I recited are not really my sort, you know, predominantly lyrics full of images, not a single love poem which I now do so well, some of it very nicely and delicately interpreted, I did very well with "the ballad of the yellow death," you know from Edgar Allen Poe's novel "The Red Death," which was very effective, then there was an intermission and afterwards the third act of Tyl Uienspiegel, which I did in my view most excellently, in parts strikingly so and into depths. The act lasted about 50 minutes, about the biggest challenge but one could show what one can do, and give it one's all. Big success, was called back many times. Afterwards I was and still am very tired, let the congratulations come down upon me and left for home without great pomp and circumstances. So, now you know everything in great detail, as if you had been present. I was terribly cheerful all day and kept having the feeling as if something very agree-able had happened. I hope, and now with confidence that I will be called to the telephone at not too distant a moment, and it will be You, You, I can't say unex-pected, because I expect you every moment, I already think all the time where I should give you the first kiss, it will hardly be possible in the Maria There-sienstraße or on the Franz-Josefs-Kai and I don't think, I consider it quite impos-sible, that we can hold out until we get to Schönbrunn or to the Prater. Please consider it as well, you are much more intelligent, perhaps some idea will come to you. I hope this problem will soon present itself, that is my wish for you and for me, many 1,000 kisses from your Esti.

MAY 19, 1919   (32)
    My dearest Martin,
    Today, finally after a long time I have news once again from your card from Easter Sunday. Hopefully you have meanwhile received more frequently my mail, because, surely you believe me that I write to you a lot, given that it is now my greatest pleasure of all. But you don't have to be sorry for me, I am not poor, being able to write to you can make one very rich. In Vienna it does not want to get really warm this year, I still wear my winter suit in the sunny month of May, but at least I have finally decided to buy myself a new hat, for a change a tiny crimson one which has the big advantage of being quite inexpensive, but for that, it seems very conspicuous, given that I get addressed in the street every 5 minutes when I wear it. I regularly go on Sunday excursions with your brother Olly, he is amused how people constantly try to pick me up, he told me yester-day I have something provocative, but I am not in the least in a provocative mood, but he does not court me at all, he is very nice and decent and I think, he really likes me. He is quite funny, if I did not notice the clothing, I would lose the feeling whether I am dealing with a man or a woman, except I notice it because men are easier to handle.
    Martin, you, my dear Martin, I so long for a dear tender word from you, you, when are you coming back, may I address the immodest request to fate to have you soon near me, with me.
    Until then be most dearly greeted and kissed from
    Your Esti

MAY 22, 1919   (33)
    My Martin,
    I always have to consider how to address you, the German language is too impoverished for me, dear, dearest sometimes appears too little, I want

to talk to you, be able to tell you, so soft and from my heart and tenderly, my dear dear Martin! Do you hear me, do you see me?

It is evening, my birthday is ending and I want to tell you what I received. Your congratulation arrived punctually already the day before yesterday, I thank you for it, would have been very sad if you had forgotten. From my parents I got 1,000 Kronen to spend as I wish, but I will not buy myself anything right now, some other time, until I know something reasonable, also from my mother I got gloves and silk stockings, from Marianne *des deutschen Spielers Wunderhorn* by Meyrink, from Lily a very beautiful leather-bound book to write in, but I don't need such a thing, am well provided with diaries and notebooks for poems etc., from my little friend Trude *Chinese*, meaning *Japanese Spring,* and last but not least from your brother photos from our common excursions and two lovely enlargements, I find that very friendly and attentive, he knew because he asked me a few days ago to take with him and Annerl and my sisters a loge for *Tristan,* I refused with the explanation it was my birthday, but for one my nerves could surely not stand *Tristan* at the moment, and further I want to listen to it with you the next time and second I know for sure that if I go together with your brother to a loge in the opera, especially since I quite often make excursions with him, I will be considered the next day, by the Vienna gossip society, as engaged to him.

TALKOF, WHITSUN
   Monday, 1919   (35)
   My Martin,
   I am here since Friday evening and am enjoying life. Today I was lying again, clean and properly dressed, with pretty soft slippers on my feet, the kind one can easily slip off, on a meadow, until now, 5:00 P.M., dreaming, stretching my tired painful limbs, happy with the sun, with life, that I am so healthy and strong, for total happiness I only missed that you give me a kiss from time to time. But now I have to tell you how I got painful feet and what gives me the right to be so very lazy. Saturday I was alone with a 14-year-old boy on the Schneeberg (father allowed me the Baumgartnerhaus). Got started at 10:00 A.M. thick fog, went through the Eng to the Bannsteig, then Emmysteig, Damböckhütte, Hotel Hochschneeberg then back over the Krummbachgraben, Kaiserbrunn, home by 8:00 P.M., I walked very well, the next day, start at 5:00 A.M. Weichtal, Alpenvereinsteig Otterschutzhaus (you knows all those mountain paths, don't you?), back over Seehütte, Holzknechtsteig, Edeloch, home by 9:00 P.M. It had rained all night but it stopped

when we got started and afterwards it almost cleared up. At the beginning my limbs ached from the day before, but when it came to climbing ladders and at some points to rock climbing I no longer felt any pain, felt secure, free of vertigo and fearless, and I think skillful, when you will train me, I hope you will have pleasure with me, the most unpleasant was when we had to wait beneath a waterfall until a party before us had climbed a stretch, it took them forever, I got all showered, those in front of us were so frightened, they groaned and moaned, we then asked them to let us pass ahead wherever possible.

Unfortunately it is back to Vienna tomorrow evening. I hope a grey card is waiting for me. If only one came which announces your arrival, may I get you from the station. Listen you, how will it be when we see each other again eye to eye, able to hold hands.

Sometimes it all seems like a dream, which would be unbelievably beautiful, to let oneself be loved, that is so soft, so warm and you are a prince a real fairy tale prince,

Your Esti

JUNE 18, 1919   (36)

Martin, my dear boy,

You will be coming home soon, and so that you should not be too surprised, I must tell you for once how it actually looks in our postwar republic and in the hydrocephalus Vienna. Since you were here last, basic changes have occurred, imagine the mailboxes are even painted grey! To take the trolley car, one has to be almost a multi-millionaire, my modest pocket money circumstances allow me this pleasure only very seldom, one trip actually costs 60 Kronen; going for walks too often is however also not recommended because the Vienna streets, due to our lack of progress, are nothing but trenches with overhangs to protect against bullets. I would put up gladly with this smaller troubles, but I am annoyed that the suburban rail is not running given our intentions for a trip to Schönbrunn and that one icecream costs 4 Kronen, is that not a misery, 4 Kronen for a mixed ice!

Graben and Kärtnerstraß [elegant midtown streets] have remained unchanged, except that one can admire in the shop windows ravishing little shoes in all colors starting at 200 Kronen and up, but you will probably be more interested in the women who wear them, they have also remained approximately the same, pretty and elegant as always, some, the more mature ones, put on a bit more color, you know, like trees that have rings for each year and a few young girls promenade their fiancé triumphantly, after the satisfied Papa has put an ad in the *Neue Freie Presse* to inform the world that his Miss daughter has found a taker.

In contrast, the men have changed a lot, for one there are now many of that species, wherever one looks there are men, and second they no longer wear a uniform, meaning the old Austrian uniform, the Viennese are in civil apparel, with the others one is confused, one wears stripes on his trousers, another on the sleeves, a third on his head, those are the differences between the nations, the remnants of the former monarchy. The few folks who still speak German have now become old acquaintances ... oh, I almost forgot, there are cars in the streets and if one is not very careful one can even get run over. Tiritiri honk the Italians, the other military missions are less individual in their honking signals, but they are different in other ways, I concentrate on the latest racial studies—The English are giant guys, blond and tanned with a smart gentlemanlike [*sic*] brutal expression in their face, dismissing all women with their looks, the French here, are small, graceful, with narrow hips, always in dubious female company, the Italians broad strong compact shapes, I am very popular with them, in passing I am always the subject of very fiery looks.

The other day I was with the parents for dinner at the *Stadtpark*, it was a regular beautiful warm summer night, made, if not for kissing, at least for flirting, but since I released all this year's shy admirers in the course of the winter to my sisters, I was very well behaved and totally alone, no soul nearby even for an exchange of looks, a situation which is perhaps very upright and decent, but extremely unamusing, in plain German, boring. Before that I was together with a very pretty same-aged young woman, whom I have known since girlhood, now the mother of very cute six-month-old twins, her husband, after a not quite two year long marriage lets her have dinner alone with six free-floating men ... ! Martin, should I tell you some more gossip?

I think you will laugh about my letters, quite nice for a change something else from me, don't you agree? If you knew how little I feel in a laughing mood, your last news was of May 11 ... !

In affectionate inclination, and heartfelt thoughts, Your Esti

JULY 14, 1919   **(41)**

My Martin,

Today I received your card from June 22, I am very glad that you get at least regular news from me. I would certainly like to make my letters deeper and more affectionate, so that you are satisfied and feel pleased, but the thought that they are read by several strangers and some force inside me keeps me from writing down my truest and most tender thoughts.

Dearest: "I am not a poet" you once said, and the same is true for me.

Martin, you, I have very much hope and very much confidence and much courage, first of all I have invincible self-confidence, and second, or rather first, even more confidence in you, you should have it, I think, it is half the way to success.

Sometimes, on totally sad and bad days, I imagine that you no longer love me, then I take for comfort your old letters and read them again and again, I even have my favorite letter of September 23: "My dearest, big, beautiful girl!" This letter is the most beautiful, there you are just the way I want you to be, you know it is the one, in which you tell me about the big success at the military court.

Have I mentioned that there is in Vienna a new and lovely park the former emperor park next to the *Hofburg* [the emperor's domicile] is now available to the public, then there is a new theater, the Schönbrunner-Schloß theater, where *Burgtheater* actors are playing. . . .

In the next days I will telegraphy you again, hopefully a last time. If you can come to see me at Puchenstuben, write me with what train you will arrive, I will then meet you on the way, at Lannbach-Mühle.

Dearest, dearest Martin, I love you so incredibly, kiss me until I say "stop," Your Esti.

JULY 17, 1919   **(42)**

My dearest, dearest Martin,

Today I telegraphed you again, hopefully for a last time, in Italian, they no longer accept German. . . .

Martin, I am hopelessly sad today, the newspaper keep mentioning the delay of peace, everything is against us. [*Torn parts of the letter, some sentences about difficult economic and employment conditions.*] Everything has become so bleak, my laboriously gained optimism, partly due to my ostrich attitude, partly due to your news of the last weeks is all gone. What is it all for, I can't see the necessity of all these events. Does one have to go on living? I am quite convinced of my uselessness. The only thing that gives me, in my eyes, a right to live is YOU. But maybe that is not true; what do you need me for; to be kind to you, to care for you, perhaps others can do this much better. I have self-confidence, but will you experience me as an obstacle, a burden.

Martin, forgive me that I write you all this, but when I write to you, in this intimate contact of souls with you, I regain hope and pleasure. You, Dearest, I think my letters will bore you, do I not write again and again the same things, I am tormented by this one-sided correspondence, I keep thinking all the time, what would you respond. I can generally undertake nothing without bringing it in some connection with you. Would you approve of my going someplace, of reading a certain book, wear a particular dress ... by the way I wore the other day, on my mother's wish, a light blue summer dress, in which you had not liked me, the afternoon was spoiled, is that not childish.

A man has one love—the world!

A woman has one world—love!

I just read this in P. Altenberg. How accurate is the second sentence of this aphorism. Since I love you, you are my world. I am ashamed in front of you ... in former times ... and now. I never loved before, I was perhaps once in love, but never in a way that affected my thinking, my acting, now they could deprive me of this whole colorful beautiful God's world and stick me into a dark hole, I would hardly notice it, because my thoughts are with you.

Martin, dearest to my heart, may I tell you everything. We have not seen each other for 10 months, but the long separation has not called forth any estrangement, as one would expect, maybe a little at the very beginning but now you are closer to me than ever, and I so long, so long for you and when you will come, I will surely make a stupid face and not dare to give you a regular kiss.

Has my love, my yearning, my wish of all wishes no power to call you back to me?

I remain forever your Esti

END OF LETTERS TO A PRISONER OF WAR

In the summer of 1919, when the family was staying at an inn in Puchenstuben, a telegram arrived for me saying that Martin had arrived in Vienna and would come to see me even before he saw his parents who were spending the summer in the Tatra mountains.

EXPRESS LETTER.

Dr. Martin Freud
Berggasse 19.
Puchenstuben, Hotel Burger
August 7, 1919   **(43)**
My Martin, my dear, dearest,

About an hour ago at 7:30 P.M. I received your telegram. You are here, finally here, it is like a dream, I cannot believe, I am stunned, am frantic wondering whether someone is playing me a dirty trick. I shall call you right away, tomorrow morning, hoping to still get a letter from you.

You, you are coming to visit, for sure, won't you? If nothing else is possible, at least over Sunday, there is a train that leaves Vienna at 6:00 P.M. from the *Westbahnhof* [West Station] which arrives here about 10:30 at night, we then make some excursion, or whatever you want, you don't need to bring along food, you get very good food here and much less expensive than in Vienna. Please be sure to take along *very warm* clothing, it is very chilly and you come from a warmer climate. Will you still come on Saturday? If I should not be able to reach you by telephone, please telegraph me or write when I may expect you.

Martin, I cannot continue to write, my head is in turmoil and my hands are trembling. I welcome you home most affectionately and wish you a wonderful time. I love and I long for you, am so very happy about your return, kiss you many many times and cannot wait for the reunion and your visit.

Your Esti

No DATE. IT SEEMS TO BE A PIECE OF PAPER LEFT FOR MARTIN IN HIS ROOM.   **(44)**

Dearest Martin,

Please forgive my not welcoming you, I would so have liked to meet you at least at L. Bachmühle, but supposedly that is not done, people could talk etc., and so I must go to sleep. Please forgive me that I have left traces in your room, cupboard etc. are of course at your disposal.

Sleep as long as you wish tomorrow, without consideration for me, and be much embraced and kissed from your Esti.

I am so happy to be able to be together with you. Forgive the scrap of paper.

SOPHIE'S DIARY: NEW YEAR'S EVE, 1941

While mother was in Marseille, I found and secretly read the letters that she had written father in the years 1918–1919 as his fiancé and a little before that, but above all during his nine months as prisoner of war in Italy. She never talks about that. They are the most charming love letters I have ever read. She must have been very sympathetic. So much love and youthfulness is contained in these letters; one gets a good picture of her life at that time. There is even a big and earnest Yes letter among them. She must have loved him most crazily. How could he then have left her so heartlessly? It makes the whole marriage very black. One hears everywhere about the bad result of marriages and in general it is a true wonder with how many illusions each young girl, probably myself included, gets married.

I see this a little differently now, 65 years later, although I am still moved and saddened by so much love and hope gone awry. But reading this as an old woman who has forgotten about youthful passions, I am taken aback by the expression of so much dramatic emotion of love and worry and hope. We can only assume that my father too felt love, sufficiently so to marry my mother. His sister Mathilde (Tilde in Mother's letters), according to my brother, advised him against this marriage, and according to my brother, she reported that he answered: "it is too late," thus perhaps expressing last-minute doubts. But Tante Mathilde told me once, when she was already quite old, that my father had always been incapable of loving anyone, not his mother, nor his sisters, nor his wife, perhaps not even his children.

These two people hardly knew one another—there were, after all, only a few fleeting meetings during exciting war times. In the apparently mostly one-sided correspondence, Mother does not give away much. At times she realizes that she may have invented her prince and that she actually hardly knows him.

Her great need to be admired is very obvious. It is a trait that will lead to endless insulting incidents created whenever she does not feel sufficiently appreciated. We presume that underneath such a great need lies deep insecurity about being lovable, which may also be a subtext of these letters and possibly the reason why she constantly reminds her prisoner-of-war fiancé whom she loves so deeply that she is surrounded by men who are courting her. She wants to make sure he knows how much her favors are sought after, perhaps not a bad strategy given that she is plagued by uncertainty about his true feelings.

The love and the worry and the yearning are surely authentic and very persuasively expressed, yet I doubt her when she writes that without him life would be meaningless, purposeless, etc. All the grief is in contrast to much enjoyable dancing and suitors, a crimson red hat, recitations, excursions, and so on. At one point she writes that she could have killed herself, her life had been so lacking in purpose, and while I know that Mother suffered from depressions, she appears to have considerable zest for life in these letters.

Part IV

Married Days

CHAPTER 10

Joys and Sorrows of Married Life

In September 1919, Martin and I became officially engaged. A cup from my mother's best china set was broken for "mazeltov" (good luck). My father mobilized all his friends and connections to find a job for Martin. One of them, the director of the *Wiener Bankverein* (bank company), Mr. Markus, advised Martin to emigrate to the United States. Father was furious at this advice, but now, with hindsight, it does not seem like such a bad idea. Eventually Martin found a job as a clerk in a newly created bank.

Apartments were scarce in the postwar period. We found a three-room apartment on the second floor of the building my parents lived in. My father promised to pay the rent and the marriage date was set for December 7, Martin's 30th birthday.

We have two memorable birthdays in our family, December 7, my father's birthday, Pearl Harbor Day, and August 6, my own birthday, Hiroshima Day. If we continue our savageries, we shall find that soon, every day of the year, and therefore every birthday will be covered by some huge historical shadow.

But it is not because of Pearl Harbor Day that I become uneasy when December 7 rolls around. It was the day when Mother expected her husband, even years later, her estranged husband, to send her red roses, the number of roses to match their years of marriage. Would Father remember to send the roses on time, would they be as fresh and elegantly wrapped as Mother required, would he get the number of roses right? It was definitely an anxious day.

WALTER'S *ERNESTINE*

Mother was born in May 1896, but she made herself two or three years younger. She married in 1919, i.e., when she was 23. She was very lucky to

Esti as a bride

find a husband at all, considering that of the 7.8 million mobilized Austrian soldiers, 1.2 million were killed and another 3.6 million wounded and crippled during World War I. Her sister-in-law, my Aunt Anna, father's youngest sister, was not so lucky. Had Esti not married, her two younger sisters could not have married either, because in Jewish families a younger daughter could not marry before her older sister. Esti's parents were relatively observant Jews, in contrast to us.

What nonsense. The reason Tante Anna did not marry was not because there were no suitors for her, but because she wanted to stay home with her beloved father. Besides, she was to find a woman, Dorothy Burlingham, with whom she shared her life. Neither were my maternal grandparents observant in any visible fashion, except for celebrations of Jewish holidays. The three sisters could certainly have married whenever they wanted.

I received a dining room set previously owned by the uncle who died of leukemia and took the furniture from my own room to which two brass beds were added.

How well I remember these shiny golden brass-frame beds, given that one of them later became my own bed. The beds had never stood next to each other, at least in my mind's eyes, but back to back, at some distance from each other in this very large room. Still, in 1920, Mother looks forward to sleeping in one bed and I was born in 1924, so they must have shared the same bed, at least temporarily, in the early years of their marriage. But not so, within my memory.

It was very difficult to obtain things and everything had to be carefully planned. It was a period of terrible inflation in what was left of Austria—the German-speaking provinces only—and cash melted away like butter in a warm oven.

We were married in the Pazmaniten temple, the one erected with my grandfather's money. In the afternoon there was an at-home tea limited strictly to the family. I think my parents might have done better for the wedding of their eldest daughter, but it was their way of demonstrating their disapproval of our marriage.

In spite of some reservations in both families—with Mother being recognized as not prepared for the thrifty Freud family lifestyle, and Martin not being "eine gute Partie" (a financially favorable linkage)—it was, by all accounts, a highly suitable alliance. Both families were assimilated educated high-status Jews and the sorry outcome could not have been foreseen. It could indeed have become a positive connection in which the two partners adapted to their differences, especially given the great love with which Mother had started the marriage.

For a honeymoon, we went away for three days to *Baden bei Wien*, a spa about half hour away by train from Vienna. Martin wanted to be present at a meeting of the trustees of the bank where he worked.

After those three days, life's realities started to impinge on me. Two beds had to be made, fires in old-fashioned ovens had to be lit, shopping had to be done, and lunch had to be prepared. I was not at all used to housework. I remember once, when ironing a pair of my husband's pants, I burned a big hole in one of the legs with a too-hot iron. Fortunately it could be invisibly mended. When Martin was promoted, I hired a maid to make life a bit easier for me.

Everywhere in Austria, even today, lunch is the main meal of the day. My mother's household included a cook and two maids and we had a permanent invitation to eat dinner in my parents' house. Unfortunately my mother took this occasion to make life miserable for me. She did not regard me as a daughter who needed temporary help, but I became a poor relative who could be treated with disdain. Martin promptly reported what he observed to his parents, a fact which did not increase esteem for me in the new family.

Mathilde told me of the brilliant marriage Martin could have made if he had followed her advice and wooed the daughter of one of her friends. As it happened, one or two years later the father of this girl had to go into *Konkurs* (bankruptcy) and the family became quite poor.

Being expected to turn every penny around three times before spending it, made me very depressed. Once, when I overstepped my monthly budget when buying something essential for the household, Martin instituted a daily household money stipend, something I felt most degrading. "It is easy to spend money," he said, "but difficult to earn it."

About this time Martin started to gamble my money on the stock exchange. He sold my sound investment, the Jud Süd stock, to buy some worthless foreign exchange. Polish marks dwindled to nothingness before one's eyes. I didn't dare object to Martin's unfortunate monetary ventures until it was too late and my money became a mere pittance.

Although my mother never directly addresses or questions her low status in her in-law family, we see her searching for reasons here, in her old age, wondering what had gone so wrong. Moreover, she remembers the exact words that will soon darken her marital happiness with pennies that had to be turned around three times, while her own money is being squandered once again, this time not by her foolish father but by her improvident husband. The loss of this money, which also involves loss of her financial independence, caused a lifelong bitterness. She refers back to it repeatedly 30 and 40 years later in her correspondence with her son.

As it happens when you are young and recently married, I became pregnant. Martin told me not to tell anyone, but he told Lampl [*Father's friend*]. Lampl decided I should have an abortion because we could not afford the expense of having a baby and he immediately recommended a physician who would do it. I, stupid, inexperienced, and in love, agreed and committed the crime of having my first child aborted. We told all our parents we were going on an Easter vacation. I did not look well when we returned from this "vacation." I suddenly developed a fever and Father sent me away for a rest cure in the mountains.

Mother kept the secret of this early abortion (and the later one) all her life, and I learned about them only from this autobiography. Judging from her letters, she seems to have spent her rest-cure in the same place where she had been for her three-day honeymoon with Martin.

May 1, 1920

Dearest, dear Murksy,

I was so happy with your letter today, at noon; you know, it is just like in the summer, the mailman comes in during lunch and brings the mail. I had just started to feel a bit hurt because all the other husbands arrived today with the noon train, only ... !!

The Hotel is quite full, mostly young women with their babies, it is literally teeming with sweet little children—Yesterday afternoon it was still bitterly cold but I still laid down on the terrace in a winter coat, a wool jacket and a blanket. Today the weather is magnificent. I am very pleased that your Rax excursion will be such a success. This morning I got up at half past 7, I would prefer to stay longer in bed, but one can't have breakfast sent to one's room and gets it only until 9 o'clock. Then I went out to the terrace. After lunch I took a 2 1/2 hour nap then I went with a girl, rather a stupid goose, but quite likable, to have two cups of coffee at Weinbergers. At the hotel one gets only one cup.

Dear Murksy, would you be so kind, just in case, to ask the cook in the Berggasse or at my parents' for a kilo flour, so that they can bake me here some white bread, and send it per mail. If you do it cleverly, Tante Minna does not have to hear about it and I could bring the cook some little gift from Zell. But please, do it as soon as possible so that I am not left without it.

I feel well and happy here and must think all the time of you because it was so wonderful when we both were here together. Too bad I don't have the same room, but close to it, one with two beds. Dearest, dearest Wurschty, please write to me very soon and in detail and be 1,000 times embraced and kissed by your Esti.

MAY 5, 1920

My dearest, only one, golden husband,

I am so happy with your letter, so happy, had already been very hurt because I had not gotten anything from you for three days, when I love you so, love you so terribly.

My menstruation was very strong and lasted a long time but it was without pain. Yesterday I was in Mariazell and bought some eggs and perhaps walked too much because today I have a dull feeling on my left side. Today is also terribly cold and it pours and snows to its hearts content. But I think that I look already much much better and I feel much stronger. If the weather halfway allows I lie comfortably on the terrace. I would very much like to prolong my stay until Thursday the 13th because I really would like to be totally healthy when you see me again. Not be a sickly delicate woman and I think with all the lying down my stomach will be completely healed. Dearest, sweet little husband, don't think that I love you less and that I don't long for you, but you will surely have much more pleasure if I am healthy and blooming when you see me again. That is why I want to come Thursday on the 13th, at noon. You can get me at the train because it is a holiday. If you run out of clean laundry, ask the maid to wash the handkerchiefs, underpants, stockings, and nightgowns. Let her take the things to be cleaned to the dry cleaners, just tell her where. Then she should beat your mattress against the bedbugs (soap is in the small drawer to the right or she should borrow it from Mother)....

Actually I would quite like to stay here over the Easter holidays and you could climb the Rax again, but you probably might feel hurt. Please, dearest Puxi, send me right away 1 kilo, 4 dkg. flour which I have to hand in here, otherwise they don't give me any dessert.

I am not sure yet what the cost of the stay will be, probably over 100 Kronen. If you would like, send me also a little piece of butter, but not much, I still have quite a bit from before.

Be much kissed, you dear, dear husband You, from your Esti.

MAY 8, 1920

My deeply loved husband You,

I feel very hurt that you have not gotten any mail from me, when I wrote you already four times, and that you are worried and in a bad mood. What is making you angry, Dearest?

Today I got the 500 Kronen, meaning not yet, the mailman wanted to give me 1,000 Kronen but I said I had no change; why should I accepted perhaps an invalid 1,000 banknote! I hope I can manage with the money, I should not miss for much and if necessary I could borrow the rest. Thursday at noon you will get me at the station. Dearest, how I look forward to you. I am already the most blooming looking person in the Hotel and some people have been here for weeks. Dear Martin, Mariandel [her sister, Tante Janne] has her birthday on the 11th, ask her what she would like from me, or bring her some small gift, flowers for example, so she should not have any hurt feelings, she will get the main gift only after I get back. Let the servants get the rooms in order, the beds etc. During the evening I would like to go to the Berggasse, it is in any case our evening. . . .

Dear Puxi, I think I am almost as healthy as when you married me, no longer at all nervous.

My underwear remains totally clean, even rinsing shows no traces. only on my left side some sensitivity remains, but it will surely disappear very quickly if I take good care of myself a while longer.

This makes me very happy.

My sweet dear husband, I love you so much, as much as I am able to and becoming unfaithful to you does not even enter my mind, and I am not a bit bored, it is lovely here and I keep remembering what beautiful days we spent here together. My sweetheart, you, I shall still write you tomorrow, meaning Sunday and Monday and then I come myself. I look forward with all my heart to our reunion, to your kisses and to sleeping in one bed, until then, Your Esti

MAY 9, 1920,

Dearest Wurschti,

Your butter/flour package arrived today, many thanks. Are you already scolding me a lot, that I am always bothering you with my errands, your quick follow up is very dear of you and makes me very pleased. . . .

Now I no longer need anything and just look forward terribly to our reunion. I actually yearn to listen to lectures about the country's commerce, to news from the stock market and I am very curious regarding your muscles and breadth of your shoulders, but tell me, Dearest, you will not be in a bad mood, otherwise I won't be back until after the Easter break. I hope that I have not forgotten any member of my numerous family with my cheering-up postcards. I will write you my last letter tomorrow and remain with my very tender kisses your Esti.

MAY 10, 1920

Dearest, dearest Wurschty,

Today I got two letters from you, very very dear ones, I am so happy and radiant with them, before I had been a tiny bit hurt because you did not come to see me yesterday, all the husbands were there, and you would really have enjoyed the food here; such big portions of meat.

I continue to look very well, feel totally fit and sleep and eat into infinity . . . : at the train station I will whistle, will wear a red hat. . . . Dearest, you will have me in our flat all alone for you, it's great, so great, don't you think!

So much love, but perhaps Mother would have liked to stay a little longer in her rest cure, especially if her Beloved should be in a bad mood upon her return.

CHAPTER 11

Young Motherhood

Six months later I was pregnant again and my son was born April 3, 1921. My pregnancy was a very easy one, but I was worried about disfigurement of my body and whether I would look normal again. I had no nausea or any other kinds of spells, just a craving for meat, which, in those early postwar years was still hard to obtain. I became very heavy and it was difficult for me to turn from one side to another when I was lying down. My maternity dress was made from an old suit and someone from the Freud family said I looked like an *angepumste* (pumped-up) governess, a remark that upset me very much.

Giving birth for the first time was hard for me. After 40 hours of pain the obstetrician said in my presence, "the life of the mother goes before the life of the infant" and I started to worry lest I gave birth to a dead infant. It was decided to use forceps. I was put to sleep and when I awoke I was presented with a boy whose head was egg-shaped from the use of the forceps, and was voraciously hungry. My breasts were full of milk and I let him suck and suck. At this time it was thought necessary to keep the young mother in the hospital for 10 days. I had to share the room with a woman who was lovely and good company, but the visits of each husband disturbed the other one, and I was permitted to go home after a week.

I had plenty of milk and let the baby drink too much, which did not agree with him. Shortly after my return home my mother-in-law announced that she had hired a baby nurse, since I was not competent enough to rear an infant, and that Papa-the-Professor would pay her salary. The baby nurse was an old dragon, who had just been discharged by a wealthy family, and who, with some grumbling, had to adjust to a much simpler household. The baby's weight was taken before and after each feeding, and he was allowed to drink only a certain amount. He gained weight and thrived normally.

After the baby's birth I asked the pediatrician, *primarius* Dr. Paul Moser, the one who had looked after me from early childhood, to take care of my son. This was vetoed by "Papa." Freud rarely interfered with the education of my children. However the advice I received had to be accepted. It never occurred to me not to heed strictly to his rules. I was informed that *primarius* Moser had prematurely published a paper claiming to have discovered a serum against scarlet fever. When tested it had proved to be without any value. One of the worst crimes in Freud's eyes was an unfounded scientific commitment. A person who made unqualified unserious scientific statements was not to take care of his grandson. Doctor Hans Abel was recommended and he proved to be a faithful, reliable physician who took good care of both of my children.

Shortly after my son's birth, Martin changed jobs. This new employment also did not last long. Weekends he took up his former hobby, which was leaving Vienna for two days and hiking or rock climbing the Alps. Before my pregnancy I had gone with him, but with a baby to feed every six hours, this was no longer possible. One week he and his climbing companions decided to do some difficult rock climbing in the Gesäuse. He did not return Sunday evening as he was supposed to and I was beside myself imagining him with a broken skull lying in some mountain abyss. He returned unscathed on Monday morning when I was already half crazy with anxiety. He had missed the last train going back to Vienna. The idea of telephoning me had never crossed his mind. My baby nurse was most indignant, predicting that the infant would cry because my milk was contaminated by worry.

That year I went on a summer vacation with my parents and youngest sister to a place in the northern Alps my father had discovered. My parents and sister left since they found the place too lonesome, but I stayed with the baby and nurse until my husband arrived. This time I accompanied him on his climbing tours, cow's milk replacing mother's milk until I returned to feed the baby.

VIENNA. JULY 23, 1921
> Dear Murri!
> The milk
> I have given to Mrs. Kalhammer
> who was very sick

I think bleeding kidneys
and is superhappy with it
I wont go up the Rax
because it is not worth while
since I am already leaving Monday
I have already bought the tickets
third class
the same train that you took
I will go until Innsbruck, but will
look out of the window
and if the train should stop in Halle
of course get out in Halle.
I was extremely active
Have paid the tax for the synagogue
Taken care of tax regulation
Handed in the earning document
Caught up with all old sins at work
Telegraphed Mama for her birthday
At home it is wonderfully quiet
and very cozy
Only my stomach is a bit irritated
I thus hope very soon
To see you already quite recovered
And meet you in a cheerful frame of mind.
As ever with kisses
Your faithful Murrer
Don't forget to oil my climbing shoes.

VIENNA, AUGUST 3, 1921

Dearest Murri!

I hope you and the little one are well and you are getting a good rest. Ernst and Lux [*his brother and wife*] have also had a son, as Papa writes. So far I have not had any news from you.

Business: Eisler has returned, very amiable and agreeable.—this week is naturally especially exhausting and eventful. Eisler gave me from his wife for our "little girl" a small sweet coral luck-necklace. I leave the office very late, then usually go to the movies in spite of the great heat, to pass the time, which it does. The evening before yesterday I spent with Uncle Alexander, but it was not very stimulating.

I would like, if possible to leave once again, and hope that this can be arranged. I think we could go together in the Stubai, or wherever you would like, we could take a place on the way, for example Zell am See, what do you think? Then we would save a part of the way back. But I leave it totally to you to decide where to spend the rest of our vacation. I shall telegraph you once I am sure of a vacation.

Let me also know how the child is and how you spend the day, is it still so terribly hot? In Vienna the temperature continues at the boiling point. I am very eager for your news and remain with

Many kisses

Your faithful Murrer

Soon I suspected I was again pregnant. I went to the obstetrician who diagnosed an extra-uterine pregnancy and said I might start bleeding to death. Since I felt so well I did not believe Dr. Schiffman, the Freud family insisted on a second opinion. I was referred to Professor Halban. He did not diagnose an extra-uterine pregnancy but nevertheless suggested an abortion. As an obedient child, without money, I again went under the knife.

I was 26 and it was between Xmas and New Years of 1922. Martin wanted to go out and celebrate the last day of the year. Although I told him that I did not yet feel very strong, he promised that he would go to some nightclub and simply watch a performance. By the end of the evening I had walked all around the Ringstraße (4 km) because my husband could not find a place where he liked the ambiance. The following morning I had a fever of over 40 degrees C (about 103 F). Dr. Schiffman was very upset. Obstetricians do not like it when a patient of a prominent family dies in the wake of a legal abortion, since it is detrimental to their reputation.

After this incident I made up my mind no longer to follow blindly some of Martin's unreasonable wishes and to start a more independent life. I had no money and my abilities were limited. I felt I had become a financial burden. Martin often spoke of a girl he had been interested in who had begun a business manufacturing sweaters and exporting them to the United States and had thus made good money. As it happened, the poor girl worked herself into a case of tuberculosis and died some months after the onset.

I would not have liked to be Mother's enemy in those days, given the terrible fate that befalls all on them. Erich Bruckner who had not been interested in courting her, had two unhappy marriages and ended his life poverty stricken. The father of the rich girl Tante Mathilde had proposed for Martin went bankrupt within two years.

Another rich girl on whom Martin had had an eye overworked herself and soon died of tuberculosis.

The only thing I had a talent for was acting, reading poetry, and perhaps, teaching speech techniques. Acting was out of the question, because as a beginner I would not have found an engagement in sophisticated Vienna, but would have to go to some small-town theater in Germany and that would have meant leaving my son. Poetry reading was far from lucrative. What remained was teaching speech, but I was not known well enough to find students to teach.

When my son, whom we called Anton Walter (Anton in memory of Anton von Freund, whose donation had enabled Freud to establish the Psychoanalytic Publishing House) was two years old I dismissed the baby nurse. The child had suffered frequent colds all winter long and Dr. Abels recommended the seashore for a vacation. I selected Grado, a beach at the northern end of the Adriatic sea, a place I had known from childhood.

The baby took the separation from his nurse very much to heart. He whimpered many nights, calling her name and became difficult to handle, making life miserable for me. When I left him on the beach and went out for a swim he stood on the shore, desperately howling until I returned.

One day, after speaking a while with an acquaintance, I assumed Walter was building one of his sand castles, but when I looked for him he was gone. I ran along the beach calling his name, but no Walter answered. I went to alert the lifeguards, imagining him already drowned, with me as the culprit. Anyone who knows the constellation of the Grado beach knows that with the exception of an infant who can barely walk, drowning is highly improbable. While I was searching desperately a bambino pointed to a little boy who was sitting in one of the small boats along the shore, paddling out to sea. It was my son, the 27-month-old boy who had pushed the boat from the beach into shallow water and had started to paddle. I would not have needed to worry for the boats are well watched and the bambino had not yet received his obolus [fee] for the use of the boat. I had to take Walter with me to the toilet also, because once, when I did not, I found him standing on the sill of our third-story room window.

In contrast to the abortions, which had remained a family secret, the above story was a well-worn anecdote and even retold several times in letters to Walter.

JUNE 3, 1951

... When you were two years old we were for the first time in Grado. You were quite naughty, often had stomach aches and once, while I was in the toilet, you crawled out of your crib, over the railing and I found you standing on the windowsill; I gave you a hard spanking.

You also once climbed into a canoe, unfastened it and started to paddle. You were then 27 months old. Always while I went for a swim, you stood at the shore and screamed bloody murder, so that people came toward me in the water to tell me that I was a cruel mother without heart who lets her poor little child scream and scream.

Who would leave today a two year old standing alone, unsupervised, and upset at the edge of the sea? She expressed no guilt, but the story served to illustrate her hardships with such an obstreperous little boy, although there might also have been a note of pride about his enterprising spirit.

Martin arrived later on to spend some time with us and go with us to the mountains. Traveling in 1922 was not easy. Railways had been constructed for the Austrian Empire, but at that time when we traveled from northern Italy to the Austrian Alps, the trains went through the newly created Yugoslavia, which meant going through three frontiers. We went by boat to Trieste, where we had to spend the night. Martin had chosen a train that left at 4 o'clock in the morning. In order to save a few lire, we took a room in a third-class hotel that looked out into a courtyard with no air at all.

I gave Walter scrambled eggs for dinner and in the middle of the night he vomited. Without having slept, we got up at 2:30 in the morning in order to be on time at the station. The child vomited the tea I gave him for breakfast. At the Italian-Yugoslav border, the train stopped for two hours and Walter vomited again. One of the border guards brought some tea to the train, which he also vomited. We were not permitted to leave the transit car. Walter whimpered for something to drink, he became dehydrated, but he vomited as soon as he had drunk a drop. The trip became a nightmare. When we finally arrived in Villach, the second largest town in Kärnten (Carinthia, an Austrian province), we left the train and went to the best hotel in town and called a pediatrician. Villach's pediatrician's prescription helped. It took days until he could digest solid food (fresh brook trout and mashed potatoes). Martin had to return to Vienna, his short vacation completely spoiled.

I am uncertain who is the culprit in this story. Is it the sick baby who spitefully vomits everything desperately offered to him, or rather is it the cheap husband who chooses inconvenient trains and third-rate hotels to save a few lire?

WALTER'S *ERNESTINE*

Returning to our health, at the least sign of constipation, we were given a generous dose of Castor Oil mixed with raspberry juice. As a result, I could not stand the taste of raspberry juice for the next 30 years. Alternatively, we were given an enema (not with raspberry juice), which was less unpleasant. We had a special gadget at home that could be hung on the wall over the bed for this purpose. There can be no doubt that in our home in Vienna, the digestive organs were considered the be-all of the body, its soul and spirit. I do not know if this belief was general among Austrian Jews, but it was certainly so with Esti. Her parents, who lived next door to us (our flat used to be her father's office before he retired), were more concerned with the intake, rather than with the expulsion, of food. At dinner, they used to eat the main course first, before the soup, so that the latter should not spoil the appetite of the main course. The excuse for this indulgence had something to do with the Messiah. If he should come during dinner, at least the main part of it was already eaten.

It becomes clear that neither Mother nor Father had separated from their parents. Both families were supportive with money while taking over important decisions. Father Drucker pays the rent and sends his sick daughter on vacation; Mother Drucker is ready to provide meals, but at the price of contempt; Mother Freud hires, and pays for, a (hateful) baby nurse, making mother feel incompetent to take care of her own baby. Father Freud makes the medical decisions and someone from the Freud family calls her angepumste *governess, a hurtful comment remembered after 60 stormy years. And husband Martin is miserly and appallingly inconsiderate. The blue sky of marital bliss is darkening with thunderclouds. The walls of oppression are descending down on my poor young mother from every side. She gets ready for a change. She is about to make the decision to enter professional training, which will financially, emotionally, and socially, save her life.*

Part V

Training as a Speech Pathologist

CHAPTER 12

Starting an Independent Life

In 1923 my father-in-law had his first palate operation. A malignant growth was removed. Surgery was performed by Prof. Dr. Hajek, *ordinarius*, of the Ear, Nose, and Throat Department of Vienna's medical school. The surgery was done at the outpatient clinic and Freud was left sitting there after surgery, with blood all over him, until someone took pity on him and summoned Mrs. Freud. After this Dr. Hajek was not too well spoken of by the Freud family.

In spite of sickness and pain, Freud did not stop working. Not only did he have a considerable load of patients, but he continued to write. Patients and disciples arrived from all corners of the earth and he asked his patients to pay in the currency of the country they came from. The family's economic situation took a turn for the better. I watched as Freud became more and more famous.

In 1924, the year my daughter was born, Monsignor Ignatz Seipel was in charge of the Austrian government and undertook the stabilization of the Austrian currency. The Austrian Krone, which inflation had made worthless, was reevaluated on a more solid monetary basis and a new currency, the Schilling, was created.

In the wake of this economic upheaval, the bank where my husband was employed had to close, and Martin was again without a job. When he came to visit me at the Rudolfinerhaus, where I was confined, he spilled out all his frustration and disappointment from being unemployed and looking for work. The situation, however, was not as bad as it had been previously. Father had carried Martin as a *Konzipient* (apprentice lawyer) since our marriage, and Martin had just taken his bar exam and could therefore set up as a lawyer if he wanted to. Members of my family and friends began to refer law cases to Martin. My father's secretary did the necessary typing. In addition, Martin developed an association with the private banking house Spielberger, where he worked at financing the credit-buying of automobiles—buying in installments was a new business phenomenon in Austria.

VIENNA, JUNE 17, 1927

Dearest Schnups!

I hope your trip was pleasant and you enjoyed yourself and found everything in good order upon your return. Please allow yourself an "all right" telegram as soon as your return.

Papa has given me 25 dollars for you. I have already spent:

S 73 Reiser

S 60 Koppelwagner

I still owe you S 42. I think there was still a third bill to pay. Help me remember! Foldstein? Drycleaner?

No new successes to report. No news from Magnus, whether he could place anything, nor from America. I will only know next week whether the matter with Director Spielberger has any chance. I am pessimistic. If the matter fails I will throw myself with renewed energy into writing.

The sun shines on principle only during business hours, when I go kayaking an icy wind always blows.

Until the various decisions have turned out I shall decide on vacation plans. I am already sufficiently sick of looking at the caserne vis-à-vis.

Affectionate kisses from your faithful Murri

My daughter was born August 6, 1924. We called her Miriam Sophie, in memory of Martin's sister Sophie who had died of the lung plague [influenza] in the winter of 1920. I had changed obstetricians and had a physician recommended by Dr. Abels. Her birth gave me the least trouble. There she was, one, two, three. "That's a good girl," the midwife said, and a "good girl" she remains to this day.

Sophie was reared without an experienced baby nurse. The only help I had was a girl-of-all-work and she was inexperienced indeed. Walter was now a big boy all of three and a half. Alone with me he was a perfect little gentleman, but he was jealous of his little sister. I had to watch him so he did not harm her; his antagonism was serious. This open animosity toward his sister lasted until he was in his early teens when they became close pals.

Esti's children, Walter and Sophie, before leaving Vienna

*I remember my brother as disliking me, threatening me, beating me many times—
albeit not dangerously—never including me in his games or friendships and either
offending me or ignoring me. I loved to visit my best friend who had a caring, interested, and supportive older brother who extended his kindness even to her friends.
But my mother was right, all that changed suddenly in the last year just before we
were parted when he became friendly and, in response, I grew to care about him*

above all others. I would spend the entire war years constantly thinking about his welfare and his safety.

It is not far-fetched to speculate that he greatly resented my mother loving me more than him, something I also sensed as I grew up and which made me feel uneasy. I would rather not have been her favorite child.

As I mentioned earlier, I had begun to teach speech techniques, but it was hard to find students. The first opportunity was given to me by my former high school, *Die Schwarzwaldschen Schulanstalten,* where I was given permission to organize a speech technique course for pupils who "mumbled." It is there where I got my first experience in group instruction.

In the course of my work, I heard about a clinic dealing with speech impairments, led by Dr. Fröschels, the head of the outpatient clinic for speech and voice disorders. This information provided me with much food for thought. I decided to write a letter to Dr. Fröschels, asking whether he would accept me as a student. The prompt reply invited me to an interview. It resulted in my being accepted as a trainee at the clinic. The fee for the courses involved all the money I still owned. Martin was upset about my decision. His main objection was that I would not follow through with my apprenticeship and the invested money would be lost. The second argument was: "What will happen to the children?"

The inexperienced girl-of-all-work was exchanged for a cook and a Fräulein to take care of the children, one chosen by my mother-in-law, whose help and support I had gained.

In September 1926, when I was 30, I began my education for becoming a speech, voice, and hearing therapist. The *Ambulatorium für Sprache und Stimmstörungen* (Clinic for Speech and Voice Disturbances) was part of the Ear, Nose, and Throat Department, which Dr. Heinrich Neumann was in charge of. My life had been limited to household chores, taking children to the park, waiting for my husband to come home, and visiting the Freud family. Suddenly my world expanded. Having been a nurse during the war greatly helped my new activity. I knew how to behave in a hospital environment and how to get along with all kinds of people. The training was rigorous. Every morning I had to be at the clinic at nine and work until noon. Selected readings were assigned for the afternoon. Dr. Fröschels had a contract with the public school system. Children with speech, language, voice, and hearing impairments were instructed in special classes. Every day, a teacher, whose specialty was communications disorders, brought his or her class to the Clinic for a consultation with Dr. Fröschels. The students sat in a semicircle by the side of the professor who taught by discussing the different cases.

At the beginning of my training, case histories were dictated by me. Following the school children, cases referred from different departments of the hospital were seen and the means of therapy explained. Three times a week, there were formal lectures on subjects involving a great variety of speech disorders, such as aphasia, cleft palate, stuttering, voice loss, the consequences of hearing impairments, etc. I do not think that in the course of this lecture series any valid information about existing communication disorders were omitted.

Fröschels' favorite lecture theme was philosophy, and he used this lecture to attack Freud's concept of the unconscious. The attacks on Freud detracted from Fröschels' reputation as a philosopher. He should never have deviated from his field of specialization.

Although Fröschels called me "stupid goose" several times in front of the whole Clinic, I soon became one of his most prominent pupils, and when the formal training was over, he asked me if I wanted to become his unsalaried assistant. This I remained until the occupation of Austria by the German National Socialist Party, which deprived us both of our profession.

UNIVERSITY CLINIC FOR EAR, NOSE, AND THROAT SICKNESSES
Outpatient Clinic for Speech and Voice Disturbances
(Prof. Dr. H. Neumann)
March 10, 1938

Mrs. Esti Freud has participated since 1927 in the work of the speech and voice outpatient clinic that I head.

She came to us from the art of live performances and first acquired the necessary theoretical and practical knowledge of logopedics as attested by her excellent results in the final examination. Subsequently she had the opportunity for more than a decade to successfully treat a large variety of speech and voice disturbances. The abundant case material of the Clinic and the ongoing opportunities for continuing education, which Mrs. Freud herself occasionally offered, gave her ample opportunity to give evidence of her theoretical as well as practical skills.

Since the year 1932 Mrs. Freud is also lecturer at the University for breath—voice—and speech techniques and has taught in this role graduate students of education at the university and took the opportunity to treat pathological cases among her students in collaboration with our clinic. This model setting activity has repeatedly been discussed in the literature.

Mrs. Freud also proved herself with her scholarly publications, numerous lectures, as well continuing her own activities as a performance artist. With her multiple interests and talents in our field she is a logopedist of first rank and can be recommended to the highest degree.

Prof. Dr. Emil Fröschels

I was happy at my work. It was challenging and interesting. It provided me with an outlet for my energies. Yet, gaining knowledge was not my only goal. In order to impress Martin, I had to earn money. I found a few opportunities. Just how I found them, how I learned whom to approach, and how I succeeded in almost everything, I no longer know.

There was the *Gremium der Wiener Kaufmannschaft* (Chamber of Commerce), which had a secondary vocational school. This school conducted adult educational courses. I suggested that the school authorities introduce a class on public speaking. I got the permission to teach such a class, with the proviso that at least 10 students had to enroll in it.

I visited the secretary of the *Wiener Volks-Hochschule* (adult education system of Vienna), a unique institution created to provide educational facilities for the Viennese proletariat, and offered to teach there. I was assigned first to teach how to speak German correctly and also elocution in a building located in the ghetto where the poor of Vienna's Jews lived. [*The Leopoldstadt, referred to above.*] After a few years of teaching there, I was asked to organize a similar course in Ottakring [known as the blue collar district], the center of this adult education project. I also gave a course in poetry reading at the Pedagogical Institute where teachers were trained for the public school system. I was not royally paid for either of these courses, although I put a lot of work into them, but nevertheless it was money earned by me, money which I could spend on whatever I wanted.

My new activities estranged me more and more from my husband. He was not interested at all in what I was doing and made fun of the miserly sums I was earning. Many of my courses ended at nine in the evening and he never came to take me home. As I previously mentioned, Martin had the habit of spending weekends going skiing or mountain-climbing according to the seasons.

I, through my profession, had many new friends and was invited to all kinds of meetings. At one of these meetings an elderly gentleman, upon being introduced to me, told me that he had to give a lecture in the near future and asked me if I would help him polish his delivery. It was Director Goldschmidt, one of the top employees of the *Neue Freie Presse*, Austria's

New York Times. He became one of the most helpful and influential friends I ever had. He advertised my courses without my paying for it and sent critics to my poetry readings. Through his influence, my picture appeared in magazines and newspapers and I received free tickets to all prominent events. Director Goldschmidt died about 1935 in the aftermath of a surgical intervention. At least he was saved from Hitler's invasion of Austria.

WALTER'S ERNESTINE

Soon after my sister's birth in August 1924 (when I was three), the parental marriage appeared to have struck rocks, according to my Aunts. My parents each went their own way and I cannot remember a single outing with both of them.

We children knew of course that our parents did not get on together. By about 1930, they slept in different bedrooms at the opposite ends of our flat. The relatively few occasions when they were together usually ended in nasty quarrels. But children get used to their environment; when young they take whatever happens in their home for granted. After my puberty it became apparent to me that my father must have company outside the marital home, but if so, it was done very discreetly. I never saw or much less met any possible ladyfriends. For that matter, father neither brought home any men-friends; perhaps he was ashamed of his wife. In contrast, Esti had no compunction of inviting her boyfriend home when father was out. He was a Mr. Goldschmidt, a high-up in the *Neue Freie Presse*, Austria's *New York Times*. I do not know if their relationship was sexual or platonic, but I suspect it was the former and it went on for a long time. As I said earlier, my parents lived separate lives.

Again, I must disagree with my brother considering it very unlikely that Mother had any sexual affairs while in Vienna and I further believe that her interest in sex was always peripheral to her life. But, in the course of writing this book, I received some information regarding another relationship, recorded below, that questions both of these assertions. In any case, Mr. Goldschmidt must have loved my mother and she was certainly fond of him, apart from the utility of the friendship.

In the summer of 1927, my children and I rented a cottage in Bled. Bled is a resort village on a lake in the Karawanken mountain range in Yugoslavia, not far from the Austrian border. Martin was due for a visit. The train on which he was supposed to come was delayed many hours, and there were rumors at the station that something had happened in Vienna. When the train finally arrived, the news was the Vienna's working class was making a revolution. Thousands of people were marching on the Ringstraße toward the Justizpalast (the Supreme Court building), which was already burning. Understandably, Martin was upset. He caught the last train out of Vienna. The upheaval was soon put down and in a few days Vienna was calm again. The burning of the Palace of Justice was a foreboding of horrible events to come in the near future.

When we returned in the fall, I resumed my former activities and everyone seemed to have forgotten what had happened. Walter was six years old and had to be enrolled in the first grade. On this occasion, I made one of the worst mistakes of my life. Anna Freud inquired whether, instead of enrolling Walter in a regular grammar school, would I not rather enroll him in the school Mrs. Burlingham (née Tiffany), a very wealthy American woman whose children were patients of Anna's, planned to establish. I bluntly refused. First of all, Walter would have to take an exam at the end of the year if he was going to a school not recognized by the Department of Education. Secondly, I thought the company of the children of millionaires might not be healthy for Walter. In Austria, one did not have a good opinion of American millionaires. Perhaps I wanted to be mean, I refused to do it, and with this refusal alienated Anna for the rest of my life, and with her Mrs. Burlingham—although being mean was not one of my character traits. My objection to Walter attending Mrs. Burlingham's school nearly cost me my own and my daughter's life. Having Mrs. Burlingham as a friend would have, later on, greatly facilitated my career in the United States. It is easy to be smart in hindsight.

During the late twenties, however, my own career proceeded according to plan. The teaching progressed well enough. I directed my students at the *Volkshochschule Ottakring* in the performance of plays by Goethe, Grillparzer, and Gerhard Hauptmann. In 1932, when I had been at Dr. Fröschels' clinic for six years, a new opportunity arose for me at Vienna's University, a position as lecturer for speech and voice education. In order to get the position, I had to pass a rigorous examination before the University's Appointment Committee. I believe I did exceptionally well. In this way I became a lecturer at the venerable 700-year-old University of Vienna. The position, however, was not salaried, but each student who wanted to take my courses, which were required for the position of *Mittelschule* (high school) teacher, had to pay *Kollegiengeld* (course money). I was thus again obliged to build up a clientele. If there were fewer than three students, the course had to be canceled. Dr. Felix V. Trojan, the other lecturer in the field and also a Fröschels disciple, proved to be very helpful indeed. For the winter term of 1937–1938, I had 65 students enrolled in my course.

DEAN'S OFFICE OF THE PHILOSOPHICAL FACULTY OF THE UNIVERSITY OF VIENNA

Confirmation

The Dean's Office confirms that Mrs. Ernestine Freud has been teaching since the summer semester 1932, as lecturer for speech techniques and voice development at the philosophical faculty of the University of Vienna and has excelled in this role.

Vienna, December 19, 1936.

The Dean

It was the last term I lectured at the University. Hitler's invasion of Austria resulted in my ouster. At the end of February in 1938, at the conclusion of the semester, my students gave me an ovation that lasted at least 10 minutes. I was astonished, although I knew I was popular. It was a farewell greeting, as Hitler would enter the country two weeks later. They had been informed of coming events, I, however, not.

DEAN'S OFFICE OF THE PHILOSOPHICAL FACULTY OF THE UNIVERSITY OF VIENNA

Vienna, April 23, 1938

to Lecturer Ernestine Freud

Due to a policy of the Austrian ministry of education of April 22, 1938, Bill: 12474/I/1b, permission to teach in the function of a lecturer on the philosophical faculty of the University of Vienna is being withdrawn.

Office of the Dean

But, in 1932, Hitler was not much more than a dark cloud in the back of the horizon. In 1932, the year I became a lecturer at the University, there were also changes in Martin's professional life. Dr. Storfer, who was the director of the Psychoanalytic Publishing House, had left his job and emigrated to the South Sea Islands. Martin wanted the job. He felt there was more security working for his father. I do not remember when the Psychoanalytic Publishing House was first established, but I know that Dr. Max Eitingon, a psychoanalyst from Berlin, had donated large sums of money to the *Verlag*. Dr. Eitingon's wealth came from the fur business in Leipzig. As far as I know he and Anna [Freud] were chairmen of the company. The office was located in the Berggasse, not far from where the Freuds lived. To become the director, Martin needed Eitingon's consent. I invited Eitingon to dinner, and, to Martin's astonishment, he accepted. Martin always underestimated my skill in handling people. I had arranged a sumptuous dinner with hors d'oeuvres ordered from Lehman (Vienna's famous caterer). I don't think Martin ever realized how much of a positive influence I was in his getting the directorship.

I suppose that the publishing house was a lucrative business until 1933 when Germany turned into a Nazi state and Freud's books were publicly burned. I am not aware of what arrangements were made with the translation rights. Out of the royalties, I suddenly received from Papa Freud $25 a month. I believe the other two daughters-in-law were given the same amount. Not only could I dress like a queen, but the money enabled me to make three magnificent Mediterranean cruises.

CHAPTER 13

Mother's Poems

I also built up a very effective program in poetry reading. Instead of just reading poems, I had the idea of acting them out with musical accompaniment to my words. Luckily, I found a musician gifted enough to compose music that underlined the style and meaning of each special poem. According to the content, we designed costumes. Because I did not have much money to spend, I and my children's Fräulein stitched them up together.

SOPHIE

The piano stood in the living room where Mother practiced reciting her poems, with the accompaniment of her pianist Robert Weiss. I thought it was quite strange that Mother, who fills a whole page with a piece of juicy Vienna gossip with exact names and future outcome, grants a single sentence to this absorbing activity and no name to a man who came at least twice a week for several years to our house. Then, one day, while already deep into this book, I received the following totally fortuitous e-mail:

My grandfather, Robert Weiss, was very close friends with your mother, Esti. They knew each other in Vienna and it was said that my grandfather delayed leaving Vienna because he didn't want to leave her. My grandfather knew my grandmother, Rose Hecht in Vienna, but she was already married. I spoke with my grandfather before he died in 1993 about Esti. I said, "So is it true that you went out with Sigmund Freud's daughter?" He replied, "No, his daughter-in-law." I sat for a minute and said, "but that means that she was married." He replied somewhat sarcastically, "you are very smart."

I have one letter that she wrote to him trying to help him get a job with some symphony perhaps in New York. I know that they remained friend for years, but I don't know when their romantic relationship took place or how long it lasted. My grandfather escaped Vienna in April 1938 and came to Cleveland. My grandmother then divorced her husband and married him. My grandfather was a chemist with a Ph.D.

from the University of Vienna and was also a very accomplished pianist with a degree from the Stadts Akadamie der Darstellenden Künst (academy of applied arts) in Vienna. I know that he wrote several pieces of music for your mother, but unfortunately I don't have copies. I recall that when I visited my grandfather in Florida in 1993, the piece of music that he had written for your mother was in an ornate gold frame.

Did they or did they not? It seems they did, and I hope they did and that my mother derived some happiness from their relationship.

The poems first had to be learned by heart and I was happily chosen to be her cram-master. At least I have thought all these years that this was my exclusive role, and now, with my brother's contributions to this memoir, I suddenly learn that he thinks he was the main instructor. I still think I was chosen more often than he. I was, after all, more available. For me, too, these were my best hours with Mother, when she seemed reasonably happy and neither angry nor depressed. Walter and I have forgotten many important things in our lives, but some of these poems that we rehearsed with our mother over and over have stayed in our memory and curiously we both remember the same poems.

Walter's Ernestine

The most pleasant and relaxed hours I spent with Esti were the occasions when I rehearsed with her poetry readings. She gave talks in the Urania, the planetarium of Vienna, which included recital of poems and reading of stories. The poems had to be checked for word-perfectness and she would rehearse them while I was checking. In those days, when I was a middle teenager, I had a good memory. I always learned the poems faster than Esti did. I can still remember many of them, although I have never heard of them again since. In case the reader of these lines should think that I am exaggerating or bragging, herewith is one of Esti's poems. The title and the author were not rehearsed, hence I do not know them and attempts to find their authorship were in most cases unsuccessful.

The First Poem
Ich hab im Traum mit einem Hund gesprochen,
Erst sprach er Spanisch denn dort war er her,
Als ich ihn nicht verstand, das merkte er,
Sprach er dann Deutsch wenn auch etwas gebrochen.
Er sagte: "Esti, Wissen Sie warum die Hunde ihre Schnautze halten"?
Ich schwieg und war verlegen wie noch nieh.
Da sagte der geträumte Hund

"Wir können sprechen doch wir tun es nicht.
Und wer, ausser im Traum mit einem Menschen spricht
Den fressen wir nach seinem ersten Wort.
Der Mensch ist es nicht wert dass man gesellschaftlich mit ihm verkehrt."
Er hob das Bein, sprang flink durch krumme Gassen,
And so etwas muß man sich sagen lassen!

I was able to ascertain that this poem is by Erich Kästner, called "Ein Hund hält Reden" (A dog makes speeches) and that my brother, astoundingly, remembered the poem totally correctly.

Here is a my own translation:

Once in a dream I spoke with a dog
It was Spanish he spoke
The tongue of his folk
But when, as he noticed, I did not understand
He then spoke German
athough with broken command
He said: "Esti, do you know why dogs
keep their snouts shut?"
I was silent, embarrassment made me all hot
And the dreamed up dog added:
We could speak but we don't.
And whoever, except in dreams,
speaking with humans is heard
We devour after his first word.
Humans, he added in a voice a bit hoarse
are unworthy of social intercourse
He raised his leg
skipped away as if on wings
To have to listen to such things!

WALTER'S *ERNESTINE* (CONTINUED)
Other poems that I partly recall include the following:

The Second Poem
Arthur mit dem langen Arm [*Arthur with the long arm*]
Arthur's Schwester namens Trude [*Arthur's sister named Trude*]

Fuhr einmal nach Buxtehude. [went to visit Buxtehude.]
Arthur der den Koffer trug [Arthur who her bag did carry]
Brachte sie bis an den Zug. [Took her to the train quite merry.]

It continues that Arthur would not let go of his sister's hand when the train started. As a result, his arm grew longer and longer. In later life, he found employment as a cleaner of church windows.

SOPHIE
Walter's memory is failing him here, and we argued about this. Arthur mit den langen Arm *[Arthur with the long arm] was a large amusingly illustrated children's book, indeed by Erich Kästner. I even remember how much my brother loved that book and tried through the years to find it for him, but it is out of print.*

WALTER'S *ERNESTINE* (CONTINUED)
Unfortunately, these relatively few pleasant hours when I rehearsed with Esti were rare and far between. Usually the family get-togethers were full of tension and unpleasantness, ending with a slap on my ear.

SOPHIE
Another poem that I also remember is called The Other Man *by Kurt Tucholsky. In it, the poet urges women not to exchange their probably unsatisfactory husband for a new man because after a few years the new man will be no better than the old one. At the end of the poem, he advises:*

Und hast du einen Kerl gefunden, [if you have found a guy]
mit dem man einigermaßen auskommen kann [with whom you can manage more or less]
dann bleib bei dem eigenen Mann. [then stay with your own husband.]

This is perhaps not an ideally suitable poem for a 12-year-old girl, but it was the words, not the content, not the advice, that stayed in my mind. Actually most of the poems by these between—war poets were very grim, and dealt with war, and war again (World War I), and poverty, and general despair about the state of the world. Here is a very small sample that has etched itself into my mind.

Das Knie [The Knee, translated by Andrea Loewenstein]
Ein Knie geht einsam durch die Welt. [A knee walks lonely through the world.]

Es ist ein Knie, sonsts nichts! [It's nothing but a knee!]
Es ist kein Baum! Es ist kein Zelt! [It's not a tent nor stone nor tree!]
Es ist ein Knie, sonsts nichts. [It's nothing but a knee.]
Im Kriege ward einmal ein Mann [In the war there was a man]
Erschossen um und um. [Shot dead one two three.]
Das Knie allein blieb unverletzt- [Only the knee alone stayed whole]
Als wär's ein Heiligtum. [Relic of memory.]
Seitdem geht's einsam durch die Welt. [Since then it walks lonely
        through the world.]
Es ist ein Knie, sonst nichts. [It's nothing but a knee.]
Es ist kein Baum, es ist kein Zelt, [Not tree, nor tent, nor stone,]
Es ist ein Knie, sonst nichts. [A knee walking alone.]

SOPHIE

The recitals Mother gave were accomplished, original, artistic, entertaining, and highly creative. I thought them truly delightful. She probably did not get as much recognition as she deserved. I am also awed by the energy, competence, and persistence my mother demonstrated in reaching her career goals with neither encouragement nor any sort of support from her husband. Few other married women of her generation and social standing had independent professional ambitions.

What is omitted in this proud account is our—at least hers and mine—common constant angst that accompanied these various endeavors. Would there be enough students for her classes, audience for her recitations, private patients to seek her services? Would her private clients pay her adequately and promptly? In later years my mother, not perceiving me as distinct from her, kept asking me whether people paid me enough money, whether I had enough students in my classes, enough attendance in my workshops, none of these issues of concern to me.

Part VI

The Thirties

CHAPTER 14

Grandfather Freud

I have been interviewed, in my life, about 678 times about my grandfather, yet I knew him only very superficially and learned about his life mostly through his numerous biographies. I did acquaint myself thoroughly in my later professional life with his writings and the School of Psychoanalysis that he established, and I have become increasingly critical of many of his ideas.

As long as I can remember, Sunday morning was the day to visit the Berggasse. My Fräulein, my brother, and I would set out for the short walk from the Franz-Josefs-Kai to the Berggasse midmornings, as regularly as children of other families go to church. Sunday morning was the day my Grandmother and her sister Minna, who was part of the household, received Grandfather's four sisters whom I knew as "the old aunts." Neither my father, nor my Aunt Anna, nor my Aunt Mathilde, the three of Freud's children who lived in Vienna, and certainly not my mother were ever present at those meetings. At the time, I never asked myself why Grandfather himself was not present to welcome his sisters. If Freud's only brother, Uncle Alexander, was present, he also did not mingle with his sisters, but stayed with his brother in the "oval office." I never met one of his sisters in that sacred place. At a specified moment—I believe it was a quarter to one—the three of us, although I do not remember my brother's presence as clearly as my Fräulein's—were invited to visit my grandfather in his office. I believe the reason my brother frequently did not come along was because my father took him along on hiking and skiing trips, a privilege in which I was not included.

My grandfather sat there, with his fingers in his mouth, suffering pain with each of his few friendly words, perhaps asking me whether I was a good girl, or whether everything was all right. He then tweaked my cheek and distributed a generous amount of weekly pocket money—8 schillings to be exact, which was the cost of a ticket to the Burgtheater—to me and my brother and a weekly money gift to my Fräulein. After that, the visit was ended and we returned to the living room. At exactly one o'clock, Grandfather then made an appearance in the living room and greeted his sisters as a group. I believe that was the end of everyone's visit, since it was lunch time.

During the summer, at least during the last five years after my grandfather could not travel any longer, my grandparents rented a villa, always with spacious garden grounds, in one of Vienna's suburbs—Grinzig, or Döbling, or Pötzleinsdorf—beautiful magic places to my child's eyes. Before we went on vacations, my Fräulein and I would then take the streetcar to these suburbs that I otherwise seldom visited since there were few occasions for me to leave the inner city. I should explain that my family did not own a car, which was still a luxury in Vienna at that time. The summer routine was a little different; my grandfather might sit on the terrace instead of his inner sanctum, and we would have a little more contact with him.

It was through my grandfather's generous weekly pocket money that I inadvertently became the family banker. I take after the Freud women, in terms of thrift, and thus carefully saved my money in a piggy bank, perhaps for a rainy day. Not only my brother, who was chronically out of money, borrowed from me constantly, and I am happy that he has told me I had been generous toward him, but my own mother also regularly borrowed money from me.

My frequent visits to the Burgtheater, usually with a seat in the eighth row of the *Kaiserloge* (approximately the middle of the first balcony), were important childhood events that nourished my active little girl fantasy life about kings and queens and heroes who won or lost battles. For these visits, I wore a floor-length green velvet dress with a tight bodice, full skirt, puffed sleeves, and a pink silken Peter Pan collar. My Fräulein brought me to the theater and fetched me at the end.

I keep returning in memory to the intensity of these youthful impressions, the sun downs in the Dolomites, the old Italian pictures in Venice, the first flight among the white clouds, and certainly the classical plays in the Burgtheater, with surprise that they were never quite replicated in my adult years. My love affair with Karl Moor, the hero of a play by Schiller called *The Robbers*—Karl being an innocent, well-meaning robber—nourished my fantasy. The humiliating end of *König Ottokar* (*König Ottokar's Glück und Ende*

[King Ottokar's Fortune and Ending] by Franz Grillparzer)—a Hungarian king who is defeated by Rudolf von Habsburg I, the first emperor of the long Habsburg dynasty—preoccupied me to an astounding degree. Over and over did I stage, with my friends, the scene in which proud Ottokar has to kneel in front of quite a benign Rudolf, usually taking Ottokar's role. Oh, mysteries of childhood!

By May 6, Grandfather's birthday, my grandparents were already in their summer villa, which allowed his birthdays to be celebrated outside, on a veranda, and this was also true of their September wedding anniversaries. These holidays were occasions when family and friends assembled, certainly including my father and sometimes even my mother. My father wrote poems for all family occasions, and it was my very exciting privilege to recite them.

I believe it was his 80th birthday when I had the fortuitous good luck to please the inventor of slips of the tongue by stumbling over the ending of my father's poem and instead of reciting that "God may let you live a long time," I substituted that "God may let you live forever" (*daß Gott Dich immer leben läßt*). The error was indeed well received. I am surprised, however, that my father wrote a God nobody believed in, into the poem.

After our emigration from Vienna, I regularly wrote to Grandfather during that whole year, from May 1938 until his death in September 1939, and he answered some of my letters, writing himself my ever-changing addresses on the envelope. Again, given my grandfather's importance in the world, I will give the original German version of his letters, before translating them.

GERMAN LETTER

    Mlle Sophie Freud
    I Villa Lambert, Chatou (S.et O.)
    France
    PROF. DR. FREUD
    39 ELSWORTH ROAD
    LONDON, N.W.3
    1.7.1938 (July 1, 1938)
    Mein liebes Sopherl,

Ja, Du fehlst mir auch sehr und wirst mir nächsten Sonntag besonders fehlen aber es freut mich sehr zu hören daß Du in so interessanter Umgebung und so gute Fortschritte in der Neuen Sprache machen kannst. Du wirst es gewiß leichter haben, Dich in der Fremde zu akklimatisieren als wir

PROF. DR. FREUD.
39 ELSWORTHY ROAD
LONDON, N.W. 3

1. 7. 1938

Grandfather Sigmund Freud's first letter to Sophie

alten Leute. Doch geht es uns im Ganzen recht gut nur Tante Minna ist noch schwer krank.

Da unsere Lün für 6 Monate in Quarantaine gehen mußte haben wir ein neues Hündchen angeschafft. Er trägt den Elephantennamen Jumbo ist aber ein gang winziger Pekinese, noch sehr scheu. Herzliche Grüße von Großvater.

PROF. DR. FREUD (ENGLISH TRANSLATION)
39 ELSWORTH ROAD
LONDON, N.W.3
1.7.1938 (July 1, 1938)
My dear Sopherl,

Yes, I also miss you very much and I will miss you especially next Sunday, but I am glad to hear that you are in such interesting surroundings and can make such good progress in the new language. You will surely have an easier time to acclimatize in those foreign parts than we old people. Since our Lün [their dog] had to go for six months of quarantine, we got ourselves a new little dog. He carries the elephant name Jumbo but is a tiny Pekinese, still very shy. Affectionate greetings from Grandfather.

PROF. DR. FREUD (GERMAN LETTER)
39 ELSWORTH ROAD
LONDON, N.W.3
26.7.1938 (July 26, 1938)
Meine liebe Sophie,

Nimm einen guten Rat von Großvater an. Schreib Deine Adresse immer auf den Brief, wie auf's Couvert denn das wird weggevorfen und der Großvater und wer sonst weiß nicht wohin er antworten soll. Zum Glück kam Walter u. trug Deinen Aufenthalt lesbar in meine Notes ein, so daß ich Dich heute reich machen kann.

Die Schilderung Deiner Leistungen im Heim klingen sehr erfreulich u. auf Deinen Photos siehst Du sehr erwachsen aus. Laß es Dir weiter gut gehen. Bei uns ereignet sich alles mögliche. Großmama ist heute 77 J. alt geworden u. sehr frisch und gesund. Tante Anna fliegt Ende der Woche nach Paris zum Kongreß. Onkel Ernst glaubt er hat ein neues Haus für uns gefunden, auch mit Garten, der aber nicht so weite Aussicht hat wie der in den ich vom Schreibtisch aus jetzt schaue.

Schreib nur bald wieder wenn du nicht besseres zu tun hast.
Herzlich Großvater

Prof. Dr. Freud (English translation)
39 ELSWORTH ROAD
LONDON, N.W.3
July 26, 1938
My dear Sophie,

Accept a good advice from Grandfather. Always write your address inside the letter, not only on the envelope, because that gets thrown out and the grandfather and others do not know where they should send their answer. Fortunately Walter came and wrote your address legibly into my notebook, so I can enrich you today.

The description of your achievements at the camp sound very encouraging and you look very grown up on your photos. Continue to take good care of yourself. All sorts of things are happening here. Grandmama has her 77th birthday today and is very hale and healthy. Aunt Anna is flying at the end of the week to the congress in Paris. Uncle Ernst thinks he has found a new house for us, also with garden, but not one with as broad a view than the one I can now look at from my desk.

Do write soon again if you have nothing better to do.

Affectionately, Grandfather

German letter

Mlle Sophie Freud
Groupe Hauser "Grand Maison"
Morzine Haute Savoie, France
Prof. Dr. Freud
39 ELSWORTH ROAD
LONDON, N.W.3
5.8.1938 (August 5, 1938)
Meine liebe Sophie,

Ich wünsche Dir alles Gute und Schöne zum Geburtstag und da die letzte Sendung Dich erfreut hat wiederhole ich sie heute.

Herzlich Großvater

Prof. Dr. Freud (English translation)
39 ELSWORTH ROAD
LONDON, N.W.3
August 5, 1938
My dear Sophie,

I wish you everything good and beautiful for your birthday and since you enjoyed the last shipment, I repeat it today.

With affection Grandfather

GERMAN LETTER

Mlle Sophie Freud
Paris XVIe
6 Rue Eugène Manuel
PROF. DR. FREUD
20 Maresfield Gardens
39 ELSWORTH ROAD
LONDON, N.W.3
26. X. 1938
Meine liebe Sophie,

Ich antworte Dir nicht so oft als Du mir schreibst, aber schreib mir nur recht oft wenn Du etwas besonderes erlebst oder etwas brauchst. Ich freue mich mit jedem Brief von Dir.

Gut zu hören daß Du gegen Deiner Erwartung das Examen bestanden hast. Auch Freundinnen wirst Du hoffentlich bald finden.

Wir überwinden langsame die Kinderkrankheiten des neuen Hauses. Tante Minna geht es besser obwohl noch lange nicht gut.

Herzlich grüßt Dich Großvater

PROF. DR. FREUD (ENGLISH TRANSLATION)

39 ELSWORTH ROAD
LONDON, N.W.3
October 26, 1938
My dear Sophie,

I don't answer you as often as you write to me, but be sure to write if you have special experiences or if you need something. I take pleasure with each of your letters.

Good to hear that you passed your exam contrary to your expectations. And hopefully you will also soon find girlfriends.

We are slowly surmounting the childhood illnesses of the new house. Tante Minna's health is better but by far not yet good.

Affectionately greets you Grandfather

PROF. SIGM. FREUD (GERMAN LETTER)

20 MARESFIELD GARDENS
LONDON, N.W.3
TEL: HAMPSTEAD
20. XII. 1938
Großvater schickt Dir und Mutter herzliche Weihnachtswünsche.

ENGLISH TRANSLATION
December 20, 1938
Grandfather sends you and Mother most cordial Xmas wishes.

PROF. SIGM. FREUD (GERMAN LETTER)
20 MARESFIELD GARDENS
LONDON, N.W.3
TEL: HAMPSTEAD 2002
1.5.1939
Meine liebe Sophie,
Mit Deinem Brief nach längerer Pause habe ich mich sehr gefreut. Für Deinen Schützling kann ich natürlich nichts tun aber Du hast es auch kaum erwartet. [*I had written to Grandfather, asking him foolishly whether he could help one of my friends to get out of Vienna.*]
Grade jetzt wo ich eine anstrengende Behandlung durchmache kann es mir gar nicht gut gehen. Vielleicht zeigt sich später ob sie viel geholfen hat.
Gerne möchte ich Dich und die kleine Eva bei mir sehen aber die Zeiten gestatten keine erfreuliche Unternehmung.
Nein, ich glaube nicht daß es so bald zu einen Krieg kommen wird. Für die fernere Zukunft kann—ich—und niemand verbürgen.
Herzlich grüßt Dich
Großpapa

PROF. SIGM. FREUD (ENGLISH TRANSLATION)
20 MARESFIELD GARDENS
LONDON, N.W.3
TEL: HAMPSTEAD 2002
May 1, 1939
My dear Sophie,
I much enjoyed your letter that came after some interval. I can obviously not do anything for your protégé but you did not really expect it. [*I had written to grandfather, asking him foolishly whether he could help one of my friends to get out of Vienna.*]
Since I am just going through an exhausting treatment I cannot feel well at all. Perhaps we shall see later whether it has helped much.
I would love to see you and little Eva near me, but the times do not allow an enjoyable enterprise.
No, I don't think that a war will soon break out. Neither I nor anyone can speak for the more distant future.

Cordially greets you,
Grandpapa

My grandfather had obviously included money, some English pounds, in two of his letters. We shall hear how some of this money, unspent, and accidentally unconfiscated, would safely arrive, four years later, in the United States.

LETTER FROM SOPHIE

My Dearest and Much Loved Grandfather,

Even now, in my very old age as I read your loving letters—at least this is how I experience them—I am deeply moved. Perhaps you really did care about me, even though I know I was not your favorite grandchild. You loved Heinele the most, but he died a year before I was even born, and you wrote to a friend that you would never love a grandchild in quite the same way. I think you also loved my cousin Eva more than you loved me. I just have that impression, maybe because she had visited you—was invited to visit you—that summer of 1939 just before you died. Why was I not invited to visit you in that summer before the war—the summer before the dark? Or maybe I think Eva was your favorite, after Heinele, because a picture exists of Eva sitting on your lap, just as Heinele had sat on your lap, but I don't remember ever sitting on your lap and I would not have forgotten that. I know, you saw me weekly, for many years and you always gave me generous pocket money as part of each visit, which opened the door of the Burgtheater for me, but I was not a child who really wanted money. I was a child who craved your affection and the money almost got in the way. I remember you as old and sick, with your fingers in your mouth, always in pain, a grandfather of few words. Our visits in your sacred office were short—Fräulein may have been present, or Uncle Alexander—you said a few words, looked me over to make sure I was well taken care of, tweaked my cheek, gave me money, gave Fräulein money, and the visit was over.

Just once, dearest Grandfather, did we walk in the garden together, in the summer in Grinzig while collecting nuts. During that special visit, I knew that this was a rare and precious moment, a moment of pure joy, to be ground forever into my memory. Perhaps if you had known how much this little walk alone with you meant to me, you would have arranged it more often. And why, Grandfather, was I never invited to have a meal with you and your family? Sometimes I stayed over for a few minutes when the Sunday meal had already started and I enviously watched you feed ham or other delicacies to Jofi [the dog] while you ate. I did not envy Jofi for the ham she got, even though I could tell it was the kind of ham that was only used, in our house, for Mother's jours, but I could tell how much you loved Jofi who was allowed to be present at a family meal, and that was why I envied her.

And then, when you passed through Paris, I could not spend the evening with you, excluded from other family members who surrounded you that evening. I know you would have had to invite my angry and difficult mother if you had invited me, and maybe her presence in general overshadowed the pleasure you may have had in your Vienna grandchildren.

But after we parted from each other, you wrote me loving letters, addressing the envelopes yourself, thanking me for my letters, expressing satisfaction with my progress reports, giving me the impression you cared about me in a way I had not felt before.

Dearest grandfather, being your grandchild has stamped my life. You were a kind and protective presence in my young life, even if emotionally distant. My early identity as a princess helped me to remain steadfast during some difficult years, shielded me from the destructive self-doubts that tormented my poor mother, spurred me on to start thinking for myself and raise my voice, and even gave me the courage to critique your theories, which, I know, you would not have forgiven me. There were times when I wanted to be seen as other than your grandchild, but altogether your mighty shadow has enriched my whole life, rather than curtailed it. It was my good fortune, my enormous privilege, to be born your grandchild and I thank you for all you have done for me. Your Sopherl

Chapter 15

Franz-Josefs-Kai 65

*A*lthough my mother would eventually spend time in three continents, her first 42 years were not only spent in the same city of Vienna, but, since age 11, even in the same house. We hear that she did not even need to change her address when she got married.

My maternal grandparents rented the whole second floor of quite a sturdy house. It was really the third floor, given that there was a first floor called the mezzanine. The first floor of many houses in Vienna is called parterre and the second floor mezzanine and sometimes there is even a high parterre (Hoch-Parterre), making the first floor often a fourth floor. Legend has it that this custom arose to sidestep the prohibition to build houses of more than a certain number of floors, or else that houses were taxed per floor and the parterre and mezzanine, not being true floors, thus escaped taxation. But our house only had a mezzanine and a well-functioning elevator, which we used most of the time. It was not the kind of elevator that visitors had to activate with coins as in some other houses.

My grandparents' apartment had two entrances next to each other, one leading to the front end of the flat and the other to the rear end, where Grandfather Drucker's office had been located. It was the exact same arrangement as in my other grandparents' apartment in the Berggasse. By the time my parents had outgrown their three-room flat, soon after my arrival on the scene, my Grandfather Drucker retired. Mother's two younger sisters had left the family and moved with their husbands to Berlin and to Prague, respectively. My grandparents were thus reduced to a family of three people, counting their live-in servant Mitzi—who naturally lived in a dark cubicle off the kitchen—and they no longer needed so much space. The office and perhaps some other rooms were converted into a separate flat. Times were hard, housing was scarce, and so was money, and it must have been lucky for the *young couple to have such a nice relatively large rent-controlled flat to move into. Thus, it came about that it was my mother, the oldest child, the one who should have been a son and I suspect was the least loved of the three daughters, although she claimed she was her father's favorite, came to live next to her parents for the first (and de facto only) 19 years of her marriage.*

The house in which we lived and where I grew up, Franz-Josefs-Kai 65, stood at the corner between the Kai and the Theresienstraße, both with names of the Habsburg royalty who enjoyed the love and gratitude of Viennese Jews, including my parents. The windows of my grandparents' flat all looked down on the elegant Kai bordering the Donaukanal, but all but one window in our apartment looked onto the quite humble Theresienstraße and more specifically onto the Rossauerkaserne. The latter is an imposing large red brick barrack—a building stretching over several blocks with battlements on top, all around. It was then and I believe it still is, in active use. "I am sick and tired of looking at the barracks," writes my father, in 1927, eagerly planning a vacation. The Rossauerkaserne was not within talking distance, but close enough for some friendly visual interchanges between some of our household help and the soldiers who lived there, although my last Fräulein, the one I remember best and who stayed with us for the last six years in Vienna, was above such fooleries.

Twice, in my later life, I had occasion to return to this childhood flat. The second time, only a few years ago, the flat was empty, about to be redecorated. I bent out of that corner bay window and saw a magnificent view, following the Donaukanal, with the Kahlenberg and the Wienerwald still visible in the distance. But it was nothing I had ever noticed in the almost 14 years I lived there, nor when I revisited the house the first time, in 1960, eager to show my husband all the places where I had grown up. This turned into a very short visit because the inhabitant of the flat, a physician, still the same who had taken over the apartment when we left, spent the entire time cursing our cook, "that disgusting tramp" who was the last to leave the apartment and had ripped out and taken along the bathtub when she left.

Straight ahead, from this same window, one could see the Augartenbrücke leading from our first Bezirk *(district) across the Donaukanal to the second* Bezirk, *the Leopoldstadt. We seldom had occasion to cross that bridge. The Leopoldstadt was the universal point of entry for all Eastern Jews who immigrated into Vienna, including the families of three of my grandparents and the then-current domicile of two of my great-grandmothers. Many families moved out if they became sufficiently affluent, the next stop being the ninth* Bezirk *where my paternal grandparents lived, within a 10-minute walk from our house. Our house was in the very respectable first* Bezirk, *yet it was not only across the Leopoldstadt, but it bordered directly on the ninth* Bezirk, *which started across the Maria Theresienstraße. If you were not born in Vienna, you may think that such a long discussion on the districts of Vienna is out of place, but when two people born in Vienna meet each other anywhere in the world, they determine almost immediately in which* Bezirk *the other person lived, indicating their probable religion and social status, arguably what we need to know most when we meet strangers.*

CHAPTER 16

Rooms Full of Memories

A long the Donaukanal was a park, the Kaipark, which has given way to the U4 underground station called Schottenring, but the house itself still stands there, unharmed, with the same wrought-iron door that I now consider quite beautiful but did not notice as a child.

I spent many hours of my childhood playing diabolo, alone, in the Kaipark. I can't imagine why American children, and perhaps today's children in general, are not familiar with that interesting challenging game. It consists of two separate sticks connected by a string and of a spool about the size of a hand, which is to be balanced on the string, thrown into the air, and caught on the string along with other balancing acts. I pretended to be a whole group of children who competed with each other, including myself, but I did not insist on winning. Often other characters that I impersonated threw the diabolo-spool higher than I did, or else caught it on the diabolo-strings more consistently. One day, I was perhaps already six or seven years old, the same age child of our janitors joined me in the play. Even though we lived only a few floors apart, we had never played together. I should perhaps explain that being a janitor was a very low status occupation in those days, and the word Hausmeister was used as an insult to denote vulgar behavior.

Having a real rather than imaginary competitor in my diabolo game naturally led to vigorous arguments. I later complained to my mother about our fights. She screamed crazily, "I don't send you to an expensive private school to have quarrels with Hausmeister children." More than 70 years later, I remember the pounding heart and the restless night that followed this introduction into our class system. It taught me early not to run to my mother with childish complaints. I never played with that little girl again.

113

My mother would later teach at the Volkshochschule *(adult education center) in Ottakring, Vienna's working-class district, and I never heard a derogatory word about her students. Moreover, she voted for the Social Democratic Party, the Reds, not the Blacks, in Austria. She was sympathetic to Communist Russia, at least during the war. Yet her class consciousness was profound and may have sustained her through the periods of poverty that followed our arrival in the United States. When American sailors came aboard our Portuguese ship, as we entered the United States near Baltimore, our passengers, all of them refugees, embraced these gentle-looking young men in their trim white uniforms with fierce and tearful affection. Not so my mother. Arriving in a new strange land, homeless and penniless, she scornfully whispered to me, "how ridiculous, they are only uneducated sailors."*

*Our flat was T-shaped. The top of the T consisted of a string of four rooms along the Theresienstraße, opposite the Rossauerkaserne. The corner room, with the bay window that adjoined my grandparents' flat, was my parents' big bedroom with the famous brass beds. Next to it was the large living room called the gentleman's room (*Herrenzimmer*). From there, one walked into the large dining room and finally into the children's room, the end of the top of the T, which I shared with my brother and the current Fräulein and which had only linoleum on the floor. The only bathroom, without a toilet and looking into the courtyard, adjoined the children's room.*

The stem of the T was the hallway, which landed halfway into the dining room. Off this stem/hallway, was the toilet, exactly opposite the entrance and separate from the bathroom, as is still often the custom in Austria. Since one had to walk, at night, either from the bedroom through the living room, dining room, and hallway, or from the children's room through the bathroom, the kitchen, and the hallway, to go to the toilet, people used chamberpots that were stored during the day in the night-table next to the bed. Adjoining the toilet off the hallway, was the maid's room and kitchen. These three rooms had a window into a courtyard so bleak that it resembled an air shaft. The flat was built for families in which cooks, rather than the lady of the house, spent time in the kitchen, and the kitchen was thus not deemed worthy of any sunshine. I already mentioned that Mitzi, who sustained my maternal grandparents in their older years lived in a dark cubicle. Our cooks, too, inhabited a dark and poorly furnished enclosure, not much bigger than the next-door toilet. This kind of maid's room was standard in all the families that I ever visited and absolutely taken for granted. When the Freud family moved to London, where they were fortunate to live in an elegant two-story house with a garden, the servant Paula, who had come with them from Vienna, lived in a small room off the kitchen that was as unattractive as her room in the Berggasse flat had been. I feel sure that she had been given a choice where to live, but had felt out of place in a larger, sunnier room.

This might be the point to take a small detour and describe our household help-ers. There were many changes of Fräuleins and cooks in my early years. Some depar-tures must have been due to my mother's quarrelsome nature, but not all of them. I remember one Fräulein who came to us from a more distinguished family, as she reminded us frequently, and insisted, among other arcane rules, that children are to defecate at an appointed hour. It was a great relief to us when mother asserted her authority in this situation and thus established a protective presence. Children tend to learn quickly who calls the shots. One can appeal to a mother if a Fräulein is too harsh, but not the other way around. In any case, I never had reason to complain about my last Fräuli.

Indeed, some stability came to the household when Amalia Schober from Wolfsberg, Kärnten (Carinthia), and Rosa Schwarz, also from the country, entered our household. I believe both had been selected by Grandmother Freud, and for both of them ours was their first job in Vienna. Fräulein came to live with us when I was seven years old, Rosa a few years later. They each had their assigned tasks, Rosa being charged with most of the daily cleaning, food shopping, and cooking. Fräulein was initially in charge of the children, the children's room, and our light evening meals, my parents eating seldom at home in the evening. They each had their days off, I believe one-and-a-half days a week, and probably not the same days. There was never any question that Fräulein's social sta-tus was clearly superior to Rosa's status, signaled by her eating with the family and sharing her room with us children, neither matter much of a privilege in my current view. If there were conflicts and jealousies between these two household servants, they took care to keep them private. Like most middle-class households at the time, we had a washerwoman who came once a week and did all the heavy washing. This involved, for some reason I wish I had asked my mother, counting all the sheets and napkins, and pillow cases, before they were washed, and then again, when they were finished, all beautifully ironed and folded. In addition, a very nice seamstress came perhaps twice a month to do all the odd sewing of the household, mostly repairs, because we went to a dressmaker for our clothes. I think ready-made clothes appeared in Vienna only in the last years before we left, since I remember it as a big occasion when I received my first store-bought dress at Gerngross's.

As we grew older, and we no longer needed a Fräulein, she actually became my mother's (what shall I call it?) personal assistant, chambermaid, only ever-present confidant, financial mediator between her and her husband, all of the above. Mother mentions how Fräulein helped her sew her costumes for her poetry recitals, meaning Fräulein surely did all the sewing under my mother's direction. Mother hardly men-tions Fräulein in her autobiography, and I, too, did not give Fräulein the apprecia-tion she might have deserved. When I wrote stories about "My three Mothers," Fräulein was not one of them—she was a Fräulein, not a mother.

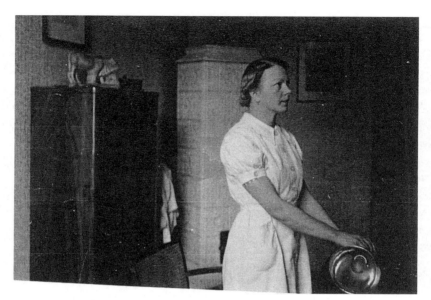

Amalia, Fräulein in the Freud household

Rosa, cook for the Freud household

The living room (Herrenzimmer) *was the center of mother's receptions, although they naturally extended into the dining room. It was certainly also the center of family life—well, family life without my father whom I don't remember ever seeing in the living room, which is absurd since he surely must have been there many times. Its floor was covered with a Persian rug, and the room, like all other rooms in the house, was wallpapered. It was a cozy dark room, warmed by our precious* Dauerbrandofen *(stove), which Rosa, the cook, fed with coke every morning and which kept most of the flat reasonably warm. I see myself sitting in one of the two overstuffed easy chairs placed at each side of the fireplace bitterly crying for days about the fate of young David Copperfield. I still remember the picture of the Mona Lisa on the wall and the nearby Dürer print of Adam and Eve and the snake curled around the apple tree, which I could describe exactly since it made it all the way to Paris, to Nice, to Mother's flat in New York City and from her estate, to my own living room where I can look at it, while writing these lines. In one corner stood a black high chest of drawers with an opening for a desktop, chiseled out of black wood, my mother's graceful bureau that was forwarded after us to Paris, but no piece of furniture made it all the way to New York City. On the chimney stood, among other knick-knacks, two brass menorahs, only as decorations, because we did not celebrate Chanukah and they are also mere decorations in my living room.*

I have mentioned that it was the room in which Mother prepared her poetry readings with us, and with her pianist. It was also the room in which Mother saw her private patients. It was also in this Herrenzimmer, *in front of the* Dauerbrandofen, *that the unforgettable following scene happened.*

Did my mother have an umbrella in her hands all along, or did it happen to lie nearby in the living room? Why would an umbrella lie on a chair in the living room? But there she stood, in front of the cozy oven and asked my brother whom he considered the best mother in the world. She asked this in a nonthreatening deceptive tone, as if open to honest information. He hesitated, he choked around, and then admitted his opinion that Reserl Schaar's mother seemed the best. Thereupon she screamed at him and beat him. Enraged, she hit him again and again, with an umbrella, I remember that for sure.

WALTER'S ERNESTINE

It must have been soon afterwards that she asked me in a mealy-mouthed voice "Who do you think is the best mother in the world"? Obviously expecting the answer "You, dear mother." But I had met the mothers of many of my friends who compared very favorably with my hysterical mother. So I said truthfully: "It is Mrs. Schaar," who was the mother of my friend Reserl, and a truly delightful person. For this bit of truth Esti beat me up.

Sophie's childhood living room corner

Many years later my poor and wounded mother asked my children, not once, but repeatedly and perhaps desperately, which grandparents they loved most.

How strange, that my brother and I remember this same event in such similar terms even though I had written my memoir a year before he sent me his contribution and he had never laid eyes on anything I had written. The reconstruction of memories has recently fallen into bad repute, and as we can see in these pages, not without reason, but I am also offering an example of one event, apparently traumatic for the little girl and her bigger brother that must have really happened in quite this way.

It was in the Herrenzimmer as well, where Mother's receptions took place, although they naturally extended into the dining room. We called them jours, a French word defined by the Larousse as the day on which a lady receives. Many guests were crowded in a rather tight space. Apart from helping with the preparations, I was allowed to pass the prepared hors d'œuvres and curtsy when introduced to newcomers.

Freud's patients consisted mainly of people from foreign countries and Martin took care of their financial affairs. He needed a connection with a specific banking house in order to get a better exchange for these foreigners' money. He could not find an entrée into this banking house. In order to further my private practice, I had a reception in my home each month, a kind of literary salon. Musicians played their compositions, novelists read the newest chapters of their novels, and poets their latest poetry. Martin pooh-poohed and sabotaged my receptions and never attended them. On one of my cruises, I met a young charming couple on their honeymoon. I invited them to my parties. It so happened that the young man was the junior partner of the same banking house Martin needed for his valuta transactions. The business introduction became a cinch and Martin was not only able to make a more advantageous exchange for his foreign customers, but he could make a nice profit himself. Martin became less hostile about my entertaining.

Much the same anxiety that accompanied her recitals hung in the air about the jours, in this case as to whether certain people would accept my mother's invitation. Not doing so would be viewed as a personal insult and the name of the offender forever crossed off her list. I had a Latin tutor, a girl only a few years older than myself, still at the same gymnasium but in a higher grade. She was not only a very effective tutor, but also a much admired older friend. She did not come to one of Mother's jours, even though invited strictly as a favor to this young woman. Her being instantly blacklisted seriously threatened this important relationship. I usually tried not to introduce any adult I admired to Mother, because of the danger of some similar quarrel, but sometimes this strategy simply did not work.

My mother's quarrels, either listening to them, or hearing about them, were the background music of my childhood and years beyond, since her quarrels continued all through her life. She quarreled with my father, my brother, her sisters, my Fräulein, the cook, members of the Freud family, many of her colleagues, and her friends. I learned to pray to our Jewish God. Sh'ma Yisrael, I prayed, "please let my mother not quarrel with anyone tomorrow, or let her quarrel with me, rather than with anyone else."

Not that Mother's quarrels were the only matter for me to worry about. I also worried about burglars, Mother getting run over, earthquakes, and getting leprosy. I had read in a junk magazine that leprosy started with a white spot on one's palm and examined the inside of my hand quite frequently. Fear of earthquakes came from my brother assuring me that Vienna lay on a fault line. Mother did get run over, one evening, after a fight with my father, and burglars would certainly turn up in our flat, even if in the guise of Nazi officials doing a "house search."

It is obvious that our living room was seriously overworked and that our family of four, plus two live-in servants, presented a serious space problem. I have explained how the big corner bedroom adjoined my grandparents' apartment, with a firmly locked door that was never opened. I have no idea how the original big apartment was divided when my parents moved in, and whether conflicts had arisen at that time, but I remember later angry quarrels between my mother and her mother about where the division should have taken place and how it should be changed. Mother wanted the boundary between the two flats moved by one room, naturally the one adjoining our big bedroom, a room that was not ever used by my grandparents and was currently not even heated. It was a little museum room of what appeared to me extraordinary beauty. It could have been a room in Schönbrunn (a royal castle in a suburb of Vienna) with chairs of blue silk brocade, an inlaid wooden desk, and a glass cabinet full of china figures. My grandfather's picture collection hung on the walls. My brother still mourns this disappeared picture collection—who knows, there may have been a Klimt among them—but in the light of later events, their loss was a small indignity. I visited the room perhaps once a year, naturally only with the express permission of and admonishments not to touch anything from my grandparents, and found each time some new and precious treasure I had not formerly noticed. Well, it was this blue room that my mother wanted, arguing again and again that we were too crowded in our apartment, that she needed an extra room for her jours, *pleading with her mother to give her that extra room. But my grandmother remained adamant in her refusal.*

Instead, a change was eventually made that also mirrored our family's development. The dining room was divided into two halves, one half for my growing brother who now had his own room.

WALTER'S ERNESTINE

When I became a teenager I got my own room, which was detached from the dining room. I very clearly recall my discussion with the architect about what sort of lights I wanted in my room; it was the first and last time that I could make a family decision. Usually any comments, suggestions, or wishes were completely ignored or ridiculed by my parents. In my room I could play relatively undisturbed.

My Fräulein was asked to rent a room in the neighborhood, I imagine at the family's expense. In a few years a picture of Hitler would "decorate" the room, hanging above her bed, no doubt to proclaim my Fräulein's political correctness. It would have given me nightmares, but my Fräulein did not care. My father moved into the children's room, which became carpeted and redecorated with all new modern furniture clashing with all the old pieces in the rest of the flat. I was assigned my father's bed in the master bedroom. I was perhaps 10 years old at the time. It gave me little pleasure to take my father's place, be it in his bed, or in my mother's life. It settled the matter that I had already realized for some years, that it was I, rather than my father, who was officially responsible for my mother's welfare.

The Bedroom

The Franz-Josefs-Kai had a trolley car running all along its length. In my last four years in Vienna, I thus slept in a room which had a bay window on the Kai. I got used to falling asleep to the soothing clanging of that trolley car and I always thought I would want to live among city noises all my life. But the trolley car jingles alternated with frightening rumbles. Endless chains of what I remember as tanks, but must have been trucks, with warlike faces frequently rolled along the Kai. I know not from where they came, and where they went to, but they were connected with the fear of war that had always been part of my childhood. One war had just ended, my brother and I were postwar babies, and another war was already in sight. At school, in the second grade when we had learned to write, our beloved young male teacher asked us to start our composition book—the orange one that was firmly bound and accompanied us through the whole year—with the words Never Again War (Nie mehr Krieg) almost as a title for that book, on the very first page. Then there were the cries of Extraausgabe (special edition) of the newspaper boys on the street. Extraausgabe meant something terrible had happened, perhaps a civil war in our own city, or Dollfus had been murdered.

The Kitchen

I raised my children and continue living in a house in which the kitchen is integrated with the living area. In a household without servants, there would have been no other practical way to prepare meals while supervising small children. Not that there was an upstairs and downstairs in my childhood home, but the kitchen (along with the toilet and the maid's room) was one of the few self-contained rooms in the flat that could be entered without going through several other rooms. In spite of its darkness, its windows going into the bleak inside courtyard, it was a large and comfortable kitchen, no doubt well equipped by the standards of those days. The iceman delivered huge ice blocks, once a week, which were inserted into the wooden icebox; there was a regular gas stove and a big table for preparing meals, and of course for eating, since Rosa, unlike Fräulein, ate by herself in the kitchen. I only remember our last cook, Rosa Schwarz, who stayed with us for the last five years of my life in Vienna. She was unfailingly kind and friendly and often told me about her own little girl she had left behind, with her parents "in the country" (am Land).

Yet, I did not spend very much time in the kitchen with Rosa not recognizing how much I could have learned from her, and so I only have my Viennese cookbook when trying, over the years, to imitate some of the delicious dishes she had prepared for us. Mother spent even less time in the kitchen, but once a month, or at *times even twice a month, Rosa, Fräulein, myself, and Mother sat around the big kitchen table and prepared the sandwiches for that afternoon's jour. Only at Gerstner's or Dehmel's, the two finest Viennese teahouses, have I tasted little open sandwiches that were as delicious and looked as appetizing as the sandwiches we made at that time. There might be a row of white cream cheese with black caviar, and next, a slightly overlapping row of yellow egg salad sandwiches with a cross of red ham strips on top and next in line were perhaps the tips of two canned asparagus with a snippet of tomatoes in between. We made trays and trays of sandwiches, which I was then allowed or expected to help pass around among the guests. Actually Rosa herself did not sit with us much of the time, since she was busy baking the sweets for the reception, but my own interest was focused on the sandwiches, especially with eager anticipation of leftovers. In spite of my later efforts, I have never been able to duplicate these particular sandwiches in my adult years, no matter how much pink smoked salmon, green pickles, and black caviar were at my disposition.*

The Dining Room

It was in the dining room that the most unpleasant events of my childhood took place. It also had a Persian rug and was elegantly furnished. I am talking of the time after my parents had separate bedrooms, with neither of them visiting the other's bedroom very often. Family members had separate breakfasts and separate evening meals, but we did share the midday meal. And since, as mentioned, father even seldom entered the living room, the dining room was the main space and the noonday meal the limited time when my parents were together.

The meal was scheduled for around one o'clock, although it usually did not start until one-thirty since my father was late, stopping at his parents' house on the way home. My mother who had spent the waiting time at her parents' complaining and sometimes crying, was thus always angry from the start.

Unfortunately my husband's being employed by the *Berggasse* made me see less and less of him. Day after day, he visited there at noon, before lunch and went in the evening after work. Over the weekends, he traveled to the mountains.

Fräulein sat at the table with us, and Rosa served the meal. Fräulein might have had a much better time eating with Rosa in the kitchen, but her status dictated her place at our dinner table. For a time there was an impoverished pale and thin Jewish boy who came to eat at our house—something arranged by the Viennese

Kultusgemeinde [*Jewish Community Office*], but it was his good luck to be relegated to the kitchen, certainly not invited to our dinner table. There was thus another child close to my age with whom I never conversed, let alone played, although he visited our house regularly.

The meal consisted of soup and then meat (or fish) and perhaps potatoes or rice and a vegetable and fruit, seldom a sweet desert. Because my mother received a certain amount of household money from my father—later via my Fräulein—she tried to divert some of the money to her own needs and so we also had meatless days, at least once or twice a week. There were delicious dishes on meatless days, such as noodles with sugared poppy seeds or sugared nuts on top, or even fruit dumplings or milk-rice. Naturally my father never had a meatless day, and surely would have been irate if this had happened. My mother was always on a diet, afraid to become as stocky as her parents, and so she ate little and I followed suit, soon to be declared a fussy eater.

My father instantly hid behind the newspaper, Die Stunde, which he read throughout the meal, which is how I remember it, although did he not put the paper aside while he ate? It was during fruit time, during the end of the meal, that my mother raised some difficult subject, usually having to do with needing money, at which time my father started to shout at her and my mother might fall into a seizure-like attack in which she threw herself on the floor, flailing her arms and legs and screaming.

WALTER'S ERNESTINE

I like to stress that I was not the only recipient of Esti's fits of rage. The fairly unusual communal meals frequently ended with Esti getting furiously angry with father, throwing something at him. The meal thus ended among screams and tears. This was disappointing from a culinary aspect because Rosa Schwarz, our cook, was very good at her job and prepared excellent meals.

After the unhappy meal, father left the house as quickly as possible, perhaps only return-ing late in the evening. A gas space heater was in the corner of the dining room, and at the end of the crisis my mother would light the heater and huddle next to it, crying and expecting my comforting company next to her. I understood that the space heater was expensive to operate and since there had just been a huge fight about the need for, and lack of, money, I worried acutely about the unnecessary expense of the gas heater.

Father's Room

I was allowed to visit my father in his newly furnished elegant room, especially Sundays during breakfast. It was the main time we visited with each other.

Naturally, I remember the furniture of that room especially well, since it would later become the furniture of my room in Paris.

While spending little time with me, my father was unfailingly kind toward me but would get extremely distressed and helpless if I ever cried. What I remember best was watching him eat a soft egg—something that was forbidden to me since I was supposedly allergic to eggs. There, on his own breakfast tray was a blue and white delicate china egg cup with a soft-boiled egg sitting inside. He carefully beheaded the egg with a knife, scooped out the top of the head with a spoon, salted the rest of the egg and ate it spoon by spoon. Need I add that I have eaten a soft-boiled egg daily for most of my adult life, in spite of its probable disastrous influence on my high cholesterol count?

My father's room was also the place in which the monthly (or perhaps weekly) accounts were settled between Fräuli and him, which I was welcome to attend. Apart from the agreed upon household money for food, she had a long list of expenses: Latin tutoring for Sophie, new sneakers for Walter, dancing lessons for Sophie, repair of a window sash, money for a school outing, money for the iceman, a tip for the janitor for some extra service, and so on. It was a long list. My father moaned and groaned and argued about particular items, but the money had already been spent, it was a lost cause and he had to come forth with the money. The little girl wished he did not have to pay for her dancing lessons, which she hated anyway, and she would even have given up her new black patent leather shoes, which she liked a lot but had not really needed.

CHAPTER 17

Waiting for the Apocalypse

In the winter of 1934 Martin became seriously ill with what proved to be a kidney stone. He did not take care of it, went skiing, and one day returned from a weekend with a terrific pain and had to be operated immediately. When he came home from the hospital, there was civil war in Vienna. An Austrian fascist group called *die Heimwehr*, patterned after Mussolini's fascism and headed by Count Starhemberg, took over the city of Vienna. The very popular major of Vienna, Karl Seitz, was deposed, and when Vienna's working people rallied to protest, they were shot down with cannons. When Martin's physician told me to provide a peaceful environment for the convalescent patient, there was gunfire outside the apartment windows.

Grandmother Freud wrote to her son Ernst at that time (January 15, 1934) that "Esti behaved very well," meaning she took good care of Father but, she adds, "only he cannot stand her" (nur daß er sie nicht verträgt) (From The Diary of Sigmund Freud, *p. 166).*

Austria's Heimwehr was an attempt at fascism organized in the hope of preventing Austria's falling into the clutches of Nazism. Graf Starhemberg, a scion of the major who had defended Vienna against the siege of the Turks, proved to be an unpopular leader, although he had an affair with one of the city's most beautiful Burg-theater actresses. He was supposedly financed by the heir of one of Austria's armament factories. For me, the consequences of the Heimwehr revolt consisted of being asked by the management of the *Volkshochschule* to relinquish one of my speech instruction courses to a member of the Heimwehr party. A few weeks later, I received a call from the newly appointed instructor asking me, as a favor, to take over his course as he had lost his voice and become incapable of continuing group teaching.

In the summer of 1934, Austria again suffered a terrorist shock. Austrian's Chancellor Dollfuss was assassinated by a gang of Nazis who, unobstructed, entered the *Hofburg* (Imperial Castle) where the Dollfuss offices were located and cold-bloodedly murdered him. It looked as if the National Socialist Party would immediately take over the Austrian government. The coup was aborted. Hitler was perhaps not ready for such a big bite, or perhaps Mussolini did not wish to have the Third Reich as a direct neighbor. Kurt Schuschnigg, a Christian Socialist, became the last chancellor of Austria.

When this occurred, I was in Grado with the children and was at a total loss of what to do, whether to return immediately to Vienna, or to wait it out in Grado. The children, who loved it in Grado, voted for staying and they were right, as things calmed down again. Austria got another reprieve, for another three years and six months. The following years were lived with the knowledge of catastrophic Nazism approaching.

My youngest sister Marianne lived with her husband in Berlin. He was the manager of a large department store and was put into what the Nazis called "protective custody," which meant being put into prison. My sister was able to free him with a counterfeit passport and they came to Vienna to leave shortly for Paris. Luckily he was able to establish himself there as a successful banker.

Both of Freud's sons who had lived in Berlin and had married German girls, returned to Vienna. Ernst, Freud's youngest son, eventually went with his family to London. Oliver Freud went to Nice in the south of France. All prophesied the early fall of Austria. The Austrian Jews waited for the impending apocalypse until it was too late.

During the first years of the Third Reich, those German Jews who emigrated were still permitted to take their properties with them. Later on, a *Reichsfluchtsteuer* (flight-from-Germany tax) was introduced, which meant the Jews were expropriated and had to leave the country without any means whatever.

The events that brought Hitler to power were rooted in the Treaty of Versailles, the treaty ending the first World War, which had ruined Germany's economic existence. Heavy reparation payments to France had undermined the Weimar Republic. Weimar Chancellor Brüning had tried at Locarno to alleviate these burdens. Being unsuccessful, he abdicated and was succeeded by Von Papen and Schleicher. They had opened the door for Hitler. A very peculiar story is connected with Hitler's nomination. The German government had subsidized the Prussian estate owners (*preussischen Junker*) with huge sums of money in order to enable them to buy equipment so that they could administer their farmlands more profitably. One day a French newspaper published a story that Monsieur X, a member of the Junker class, had lost a few hundred thousand francs at the roulette table in Monte Carlo. A few of these gentlemen, instead of modernizing their lands, spent the government money they received on champagne, women, and song. Hitler, when he learned about it, went to Hindenburg's son, who was Hindenburg's gray eminence, and threatened to publish the news in Germany. This would have provoked a serious scandal, followed by public investigations, thereby compromising the entire Junker clique. All the men involved were the younger Hindenburg's friends or belonged to the same fraternity. Hitler promised that, if he were made Chancellor, he would suppress the publications of these happenings in the newspaper. Supposedly this was the way Hitler blackmailed Hindenburg into making him chancellor.

In 1936, Freud celebrated his 80th birthday. He was the recipient of a number of honors bestowed upon him. My contribution to this birthday was a huge cake more than one meter in diameter. I ordered it from Demel, Vienna's most famous pastry baker. The icing on the cake was a map of the world made of sugar. In Australia, an Aborigine read "Totem and Tabu," on the North Pole an ice bear read "Civilization and its Discontents," and at the Cheops pyramid a camel driver contemplated "Moses and Monotheism." This birthday gift was a huge success.

Sophie, my daughter, was then a delightful girl not quite 12 years old. She had the oriental eyes of her father, and on this occasion Freud wrote in her scrapbook: "To the youngest but most precious piece of my Chinese treasures."

A videotape exists of this girl who looks like me, except with long corkscrew curls, coming to congratulate her grandfather with some flowers. He laughs and plays with her curls and her grandmother laughs as well. Suddenly, after many months, I retrieved the memory that my parents made me wear a wig that day, as a little joke.

In the summer of 1937, I took my children again to Grado, since they simply wanted to go nowhere else. It was the last time in my life I spent the summer vacation with both my children.

Grado, that vacation island on the Adriatric Sea, my childhood Garden of Eden. For many years we went there for both summer months, living in an apartment, in the

Villa Bauer, with a full-time Italian servant to minister to our family's needs. We could freely roam about on the beautiful sandy beach, a special treat for a confined and overprotected city child. The Adriatic is more a salt lake than an ocean, usually smooth and mild, and deliciously warm. A little tower, a sort of dock, was placed at just the right distance, and my mother, a strong swimmer, would take me on her back, back and forth to the tower, until I learned to swim there on my own.

I spend my summers, in this my old age, swimming back and forth across Walden Pond in Concord, Massachusetts, every day from June to the end of September—it was certainly in Grado that I acquired my love for swimming.

Without the daily conflicts with my father, who would come to visit us perhaps once or twice a summer for short unremembered visits, and in later years not at all, Mother, surrounded by admirers, was more relaxed.

WALTER'S ERNESTINE

I loved the Adriatic coast at a place called Grado. It had a very long beach of fine sand and the water was warm and shallow for a long distance from the beach. I was allowed to roam the beach at will and could play with the many other central-European children who were holidaying on this then-beautiful island. While we were playing in the hot sand and warm sea, Italian pilots from a nearby air base entertained Esti. When I thought that the entertainment had continued long enough for Esti's reputation, I would come running, screaming at the top of my voice: "Mother, mother!" The sight and sound of an obviously obnoxious little boy was enough to cool the ardor of the most persistent admirer and he soon made his excuses to find more suitable subjects for his entertainment.

At some point, my mother must have decided that the combination of seaside and mountains was even healthier than spending time only at the seaside. Thus, we spent only one month in Grado, and the second month either in Mallnitz, a high mountain village in Kärnten, Austria, or in Bolzano, in Italy's South Tirol, in the Dolomite mountains. I have seen numerous spectacular places in my many travels, but no sunset can compare to the long-lasting dark pink sunsets of the Dolomite mountains.

WALTER'S ERNESTINE

If Esti had looked after our, my sister's and mine, mental health to the same degree as she watched over our physical health, we would have been the most normal and balanced children in Vienna. In the summer of every year, we were taken for one month to the Adriatic Sea, followed by another month in the Tirolian mountains.

Esti in Grado, with Walter "spoiling" the picture

In the last years of his life, my brother checked out these childhood paradises and was bitterly disappointed. Grado had become connected to the mainland with a bridge, and by the time my brother and I individually revisited it, it was invaded by cars. The graceful villas had been replaced by monster hotels appropriating the beach. He also visited Mallnitz and declared it a dead place, at least in terms of tourism, although the postcard he sent me looks idyllic.

We went to Venice and I took them sightseeing to the famous churches and galleries. Walter found these museum trips rather boring and resisted coming with us. He was a handsome youngster, had excellent manners and considerable charm, which he could use to his advantage. However, he gave me plenty to worry about when he was a teenager.

Actually Mother and Walter were in constant conflict, as early as I can remember. I cannot remember what the conflicts were really about, only that he was considered disobedient and "a problem." He was also failing in school and eventually had to be moved from the RG1, the public gymnasium in Vienna with the best reputation, to a private day school, which represented a comedown at the time. Although I was also failing in school and needed tutors in both Latin and mathematics, my mother viewed me as a model child. I think my brother believed that my Mother preferred me over him, or at least did not really love him.

WALTER'S *ERNESTINE*

My favorite toy was a Matador set. Matador was similar to Mechano but all parts were made of wood instead of metal. This gave the models, which one could build with Matador, a much more three-dimensional effect. My friend, with whom I worked on our constructions, Georg Pollak, now George Parker, is still alive in New York City. One day when we had just completed a lovely large locomotive, Esti came in, as usual in a fury. She picked up my locomotive and smashed it on the floor so that it broke. This wanton destruction in an attack of hysteria, of which I was completely innocent, upset me greatly, as can be imagined, and was remembered all my life.

One of the few subject matters which I could discuss with Esti with little fear of ending in tears was geography, particular traveling by train. We both knew the train timetables well and could speculate on the best and quickest way of getting from A to B.

Mother was very busy and we did not have much time together during the year, except for the unpleasant meal times, but we did have happy vacations. After my brother spent part of these vacations in a summer vacation camp with his friends, mother took me on memorable travels, the most beautiful being a trip to Venice. No place on earth ever again left the impression of the dreamlike city of Venice (including later visits to Venice itself) nor of the magnificent paintings that have stayed with me.

There were, however, also happy times with Mother in Vienna. Sometimes I was allowed to pick her up at her clinic, where Mother looked in her element, in her white doctor's coat. After introducing me proudly to her colleagues, she would take me to one of the elegant pastry shops in Vienna. These were red letter days, but if I had known then, as I do now, how expensive those shops are, I might not have enjoyed these outings even then.

Before leaving for her evening activities, Mother, in her glamorous clothes topped by an elegant fur coat, with lipstick, powder, and eye shadows, radiating perfume, would often bid me good-bye. I remember contemplating her and deciding I would not want to become that kind of woman. I made a similar vow when watching mother in her elaborate and endless cosmetic activities, such as smearing her face with all sorts of thick white creams that had to be left on for hours, not to mention whole Saturday mornings spent pulling out white hairs and the hairdresser's at least twice a week visits, with her elaborate services. I believe Mother thought that people might love her, or if that was an impossible goal, at least respect her, treat her well, admire her for her beauty, and she did everything in her power to preserve it. She had, moreover, bought into the American cult of youth, long before she came to that country and she waged a relentless war against encroaching old age. When her old age really approached, she searched for the fountain of youth in Bulgaria; she had at least two face lifts that disfigured her appearance in old age and she submitted to various hormonal youth therapies.

Curiously enough, I have held to my youthful resolve. I have avoided cosmetics, including lipstick, even in my youth, I have eschewed outward glamour and I never died my hair, all of which simplified my life and gave me energy for other pursuits.

During the winter months of 1937–1938 rumors in Vienna were increasing to the effect that Austria's becoming National Socialist was imminent. I went to see Anna Freud and said with urgency, "Papa has to emigrate." I can still hear her reply: "*Ein Professor Freud wandert nicht aus*" (A professor Freud does not emigrate). She could not conceive of the fact that Hitler's intention was first to humiliate and then to annihilate the Jewish spiritual leadership. Anna Freud was unable to appraise the situation realistically and had to pay dearly for it. Besides, Freud was deathly ill and needed Dr. Pichler's constant ministrations.

In my family, it was nigh impossible to come to a decision. Marianne my sister, who had settled with her family in Paris, came to Vienna to implore my parents to liquidate their assets and emigrate. Father refused. He had real estate that could no longer be sold at a sensible price. "I will not accept economic help from my son-in-law," he said. He died still at home a year later of cancer and a broken heart. When he died, I was already in Paris and could not return to Vienna without endangering my life. His last words were *"Die Esti kommt nicht"* (Esti is not coming). I was his favorite daughter.

A few years later, Mother and I almost stayed in Nice, a sure death sentence, because Mother, according to family tradition, could not bear the thought of becoming financially dependent on her brothers-in-law in the United States.

In January 1938, Dr. Kurt Schuschnigg, Austria's chancellor, was blackmailed by Hitler into nominating into Austria's cabinet a number of National Socialist ministers. Shortly afterward, Schuschnigg suggested holding a plebiscite in Austria as to the preference of the Austrian people regarding whether they should remain an independent country or become an annex of the Third Reich. Hitler regarded this attempt as a subterfuge and a personal affront. Schuschnigg made a farewell speech on the radio, saying he did not want to shed German blood and surrendered his country without the least resistance. On March 13, 1938, a German army marched over the Ringstraße and Austria had ceased to exist. At night torch parades tramped through the city. All night long the shouts *Ein Volk, Ein Reich, Ein Führer* (one people, one country, one leader) reverberated through Vienna's streets.

CHAPTER 18

Heroes of Their Own Lives

During these years, my relationship with my husband was steadily deteriorating. He was not only completely indifferent, but sometimes openly hostile. My presence made him noticeably nervous. I sensed by his behavior that he had a serious affair going. Until a short time earlier, he had spoken to me about his business in the *Verlag* (publishing house) and all the other enterprises he was in, and I had advised him and he had learned to trust my advice.

We might think Mother exaggerates the help she gave her husband, such as in the examples of getting Mr. Eitingon's approval, or the connection to the bank, but Father, on his own, was unable to establish himself professionally in London, so she might indeed have helped him in Vienna.

Now he hardly spoke except to criticize me. But, on the night of the Austrian Anschluss, we were returning peacefully from the Berggasse. There was too much turmoil around us for us to fight.

Indeed, one of the strangest things that happened in those strange days was Mother and Father leaving the house together one morning. They looked grim and, watching them from the bedroom window, I wondered whether they were on their way to the infamous Gestapo. Why else would they leave the house together?

I knew that Papa, from the royalties from his books and fees from patients, had some money in foreign countries. This was permitted in Austria but was against the law in the German Reich. I asked Martin whether he had destroyed all the papers dealing with these foreign accounts. My warning was ridiculed. Two days later 13 Austrian Nazis stormed the entrance to Freud's office and apartment and stole all the money they could find, so there was not even enough money left to buy food for the next day. I do not know if they went to the Verlag before or after this "visit," but I know that they searched Martin's desk there and found a list of Freud's foreign assets. Martin succeeded in bribing one of the gangsters with a considerable amount of money and was able to burn incriminating documents. The office had no curtains and the people on the other side of the street were watching the events with opera glasses. Martin's attempt at bribery was discovered. While all this was happening at the Verlag, a group of Nazis entered my home and searched it. They took Martin's gun, which he still had from the war, and our passports. The men did not behave too badly and I suspect that some of them knew me from my teaching in Ottakring, and perhaps one or two of them had girlfriends who had acted in one of the plays I had directed.

I had no inkling of what was going on at the Verlag when Martin phoned and said I should send him his pills (since his kidney stone operation, Martin took some medication). Then I knew. I told the men that, if they were returning to the Verlag, I wanted to go along so that my husband could get his medicine. When I arrived there, I was told of the ongoing investigation and the fact that my husband would be taken into custody. I do not remember what I said and how I did it, but I was able to talk those men into allowing my husband to go free.

My father also wrote an account of this incident in his book about his father:

The next day, Sunday, 13 March, The Austrian Nazis ... were in full possession of Vienna ... [206, 207]: I was, of course, naturally anxious about my parents that Sunday morning, but I determined, nevertheless, to go to my office first.... I knew that I must destroy legal documents of great importance. I had, in the course of my normal duties as a lawyer, invested money of my clients in reputable and stable currency abroad, this having been perfectly legal under lenient Austrian law; but I knew that it would be a crime in the eyes of the dollar-hungry Nazis, the punishment for which would be at least the confiscation of such funds. It was plainly my duty to protect my clients, including my father, by destroying all evidence which could lead to detection.... [T]he Nazi-controlled radio [had] warned the people of Vienna against unauthorized bands of armed raiders ... but I could know nothing of this when such a band came to the office before I had had time to destroy any papers.... Although unaware that my unwelcome visitors were hardly more than bandits whose activities were unpopular with the new authority, the fact that they were without a leader made me suspect that the raid I was enduring was an unauthorized implementation of the confused situation caused by the Nazi occupation. All their decisions were reached by majority vote as in adventure stories written for boys. There were a dozen of them, ... the most aggressive was a small haggard-looking man who, unlike the others who carried rifles, was armed with a revolver. At intervals throughout the incident whenever I showed no desire to co-operate, he displayed a blood-thirsty spirit by drawing his pistol and noisily pulling out and pushing in the magazine as he shouted, "Why not shoot him and be finished with him? We should shoot him on the spot."

One of the curious aspects of this raid was the fact that across the narrow street from the office there lived a staunch Nazi who, now sitting at his open window, enjoyed a grandstand view of the proceedings: something I was unaware of at the time; ... Although I was held in awkward imprisonment in my office chair, two of my guards keeping their rifles pressed against my stomach for much of that Sunday, the time passed quickly enough.... The safe had been rifled and the contents of the cash drawers, a considerable amount of money in coin and notes of a number of countries, had been placed in piles on a table, but I had removed the papers I wanted to destroy from the safe and placed them on a shelf where they had not been noticed by the raiders.

After some hours, when the initial enthusiasm of the raiders had tended to settle into something less ebullient, I asked if I might have a cup of tea. This request was instantly put to the vote, the result being indecisive until the fat boy suggested that I might be allowed to have a cup of tea provided I agreed to wash the cup and saucer myself. This was passed with applause, but I offered an amendment to the effect that the office caretaker should be ordered to wash up the dishes. This inspired further discussion, but when it was agreed that the caretaker (who had become a Nazi without undue delay) was still my servant, I was allowed to have a cup of tea.

During the early part of the afternoon, the ranks of the raiders began thinning out until I was left with only one guard, a seedy-looking man of middle age whose appearance suggested an unemployed *Ober-Kellner*, a head waiter, one who would have felt happier with a napkin over his arm than with a rifle held at my stomach. Being happily ignorant of the fact that the raiders who had withdrawn had gone to my father's flat, I was relieved at this turn of events.

Now that we were alone, my guard took his rifle away from my stomach and invited me to stand up to stretch my legs, thus giving me great relief.

All this, I might say, was closely observed by the Nazi gentleman watching from the window across the street.

My guard now began a tale of woe about the hardships and privations he had had to endure in recent years and it was soon plain to me that a generous tip would be welcome. I responded at once, giving him all the money I had in my pockets, including some gold coins and a roll of notes. He was deeply grateful, so grateful in fact that I felt I might hazard a request to be allowed to visit the W.C. This was granted at once and he agreed to escort me there, a short journey across a passage which would take me past the files of documents I wanted to destroy. I managed to organize quite a number of journeys until all the papers were torn up and all had begun a procession along the elaborate Viennese sewer system.

As it was the Nazi gentleman [from across the street] observed ... that during the guard's and my absences from the office when we crossed the passage to the W.C., some members of the gang returned for quick stealthy visits, to help themselves to some of the notes and coins stacked on the table. The outraged Nazi at once gave the alarm to Nazi headquarters, and the result was that within a few minutes ... the *Bezirksleiter*, the District Commander of nearby S.A. headquarters [arrived].

And so my father was released.

The two accounts of my parents of these life-threatening events are not totally different, except that my mother does not even appear in my father's account, while she remembers having rescued him. Even my brother who tends to be charitable toward his father is sure that my father had been careless and negligent with his father's and his clients' important papers. My father, who was almost shot at the time, chooses to make a circus out of the scene, the account focusing on his keeping his cool and his cleverness on managing to throw the documents into the toilet.

Not only did my father throw the questionable documents into the toilet, but he wanted to completely absolve himself of any reproach that he might have been careless by not destroying these documents at the proper moment.

Happily, the new Vice-President of Police, a man with a criminal record, was a close friend of my cook. Through this contact, I was able to buy back the documents quite cheaply.... (p. 215)

I believe it is my father who spread the rumor, unless it was Freud himself, of Freud's final courageous defiant gesture against the Nazis. He writes:

This was when an S.S. party had come to ask father to give a certificate proclaiming that he had been well treated by the authorities. Without hesitation, father wrote *"Ich kann die Gestapo jedermann auf das beste empfehlen* (I can recommend the Gestapo very much to everyone)," using the style of a commercial advertisement. This irony escaped the Nazis; although they were not altogether sure as they passed the certificate from man to man. Finally, however, they shrugged their shoulders and marched off, evidently deciding that it was the best the old man could think of. (p. 217)

The document was later found by historians, and no such sentence appears in it. I can imagine a scenario in which Freud told his family what he almost wrote. It would indeed have been unthinkable for Freud to jeopardize the lives of 17 people for the sake of a clever joke.

Events followed each other rapidly. The American Ambassador, Mr. Messerschmidt, following a direct request from President Roosevelt intervened with the Nazi authorities who had no wish to alienate the United States. Martin did not sleep at home, but in his pied-à-terre; over the weekend he went with his girlfriend to Baden. Anna had to go to the Gestapo headquarters to be interrogated, but was released with flying colors. Dr. Ernest Jones from England and Marie Bonaparte from France arrived to act as guardian angels for the Freud family and soon procedures for emigration were initiated.

It is by now well known that Freud only decided to leave Vienna the day after his daughter had been detained by the Gestapo for an entire day. (I am certainly not sure what Mother means with being released by the Gestapo "with flying colors.") While I worked on this book, I asked my brother why nobody focused on the younger members of the family, especially on him, who as a 17-year-old young man was in great danger, regardless of whether grandfather wanted to emigrate or not. The thought that neither my grandfather, nor my parents, had concerned themselves with his fate still upsets me. He replied that it never occurred to him that anyone would consider his future safety. But when grandfather decided to emigrate, and important and affluent people came to his help, our family received 4 of the 17 exit visas that he could procure. I thus owe it to my grandfather to be among the few lucky ones to have escaped Vienna before the murderous persecution of its Jews. When my brother, many years later, heard of my criticism of one of our grandfather's theories, he said to me, "Without Grandfather the Nazis would have made lampshades with your skin."

Later in his book, Father extolled his mother's defiant courage during the house searches; his wife's courage during these situations remains unmentioned.

I was a witness to both searches of our apartment, which my mother dismisses rather lightly given how extremely upset she was afterwards at the time, although it is true, she played "good hostess" to the hilt. Both my brother and I were at home, playing chess, when a group of armed men in boots appeared at the door. It is true, they did not shoot us, or even threatened to shoot us, or break anything, they merely tore the place apart. What Walter and I remember most keenly was the hacking open and strewing about the flat the provisions of flour, sugar, tea, and such, which were kept in white bags, as emergency food in those uncertain times. Any loose money disappeared, as did the collections of small gold coins my father kept for each of his children. How amazing that my mother does not mention the second frightening house search a few days later.

Mother also mentions, oh ever so casually, Martin's pied -à-terre, although she had not known the existence of such a flat where he presumably met his lovers. But, while indeed hiding in Baden, so my Fräulein explained to me many years later, vital papers that had been left in that place needed to be fetched. My Fräulein made several dangerous trips on her own to the apartment, but on one trip, my mother accompanied her. "And when your mother entered the place," my Fräulein said, "she shook with rage, grabbed a desk lamp and smashed it against the wall."

In my personal life everything I had was gone—my work, my marriage, and my home. What I was left with was my life and my health, and as it turned out later I still had considerable strength. Martin emphasized that my work in speech rehabilitation was language-bound, and since I could hardly speak a word of English, I would not be able to work in England, and would thus be a burden to the financially hard-pressed family. I spoke French fairly well. Compared with England, living conditions in France were much cheaper. I had a sister in Paris who was comfortably established. Moreover, after the recent events, I could not see how I could go on living with Martin as if nothing had happened. I suggested that, at least for the time being, I would prefer living in Paris. Martin was to take Walter with him, and I Sophie. We agreed on a monthly sum that I was to receive to support me and my daughter modestly, with the hope that eventually I would earn my keep. Perhaps we would resume our family life if conditions improved and Martin found a job in England. Marie Bonaparte, one of Freud's disciples, had the pull to secure the necessary papers for une *permission de séjour* (permission for residence) in Paris.

We children were not consulted about this decision and, although I might have secretly preferred to go to London with the rest of the family, I would never have admitted that, knowing my role as my mother's caretaker. In any case, the family division along these lines had happened some years ago. One day my father obviously decided to rescue his son from the influence of this awful woman whom he had unfortunately married. He suddenly started to take Walter on hiking and skiing trips and thus built a relationship with him. I was never included in such trips.

I saw my father very little. When I had been small, I was sometimes dressed up to go for a walk with him. Did we go for five walks, or a few more than that? Once, when I was 12 years old, he invited me to go to the theater, a thrilling experience. That night Mother woke me up, somehow in a rage—with whom did father talk during intermission, what else went on, did we come home immediately afterwards and so on. I was her child, it was all she had, and she was not going to share me with father, or so it seemed. It is also possible that I had become, in her eyes, yet another competitor for his love. He never asked me to go to the theater, or a movie, or any other outing, again.

Life in Vienna was more and more horrible. Signs appeared on coffee houses: JEWS AND DOGS NOT PERMITTED. Nazi bands roamed the streets looking for Jewish women whom they took to public lavatories, which they had to scrub with some acid so that the skin on their hands were burned. Jewish doctors were taken into custody, with the accusation that they had carried out abortions, which in Austria was strictly forbidden by law. One heard of people jumping out the window when the Gestapo came to jail them. Some took poison. In a few days Vienna's Jewish community, which had contributed so much to its scientific and cultural life, was annihilated. A letter received from the Department of Education informed me that my teaching contract at the university was revoked.

When I visited the Fröschels Clinic to say good-bye, Dr. Arnold, a prominent Nazi at the Neumann Clinic, threw me out by hand. Dr. Arnold is now a highly esteemed ear, nose, and throat specialist in Jackson, Mississippi.

Fräulein and cook remained faithful. The cook's boyfriend was a well-placed dignitary in the National Socialist Party and sent a message that, if I needed help in any matter, just to let him know. It was my parents who now became my greatest concern. Father was 78, mother 10 years younger. What would become of them if they were to remain alone? I was helpless. In the middle of May, we received our passports to travel. Carol & Jellinek was given the orders to ship our furniture to Paris and to London. With a trunkful of clothing, my children and I were ready to leave. Separating from my parents was the hardest thing to take. My father cried, "I won't see Esti anymore!" Half a year later, father was dead.

Fräulein accompanied us to the station. We took the night train via Germany to Paris. Martin left the next day by sleeper. To take sleepers for all of us would have been too expensive. The trip was uneventful. When we arrived in Kehl without incident, I felt relieved, although I was traveling into an unknown, insecure future.

In Paris, my sister had rented rooms for us in an awful pension with a witch as the owner and the metro crossing on a bridge outside my window, waking me up from sleep every five minutes. Even if it was only temporary, it appeared as if she had not searched for our quarters very hard. There was nothing I could do as I was completely dependent on her.

Martin's Book

[through the cook's Nazi friend] I was given timely warning of my projected arrest. Under these circumstances, it was decided that any delay in my departure might only cause embarrassment, and I decided to make for Paris to join my wife and two children, who had been sent there some days earlier. (p. 215)

Martin, who arrived the next morning was horrified and wanted to move immediately, although he planned to remain in Paris for two days only. I persuaded him to stay because I did not want to offend my sister.

The following day I prepared breakfast on the simple cooking facilities we had in these rooms. Martin was used to having scrambled eggs with ham for breakfast. I got up early to shop for the needed ingredients. In Paris, good quality ham is bought at a *charcuterie*, which closed once a week, but I did not know that. It was on one of those days that I had to buy Martin's ham at a grocer's, and after having gone to all grocers in the Rue de Passy, was glad to find ham. When I prepared the dish and served it to Martin, he criticized the ham as much too fatty and stated that I could not even shop for decent ham. It was the last meal I had to serve my husband.

A day later, Martin and Walter left from the Gâre St. Lazar for London. It would be 12 years before I met my child again. I saw Martin again in 1950 from a distance only, but we corresponded for some time.

My parents had been robbed, overnight, of their upper-middle-class lifestyle. They had lost their country, their friends and relatives, their work, their belongings, their language. Perhaps they would have appreciated their new freedom more fully if they had foreseen the future. But nobody could suspect, at the time, the transports in cattle cars without water, food, or toilets, the murder in gas chambers, and that Mother's mother and Father's four aunts and their friends and colleagues were to be cruelly murdered. For Mother and Father, the present was difficult and the future dark and uncertain. They found no way to comfort each other, no way to conjure up some hope. They tormented each other up to their last common meal.

FROM THE NÜRENBERG TRIALS

I beg you, Mr. Witness, to tell how Kurt Franz killed the woman who identified herself as the sister of Sigmund Freud? Do you remember? And Rajzman's answer was: "It was like this. The train from Vienna arrived. I stood on the platform as people were led out of the wagons. An older woman approached Kurt Franz, produced an identity card and said that she was the sister of Sigmund Freud. She asked to be used for light office work. Franz looked at the card very thoroughly and said it was probably an error, led her to the train schedule and said that a train would return to Vienna in two hours. She could leave all her valuables and documents in place and go to take a shower and after the shower her documents and a train ticket would be ready for her. Naturally the woman went into the bathhouse from where she never returned."

FRANCE

Part VII

Paris Years and Exodus

<small>CHAPTER 19</small>

Getting Settled in Paris

<small>RÉFUGIÉE A PARIS,</small>

la belle-fille de FREUD fait parler les SOURDS-MUETS

Elève libre du professeur Lemaître, le chirurgien du silence, elle poursuit avec succès et désintéressement — et dans la joie — ses expériences de rééducation

PAR
Merry BROMBERGER

Le hasard d'une visite à l'hôpital Lariboisière, dans le service du professeur Lemaître, le chirurgien du silence, des sourds, des muets, qui corrige les malfaçons de la nature, réséque des cordes vocales, enlève des larynx, refait des palais...

Dans le couloir du pavillon, une musique étrange s'élevait. Des voix exécutaient des gammes prolongées comme des exercices de plain-chant. Cela venait de la salle de consultations du dentiste.

— Une maîtrise dans le cabinet de prothèse?

— Mais non, me répondit une infirmière en riant; c'est Mme Freud qui fait parler les sourds-muets.

Depuis un an...

Depuis un an, en effet, une jeune femme souriante, qui n'est ici qu'une élève libre du professeur Lemaître, apprend à parler aux aphasiques, s'efforce à ren-

Article in *l'Intrasigeant* that made life easier for mother

Refugee in Paris: The Daughter-in-Law of Freud Gives Language to the Deaf and Mute

A volunteer student of Professor Lemaître, surgeon to the deaf and mute, pursues with success, selflessness, and pleasure her efforts at reeducation.

by Merry Bromberger

The accidental visit to the Lariboisière Hospital, in the service of Professor Lemaître, who corrects the mistakes of nature, [leads one to] Mme. Freud, who gives language to the deaf and dumb.

A young and smiling woman, she teaches people who are aphasic because of a stroke to use their lips—or how to draw sounds from the esophagus, for those who have no larynx. It is the daughter-in-law of the master of psychoanalysis, who, a refugee in London at age 83, is correcting the galleys of his books translated into French.

In Paris, two facts proved to be extremely helpful. The first was my being the daughter-in-law of Sigmund Freud, whose persecution in Vienna had made big headlines throughout the world. The second was my friendship with a well-connected woman who had studied at our clinic and remains until today my friend—Isabelle Martha Vié. Isabelle introduced me to Professor Lemaître, the chief of the E.N.T. [ear, nose, and throat] clinic at the Lariboisière Hospital, who permitted me to organize a speech and voice rehabilitation clinic in his pavilion. The appointment was not salaried, but Lemaître told *l'Intransigeant* about me, and the paper published a long article about my activities on the front page complete with a photograph. Isabelle also provided introductions to the best-known E.N.T. specialists and pediatricians in Paris. I diligently visited each of the physicians although it took a lot of time and energy.

On June 17, 1938, Papa and Mama Freud came through Paris on their way to London and stayed overnight at the *Hôtel particulier* (mansion) of Marie Bonaparte. They both looked frail and lost. We took leave of them at the *Gâre St. Lazare* and Sophie, in tears, sobbed, "I won't see grandfather ever again."

For once it is I, not my mother, whose feelings are hurt. Princess Bonaparte took home movies during the evening the Freud family were her guests. I believe the movie is available at the London Freud Museum. There is a whole group of relatives and friends but neither my mother nor I were invited. I presume they could not have invited me without my mother who would have been unwelcome and so neither of us got invited. Yet I feel sad and rejected that I could not have spent that last evening with Grandfather.

Soon we left the awful boarding house and were spending the summer in Chatou, a town in the *banlieu* of Paris, in a big house with a beautiful park. The wife of the owner tutored Sophie and me in French and I commuted every day to the hospital clinic.

One day, to my surprise, I received a call from Dr. Eitingon who had come to Paris to visit his sister, inviting me to have dinner with him. I still do not know how he found out where I was staying. It was a most pleasant evening and it cheered me up. He asked for another date two or three days hence, when I would meet his sister, but weeks passed and I did not hear from him. Eventually his sister phoned to tell me that her brother had had a heart attack after bringing me home. She asked if I wanted to see him, and I did so soon afterward. Eitingon left shortly to return to Jerusalem, which was his home, only to suffer soon a crippling stroke from which he never recovered. I felt like a *femme fatale* who destroys her admirers. With his death, I lost a valuable friend.

Marianne suggested I enroll Sophie in a private social dancing school to make her life a little pleasanter. She knew of a German refugee couple who gave such classes and Sophie signed up for them. One of the pupils became Sophie's husband in 1945. The same people had a summer camp in the Haute-Savoie and I sent Sophie with them for her summer vacation.

I was very happy in that summer camp, liberated for a while from my complaining mother and among young people who were also all refugees. The young couple, Harald and Edith Hauser, who ran the camp were fervent Communists and, while in France, they became my closest young adult friends, and I became deeply attached to them. For them I was a possible recruit, "a soldier of the future," although this never quite worked out.

Father announced that he would come to visit me at the camp, and I made the mistake of telling Mother about his coming visit. She appeared unannounced, at the same time. I was very angry that Mother chose my time and my turf to make tremendous scenes, and wrecked weeks of my precious vacation. The following year I attended the same summer camp and, while I was very cool toward father during his visit, I had not informed Mother that he was coming. When she later learned about his visit, it was her turn to be enraged at me, accusing me of a major betrayal, of siding with the Freuds against her. Our time in Paris was generally punctuated by such accusations. I was, by any standards, the best-behaved adolescent one could wish, but I objected vigorously to Mother's constant yammering and complaining about father or lamenting how Walter was surely lonely and neglected. I might have said such cruel words as, "Perhaps I would be happier in England."

"Your father is paying you to torment and persecute me," she screeched. One day, I believe it was during the memorable fight about hiding father's visit at the summer camp, I said that I was sick tired of listening to her anger at her husband; those were her affairs and not mine and I no longer wanted to hear about these matters. "You are a ruthless girl," she replied, "you have inherited your grandfather's famous stony heart." The accusation of being merciless and cold-hearted was often enough repeated that I incorporated it into my identity. In retrospect, I feel that this was both a curse and a blessing that has stayed with me through life. Yet, was it really my mother who cast the spell of an icy heart on me or did she merely recognize a certain character trait in me? I now remember how captured I was by Andersen's snow queen turning the little boy's heart into ice and by the Faustian fairy tale by William Hauff, called The Cold Heart.

Marianne had invited me to Lavandou, a beach in the South of France where she had rented a cottage. I was there three days when a telephone call from her husband obliged her to return in a hurry. She never told me what happened. I decided to go to Grenoble, to study French at the University's summer classes.

I suspect, and I presume so does Mother, that Tante Janne could not bear Mother's visit and had arranged with her husband to call her back.

On July 14, in memory of Bastille Day, the Parisians danced in the streets. The president reviewed a large army parade on the Champs Elysée, displaying all the military hardware, including fighter planes flying in the sky above, with Hitler looking in over the border. The *président du conseil* (prime minister) was Monsieur Blum and some stickers in the Paris Métro read, *Mieux Hitler que le juif Blum* (Better Hitler than the Jew Blum). Anyone with any sense could interpret this message as a forecast of coming events, especially after Hitler's blackmailing of Czechoslovakia into ceding part of their country to the Reich. It is the story of Chamberlain, with his umbrella, meeting Hitler in Göttesberg and promising peace for the next hundred years.

Around this period, I wrote a letter to Anna Freud asking her if she could help Sophie and me emigrate to the United State. With her connections, she could easily have done it. Martin wrote back saying that I was making peculiar demands on Anna.

My tasks for the fall were to enroll Sophie in a lycée and to find a decent place to live until our furniture arrived from Vienna. Sophie was accepted at the Lycée Jean de la Fontaine, but lost a year due to her poor French.

CHAPTER 20

Tante Janne

*W*hile Mother mentions the name of Freud and the presence of a friend as the
*factors that helped her getting settled in Paris, for me it was unquestionably
the presence of Tante Janne who made all the difference. She received me with open
arms, surely as the daughter she had never had. For me, she became an oasis in a desert, a safe harbor in a stormy sea; she made up for many of the losses of my life at
the time. I had found a second mother when I needed one the most, a mother I would
secretly prefer to my actual mother. Naturally, my mother sensed my perfidy—after
all everyone always loved Tante Janne more than her, why not her own daughter—
but in spite of her jealousy, she did not interfere with our relationship, as she had
done in Vienna with my grandmother and my father. I am totally certain that
Mother always wished me well and I think that she realized how much support
Tante Janne gave to me in my great need in those days and she thus allowed me to
relate to her. Besides Tante Janne, a sister, was at least not a member of that hostile
Freud tribe. In any case, conflict between the two sisters remained under shaky
control.*

My sister used the occasion of my being a poor and hunted refugee to say to
me that Walter was a complete idiot. She should not have said that. A few
years later, her son became schizophrenic and is to this day seriously disturbed. I have every reason to be proud of my son and his family.

*My mother's gloating over her sister's immense misfortune might strike some of us
as so repugnant, as to deny Mother any further compassion. At least that was my
own reaction for some years after I read her autobiography.*

*This was the outrageous time when desperate parents of severely disturbed chil-
dren were accused of having caused their illness. Does it make a difference that Tante*

Janne would say to me, in a puzzled tone,after her son fell ill, "we were always so careful not to quarrel in front of Herbert, while your parents made your life miserable with their fights." She thus implied that fate had been unfair, punishing the wrong sister.

I will introduce Tante Janne as a young woman through a letter from Father to Mother, early in their marriage, in which he jokingly tells about a visit to his sister-in-law and her husband.

VIENNA, JUNE 26, 1923

Dearest, best Murrer!

I just want to describe to you, very briefly how I spent Saturday and Sunday. Saturday was still bad grey weather, I was invited for lunch at your sisters [Marianne Zittau] which did not proceed without some complications. First Heinrich and I had to wait for the woman of the house until half past one since she was apparently delayed in her shopping, hence a certain storm-sultriness in the air. Barely had we sat down at table, did the bell ring. A messenger from Henry's bank appears and brings the entire day's mail for signatures. The man of the house thus puts down his soup spoon and retires into the living room and signs letters for about 20 minutes. The woman of the house remains mute at table and refuses to take in any nourishment. The guest dips now and then, embarrassed, his spoon into the already cooled-down soup.

The man of the house returns, with documents under his arm, visibly uplifted for having accomplished difficult intellectual work. The woman of the house, probably activated by feelings of revenge now takes her turn at jumping up, remembering a telephone appointment that she has to take care of instantly. One hears the telephone ringing twenty times in succession from the bedroom and snatches of an ever more nervous negotiation between the telephone operator and the woman of the house. The man of the house and guest sit opposite each other scrutinizing each other in silence. Another 15 minutes pass. The three protagonists are united once again around the table. The soup is cleared away. The roast is being brought in. Behind the roast appears in beaming friendliness the father-in-law and greets all present. He is urgently looking for a recent issue of the *Prager Tageblatt* (Prague's Daily) which reports, apparently from a new sensational perspective, a much discussed suicide of a prominent member of Vienna's society. The man of the house puts down fork and knife, jumps up and hurries into the bedroom where he combs through a thick stack of newspapers for that particular issue. The woman of the house also puts down her cutlery, and looks heavenwards, a picture of quiet but not piously resigned despair. The sauce of the roast starts to coagulate and get stuck on the still full plates. The guest is prevented in his attempt to bring the purpose of the cooling roast to fruition, by his father-in-law who embroils him in an interesting debate full of backward looks and future developments about the course of the stock market. The bell rings. The guest is called away because his tailor appears with a suit ready for a fitting. As the guest returns to show off the new suit he finds the couple, without father-in-law, in a state of having-found-each-other-again, and disappears as totally superfluous without exchange of any special formalities.

In this way it got to be Saturday, 4:00 P.M. I went to the Diana Bad [Vienna's main public swimming pool] where they just had an evening of waves and with this North sea substitute I shortened the time until 6 h quite pleasantly. Freshly bathed and correspondingly hungry, after a scant hour of reading at the coffeehouse, I went out to eat at the *Linde,* quite badly and expensively (an over-salted veal cutlet with a dried-up cucumber and a compote, 50,000 Kronen)....

Tante Janne and Heinrich Zittau soon left for Berlin where Tante Janne became part of the leftist intellectual scene of the Weimar Republic. We hear about her next in another letter. This time a letter from Grandmother Freud to her son Ernst who had left Vienna to live in Berlin, was married, with a growing family and establishing an architectural practice. She is happy that the wealthy Zittau family is providing her son with some badly needed architectural commissions.

GRANDMOTHER FREUD'S LETTER TO ERNST AND LUX

Vienna, April 3, 1925

My much loved children,

Here everyone and each one leaves for Easter, one almost has to apologize for staying home. Papa, who used to have a passionate love for traveling is unfortunately no longer able to do it, and I feel infinitely sorry for him but after all we have to be glad that he feels so comfortable between his four walls which is thank God the case!! For the three summer months we have once again rented the Villa Schüler on the Semmering. [A vacation resort near Vienna.]

Naturally I wish for you with all my heart that Ernst should have sufficient and well paying work, but who is in that position these days. Martin, who wants nothing else but work and earn a living is practically paralyzed, only has, through connections, a paying job which he does not enjoy and our poor Oli slaves away like a worker without being able to afford the least little thing.

So really, on every side there is a standstill. There is no point complaining, one has to try to comfort oneself with the thought that it will not always stay this way and will also change again.

Thank God that Ernst is in good health and that the much loved children are also thriving, one hears from all sides enthusiasm about them, just now again from Mother Drucker [who must have been visiting her daughter in Berlin].

By the way I recently received a lovely little letter from Marianne Zittau in which she thanks me that I recommended her to you and how totally unhappy and forlorn she would feel if she did not have the two of you. You see my dear, how good deeds get rewarded. . . .

But let me get to the birthday child! Unfortunately I have no gift for you, my Ernst, only good wishes. Stay well and happy in the circle of your loved ones; keep up your head even when things go a bit differently that you had wished for. . . . Be well, both of you for today, my loved ones, and be fervently greeted and kissed from Mama.

Beautiful Tante Janne

I was not told at what exact date my grandmother went to Berlin to break up the love affair between her married son and her daughter-in-law's sister, but Tante Janne confirms the story. This was the true reason, Mother later explained, why the Freud family had held her in low esteem. "I paid dearly for your Aunt's bad behavior," my mother said to me when I inquired more closely about what had happened. "The family never forgave me."

I myself faintly remember quite another episode. I have the curious impression that I had opened a door and found Tante Janne, during one of her visits to her parents, sitting on Father's lap. In any case, there was a huge fight between the sisters and some months later the gift of silk stockings for my mother as a peace offering arrived in the mail. It was only in retrospect, as an adult, that I came to understand the connection between these events. "No, I did not care for your father," Tante Janne claimed to me when I reminded her of this episode years later, "but I surely loved your Uncle Ernst."

Both my mother and Tante Janne were beautiful women, but my mother was cold and soon grew bitter and ever more certain of being unlovable, while her younger sister was charming and charismatic, conquering hearts with seemingly no effort wherever she went. These were not only the hearts of lovers, often distinguished men with worldwide reputations in science, or politics, or the arts, but everyone she met seemed drawn to her.

CHAPTER 21

Liebstes Herzenspuckerl

A *lthough my brother had contributed a memoir of his mother to my project, he had never mentioned that he had in his possession hundreds of letters his mother had written him through the years. He had saved all the letters he had ever received, and he may, in some ways have forgotten about them, since there is no mention of them in his* Ernestine. *Had I been hounded by so many parental letters though the years, many of them full of despair or anger, I might also have been tempted to forget them. My mother also never mentioned this voluminous correspondence with her apparently much-loved son, so it was almost a secret not only from the Freuds but from me as well. They were written almost entirely in German, especially in the early years.*

Father and son had left Paris for London toward the end of May and within weeks Mother started to agitate for a reunion. She yearned day and night, she explained, for the presence of her 18-year-old son at her side. The style of her letters is almost identical in feeling to the letters she wrote to her fiancé while he was a prisoner of war in Italy, the loving and the missing is all there, once again.

Letters overflowing with affection are certainly easier, in both cases, than actually being together.

JUNE 10, 1938

Dear nasty Puckerl,

I find it incredibly nasty of you that you have not written to me a single time, especially considering how much I miss you. I know nothing of your school except that you have become their dancing teacher; are you playing tennis, or are you riding horses? How about your health and the English language?

I am getting by. I work three times a week in a big hospital, naturally without pay and otherwise I run about all day introducing myself to doctors in other hospitals to also get paying cases, but it is naturally all terribly difficult. I will surely still need years to earn money here, hopefully I can stick it out. . . .

Dear big Muckerl, do write your Mother who misses you so very much, and be embraced and kissed from all my heart.

JUNE 17, 1938
Dear big Muckerl,

My heartfelt thanks for your dear long letter that gave me terribly much pleasure. I miss you so very very much, nobody I can nag. It is very lonely and I feel abandoned and cast out, the only thing that comforts me and makes me very proud is that it was I who managed to rescue Grandfather Freud's property and I beg you in your interest to *be sure* to remember that.

I am always terribly tired, since I need to take all sorts of steps to start earning, but until now all in vain. I wrote father that I would terribly much like to come to England for a few days, to be a little bit together with you, but father has responded that it costs too much, although there are weekend excursion tickets for about 300 francs. If I earn money once again, given I can do with that money whatever I want, we shall give each other a weekend rendezvous. You could meet me at the coast so that I would not have to travel so far. Find out what place might be the most favorable, father need not know anything about this. . . .

I kiss and embrace you with all my heart, from your Mother who loves you, Esti

JUNE 27, 1938
Dear Puckerl,

You are a wicked son of a raven that you don't write me for so long. I am already very anxious. I am already sufficiently miserable and lonely, and even more so when nobody writes, because Father does not write either.

Mother tries again to organize a summer visit from Walter.

JULY 7, 1938
Dear Puckerl,

My health is definitely better . . . and I also sleep better and no longer cry all day. . . . Don't foul-mouth the hospital, it is very important for me, the only way I can get established. Since Father will in a shorter or longer time, more probably shorter, send me either no money at all, or as little as possible, so he can have more for his whore, I have to see to it myself, so I shall be able to bring up Sophie properly.

JULY 17, 1938
Dearest Herzenspuckerl,
Schnapserl is since Thursday in the Haute Savoie [*I am on vacation in a summer camp*]. I am now totally, totally forsaken, and it is Sunday, on top of it.

I was quite poorly for several days, you know there is nothing worse than lying ill while all alone in a bad hotel room without service or help, I wish that fate some day for Annerl [Anna Freud] so she should see how that feels, if there is justice, she will catch her full share ... if I can hold out for two years with my heart etc., I will have quite a bit of work. Then all the F's can, you know what. My parents are very upset, they want to emigrate as well. I don't know what is happening, am very upset ... pretend only to the outside that you are on good terms with the Freuds, between us, except for Grandfather, they are the most malicious pigs that one can imagine, including Father, but maybe the latter is only stupid.

Dear Puckerl, don't be surprised that I write to you in such detail but there has to be somebody one can discuss things with, but don't tell anyone, especially not Father about my affairs, otherwise they will spoil things for me out of malice, these are only my connections and have nothing to do with the Freuds. Keep your fingers crossed and above all your mouth shut. *Don't tell* Father anything, my life is not his business after the way he has treated me.

Please see to it that we can be together and be embraced and kissed with all my heart, Your Mother Esti.

Mother's hatred of the Freud family was quite mysterious. She writes to Walter in 1946 that "I would have liked to see Grandmother Freud again, I think she always liked me, but I might be mistaken." Thus, if Grandfather, Grandmother, and perhaps even Father are excluded, that leaves only Tante Anna and perhaps Tante Mathilde, the only other Freud family members who lived in Vienna, to be hated.

JULY 29, 1939
Dearest Herzenspuckerl,
Our furniture has arrived and now I am sitting in official offices to get my *carte d'identité*. Everything is more difficult for me than for other people ...

maybe the princess is agitating against me and they will imprison me, here in the prisons there are rats who kill people with their bites. Sometimes I wish the Nazis had beaten me to death, at least it would have been at home and I would now have it all behind me, this way it lasts much longer. I keep wondering what crimes I have committed that they have banished me into total loneliness.

I hope you at least are doing well. I so much would like to see you. Thousand kisses, Mother Esti.

In actuality Princess Bonaparte would later facilitate asylum in France for Mother's mother. While we lived in Nice, after the armistice, she either paid or transmitted regular monthly money amounts to us.

MARTIN TO ESTI

November 27, 1938

The Princess has written to the authorities regarding your mother, hopefully it will be successful.

AUGUST 1, 1938

Dearest good Herzenspuckerl,

I am very pleased that you are finally getting some vacation.... Please *take good care* in your swimming, the Atlantic Ocean is not the Adriatic.... I am just reading in the newspaper that Grandfather bought himself a magnificent palace in London. Although I am living in the cheapest boarding house in Paris, the Princess accuses me of using too much money so that I really hardly dare to eat enough and they buy themselves a palace. Besides, it is professionally very unfavorable for me. Nobody will help me to earn anything when the father-in-law owns a palace in London.

I am absolutely opposed to your going next year right into a film atelier, if you have no engineering degree you can never become anything better than a cameraman, if you do get an engineering degree, you can become the director of a film company.

Don't be so stupid, you don't have to become a Proletarian, just so your relatives can save money on your studies. You are *entitled* to a decent education. Besides, especially for film studies, France is a much better place. Please write me much and often, it is the only thing that keeps me halfway going. Have a good rest, and be affectionately embraced and kissed by your loving Mother Esti

AUGUST 3, 1938

Dear Herzenspuckerl,

Today many good news ... tomorrow I am getting a permit to travel in and out of France. If I am able to get an English entry visa, I shall come to visit you in the second half of August, I will wheedle money out of Grandfather. Please don't mention this to Father, otherwise he will prevent it. Ask your landlady whether I can also stay with her.

AUGUST 5, 1938

Dear Puckerl,

... Father seems to be *nebbich* totally *meschugge,* he wants to go as a bank clerk to Israel, which would entail for him certain death, considering the state of his health.

That the Freuds have bought a beautiful house, I do know as a fact but it is kept secret from us.... Please ask your landlady to use her well-placed connections to get me a reference for the British consulate in Paris, that I can come for one month to England.... I have also asked Grandfather, *please,* ask him *as well,* he should give it to me as a birthday gift. I do fear that Father will interfere; I won't have any time in the winter, and I want to see you again, I miss you so so much and I am horribly lonely and have a very very difficult time.

Thousand, thousand Pussis, Mother Esti

Grandfather seems to have had as little desire as Father himself to welcome his daughter-in-law in London, as suggested by his diplomatic letter:

PROF. DR. FREUD (GERMAN LETTER)

39 ELSWORTH ROAD
LONDON, N.W.3
August 7, 1938
Meine liebe Esti,

Dein Brief an mich hat sich offenbar mit den letzten Brief Martin's an Dich gekreuzt, sonst hättest Du andere Pläne gemacht. Du weißt jetzt daß er nach dem 18. D/M von der Prinzessin (jetzt gerade unser Gast) nach den Süden eingeladen ist-daß er über Paris fahren auf den Hin- wie auf den Rückweg mit Dir sein wird so daß es keinen Sinn hat, wenn Du nach London kommst wenn er nicht dort ist. Sollte sein Reise auf Schwierigkeiten stoßen und aufgegeben werden so wird es allerdings notwendig sein, so werden wir auf Deine Absicht zurückkommen müßen. Das erledigt den ersten Teil Deines Briefes. Was den zweiten Teil betrifft so anerkenne ich gerne Dein historisches Recht auf eine Geburtstagsdonation das nur in jenen dunklen Tagen vernachlässigt wurde und lege Dir einen kleinen Cheque bei den Du hoffentlich ohne Mühe zu Geld machen kannst. Mach Dir die Zeit bis Du Deine Arbeit beginnst recht angenehm. Mit herzlichen Gruß Papa

Prof. Dr. Freud (English translation)
    39 ELSWORTH ROAD
    LONDON, N.W.3
    August 7, 1938
    My dear Esti,

Your letter to me crossed itself apparently with the last letter Martin wrote to you, otherwise you would have made other plans. You know by now, that he is invited on the 18 of the month by the Princess (who is currently our guest) to join her in the South and that he will travel via Paris and stop with you going and returning and that it thus makes no sense for you to come to London when he is not there. If his travel plans should meet difficulties and need to be cancelled, then it would however be necessary to have to consider your intentions. That takes care of the first part of your letter.

As to the second part, I do recognize your historical right for a birthday donation which got only neglected in those dark days and I am enclosing a little check which you hopefully can convert without effort into money. Do arrange your time, until your work begins, in pleasant ways. With cordial greeting, Papa.

August 8, 1938
    Much loved Herzenskind,

Please be so good and ask Father that he should help me to get the English visa, I so much want to spend a part of your vacations with you, and since I have to work in the hospital starting September 6, a year might pass before I can see you again. Up to now we have always spent all our summers together and you always had a pleasant and cozy time. Since our emigration I have not granted myself a single good hour and I would like gain new strength at your side. The Princess did not want to confirm my money situation, I am not sure why, if you guys don't help me, I will get a false passport, come what may, I don't care.

Please, please, write Father, I miss you so terribly. Kisses, Mother.

P.S. The Princess has invited Father to St. Tropez. Naturally not me. If the Freuds can buy themselves a palace, there has to be enough money for me to come to see you. Without me they would not have a penny!!

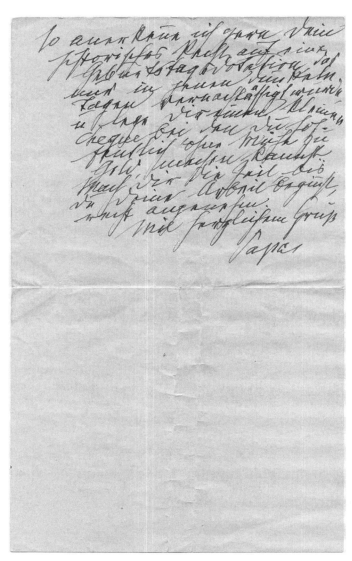

Letter from Sigmund Freud to Esti: Don't Come to London

LE LYS DE MER
SAINT-TROPEZ, VAR
August 26 [1938]
Lbst. Mr!
I was charmingly received here and everything is very informal, every-one walks around barefoot and also otherwise barely dressed. Only the

living situation is not working out very well, I sleep on a couch in the dining room and am somewhat homeless during the day. The weather is changing, many clouds and stormy. I don't think I will stay any longer than until the 29th, as nice as it is, it is still the opposite of a true vacation. Visitors arrive constantly and to get to write even one line is the greatest magic feat.

I will telegraph again when I come through Paris. A letter lasts four days, so I won't write again.

With affection, Mr.

FATHER TO SOPHIE
    August 29, 1938
    . . . I visited mother in Paris, she was quite recovered, compared to May 21.

CHATOU, AUGUST 22, 1938
    Dearest Herzenspuckerl,
    . . . I am staying this summer outside of Paris in a big house [now a boarding house] that once belonged to rich people, surrounded by a lovely garden with a pond. I am very anxious about all I have to accomplish. Enroll Sophie in a school, find an apartment, have my teeth fixed, apart from the professional work. . . . I hear little about our furniture. Rosa and Fräulein behaved scandalously, and have stolen the best things that I owned.

AUGUST 23, 1938
    Dearest Herzenspuckerl,
    I have not seen you for so long, I no longer know how you look. I miss you so terribly, you are horribly mean not to write. . . . Imagine, one of my front teeth has broken, that is all I needed added to all the rest. I miss you so terribly, please, please write me a detailed letter.
    Thousand million kisses, Mother

PARIS XVIe,6, RUE EUGENE MANUEL
    September 18, 1938
    Dearest Puckerl,
    Since Thursday I am once again in Paris. . . . I miss you on all nooks and crannies. Of all the nastiness and perfidies that I have been exposed to, in the last four months, what upsets me most is that one has taken away my son. Let us hope there will be no war, that would be terrible for the emigrants; those in France will be sent to concentration camps. . . .
    Please write your grandparents in Vienna!

OCTOBER 14, 1938

Dearest good Herzenskind,

I am very sad that I am not allowed to see you for a long long eternity. I will pack up with the Schnapsin and visit you all, as soon as I earn money again, which will be the case quite soon. Now I have not seen you for six months, this viciousness is really beyond belief.

The Schnapserl passed the exam to the Lycée very well and is going there starting today. I have gotten a second hospital, which is very honoring— You see I am totally busy. If I had you with me things would not be so bad, but I am so very much alone.

The many planned visits never materialized after all. Father made it quite clear that such a visit would mean the end of his alimony to her.

FATHER TO ESTI

June 6, 1939

You write to my father that you have started to earn quite well and want to come to England. I will regard such a visit as a sign that you are materially independent and no longer need my help—then you can really do whatever you want.

CHAPTER 22

Miraculous Acceptance at the
Lycée Jean de la Fontaine

*T*he acceptance at the Lycée came as a huge surprise and relief. I had indeed been *helped to prepare for it at the lovely summer place in Chatou but my French was still elementary and I did not expect to pass the entrance examination.*

SOPHIE'S DIARY

October 10, 1938

Today was the first day of examinations. In the morning I already got up at half past 6. It was dark and it had rained. At school we were all led into a big hall and from there to the classrooms. The first hour was French. A dictation with insanely many mistakes and explanations of which I did not understand a single word. Surely I got a 0 or 1. Then we had geography/history. In history we had to explain words and the dynasty of Antonius and in geography Japan and South Africa. I think I fared quite well in that. Let's say a 10. At 11 o'clock it was finished. Afternoon school was from 2 to 4. I arrived an hour too early. The German exam naturally turned out very well. Nevertheless I have naturally absolutely no hope.

October 11, 1938

Okay, now I am through with the exams. Today was Latin, zoology (I had the incredible luck not to get botany). Results are mediocre. Zoology even very well because I happened to get the crab. [My teacher in Chatou had predicted the crab and we had gone over it carefully.]

Thursday we have the results. But I am not at all curious. I will in any case not find myself on the list of passing pupils. . . . During breaks between the different exams I was terribly lonely . . . I stood there against the wall and waited for the break to be over.

But then the unexpected happens, and I am accepted—is it possible that the authorities had pity with me? Perhaps the name of Freud made the difference?

SOPHIE'S DIARY

October 14, 1938

I can't believe it, but it is so, I passed. Such luck. Mother was also very pleased but now everything is back to the usual. Today I was for the first time at the Lycée. It is called Jean de la Fontaine. I don't know, I don't feel I belong and never will. Most of the others are younger than I. They are very naughty and make incredible noise. I don't belong to them and never will. Because I am Austrian and they are French. One cannot bridge such a difference, at least not for the time being.

October 17, 1938

The cleaning woman comes at 7:00 A.M. She wakes me up and quickly fixes my breakfast. I get ready quickly and just miss the bus and have to wait a quarter of an hour for the next one. In this manner I am usually late. But up to now I have not had special unpleasantness because of it. Then I have school until 11:00 A.M. At 11:00, I go with the other day students to the Institute Maintenon. That is a big private school quite close for pupils who do not go home for the midday meal. At noon we take in our serpent-slop. We are ready by one o'clock. Then we take a detour, in guise of a stroll, back to the Lycée which starts at 1:30 P.M. Around 4:00 or 4:30 P.M. the Lycée is over. Then we go as a group back to the Maintenon where we work under supervision until 6:30 P.M. Well, not magnificently amusing. But thank God there are Sundays, Saturday afternoons and Thursdays in the world. Because those are the times when we are free. And yesterday I did something new. I joined the Jewish scouts. I enjoyed that so much, I decided to become an excellent girl scout.

Coming late to class did not fit into my new ambitions of becoming a respected student. A solution had to be found. I had acquired and learned to ride, a bicycle, that first happy summer in the vacation camp.

I had grown up as a protected city child and the very idea of riding a bicycle had never entered my assumptive world. It had been a very important achievement, perhaps comparable to how it had been for my children to learn to drive a car. Mother had, however, forbidden me to ride my bicycle in the city, when I returned to Paris at the end of the summer. She regarded it as too dangerous and could not be persuaded otherwise. The bicycle was stored in a shed in the courtyard of the Avenue Marceau.

The Lycee Jean de la Fontaine was located in Passy, near the Bois de Boulogne, about eight miles from our flat. My mother gave me the weekly bus fare, plus a very small amount of pocket money. I decided to disobey mother and ride my bicycle back and forth to school. There was no provision to park the bicycle at the school and I could not contemplate the threat of my most precious possession getting stolen. I negotiated with a nearby garage to let me park my bicycle there, for the cost of the daily bus fare. Mother, preoccupied with her own survival, was not overly inquisitive of my pursuits. She knew that I was an extremely obedient girl who did not need supervision. My rides to school became daily triumphs of mastery and independence and I never needed to be late again.

At that moment in French tax history, a tax on bicycles was instituted. It was in the form of some plaque that had to be attached to the bicycle in visible fashion. I cannot tell how much money it would have been in American dollars, but I imagine it was perhaps $25, a sum that was completely out of my reach. If my own children read this story they will not understand it. When they were 14 years old, they not only received pocket money that was adequate for their needs and could be saved for special wishes, but they could also earn more money than they could spend. They babysat, they raked leaves for people in the neighborhood, their services were much in demand. But I lived in a strange city, in a house in which I knew no other tenants and I could not imagine a single way in which I could earn some money. If I received one dollar a week of pocket money, it would have taken me 25 weeks of never spending a penny before I could afford this bicycle plaque.

I took the $25 from my mother's pocketbook, bought my bicycle plaque and all was well. A few days later my mother asked me whether I had taken money from her purse. She missed $25 (perhaps 200 francs?) and could not imagine how the money might have disappeared. I admitted to having stolen the money. I hung my head and waited for the verdict with dread. Would my mother brand me as a thief, threaten me with reform school, heap me with reproaches about having to raise me as a single mother in a foreign country, ask me whether Father was paying me again to make trouble for her?

But my mother said quietly and matter of factly, "You must let me know when you need money, rather than take it." She did not even ask me why I had needed money so badly. I don't remember her ever referring to it again. Stealing was apparently not one of her cardinal sins, perhaps knowing from her own experience with Father's things that people need to steal in times of emergency.

Chapter 23

Twelve Years Would Pass before I Met My Child Again

No doubt, dreading her visit, Father did cede to her constant pressure for a reunion with her son, by sending him over for a few days. Mother had never told me that she was either going to visit Walter, or that he might come for a visit, so his visit came as a complete surprise to me.

SOPHIE'S DIARY

October 27, 1938

This evening I came home from school and—Walter is there. I was so happy, more happy than I can describe. He is so tall and handsome and grown-up. He brought me a beautiful white pocketbook. But I don't care about that. I just talked to him and showed him everything that I own. I can feel it with certainty, he is the one I love most in all the world. After that Tante Janne, and Mother (now and then) and Grandfather and [my girlfriend] Mitzi, no, before that Father. Mother claims he looks so rundown. Tomorrow I still have school, but not the days after tomorrow. I will cancel my appointment on Tuesday, although I find that disagreeable, but I want to be together with him.

October 28, 1938

Today he picked me up at school, and I wanted to show him off, but we were out one hour earlier. So I had to wait for him for an hour and when he arrived he was tired and we just quickly took the bus to go home. This afternoon we sat at home all day. He does not want to go out. This evening we are going to the movies—

The movie was not especially interesting. I explained everything to him [it was of course in French] but he still did not get it. He has changed so. No longer the old fun-loving polite Walter. He dislikes being here. He wants to leave, go off, back to England. He does not speak French, cannot tolerate Mother's ways and everything else. Does he still care about me??? At most half as much as I care about him. He is tired all the time. If only Tante Janne were here!! This evening I had to cry to terribly. He wants to leave, already Tuesday morning. But Mother only wants to let him leave on Wednesday. Me too. My inside self is all torn up. The letters were different, mine and his. I do everything I can for him.

October 29, 1938

My inner self is in total turmoil. This morning I was at the scouts. In the afternoon I wanted to be with Walter. We played cards. It would have been quite enjoyable, but Mother suddenly staged fits against the "Freuds" in general and Father in particular. I already know what she is going to say.

This rather moderate account of my mother's behavior, which I still recall as a horrid scene, shows that I had become inured to my mother's pseudo-grand mal seizures with which she had punctuated her son's obligatory, reluctant, and finally disastrous visit.

When I came upon the above section, I sent it to my brother who was then close to dying of metastasized cancer. He was very moved to the point of making an effort to write me the last letter I would receive from him:

ENGLISH LETTER

January 16, 2004

Liebes Sopherl,

I am trying to write, but the right arm is the bad one, so please excuse effects. I was very touched and moved by the extract from your diary, I did not know that your feelings for me were quite so positive. I have forgotten everything about my October visit, you, mother, Paris, the cinema and game of cards. It must have been mother's behavior which made me suppress this part of my life. A shame that you did not come for a visit to London. It must have been terrible for you to be suddenly and forcibly removed from your family particularly from that part which you liked best. I liked you but not to the same extent as you did. I felt very mixed up at that time, did not know whether I was coming or going. Certainly glad to be away from Mother. I recall with great pleasure that you were a reliable and ever-present money lender, my pocket money seemed to run out earlier than yours. . . .

To break up the family in face of the Nazis was an utter contemptible step to take. Unfortunately you and I were not old enough to take the matter into our own—and much better—hands. I must confess that I thought little of you during this time. I was interred [in England], sent to Australia, in the war, and generally driven around like a loose leaf without any action created by myself. There was always enough to eat and dress and the danger of death was not too close most of the time. I was, probably subconsciously, fairly sure that your life would be similar to mine, unpleasant but not worse.

I am very touched about your affection. Had we been together, we would not only have been fond siblings but also good—very good—friends or even lovers. What a shame that we missed all that. We missed a great deal and in exchange we got some rubbish.

Herzlichst und alles Gute, Dein Walter.

I am very touched by my brother's response to my youthful declarations of deep love. It was the most personal and feelingful letter he had ever written to me. His willingness to collaborate with his memories in my endeavor of writing this book about our mother's life was a generous and unexpected end-of-life gift to me. My friends have suggested that I omit his incestuous comment in this account as it would give the wrong impression. Indeed, my brother died three weeks later and was already heavily sedated with morphine to kill his pain, when he wrote this letter. We must thus discount his incestuous fantasies, but we must also discount his fantasies of the affectionate relationship we might have had. We could have had a lifetime of an adult friendship, since we both fortuitously survived the events of our youth. But instead, I had experienced my brother as unsupportive, ungenerous, and harshly critical of me and my family. I am sad to affirm that most of the time he had not been a friend to me.

Mother's next available letter announces the death of her father. She makes no mention of Walter's visit and laments about their separation continue.

DECEMBER 5, 1938

Dearest Herzenskind,

I have to tell you the sad news that Grandfather peacefully passed away on Friday, second of December at 6:30 in the evening. You can imagine how sad I am, that I could not see him again, and that none of us can be with Mother. I beg you most affectionately to immediately write Grandmother a detailed warm letter. Although Sopherl is very dear, I would so much see you now with me; you can't imagine how horribly lonely and abandoned I feel. Uncle Heinrich is very loving with Tante Janne, only I have nobody at all. Uncle Rudi is now also present and he says he would not have been surprised, if I had committed suicide after all that has been done to me.

Dear Puckerl, I am now trying to get permission to go to Australia, New Zealand or America. Because there are about to be laws to deport all immigrants, as happens in Italy, and since I am not allowed to go to England, I don't know what will happen with me, perhaps I will put an end to things, as so many of the immigrants here are already doing.

I am very glad that you are doing some horseback riding, because you had already a very bad posture....

Our things are lying about at the customs office.... Unfortunately they include all my winter things and since it has become very cold and I only have light clothing, I am freezing most miserably and already have horrible rheumatism and sciatica pains.

Dear Herzenkind, please write to me soon and in detail, then I feel at least for an hour as if I had you again with me, and be most affectionately embraced and kissed from your Mother Esti who loves you.

JANUARY 15, 1939
Dear Herzenskind,
I thank you for your dear letter although I had to wait for it a long time. Did you receive the fruit-jelly-candy? I want to see you soon again and have the intention to come to England this time. I think I managed to get a French immigration permission for my mother, the princess does not care a hoot about it. I am very proud about this.... About Father one unfortunately does not hear very pretty news, but I am already used to it....

It was of course Tante Janne who finally got their mother out of Vienna.

We must never forget, appalled by this troublesome correspondence that, at the same time, Mother was building up her professional life, step by step, in her own indomitable way.

CHAPTER 24

Baggage from Vienna

I found an *appartement meublé* (furnished flat) in the Rue de Passy, not far from where Marianne lived. I cannot remember when I started to earn money in Paris, but I know I did. I still have occasional dreams about what would have happened if I had stayed in Paris because I began to get established there.

Eventually we were notified that our belonging had arrived and I went to the warehouse to see them. All the rugs and half the furniture was gone. Caro & Jellinek said they were unaware that anything was missing and could do nothing about it. Now I had to look for an apartment. Just as in New York, addresses are very important in Paris. I found what would be called in New York a five-room apartment in an elegant quarter, Avenue Marceau. It was located in the back of the building and one had to walk through a courtyard to get to it, but the address was a good one and the rent was reasonable. The place had a large living room and I was able to entertain, although it did not look too sumptuous without rugs and with very little furniture.

I had to sign a lease with the *Societé Fancière et Financière*, which was not an easy thing to arrange with the landlord because in France, at least in 1938, the law did not permit a married woman to sign such documents. The place fortunately came with a beautiful big Chinese-styled bed, since no beds had arrived from Vienna. Sophie had her own little room and had to sleep on a sofa.

This, however, is not how I remember the matter of the furniture and other things that also arrived, some of them addressed to my father in London, sent via Tante Janne's address in Paris. First of all, mother decided to keep the elegant furniture of my father's room and assigned it to me. So, no way did I sleep on a sofa, at the

Avenue Marceau, instead, once the furniture arrived, I was actually living among very nice, albeit stolen, furniture.

Then there was the awkward matter of Father's photo album mentioned in a letter to Walter.

OCTOBER 19, 1938

... Three times already, I was at the customs office for Father's things, horribly far from Paris. Finally I managed to expedite one basket with the winter coats. Yours is among them, I hope it still fits you. The other basket with the pictures and things they have still held back, but I had to unpack everything and the photos of Father with more or less dressed ladies flew around at the furniture warehouse, and I was terribly embarrassed in front of the custom agents. You can imagine the kind of jokes they made, it made me quite sick and I am still trembling in my whole body....

I am surprised Mother discovered the album because it was not a photo album, but looked on the outside like one of Grandfather's books, part of a collection in green linen with the label on the back, Freud—Vier Krankengeschichten *(Freud—Four case studies). But after only a few pages, it became my father's photo album with many pretty ladies in it, some with him in the picture—always smiling and looking very happy—but most of them just the ladies, in vacation settings, in bathing suits on the beach, or else formal studio pictures.*

SOPHIE'S DIARY

October 25, 1938

I cannot honor my father's taste. Among the 10 little ladies I find two halfway nice, none of them can be compared by far with Mother. And father grins so terribly on all of them, and looks young and handsome. I can imagine how these photos must have broken Mother's heart, they scream adultery. They leave me rather cold, although they do give me heart beat and sad feelings. If I had ever doubted of Father's infidelity, here is the infallible proof. I do know, he is a free person and I am not here to judge him, and surely it was also Mother's fault, but still, but still.

MOUNT ROYAL (HOTEL & RESTAURANT)

Marble Arch, London, W.I

November 2, 1938

Dst. Mr.

I would like to know more details regarding what has been salvaged of our things, has your silver arrived? What about my old furniture? Have our two engravings been delivered? I know, never mind how, that some of my photos and souvenirs have arrived and I would like to have these things namely without censorship and immediately. Bad enough what the Nazis have done to us, we don't have to also torment each other!

But Mother kept his photo album and she kept his furniture.

SOPHIE'S DIARY
October 1938
And Mother then showed me this letter from Vienna that was addressed to Father, and sent to him by express mail via Tante Janne's address written 10 days after she had accompanied him to the train station when he left Vienna. After all of Mother's anxieties for father, it surely was a horrible shock for Mother to read such a letter. Given Mother had loved him so, and had greatly helped him in the Nazi danger.

The letter arrived at the time when Mother was staging a nervous breakdown, soon after our arrival in Paris, and this was just one more shattering wound. She explained to me that this was the woman, an Austrian countess, with whom Father had had an affair in the midst of all the excitement of the Nazi occupation and with whom he had been while hiding in Baden. One cannot tell which of the pictures belong to this letter.

WRITTEN IN ENGLISH ON BLUE PAPER IN CAPITAL LETTERS
Addressed to Mr. Martin Freud c/o Mr. Zittau
Paris 16 28 Avenue Lamballe
(sent Express on May 22, 1938)
DO YOU HEAR THUS, THAT I CALL YOU?—BUT DO YOU HEAR ALSO HOW MUCH AND HOW OFTEN I CALL YOU? AND DO YOU NOT GET TIRED OF IT? YOU WRITE THAT YOU NEARLY LOST YOUR BALANCE, BUT I HAVE LOST IT TOTALLY, IN THE MOMENT WHEN THE TRAIN LEFT THE HALL AND VANISHED FROM MY EYES—
NOW, HERE, ALONE, I DO NOT DO ANYTHING, I HAVE NOT THE FORCE TO DO SO AND NO MORE THE COURAGE AND—PERHAPS ALSO NOT THE WILL—TO TRY TO HELP ME. EACH SINGLE DAY CREEPS LIKE A VICIOUS ANIMAL TOWARDS ME, BRINGS ME HUMILIATION AND SORROWS BEYOND ALL DESCRIPTION, AND ALL THIS TOGETHER HAS BECOME TOO MUCH ALREADY, UM NOCH WEH TUN ZU KöNNEN [*to be able to inflict pain*]—WHEN YOU

LEFT ME I WAS FILLED WITH APPREHENSION, TERRIBLE ANXIETY—
NOW THAT I KNOW THAT THERE IS NO HELP FOR ME—ALL WHAT
I LIVE AND SEE IS LIKE A TERRIBLE DREAM—AND SOMEWHAT
VISIONARY—

BUT I HAVE STILL MY FAITH, AND DO YOU STILL REMEMBER, AS
ONE SAID: "IF IT PLEASES GOD, IT MUST BE AGREEABLE TO ME."—
BUT YOU ARE DISTANT FROM ME AND LEFT ME ALONE—AND I AM
HERE LOOKING FOR YOU EVERYWHERE—AND I CALL YOU—

I DARE NOT THINK OF IT, WHAT LUCK HAD COME, IF ALL OUR
PLANS—ALL OUR DREAMS WERE REALIZED—AND I DARE NOT
THINK, THAT IT IS MONEY THAT CAN BREAK EIN MENSCHEN-
SCHICKSAL [*a human destiny*]—

WRITE, WRITE, WRITE! WRITE OF YOUR HEALTH—OF YOUR
PLANS—AND OF YOU—WRITE MUCH AND OFTEN—YOUR LETTERS
ARE THE ONLY JOY I HAVE—

I copied the entire letter into my diary, and had angry things to say about the letter and then concluded:

SOPHIE'S DIARY
October 1938
The letter leaves one flabbergasted and opens many puzzles. One thing I am sure of, I never knew my father better than any old stranger. The most important part of his life was totally foreign to me. None of his hopes and plans was I told about. But here this letter, it is well worth being eternalized, I must admit, a model love letter, she really seems to have loved him. The funny part is that in the long run Father loved himself more than any woman and their famous plans would probably never have been realized because a divorce from mother in Vienna, for example, would have disrupted his daily habits much too much. This woman was surely very unhappy but I am not sorry for her, I have a stony heart. Before one gets started with someone one has to consider whether he is free and if not— à vos risques, Madame.

This letter sent special delivery never reached its destination.

People have been speculating whether my father ever had a sexual liaison with Dr. Edith Jackson, one of his father's patients. My mother whom I remember frequently mentioning that rich ugly American witch had told Dr. Paul Roazen in an interview that this had been the case and he had spread that information in his writings. My Fräulein thought it was unlikely, given my mother's description of her. Dr. Jackson's biographer once came to see me to discuss the matter, bringing Father's letters to her after he had left Vienna. Their common picture was in the photo album, sitting next to each other on a mountain, but their correspondence was one of friendship, not sexual love. We decided together that she had probably loved him but that their admittedly close relationship had been one of genuine friendship, not sexual love.

CHAPTER 25

But We Corresponded for Some Time

*M*y mother should have written "we continued to torment each other for
another two years," until the German invasion of Paris. After Mother's
death, I found some of my father's letters in her estate. Sometimes one can guess
from his responses what she might have been writing about and I presume her own
letters matched his tone, but with her own brand of desperation.

Father's letters, between Lbst Mr and Lbst. standing for Liebster (dearest=
Drst) and Mr standing for Mur—and Herzlichst (affectionately?) Vater, were
mostly about his frustrating unsuccessful exhausting efforts to earn money and the
overall depletion that her excessive alimony is causing him. All their correspondence
is in German.

MOUNT ROYAL (HOTEL & RESTAURANT)
    Marble Arch, London, W.I
    November 27, 1938
    This is not the detailed letter that you expect, but meanwhile a shorter bit
of news. I was totally stressed out this week and have a bad infection, ordinary
cold and cough, not the flu. Walterl is well and went riding this week.
    I do count on sending you a bigger sum toward the end of the year, but
I was of the expectation that your rent will be paid in advance with the
money, not that 150 pounds are spent on purchases. Beds and linen could
not possibly cost that much! I can't ask Papa for money, he has to sell stocks
all the time because he and Anna do not earn enough.
    With my enterprises I am so far that there is already a talk of numbers
on both sides, unfortunately these numbers are pitiful. At the beginning I

would not get more than 6 pounds and without investments on my part only 4 pounds per week. I would thus earn scarcely half of what you want to use up for yourself. I hope that I will make some money with my book, but it is not yet ready, and it is totally unsure if and when a tangible income will emerge from all that writing. With luck, quite a lot of money could come out of it, and then you can be sure that you will not be on the short end—but one cannot count on it. . . . You have not been writing about your own professional prospects.

With affection, Father

Given Father's complaint about the bed linen, Mother then seems to have decided to ask her poor mother to send her some bedding from Vienna.

IDA DRUCKER FROM VIENNA TO MOTHER IN PARIS (GERMAN LETTER)

Vienna, 2/1, 1939

Dear Esti!

I thank you for your dear letter. I sent you the desired bed linen, since I have two assigned guests, I could not spare more. Unfortunately I could not have them dry cleaned any more. Since they would only accept them after the holiday—I had tried for weeks. So many stores are shut up and the others are overwhelmed with business. There were also rumors that it will be forbidden to send anything abroad, so, whether true or not, I sent them quickly, so you should not be in a predicament. If you find it necessary you can have it done yourself at some point.

I sent them to M. [Marianne] since you are not always at home. Wrong?

I have, as you will see from my letter to M. much work behind me, which I am very glad about. Because at the moment I am again in bed with a bronchitis. . . . I am so abandoned and alone; it is awful and am for the first time in my life faced with difficult duties. My dear child, Father thought shortly before his death with yearning of you—you have indeed always been his favorite child. Four weeks have sadly passed since his last breath. I am disconsolate as on the first day.

I am anxious to know whether R. [Rosa, the cook] left you the tray and the bowl which you always borrowed from me for your guests.

You old acquaintance, Miss Lia [Fräulein] will marry a private and has received a very nice flat and would like to buy one of my big carpets. Be embraced in love, your faithful M. Ida

MOUNT ROYAL (HOTEL & RESTAURANT)
    Marble Arch, London, W.I
    December 8, 1938
    Dear Esti!
    I can only send you belated condolences for the death of your father. You did not inform me and I heard about it through detours. While I did get your gift but no birthday greetings, supposedly a telegram came from you to Maresfieldgardens [his parents' address] that was meant either for Anna or for me, I never got to see it, it got mislaid.... Please acknowledge my letter with check. Unfortunately I make no progress with my plans. I meet at every corner acquaintances, it is getting too much.
    With affection, Father.

Her letters, judging from my father's responses, were apparently a series of reproaches and descriptions of her hardships.

JULY 5, 1938
    ... Could you not write me something a little more pleasant, I am already scared of opening your letters.

NOVEMBER 6, 1938
    ... You write me six long pages of unpleasantnesses, I don't want to retaliate in the same coin.

After her son's unfortunate visit, Mother must have complained that he seemed not well taken care of since Father writes:

NOVEMBER 1, 1938
    Walter was certainly not in a deplorable condition when he departed here, certainly not!

NOVEMBER 6, 1938
    Drst. Mr, today Walter visited again, he looks very well, and has grown, I see no reason whatever for worries.

Reading those old letters, I was surprised to learn that Mother had occasionally played with the idea of joining the English family judging from discouraging comments in my father's letters to her. Actually she was establishing herself in Paris and would not suddenly have left, but she might have tormented Father by threatening to do so.

Mount Royal (Hotel & Restaurant)
 Marble Arch, London, W.I
 December 8, 1938
 Dear Esti,
 ... someone in our family has spoken to the president of the London logopedic society and learned that not a single immigrant speech therapist is being admitted because supposedly the native ones are doing quite poorly.
 Affectionately Father

Martin's Preparations (1939) Limited
 Directors: C. BARNETT; S.R. BRIGHT; J.B. BOULDERSTONE; H. BROWN; M. DAVIS; K. WELDON
 Chairman of Directors:
 J. MARTIN FREUD, LLD. (Ex-Austrian)
 3 HANOVER COURT,
 MILTON STREET, E.C. 2.
 June 6, 1939
 Drst. Mr, you must have received the money long ago. It is becoming increasingly difficult to raise the amount, the business is not yet bringing in any money and on the contrary, my colleagues expect me to invest more money in it, and I have none left.
 I don't think I can stick it out any longer. I am working too hard and am getting too upset and I can't even go rowing on Sunday because I have to send you every penny I earn.... You also made summer plans for the child without consulting me.... Walter is going through his exams and afterwards I will send him for some respite. I also have to do something—perhaps I will sell my business and look around for something less stressful. So far I can only sell without profit.
 Hoping to hear from you soon, with affection, Mr.

Following is the final letter to Paris, written on April 18. On April 9, the German invaded Denmark and Norway. A few weeks later they started their march around the Maginot Line, toward France.

1. Holly Terrace, Highgate, N.6
 April 18, 1940
 Drst. Mr.
 I waited a long time before writing to you, because I had hoped to be able to announce some little success which would throw a less somber light

on the situation. Unfortunately everything is failing. The first book has disappeared completely, I have to return the advance honorarium because we cannot get the American rights and now they have expired.

I cannot place the second book. Publishers are trembling and writers are starving. I have half placed two nice short stories (with *Punch* and *Lilliput*) but they have not been printed and if I urge them, they return the manuscripts. I receive no more pay from Imago. All business dealings have broken down. I have not yet lost any money, but endless quantities of energy and effort.

I myself live quite miserably, am working as clerk in an accounting office from 9:00 A.M. to 5:30 P.M. for 2 pounds a week. All day under artificial light. Once a week I go to the movies for 2 shillings. Naturally I practice no sports and have not bought anything new, no longer look very elegant. And still we use up 1,000 pounds a year. You: 364£, Walter, while he is studying, at least 260£ and the rest is apparently going for my use. My part of the inheritance will be at most 2,000£ and so we will have used it up in two years. There is not much left from my savings. Can you not cut down on your expenditures? As soon as I earn more than a few pounds a week, you can naturally return to the old mode. How will the children manage if all the money is gone?

I can starve my way through as a butler, or blue collar worker, or clerk, but if the money is used up I won't be able to send you any more, and if better times develop I could make myself independent.

Think of what you can do. With affection, Father

In no way do I want to suggest that my parents tortured each other on purpose. Both had lost the relative stability, security, and comfortable social status they had enjoyed all their lives, and they were desperately trying to recover these privileges. They dumped their anxiety and despair upon each other, each in his or her own way.

CHAPTER 26

Sigmund Freud as Marriage Counselor

I do not know why my mother again and again sought ways to see her husband again. Was she so totally unaware how much my father disliked her, actually detested her, with the ever-increasing alimony burden. "Your mother," he said to me, and shook with revulsion. Although admittedly, now and then we do find some ambiguity in some expressions, like Drst. or with affection. We can only assume that she had a fantasy of reconciliation, since she apparently decided to appeal to her formidable father-in-law to intervene in the marriage.

The correspondence had started with Grandfather asking Mother not to come to London, as we saw earlier, since Martin had already left for France. Mother then had the poor taste of sending the old and dying man some papers she had written and received his civil acknowledgment.

PROF. DR. FREUD (GERMAN LETTER)
39 Elsworth Road
London, N.W.3
16.8.1938 (August 16, 1938)
Meine liebe Esti,

Ich bestätige den Empfang Deiner letzten Arbeiten, die ich gewiß auch lesen werde sobald etwas was mich jetzt beschäftigt erledigt ist.

Ich ergreife diese Gelegenheit um Dir zu sagen daß ich nie an Deiner Tüchtigkeit und Leistungsfähigkeit gezweifelt habe. Ich freue mich daß sie sich unter diesen neuen schwierigen Verhältnissen bewähren.

Ich habe nur immer—wenn ich davon reden darf—bedauert daß Du Dir duch voreilige Urteile über Menschen und übel angebrachte Leidenschaftlichkeit so viele Chances verdorben hast glücklicher zu werden.

181

Über das Thema nachdem Du fragst wirst Du so weit ich orientiert bin in der psychoanalytischen Literatur nichts finden.

Mit herzlichen Gruß

Papa

PROF. DR. FREUD (ENGLISH TRANSLATION)

39 Elsworth Road

London, N.W.3

16.8.1938 (August 16, 1938)

My dear Esti,

I acknowledge receipt of your last works which I will surely read as soon as I am finished with something that currently occupies me.

I seize this opportunity to tell you that I never doubted your competence and abilities. I am pleased that they stand the test of these new difficult circumstances.

It is just that I have always—if I may mention this—regretted that your hasty prejudgments about people and reprehensible fits of excitement have spoiled many of your chances for more happiness.

As to the subject you inquire about, as far as I can judge, you will not find it in the psychoanalytic literature.

With cordial greeting

Papa

Finally we come upon the letter in which he explains that he neither could nor perhaps wished to intervene in their marriage. Apart from the personal angle, Freud, it seems, was hardly a pioneer of couple therapy.

PROF. SIGM. FREUD (GERMAN LETTER)

20 MARESFIELD GARDENS

LONDON, N.W.3

TEL: HAMPSTEAD 2002

8.2.1939 (FEBRUARY 8, 1939)

Meine liebe Esti,

Es tut mir so leid daß ich deinen Wunsch nicht erfüllen kann. Mangel an Einvernehmen zwischen Ehegatten ist nichts was durch die Intervention eines Fremden verändert werden kann und selbst der eigene Vater ist in diesem Fall ein Fremder. Das müßen die Beiden unter sich ausmachen.

Ich sehe nur das eine klar. Der Grund den du für Euere Entfremdung angibst daß Martin dich nicht mehr hübsch findet kann nicht der richtige sein. Ich möchte sagen er klingt unsinnig. Martin ist keine Schönheit mehr, Du hast dich besser erhalten als die meisten Frauen deines Alters und um Euere Lebenszeit spielen andere Dinge eine größere Rolle in den gegenseitigen Beziehungen als hübsch sein. Ich enthalte mich jeder Parteinahme aber mir scheint es liegt daran daß Du ihm das Zusammenleben schwer machst. Rechne also nicht auf mich in dieser Angelegenheit. Ich sehe mit Befriedigung wie energisch Martin sich anstellt um die schwierige

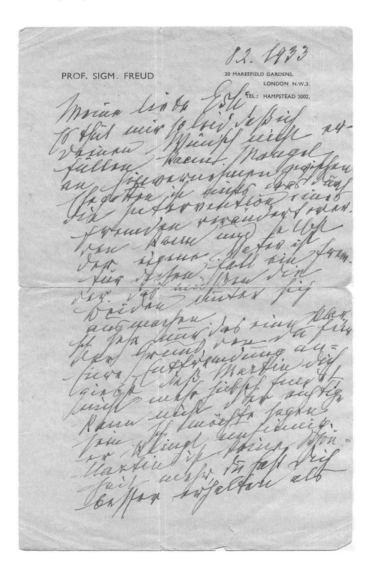

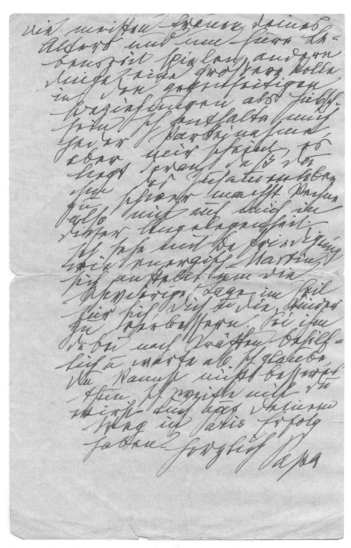

Letter from Sigmund to Esti refusing to intervene in their marriage

Lage im Exil für sich, Dich und die Kinder zu verbessern. Sei ihm dabei nach Kräften behilflich und warte ab. Ich glaube Du kannst nichts besseres tun. Ich zweifle nicht Du wirst auch auf Deinem Weg in Paris Erfolg haben.

    Herzlich Papa.

PROF. SIGM. FREUD (ENGLISH TRANSLATION)
   20 MARESFIELD GARDENS
   LONDON, N.W.3
   TEL: HAMPSTEAD 2002
   8.2.1939 (February 8, 1939)

Letter from Sigmund Freud to Esti: You Spoiled Your Own Chances for Happiness

My dear Esti,

I am so sorry that I cannot fulfill your wish. Lack of understanding between marital partners is nothing that can be changed through the intervention of a stranger, and even the father himself is in such cases a stranger. It is something the two parties have to regulate among themselves.

I only see one thing clearly. The reason for your estrangement which you advance, that Martin no longer finds you pretty, cannot be the true one. I want to say it sounds absurd. Martin is no longer a beauty. You have stayed in better shape than most women of your age and in your life phase there are other things that play a larger role in the mutual relationship than being pretty. I abstain from any partisanship, but I have the impression the reason is that you make your living together onerous. So don't count on me in this matter. I see with satisfaction with how much energy Martin tries to better the difficult situation in exile, for himself, you, and the children. Try to assist him as much as you can, and wait and see. I think it is the best you can do. I don't doubt that you will also reap success in your own way in Paris.

With affection Papa

Mother had a tormented ambivalent relationship with her father-in-law. On the one hand she revered him and his ideas. She writes of him repeatedly with admiration for his courage and genuine compassion for his suffering: "If anyone can be admired for leading a hero's life, it is Freud." But the family's rejection played into Mother's deepest insecurity of being a second-rate, unlovable person. In spite of the nearly paranoid flavor of Mother's hatred, she had not misread the family's negative feelings toward her, on the contrary, not only was her husband's dislike even deeper than she realized, but Grandfather's opinion of her was devastating.

Martin will probably leave before us with his family, leave wife and daughter in Paris, go to London with the boy. He hopes, and we all join him in this, that this will be in practice the end of his unhappy marriage. She is not only maliciously meschugge but also mad in the medical sense. (Letter from Sigmund Freud to his son Ernst Freud: May 14, 1938. From *Freud's Diary*, fortunately published only in 1992, 12 years after my mother's death.)

Grandfather refers positively to Martin's efforts to establish himself and he sounds very genuine about this. I have not been able to ascertain why my father was not invited, apparently not allowed, to continue the management of the Freud Publications. I think he might have been punished for negligence with the documents, but this is pure speculation and the matter remains a mystery. My brother did not know, but feels that Father was generally not well treated by his siblings. My Aunt Anna Freud could not remember or did not want to tell me the reason and other people who might know have died. Tante Mathilde thought "the family" might have disapproved of his "women's stories." But is this likely, given his father's attitude?

Grandfather Freud apparently knew about his son's affairs and seemed to have no objections against them. How else could we interpret the following comment written to his son Ernst on May 14, 1938, the day Martin left Vienna for London via Paris?

But what will he do in England? He cannot live without women and there he won't find the freedom he allowed himself here. (*The Diary*, p. 304. Sigmund Freud–Ernst Freud, May 12, 1938.)

Still, the old Giant was dying and his children were taking over. It was Tante Anna, his designated successor, with her favorite brother Ernst, who took over the management of their father's books and correspondences.

CHAPTER 27

The Summer before the Dark

Mother's fury had spent itself by the end of the year, she thrived under the apparent recognition of her professional work. She suddenly describes her daily life in quite a positive way to her son, although she then disqualifies the good news soon afterward in her birthday greetings to him, but still, there were some positive moments.

FEBRUARY 26, 1939, LETTER TO WALTER.

Dear Herzenskind,

My most heartfelt thanks for your dear long letter and I shal keep my fingers crossed tightly that you should pass your exam. I think the most sensible plan for you will be to study chemistry and then join Father in his business, so you can take over one day, given that Father is 50 in a few months.

Sopherl is a wonderful student and in general especially obedient and affectionate. [*Mother's exaggerations still make me wince. At that time I had finally just learned enough French to keep up with much effort.*] Unfortunately I don't see much of her since she only comes home in the evening.

I will also describe to you exactly how I live here and how things look. I live in a very elegant neighborhood but in a back building qu te a pleasant flat, a very nice working room to make an impression on patients. I have already—if someone came to consult with me, you know, one of the doctors at the Clinic asking my opinion—asked for 100 francs for one visit, and people paid it—only unfortunately such lucky breaks happen only seldom. The furnishings with all the details were horribly expensive, Father was right in scolding me a lot, but I think it will soon pay for itself—our thirgs were terribly broken down, and in bad shape, some of the things had to be thrown out, and so much got stolen. You remember how proud I was of my collection of doilies, almost all gone.... three times a week I am at the *Lariboisière* (a big French hospital) where I have a very big outpatient clinic and I am quite popular and well known. On other days I sometimes go to other hospitals, just to make new connections with doctors.... Now and then when I am very tired I stay at home for a morning, or I do errands. The thing is, I get myself introductions to doctors whom I then visit and ask them to think of me in a relevant case, I was surely already with 50 doctors. You can believe me that these are very unpleasant, tiring and stressful endeavors. Afternoons I already have a few patients and there are already occasional inquiries but unfortunately they don't all work out. I gave a very lovely successful lecture about Grandfather—*The Private Life of Sigmund Freud* in French—and will give another professional lecture next week in the Institute for Child Research (a very famous Institute in Paris). Unfortunately nothing came of the lectureship at the Sorbonne, it failed only by a hair. But I am nevertheless optimistic about my future, all the people who know me and my way of working, are well impressed—except a war breaks out—only healthwise I must stick it through, because I have become so very thin, and imagine something else, I must dye my hair, it has already turned very white, not nice at all.

Maybe I can pull myself together and come to see you for a weekend, will you then go to the movies with me? I have not visited any, for months. Imagine, Grandmother is now here, she lives with Tante Janne, do write to her. Keep an eye on Father, that he should not work too hard. I think now you know everything quite in detail. Many many kisses, from your Mother Esti. Did you get the fruit gelée candy for New Years?

Mother had generously sent me back to the summer camp run by my much-loved Communist friends. Truly, that summer before the dark was a glorious sparkle of happiness in those somber years, a first reciprocal love, a first kiss, a little sexual experimentation. Moreover, Mother had been able to arrange a visit from Walter who spent a few days with her—apparently not without ongoing conflicts—and then joined me at my summer camp in the Haute Savoie. Unlike his behavior in Paris, he was friendly and cheerful and there I was, with a my first boyfriend and my beloved brother all in one place, what else could I ask from life? Father also paid me a brief visit that summer, that fateful visit that I kept secret from Mother which truly infuriated her. But with my two men at my side and my Communist friends, and other friends I made that summer, I (guiltily) experienced father's visit more like an intrusion than a pleasure. Mother went to take some summer courses in French and did not make a great effort to join us. Walter and I had little time and inclination to write Mother many letters, which seems to have made her a little angry, although perhaps not seriously so.

AUGUST 22, 1939

Dearest Schnäuzchen,

You are both totally disgusting rascals, even if that offends Walter. I would have quite liked to join you for a weekend, but I am out of money. I am staying here until the first, except if war breaks out—and then I go back to Paris. How long is Walterl still staying in Morzine? I would have liked to be with him a bit more, but not if he keeps saying, "I have to go, I have no time," that really made me very angry. What are you hearing from father? He has not written to me forever.

Are you continuing to have a good time? Are you flirting a lot? If you do not write me in detail I will tear off both of your ears next time we see each other.

Imagine, I just heard that one of my colleagues from the Fröschel Clinic, much less famous than I, could open an Institute in London. I am mortified. Such a great pity, I could surely have gotten such a job and there we could all have stayed together, and I would not be all the time so terribly unhappy as I always am.

I kiss you with all my heart and remain your faithful Mother Esti.

Father gets a letter soon after, thanking him for his apparent monthly money. But clouds of war are gathering over France.

THURSDAY, AUGUST 31, 1939

Drst. M.

My heartfelt thanks for your letter and for the money (I have not yet been notified). I was, as the French say, totally *fauchée,* since I used up during the summer the small savings I was able to make from my earnings and could naturally not earn anything. At the instigation of the director of our hospital I bought myself a gas mask today, 180 francs, terrible, what one has to waste money on. I have no idea how to judge the situation, will stay in Paris, unless there is forced evacuation—I am not afraid, besides I don't give a darn, what will happen will happen, my family (Boykos and Zittaus) are scared shitless and they are up and gone since some time. I do worry horribly about Sopherl and Walterl, especially Sopherl.

It is very sad that your Father is ill. Should I put our silver into a safe?

Most of my acquaintances are also gone, it is quite dull to be alone in the flat, even the maid does not come any longer.
With affection, Esti

Shortly before the war I received a telephone call from two English women, telling me they had come from Martin with messages. I arranged for the first tea party in my new home. I invited my mother who had been brought to Paris with Marianne's help after my father's death. The first thing the two English women told me was that Martin had taken his Viennese mistress to London and was living with her. I could not help it, I had to cry.

I remember those two horrid proper English matrons, coming to our house just to spread malicious gossip, true or false. By then, Mother had visited her husband's pied-à-terre in Vienna, she had had a chance to inspect his photo album, she had intercepted a love letter sent to him, but oh, what a shock and surprise it had been for Mother to hear about her husband's infidelity, and what an opportunity to have a minor "nervous breakdown" in front of these two hags and what a satisfaction for them.

CHAPTER 28

(Grand)Parents Drucker Redux

*H*er mother's arrival in Paris gets mentioned only accidentally in Mother's own *story. Yet, there had been ongoing correspondence between the three sisters and their parents. I was very surprised to learn, through the following card, that my mother's two sisters apparently visited their parents in Vienna. I would not have thought it safe to go back and forth to Vienna in the fall of 1938.*

POSTCARD (TIGHTLY WRITTEN), GRANDMOTHER IDA TO MOTHER
Madame Esti Freud
Paris 16e 6 rue Eugene Manuel
October 27, 1938
Dearest Esti, you can imagine what joy the children's visit brought us. L. [Lily] left us already yesterday. My state of health is in flux, I now get injections against the pain and I spend much of the day out of bed, but am weak. Did you get your furniture? With thousand kisses for all of you. Your L. [Leopold]
Dear Esti! As dear father writes, we had great pleasure with Marianne's surprise visit and that of Lily as well. Unfortunately father's health is not improving and he suffers acute pain in spite of pain medication. We had another consultation the day before yesterday with Dr. Laud who is also not very satisfied. Father now gets injections. We are very pleased that you are all faring well. M. [Marianne] tells us how capable and hardworking you are. Rudi's [Lily's husband] sister gave birth to a girl yesterday. Lily left yesterday. Write soon to our dear father, he is very happy when he gets news from you. Be embraced in love by your faithful mother, grandmother Ida.

Next we learn that sick old people must have been assigned to live in their apartment and Grandfather's condition is worsening.

POSTCARD

    Madame Ernestine Freud

    6 rue Eugene Manuel, PARIS XVI

    Undated, but stamped December 1, 1938

    Dear Children!

We thank you d. E. [dear Esti] for the lovely picture and letter and are very glad that you are all faring well. If only we could tell you the same, but father's condition is unfortunately not well, he is very weak. Otherwise you are in the know. Regine K. came to visit d. father today, she is leaving with her children for South America, Bolivia. She is 77 years old. We did not get the visas. In terms of people assigned to our home, it is a very sick woman who is incontinent—Silence over everything else. In general there are always changes in our old age home.

    Be embraced with love from you Mother Ida.

27, 1938

    Rue Eugene Manuel, 16th

    My precious Esti!

Letters addressed to M. [Marianne] are naturally also meant equally for you.

[*Mother must have complained, even in those times of extreme crisis, that her mother's letters are always addressed to her younger sister.*] Since M. wants to get more news from me, I ask you to naturally share this letter with M. How I am? It cannot be described. Since our dear father has been torn away from me by death, all my energy for life has been extinguished and I ask myself how I can bear all that. I thank you for your efforts and your love. Perhaps you will all be writing more often a few words. It is the only thing that still binds me to this world. I just heard today that you had a visit from L. and R. [Lily and Rudi] Knowing that you, dear children are peacefully together is a blessing and gives me moments of happiness. One of father's last words is said to have been: "Esti is not coming, Esti is not coming." I really don't know how I can bear it all. It is horrible. You, dear Esti only saw the illness in its beginning—father has found peace.

    Our Walterl has written me a dear condolence letter. Also your parents-in-law and Mathilde and Martin. Everything upsets me so terribly. Be all of you embraced in love from M. Ida.

Not only does Grandmother Drucker get little copy in my mother's story, but Tante Janne's admirable rescue efforts, of which she alone in the family was capable, also only get a mere nod. She had managed to seize her husband from German clutches with a false identity card and then succeeded in rescuing her mother, at least temporarily—events I learned only recently from my brother.

Soon after Grandfather Drucker's death, Tante Janne sent a French woman to Vienna. She carried a false passport for my grandmother, under the name of Dickère and two return airplane tickets. Grandmother "casually" left the apartment with her windows open, as if going shopping. In Paris she asked for and received asylum in France, and left for Nice when the war started, but then, most unfortunately, moved on to Biarritz, in what would become the French Zone Occupée.

CHAPTER 29

Une Drôle de Guerre

In August 1939, Hitler signed a nonaggression pact with Stalin. The French and English governments had a pact with Poland to come to her aid if she were attacked. When I hurried back from Grenoble to Paris, all the trains were riding with blue lights. My son, who had joined his sister at the vacation camp, had to be sent back to England. I did not trust the French with a boy, and I was right, according to what I later saw.

Actually it was not Mother but our friend Harald Hauser whose political savvy managed to get Walter back to England, at the very last moment before the frontiers were closed to "enemy aliens."

In September, Hitler marched into Poland, and France and England kept their promises. In Paris, called the City of Lights, all the lights went out. One put thick curtains over the windows and strapped them with brown wrapping paper stripes. We had to be extra careful as the rumors were going around that the German refugees were sending light signals to the German airplanes.

Mother must have experienced the outbreak of war like a death sentence. This was not such an irrational response in the light of later events.

GERMAN LETTER
September 3, Sunday noon, 1939
Dear Murrer, dear Walterl,
I am writing at the moment of the declaration of war. I deeply regret not to be able to be with you, because perhaps you could use me after all. I am

all alone and there are almost no people in Paris. I am not afraid, as you surely know, but I don't have the intention to do anything to protect my life. Since May 21, 1938, there has almost never been an hour in which I have not considered whether I should commit suicide, but could not muster the courage. The only thing I still want from life would be to see you once again, dearest Murrer.

Dearest Walterl, I kiss you from my heart, take care of your sister.

Drst. M. greetings once again, perhaps for the last time from your Esti.

Not much happened for nearly a year. The French spoke of *une drôle de guerre* and Poland was quickly overrun. They had to fight with cavalry against tanks. Hitler consolidated his position. He did not want a war on two fronts, and waited.

Hitler needed another nine months for preparations. The French people relied on their Maginot Line, a huge underground fortress on the eastern border of France. They had erected nothing on their northern frontier, where German armies had entered in 1914. Why fortifications were not extended to the northern frontier is a fact beyond my understanding.

Everyone anticipated an imminent bombardment of Paris by air. My sister's husband had rented a little house in Lisieux, on the Normandy coast, and Sophie and I were invited to go with them. After a few days the situation became intolerable for me and I decided to return to Paris, leaving Sophie behind. On September 23, the French radio announced the death of Sigmund Freud.

Eventually we all returned to Paris and a new plan was made. My two aunts, Tante Janne and Tante Lily, each with their only child, my cousins Herbert and Bea, and myself were to drive to Biarritz and stay there for an indefinite time. My own mother clearly preferred the danger of German bombs to spending time with her two sisters, but no doubt she would have felt irresponsible not to send me to a safer place than Paris seemed at the time. The car ride to Biarritz, with two overnight stops on the way, was only memorable for the concern my two aunts exhibited for an ordinary quilt they had taken along. Surely, each motel had sufficient blankets for our needs? It was only years later that Tante Janne explained that they had sewn gold coins into the quilt.

In spite of the disastrous war that had just broken out, I experienced the few months in Biarritz, from September to December 1939, living with my beloved Tante Janne, as idyllic. Biarritz, perhaps because of its location near the Spanish border, had become a refuge for many different people and the local lycée was flooded with newcomers who were as eager for quick friendships as I was at the time. New

Sigmund sick in bed, announced dead by French radio on Sept. 23

unconventional teachers had to be hired and we had a young man teacher—naturally a subject of instant love—who was such a passionate classical scholar that I almost took up the study of Greek, although I had never even enjoyed my endless Latin classes. One could sit for hours—books on hand—and watch huge waves clash against the rocks. Tante Janne, anxious about her son's social development, was pleased and reassured that Herbert and I were such good friends. I am still sorry that I caused Tante Janne needless worries about my eating as little as possible, but I remember secretly trying to reduce the expenses that my extra food was imposing on my aunt's family. It was also in Biarritz that I incurred an immeasurable debt to my aunt. I was 15 years and had taken up smoking as a way of being sophisticated. She did all she could, in genuine desperation, holding up her own example as an ad-dicted chain-smoker as a warning to keep me from smoking. She did it so persis-tently, so fiercely, and with so much love that I desisted from smoking and never started again. Surely that was an immense and lifelong gift that Tante Janne thus bequeathed me. It is clear that both my first and second mother wished me better lives than they had led themselves.

At the end of 1939, Tante Janne felt a lump in her breast, later to prove benign, and we returned to Paris. I would visit her on a late Saturday morning and find her having breakfast in bed, surrounded by disorder. While I threw away the empty whiskey bottles that had a mysterious way of accumulating under her bed and emptied dozens of overflowing ashtrays, she regaled me with the story of her passion for her breast surgeon and with other exciting stories of love and intrigue.

While I was enjoying life in Biarritz, Mother got more and more frantic alone in Paris and bombarded the English family with cards and letters written in stumbling English.

ENGLISH CARD
> 9.IX.1939
> Dear Walter,
> I am quite without any notice about you I am very anxious to have someone. I think, life is enough difficult for me, that you at least can afford to write sometimes to your mother. I don't know neither if you are still in London. Please write as soon as possible. With thousand kisses your Mother Esti.

ENGLISH CARD
> 12.IX.1939
> My dear child,
> I am quite desperate because I have no notice of you or of Father. I am hear quite quite alone, I don't know how long I will support this, at least write me, or Father shall write me. I can't understand why you are so cruel. Is it so much work to write a *postcard*? It is the only pleasure what I would have still in life.
> With thousand kisses your Mother Esti.

ENGLISH LETTER
> 21.IX.1939
> My dear son,
> I thank you so much for your nice, long letter and the prospect of your school. I had 15 days without notice at all of nobody and was terrible anxious.... I have got for company a cat, which I found on the street, a very precious Siam cat. There are so many beasts in Paris left alone by their owners who went to the country. My situation here resembles very much to our situation in March 1938 but you get accustomed. The second time in 1 1/2 years that my whole existence broke down and that I can begin again. But now there is no possibility of beginning. I put paper stripes on all the windows. Have you done the same? And in the cellar I have an old bad mattress. So that I can sleep if there are air-raids.

I go still in my hospital but there is very few to do for me, but as long as it is open, I continue to go, because I don't want that they say I run away. My professor is working elsewhere in the country.

I always hope that I would have soon the possibility to go back home for the purpose of shooting down Mister H— and Mister R—, the men who wanted to kill father. . . .

ENGLISH LETTER

30.IX.1939

My dear son,

I have got your first letter from the school. I am glad that you like it. I am very sorry of the dead [*sic*] of Grandfather and I think that Father should now live with his mother as he can't at the moment go alone in the cellar during air raids—the English society would be very astonished if he will not do it and speak much badly about this.

I have to endure many difficulties. My social position is the same as in March 1938, I can't have money, don't get the permit to see Sophie etc. but the principal is that you and Father are in security.

. . . I will try to persuade Father, that we all should go to U.S.A. as to go away from this whichkessel where it will become always worse. But I don't dare to do that. Do you think I could make this proposal to Anna? Sophie and her aunt will perhaps go to Spain? I am very pessimist if I will ever see one of you again. Please write as soon as you have time.

With thousand kisses your mother Esti.

GERMAN LETTERS

November 5, 1939

Dear Puckerle,

I thank you for your dear letter which gave me much pleasure. I did not answer earlier because I had the flu. It was very unpleasant because I was all alone in the flat, with nobody to help take care of me, I almost starved. But now I have almost recovered.

Unfortunately it has become impossible for me to earn anything and for that reason I am trying, after the war, to emigrate with the Schnapserl to America, if you feel like it, you can come along. I have not heard from Father for over a month. I hope he is in good health. Father's book is very nice and I liked it very well. Is he doing anything reasonable? The Schnapserl goes to school in Biarritz and seems to be quite cheerful.

Write to me soon again, many kisses from your Mother Esti

DECEMBER 8, 1939 (GERMAN LETTER)

Dearest Herzenskind,

I was so very happy with your letter. Why do you write so seldom? The Schnapsin is still in Biarritz and I have become quite miserable from being alone. The prospects of earning continue to be very poor, although there are now at least some inquiries. Circumstances are very different here than in England. I am for example the only "enemy alien" in France who has been allowed to continue working at the hospital ... you can be very proud of my exceptional position. Although it does not pay, people continue to be dear and friendly with me. Otherwise life would be agreeable enough, one gets everything in surplus, I do scientific work and all my articles are getting accepted by professional journals. I already know very many people, but most rich people are no longer in Paris. Every moment there are sensational articles in the newspapers about the inheritance of Sigmund Freud. Given that I rescued everything for the F's, Father could really have congratulated me for the 20. wedding anniversary and thanked me at least for the beautiful expensive tie pin that I sent him....

Sophie and I will hopefully soon be able to emigrate, I am trying to get a job in the U.S.A., still before we get thrown out. The best would be you would join us, then we would be together once again, otherwise I judge the prospect of your ever seeing us again not very favorably. I think I shall have Schnapsin back again before Xmas and will also keep her here, being all alone makes me completely depressed. What will be, will be, I miss both of you too much. Thousand kisses Your Mother Esti.

Mother then cheers up as I return, she earns a little money, and life becomes for a few more months relatively normal.

Chapter 30

I Had to Do Something to Escape
Hitler's Clutches

In May 1940, I was still working in the Hospital Lariboisière, which is located near the Paris North Station. I heard rumors that people living in the north of France were leaving in panic. The German *panzers* had crossed the Meuse and broken through the Ardennes forest at the Belgian-France frontier at the point where there was no Maginot Line and the door had been left wide open. A battle with the English near Dunkirk had taken place and the English armies were thrown into the Channel. Mother left for Nice and the Zittaus [her sister Marianne, her husband, and her son] and Boykos [her sister Lily, her husband, and her daughter] were packing to go South. Paris became emptier and emptier. At night one heard tanks rumbling through the streets. During the day horse- and cattle-drawn wagons loaded with household belongings traveled through the City. It was an incredibly miserable sight. The news became worse and worse. Since the defeat at Dunkirk, the highway to Paris was open to German armies. This time there was no *miracle de la Marne* as in 1914.

Tante Janne and Tante Lily (i.e., "our Paris extended family"), guided by perhaps more worldly husbands, had both left Paris in the spring, while mother and I remained behind in an increasingly somber city.

Given that the Germans invaded Denmark and Norway on April 9; overran Luxembourg, Holland, and Belgium; and outflanked the Maginot Line on May 13, the two letters from Walter to Mother in April and May 1939, are totally bizarre.

ENGLISH LETTER
    Quorn Hall, Loughborough College
    Loughborough

April 20, 1940

Dear Mother!

The tie with the dogs on it is exactly like what I imagine to be a dream-wish-fashion-tie. Which does not mean that I treat the scarf and the green tie (which I am just wearing) in a stepchild way, but that you have guessed with all three gifts my taste up to the last point of the I. Unfortunately I can only send my thousand kisses, and not give in person, which I would much prefer.

... my vacations were very nice and I could have stood another month without flinching an eyelash.

I am very glad that you are well, in spite of the bad times, and that you have patients. I am well, I even work hard during times I have nothing else to do. Who told you that I got myself a hole in the head last Xmas? Do you have spies in England? Besides it was nothing serious, just that it bled a lot, at the beginning.

Otherwise everything is in good order, Father is also well, although he is in an even worse mood than ever before. But I only see him quite seldom (every three months) so I don't mind it too much.

A thousand kisses Your Walter.

GERMAN LETTER

Quorn Hall, Loughborough College

Loughborough, Leics

May 17,

Dearest Mother!

Already for the third time I cannot give you a birthday kiss but only congratulate you in a very insufficient way. I wish you the very very best (Nebbich, what good can one wish nowadays) and hope that we shall be together again next year at this time. I know that you accomplished and achieved more in these two years in Paris than most men who spent their whole lives there, and for that I congratulate you especially heartily. I hope you have a great birthday, even with only 50 percent of your offspings: tell me how many candles on the cake, apart from the middle candle?

I am so far quite well, hoping to get news from you soon again.

A thousand thick birthday kisses send you your son Walter.

ENGLISH LETTER

24.V.1940

Dear Walter,

Thank you so much for your congratulations for my birthday which I got today. I hope that your good wishes will help for something, I need them *extremely*. You can't perhaps not imagine the days of terrible anxiety which we are facing now, I lost again 4 kilos, and I am thin as a needle. Marianne and her family left yesterday Paris for Palestine. Lily is in La Boule en Bretagne. I asked for a permit to leave Paris which *I could not* get till now, and at any rate I bought a bicycle, but it is rather probable that the Austrian women here will be send somewhere. Please say Father if he or the family would not help Sophie and me to go to the United States, I will surely find some work there.

I will give you the address of the Princess, in case I can't give you notice.

Princesse George de Grèce

Les Ormeau, Benadet, Finistère

Father shall say if he leaves London his address to Barclay, so that I can find him.

Walter, many many kisses, hope always that things will turn out well at least. Your Mother Esti

At school they had distributed gas masks and told us to crawl under our desks in case of a sudden gas attack. I roamed the streets of Paris, vaguely apprehensive while the German cannons could already be heard in the distance. There was talk of waiting for the miracle of Jeanne d'Arc. I had not been brought up to believe in miracles, but it was a tempting illusion. The other talk was about the cinquième colonne, *the name for the spies held responsible for the French defeat, and people everywhere were on the lookout for those sinister enemies. I kept my mouth with its giveaway dangerous accent, tightly shut.*

"Let us leave Paris," my mother finally said, as the cannons grew louder and louder. We went to the Gâre d'Orleans, which was beleaguered by a huge crowd of people who had the same intention. All around, within five blocks of the station families with small children and belongings sat and waited for the next train. We could not even get near the station and gave up very quickly. Returning home Mother decided we had to leave by bicycle. Mother had bought a bicycle for herself some weeks before and even practiced riding it. Apparently this had been all along her final escape plan. While Mother had shared, in excruciating details, each one of her many personal hurts with me, she proceeded on her own in this situation. She neither informed me of her thinking, her doubts, her fears, nor did she ask my advice. She did write a desperate plea to her husband—avoiding the forbidden German language—but then made her own decisions in this situation of life and death.

ENGLISH LETTER

To: Monsieur Martin Freud. London, N.W.6. 1 Holly Terrace, Highgate, Westhill

7.VI (June 7, 1940)

Dearest Mur,

What now will arrive to me would be really nebbach. I do not no what to do, if I leave Paris I fear that I will never be able to work again in an hospital and in the Province where nobody knows me, Austrian are interned. At any rate please, please write to me, I have such a heavy heart and I am so terrible afraid of all the things which will still come to me and the child. She doesn't want to let me alone. For the worst, we have two bicycles. Please be so kind write to her. Marianne is already in Palestine Jerusalem 209 road Ibn Erra.

Kisses perhaps the last Esti

SOPHIE'S DIARY

November 4, 1940 [Nice]

We only decided at the last moment to leave Paris. It was stupid, but I am still quite glad because at what other time would I have gotten to know so many incredibly interesting things all at once.

I felt I had to do something to escape Hitler's clutches and save my and my child's life. I invested 1,000 francs in a bicycle and learned on the Quai d'Orsay how to ride it. Sophie had one for going to school. Trains going south were overcrowded and we did not have enough money to buy a car. Also, for driving one needed gas and that might not have been available. Bicycle riding had the disadvantage that you could not take much luggage with you. I packed a bag and took it to a shipping agent with the instruction that we would write and tell him where to forward it. Then I took my silver flatware and deposited it in the Paris branch of the Morgan bank. On June 8, 1940, two days before the German armies entered Paris, we left on our bikes.

Mother left the packing of my little rucksack to me. I took the gas mask container, threw out the gas mask, and packed into it a fancy beautiful organdy blouse I had received a few weeks earlier. I must have put in a few other favorite possessions, and off we went the next morning on the road South, toward Chartres. Bicycles were truly the best way to move ahead, since the roads seemed like huge endless parking lots full of cars filled with families and packed high with trunks and various possessions. They hardly seemed to move. From time to time there was an air-raid alarm and we threw ourselves into the ditches, but I did not experience any actual bombardments.

The highway was crammed with cars at a standstill. With our bicycles we were able to wiggle through. The rain was pouring and we were wet to our skins. At night we reached Fontainebleau [*it was actually Rambouillet*]. I asked a man who was standing in front of the door of his house if he could let us stay overnight. He said we could sleep in his laundry room where he had a mattress. We accepted the offer since we had to get out of the rain.

The next night we slept in Orléans, I believe in a building abandoned by its inhabitants who had left the door wide open. It was there that Sophie forgot her wristwatch, which she had received from her grandmother. We spent the next night in Chartres while the town was being severely bombarded. For one night we were in Amboise and crossed the Loire river just before the bridge was mined. I carefully tried to avoid the main highways and rode along country roads. Since there was no traffic on them I anticipated that they would not be machine-gun strafed by German planes. Sophie, who could bike so much faster than I, was always ahead of me. I was afraid I would lose her. Once she wanted to ride on the major highway that led to Limoge to go sightseeing in the famous China factories. I had to veto that kind of foolishness. I remember sleeping one night in the dormitory of the convent school. In Toulouse we stayed in what seemed to be a brothel. On our route we met many French soldiers, privates in *camions* (trucks), officers in Citroens and Renaults always in the company of girls running away from the German armies. We arrived now in cognac country where all the names of the villages ended in "ac."

SOPHIE'S DIARY

November 4, 1940 [Nice]

Too bad that I have not started to write my diary earlier, I would have had enough to tell. Naturally I could not write during our flight through France. Because if one arrives somewhere totally exhausted and gets some nasty room with much effort, one is not in the mood to write in a diary.

The worst was the waiting at the train station, but once we got started it proceeded okay. The first night was in Rambouillet [only about 30 miles from Paris]. There we had to sleep in a laundry because the justice of the peace would not let any foreigners enter his house. And we were all wet. That was quite a gentleman.

Rambouillet and Chartres were surely the most disgusting experiences of the whole trip. In Chartres they only wanted to let Frenchmen into the air-raid shelters. Naturally we did not say that we were foreigners, but it was sufficiently unpleasant.

I am taken aback by the moderate tone in which my younger self mentions truly upsetting, never-forgotten moments of this whole journey. We had just arrived in Chartres when a siren announced an air attack. The catacombs of the famous old cathedral were used as air-raid shelters for the town and people were rapidly lining up to enter the church. Suddenly a voice called out "seulement pour les Français" (for Frenchmen only) and I was frozen with panic lest I would be called upon to say something and be discovered and perhaps lynched. Naturally it was again all about the cinquième colonne, *the traitors in our midst.*

The other moments of terror remembered over 65 years are also barely recorded. Indeed, there were times when we drove through small seemingly deserted villages—all the windows tightly boarded up—not a soul on the streets. It is clear that the population was expecting with dread the German tanks to arrive at any minute and hoping they would not stop and ravage that village. I too thought that they—the tanks, or armed troupes, or military convoys—might eventually overtake us and I kept looking back to see if they were catching up with us, and had the impression of hearing distant rumble. But I don't think I was filled with terror. My task was to keep pedaling my bicycle as fast as possible—although I also had to adjust my speed to my much slower mother—in order to escape these very tanks.

We had no goals and no plans. Viewed in cold blood, 65 years later, the enterprise seems totally hare-brained. Mother had made a series of arbitrary and possibly foolish decisions that helped us to survive. Other people had made equally ignorant decisions that led to their deaths. I give my mother credit for having saved my life by getting me whole and alive out of Europe, but sometimes I think it is fate, rather than mother's arguably good judgment that deserves the credit. I thus lost relatively early in life the belief that we have rational control over our lives. Luckily, we also have Mother's account of that flight through France, as described to her son a few months later.

FROM MOTHER IN NICE TO WALTER IN AUSTRALIA (GERMAN LETTER)
December 24, 1940 Nice, Hotel Windsor
Dearest Herzenspuckerl,
Finally, after seven months I could find out where you are located, one could hardly be any further, but still I was quite glad. Mostly also glad that you are not with us. I would so much like to know how you are, whether you can learn something, whether you feel very alone and many other things. Schnapsin and I left Paris on June 12, two days before the invasion of the

Germans, on bicycles, up and away, because it started to be no longer quite comfortable, Paris was literally dead, it was uncanny, one could hardly find a store to buy something to eat. On the Champs Elysée, one saw only fugitives with wheelbarrows, bicycles with carts, cattle trucks, cars with mattresses on their roofs, an infinite exodus.

Thus, on the twelfth, early in the morning I shook the Schnapsin out of bed and off we went, the house was also already empty, even the concierge had left. I gave myself the bicycle as a birthday gift, because I had imagined things quite similarly, two days before we went to the railroad station, where there were tremendous masses of people, unimaginable, camped over kilometers so that one could not even approach the station, the railroad station was the most horrible thing I have ever seen. Well, we started on the main army route out of Paris—with me being still quite wobbly on my bike—for baggage, one set of underwear for change and a knitted blanket and each took also a light dress. We tried to get as soon as possible away from the crowds onto minor roads, which we managed almost always, so we managed about 600 kilometers, got bombed a few times and shot at, but we did not care much, and once we were almost in the middle of a battle, you can imagine that we got away as quickly as possible with our bicycles, with the French in front of us with their guns against us, ready to fire, and close behind us were the Germans. We always crossed bridges just as they got mined to blow them up, but we always were able to eat and also found beds to sleep, or rather one bed. People were except for once very friendly. We thus got into the South of France and we could have crossed the border, but we thought, what will we do in Portugal without money or baggage, that was, after all, too risky for us, with all the things in Paris, especially Sopherl was very much against that. Well, so we spent the entire summer in a tiny village staying with wine growers where we had a most agreeable time, very inexpensive and wonderful food. Meanwhile, we found Grandmother who was in Biarritz and unfortunately stayed there since she could not decide in time to leave there and now she can not leave any longer since it is occupied and closed off.

At the beginning of school, we went to Nice, because Uncle Oli is here, so we should not be totally all alone, Sopherl attends school, we live in a little hotel room and since I cannot work nor earn anything, I want to get a degree in French at the University. Tante Lilly [sic] who is meanwhile with her husband in New York, 255 Haven Avenue, tries to get us to join them, whether she will succeed is another story, given the many difficulties in this place.

We also got a letter from Tante Anna, they are still at home. She writes little about Father. Dear Puckerl, I am curious when we shall see each other again and what all will happen with us. Hopefully you are in good health, which is the most important, and not too sad.

Tante Janne is in Palestine, Jerusalem, 20 Ibn E road. Try to write to her. Write to me via Harry in New York.

Be embraced most affectionately by your Mother Esti.

CHAPTER 31

Reading Balzac in Castillonès

O ne evening, tired, unkempt, and dirty, we came to a little town called Castillonès and asked at a farm on the outskirts for overnight shelter. We were well received and the food was wonderful. Never in my life did I eat better food or drink better wine. The farmer had his own vineyards and he kept the best caskets for his own consumption. Sophie and I decided to rest there for a little while.

SOPHIE'S DIARY

November 4, 1940 [Nice]

Finally we stayed put in Castillonès and by good luck it became zone libre. *Then came the armistice and all those terrible things. But the French had to make an armistice. All of France was finally occupied and there was such terrible chaos due to the migrations of peoples on the roads. What had happened? Treason? Cowardice? Incompetence? It is unknowable.*

I informed the bank, which sent us Martin's money, of our new address. Martin had made arrangements with Marie Bonaparte to pay us our monthly allowance. I also attempted to seek contact with my mother. To my great dismay, I found out that she had left Nice and gone to Biarritz just when Mussolini had declared war on France. Mussolini did not want to lose the spoils of victory and did this a few days before the Germans had entered Paris. With those two decisions, my poor mother and the not-so-poor Mussolini signed her death warrant: Mother with her move to the Basque coast, which was to be occupied by the Germans, and as for Mussolini, his fate is history.

We stayed all summer long at *Les Tuileries* in Castillonès where the owner manufactured handmade bricks. After the *vendange* (wine harvest)

Sophie wanted again to go to school and we left for Nice, this time not on bicycles, but on a regular train. Things had returned somewhat to normal.

A war was raging around us, a horrible armistice had just been concluded, and yet again, this was a peaceful summer. Soldiers stopped at our little brick factory on their way home, to buy a few drinks of our host's apparently excellent wine, and we did get the news of some of the various disastrous happenings. But otherwise it might have been an ordinary summer in a little French village. I learned the art of brickmaking with interest and enthusiasm and, while we paid for our room and board, I was always eager to work along with the son of the Escat family who did most of the brick work. Mother found some fabric to make me a dirndl dress, showing unsuspected talents. But the true happiness of that summer was the discovery of a cache of books in the equally friendly major's office—the same major who would later help us by giving us a sauf-conduit *(permission to travel) to go to Nice by train. The books were meant for the general public, as a tiny public library, although, I suspect, rarely utilized. I thus spent quite a splendid summer immersed in Balzac and Flaubert. It greatly upset me that the daughter, in* Père Goriot, *does not find a husband and becomes an old maid. The worst of fates, I thought at the time, as can be seen from a comment I made in my diary a few months later:*

SOPHIE'S DIARY
November 5, 1940 [Nice]
Will I ever find a friendly husband? Certainly not in France. And not in America either . . . I shall die unmarried, of starvation.

I had had, at that point, already the opportunity to watch my mother's disastrous marriage and the equally albeit different grim one of my Tante Janne, yet the hope for marriage to Cinderella's prince far outweighed such somber observations.

I greatly regret that I did not return to Castillonès much earlier to thank those kind farmers for their hospitality. By the time I did, with my adult son, the Escat family had all died, even their son who had only been 10 years older than I, and the village had become a strange place for me.

At Compiègne the armistice between Germany and France was signed. Pétain and Laval became the leaders of the French government. France was divided into two parts, the occupied and the unoccupied zones. One of the conditions of the Compiègne armistice was that France had to return all German nationals who had sought shelter in France. This was frightening indeed, but I assumed that the French police would first begin in the occupied zone delivering German and Austrian refugees to the Gestapo. Correspondence between the occupied and the unoccupied zone was limited to postcards on which you were permitted to write about the state of your health.

Staying that summer in Castillonès was a mistake. We should have gone to Spain. There the Franco government in an uncharacteristic attack of generosity had opened its frontiers for the time being. I did not know about this. Also I would have fretted about earning a living in Spain. I did not know that the American-financed Joint Distribution Committee provided the means for making a living to refugees from France going to Spain. My two sisters with their husbands and children had chosen this means of escape. They were not thoughtful enough to look after my mother, who, at this time, was already staying in Biarritz. Marianne went to Palestine (now Israel) but this was also not a very secure residence and so they proceeded to Cuba on an Egyptian boat and stayed there until they had obtained their entrance visas to the United States. My second sister Lilly [*sic*] fared even better. Without a visa, the family embarked to the United States and were lucky enough to receive permission to disembark. A previous boat was not so fortunate. It had to return to Germany where all refugee passengers were exterminated in concentration camps. Both my sisters tried very hard to provide me and my daughter with immigration visas to America.

CHAPTER 32

Wartime in Nice

*M*y Uncle Oliver Freud und his wife and only child, my cousin Eva, of the same age, lived in Nice, where he had a photography store. Mother writes to Walter that this determined her choice, although she disliked my Uncle's wife, Tante Henny and we never came to be in close contact with that family.

Soon after our arrival, Mother informed Tante Lily of our stay in Nice and a copy of this less-than-cheerful letter later came into my hands. Here again, she writes in (somewhat incorrect but adequate) English, German having become a forbidden language. A few years ago I visited a friend from Vienna who now lives in Paris. As we took a walk, she talked German to me, but I could not get myself to openly speak German in the streets of a French city. The prohibition to speak German, in Paris, as soon as the war had started, was so powerful that I could not breach it even 60 years later.

MOTHER IN NICE TO HER SISTER LILY BOYKO IN NEW YORK CITY (ENGLISH LETTER)

Nice, le 12 October 1940, Hotel Windsor

Dear Lily,

I just got your letter. I am very happy that you, at least, are in safety. From Mother I have no nouvelles, as can't write in "zone occupped." I went to Nice as Sophie had to go to school and luckily she is accepted.

We are here in the same position as in Vienna in March 1938. It is impossible for a stranger to earn money. They are making racial laws, in the hotel were I live they behaved as with the Palais of the Viennese Archbishop after the Anschluss.

The food situation is the same as in 1918 in Vienna. I don't give 2 centimeters for my and Sophie's life.

Also I have difficulties with the *séjour a Nice* (permission for residence in Nice) and I don't know where to go, as I dare not return to Paris. The Princess wrote me a letter that she has lost money that she can give me only 3,000 francs the month.

I got a telegram from Anna in August that Martin and Walter is interned and if I need money.

Please try to send her my letter.

They have a cousin in New York Edward Bernays has a great newspaper agency, please perhaps he will know something about the Freuds. Try to see him because I am very anxious.

As I had to go from Paris on a bicycle we have no luggage at all. I am knitting the whole days pullovers so that we may have something to dress.

If the Freuds can they shall try to send me some money by the American consulate at Nice. I don't need it now but when they will have my letter it will surely be necessary.

Try to find me a position in the U.S.A. as a phonetic teacher in a school, a hospital or a university. I am so miserable.

With many kisses your sister Esti

Meanwhile, I prepared to make a living in unoccupied Nice. I had to go to the *Préfecture de police* to obtain a *permit de séjour*, the permission to stay. When I applied, I folded a 1,000 francs note in my identification papers. This helped. Sophie enrolled in the *Lycée de Nice* and continued her schooling. I was accepted to treat speech-handicapped children in the *Nice dispensaire pour enfants nerveux et retardés,* I also took a course at the university in French language, literature, and civilization. I visited physicians for the referral of private patients, but did not have much luck in this regard. However, by chance, I met a social worker who knew me from Paris and she was kind enough to refer patients. A child with a cleft palate whom I treated had a father who was a butcher and he provided us with some meat. Groceries became difficult to obtain.

Sophie and I explored the magnificent countryside of la Côte d'Azure with our bikes. The climate was balmy. It was no wonder that rich and famous people chose to live there.

SOPHIE'S DIARY
   February 22, 1941
   Two weeks ago I was on bike in Monte Carlo, or in Monaco, which is the same. The landscape is incredibly magnificent. I have never seen anything so glorious. The blue blue sky over the infinite sea.

This is already almost everything Mother has to recount about our sojourn in Nice. The stay there was apparently only a short step in her memory. But those were also the years when I kept a detailed diary and while it captures not exactly my mother's story, and I am hesitant to deflect your attention from her life to mine, my diary does throw a picture on our common life during those two years.

We lived in two rooms in a small hotel occupied mostly by refugees. Mother's room had a hotplate on which she prepared our meals. I attended the official French Lycée and to this day have no idea why I was fortunate enough to be accepted in the Nice Lycée at a time when foreign Jews were excluded from attending a Lycée. A few months after our arrival in Nice I started my diary.

Sᴏᴘʜɪᴇ's Dɪᴀʀʏ

November 4, 1940

Since the Germans occupy Paris, I am now since two months in Nice. It is not bad here, especially the school is very nice. But it was much better in Paris. Especially since I had already found a few friends and I am terribly alone here. . . . Many people in these critical days have taken flight to Portugal. Especially foreigners, of course, but also well-known Frenchmen who had agitated against Germany or who had even committed the crime of being Jews. We simply couldn't decide to leave everything behind. Otherwise we might be, like the Boykos in America, or else at father's, in England. Sometimes I am terribly sorry that we did not leave this Shitfrance far behind, that can produce nothing but laws against Jews and interns foreign Jews in disgusting concentration camps. But then I could not have continued going to school and I must finally get to finish my bachot [French Baccalaureate]. Whether I will ever manage it is now very questionable.

In England, they locked up Father and Walter in a camp. That is the last news we have from them. I felt awful to hear that they were in a camp. What will happen to them? When shall I see them again? And Tante Janne? My dear Tante Janne, how often I think of her. I am seized with the uncomfortable feeling that we shall be left all alone back in France. It is rather weird for two women to be all alone. Did Father fulfill his responsibility? I can't tell. Surely he could not have foreseen the breakdown of France.

They only renew our permission to stay here from month to month. Perhaps we shall be expelled in November. That would be awful because I want to go to school and in most places they don't accept foreigners in Lycées.

One hears such terrible things from the camp in Gürs. It seems people are almost starving, freezing to death or getting sick. It is horrible to think of it and one is so helpless in the face of so much misery.

We always listen to the English radio. That is very pleasant because it gives us so much hope. If the English win the war, everything might be good again. But if the Germans win? Better not to think about it. I am no longer a Communist in my mind, like before. I am enraged against the Russians for their nonaggression pact! Because the Russians could have avoided the war. But because their infernal world revolution they had to sacrifice thousands of people and naturally no trace of world revolution. Maybe a good economic system can exist without the need for communism. I really don't know. But at the moment the English must win. All other political considerations have moved into the background. And after they win, they should set up the United States of Europe. Will I return to Vienna? If all is as before, with pleasure. But people have left and if one has established a second home in Palestine or America, one probably does not return so easily.

Just now a telegram arrived from Uncle Ernst [*Father's younger brother, in London*]. It says that Boyko and Harry [*father's cousin, only son of Uncle Alexander, Grandfather Freud's younger brother*] will help us. But no mention of Walter and Father. Surely they must still be locked up. Oh, I would so have liked to pass my bachot.

November 5, 1940

I am very discouraged. One swims around. I might just be working for the dogs. If I should end up in America I will have to start all over again in a third language. I am really sick of it all.... Lucky there are still wonderful books about....

November 6, 1940

... Mother speaks incessantly of emigration and that she will get carted to a concentration camp, etc. I am not sure whether she really believes this or whether it is her usual way of making scenes. Whatever, it irritates me. She knows that I want to stay here to finish my bac.

Hurrah, Roosevelt has been elected. I heard about it during lunch at school and I was instantly delighted. I don't think Roosevelt will allow Europe to be swallowed up by Germany. His rival Wilky is probably a Nazi at heart. While Roosevelt is surely a totally decent guy.

Eating at school is much more fun than eating at home. There are very friendly girls whom I can ask for advice with homework and with whom one can have pleasant conversations. Morally they are different from me. Or am I just more honest? "A woman should rather give up her career than sleep with a man out of ambition" (actress). I don't think virtue is the highest goal, and I have fewer scruples. Another girl thinks (and she is always super-moralistic) that chastity is a woman's highest virtue.

My relationship with Mother, far from the Freud family, without the competition with Tante Janne and other possible threats would grow to be as harmonious and close as it ever was or would ever be in our lives. But even in those best of times, we did have terrible fights from time to time.

SOPHIE'S DIARY

November 10, 1940

I am furious at Mother for a change. I do just what Walter used to do. When she makes her hyena face, I get up and leave the room. Now I really understand Walter. The other day, when I reproached her spending 68 francs for a meal in a restaurant, she engineered a most incredible scandal. It ended at the hotel when she threw grapes at me as I closed the door to my room, and my new blouse and the walls of the hotel and the door of my room were full of squashed grapes and all the people on the floor were very upset. How can one be so out of control!

I remember this particular fight quite sharply. In her starvation anxiety mother talked constantly about our not having enough money to survive, making me naturally also extremely anxious. I considered going to a restaurant an unnecessary luxury and had tormented her about wasting money all through the meal, until she could no longer contain her rage.

My husband loved going to restaurants although he was in other ways very thrifty, while I still think it is an unnecessary luxury. We had some conflicts about this very matter.

SOPHIE'S DIARY

November 14, 1940

I failed my French school exercise, but totally and it makes me sad, especially since I also failed my Latin one. I don't know what is the matter. Am I so much more stupid than the others? I shall never amount to anything. . . . My German teacher said I lacked personality. Might she be right?

November 16, 1940

They have taken away my Walter and sent him to Australia. Oh, if he only could be well. Dear Walter. Will I ever see him again. Dear Walter. I always have to think of the many good hours we spent together and I try in vain to remember his nasty ways. Nothing holds me back in Europe any longer! On to America. Tant pis (too bad) about the new language. So I won't do my bac. It is questionable in any case whether I would pass it. I am writing so seldom because I am overwhelmed with schoolwork and I have to study so much. Besides I have read some enchanting books. . . . The other day I went to the flea market to buy antique books. Rummaging among old books is great fun. . . .

At school they are all against the Germans and the Italians and most of them for the Greeks and the English. Mother talks about going to General de Gaulle, as a nurse. It is only drivel but it would be splendid. The way I imagine things in dreams.

December 24, 1940

Xmas eve—Today a letter from Harry has arrived. So, Walter is in Australia, in Melbourne—his fate otherwise unknown. Father has become a pioneer [a lowly assistant soldier for which foreigners could volunteer]. Nothing else is known about him as well. I do hope he is feeling well. Poor Father, has to be a common soldier when he really won for himself a position of officer in the last war. If only he finds himself well. Why did his book enjoy no success [The book was called Parole d'Honneur and deals with the adventures of a soldier in WWI]. Surely it must have been a good book. He had put such hopes in the book, what a disappointment. God, if I think how cold I was to him last summer. I reproach myself. Why did I not accompany him to Chamonix? I am a revolting idiot. But maybe he is glad to be a soldier. I do hope that so much. . . . Harry writes that they do all they can to bring us to America. That is really very decent of them. Are they going to succeed? Do I want to go to America? And then, as mother rightly says, we shall spend three times as much to live in the same way in America as we live here. The Italians are being beaten from all sides. Hopefully the Germans won't come to their aid. Three days of vacation have passed. Vacations always pass horribly quickly. . . . Books, book, books.

January 17, 1941

. . . I do love Mother much more than before. Sometimes I am still furious at her, but now I feel more that she is my "Mother" and actually a very good mother. I notice that I got much closer to her, this year, and that I am now really fond of her. I now love her more than Tante Janne who is fading in my memory. The other day I heard a girl say to someone that Mrs. Freud makes such a terrible grimace when she laughs. It gave me a sting.

Is it worthwhile to fight for France and to die? I am not sure. I think it is blood shed in vain to die for a country where people say: Blum is a Jew, he had no right to govern France since he is not a Frenchman. *[Léon Blum, a Jew, had been a recent prewar president of France.] Or:* One should lock the Israelis into a concentration camp. *Is it really worth while to shed one's blood for France? Not for a Jew, never for a country, because Jews have no father-land. Only for an idea, which is more important or easier? To die is always hard, one way or the other.*

January 25, 1941

Unfortunately I have now terribly little time to read. I work all day and half the night. But the worst is I am not that good a student. How can that be? I always took myself to be quite bright. But not so, il n'en est rien (not true). Those little local provincial-geese whom I sort of despise, who have yet seen little of life and thought of it even less, get better marks than I. It is kill-ing me and throws me into a depression.

February 8, 1941

... Today we had salut du drapeau *(saluting the flag) exercises. It is dis-gusting how the girls are carrying on, all of them chauvinists. One of them decreed that we have to wear a hat and another one came upon gloves. They complained endlessly that a* few naturalisées Françaises *(naturalized French girls) sing along in the chorus.*

The English keep winning big victories in Africa. The girls express a hell-ish joy, because around here the Italians are even more hated than the Germans.

February 18, 1941

I just read Tante Lily's letter from America. They want to drag us to America and talk as if we were already there. At that thought a most horrible discouragement seizes me. My whole inner self shrinks together. I could kill myself with desperation. To start once again at the beginning. And I wont be able to learn English so quickly. I feel desperate. To be pushed around, end-lessly, from one country to another. Bea [my two-years-older cousin, Tante Lily's daughter] earns money giving skating lessons and language lessons. But since I don't know English, I can't give any lessons. Besides, there are so infinitely many others who know both German and French. I want to continue to live in Paris, or return to Vienna, but not go to New York. And then Tante Lily gives such a somber description of their lives. They have a two-room flat and we might be able to live with them. But I want to go to a college. I mean, if we have enough money—which we don't have. I want to cry, but I can't. How can I apply myself here when I think all the time it is for nothing. If I can't finish my bachot and have to start a new life in a country in which I don't know English.

March 6, 1941

I keep thinking of my Latin exam which I have probably messed up, although by god, more important events are happening. Bulgaria, etc., it all looks quite miserable. Every day I hear new jokes. Greeks have red shirts so that one can't see the blood. Mussolini orders brown pants.

March 14, 1941

At school I now have brilliant grades. I was 5th best in Latin which gave me really great pleasure, had several times the best mathematical exercise, was first in German, but that does not count. Yet today I surely messed up my chemistry composition. I simply had not understood a single word of the problem. All that does not make me happy.

I have, once again, various reproaches against mother. She is basically not at all generous. When I begged her to take on a poor guy from Gürs as "godchild" (they are starving to death) she agreed and two days later she decided they had enough. I so would have liked to write long letters, and even knit socks and assemble food packages.

Father is said to be a sort of kitchenboy. If this is true, I would feel awfully hurt for him. At his age! It seems to me he showed in the last war that he can do better. Poor Father who wanted to give his blood for Austria. And that is his reward. Supposedly it is not certain whether Walter is in Sidney or in Melbourne. J'aime autant qu'il soit là bas (Just as well that he is over there). In that way one does not have to worry about him. I don't want him to be in the English army, it is too dangerous, although it would be very good for his future.

March 20, 1941

Mother moans from morning to night about saving money, and then she goes to a tearoom for 20 francs supposedly to meet people and get pupils. (But otherwise she has also become very thrifty, never buys anything for herself although she could use various things.) I seem to eat as much as usually, but somehow I never feel full up, am always hungry. Walter's birthday is on the third of April. His twentieth! And I can't even just congratulate him! As long as it does not hurt his feelings, I don't care. Mother will say for hours (with tears in her eyes), "today Puckerl has his 20th birthday and he is all alone." And I will shrug my shoulders with indifference. She does care a lot about him and I don't know why they don't get along when they are together. Well, actually I do know. Mother has the winning habit of only talking about herself, her professional successes etc. And he probably can't bear that. My love for Walter is the most unselfish and therefore the best of all my loves. I wish only that he should be happy, very happy, and under such conditions I could renounce to ever see him again. Tante Janne should also be happy, but mostly so, that when I see her again, she must be happy in order to be the Tante Janne that I know.

322 West 72nd Street, New York City
March 16, 1941
Mrs. Esti Freud
Hotel Windsor Nice France
Dear Esti,

I thank you very much for your letter from February.

A you probably know, we all tried very hard and finally got an Affidavit for you from the First Rabbi of New York, Stephen S. Wise. You should already have that by now. I hope that it will enable you to receive the American visa and to come over. The *Times* announced a few days ago that the French government is issuing exit visas more easily and therefore hope that you will have no more difficulties in this regard. Another difficulty will be to get a place in a ship, but hopefully that can also be solved.

In terms of your shortage of money, Lily has sent you, as she told me, $50 at the beginning of the year and I hope that you have meanwhile received its value in francs.

At the same time I forwarded the content of your letter to me to the family and Ernst tries to get in touch with Martin to find a way to meet your wishes.

You already know that Tante Minna has died, but perhaps not that Max Halberstadt [Aunt Sophie's widower] is also already on the other side.

. . . I try constantly to help with the difficulties of particular family members. The worst worry children are naturally the four old aunts whose circumstances are hopeless.

I hope that your worst difficulties are over with the money from Lily and that I will meanwhile hear from Ernst what I should do.

With warm greetings for you and Sophie,
Your Harry

SOPHIE'S DIARY
March 23, 1941
I heard a horrible story, as if it had been written by Maupassant. A painter in Paris was asked to pawn a furcoat. He gave the coat to a friend to do that for him. All characters are so far dirt poor. The friend goes to the casino, loses all his money, pawns the furcoat and loses that money as well. The poor painter is naturally beside himself. How can he return the money for the furcoat? His friend was a young man from a fine family. It is very upsetting to think that all these camps and unemployment have lowered the

moral standards of a man to such a degree. Transformation from a well brought up young man to a thief. Because what he did was stealing and nothing else. It is so horrible to think what has become of the elite of the Jews of Vienna. The French have that on their conscience. No, I will not stay in France or marry a Frenchman. Above all it is of course Hitler's fault. This is such a horribly sad depressing story. It will plunge the poor painter into misfortune. He will lose his good reputation. Mother recently confessed to me that she had loaned him 500 francs before he left for Paris. This is certainly above our means, but he had no more money at all and one can't let people starve. Mother did the right thing. But this time she can no longer help him out of his fiasco. With our monthly 3,000 francs [from the Princess Bonaparte] and the money we still have in reserve, which is shrinking every day, I see us really soon going to the devil. I only hope someone will send us money before the worst will happen. How stupid that mother sold all her gold coins!! I was always against it.

April 2, 1941

... Mother wants to go to Corsica over Easter, with a ship and bicycle there. Although the birthplace of Napoleon tempts me, I shall stay here to read. We also spend too terribly much money on those excursions. And it is boring to make a bike excursion with Mother. One has to wait for her all the time, and from time to time she says: Look *... as if one could not notice it oneself.*

I received the felicitations du conseil de discipline *(congratulations of the faculty council) as the only one in my class. I was pleased but that is over now. I did not deserve it, and expect that I failed the chemistry and history tests and will fail French, mathematics, physics and geography.... The other day I had the best Latin exercise, but then I spoiled a Latin translation.*

April 11, 1941

Easter vacations, good Friday ... Before going to sleep all the various problems assault me. I must learn English, I must go to America and won't be able to speak English and will be completely perdu *(lost). Perhaps I will meet Tante Janne again. The horrible politics come to my mind en passant (in passing). But it is America* qui m'obséde, qui m'obséde *(which obsesses me, obsesses me). One is sooo terribly homeless, it is unbelievable. I don't want to stay in France, the French are too mean, with all they have done to us. By US I mean emigrants in general. The other day I heard again such a terrible story. A family wanted to emigrate to America. They already had a visa. The father goes to the Consulate, but does not get the visa because the consul notices that he has become insane. He had been in Gürs, the refugee camp where he became crazy. That speaks volumes.*

At lunch I reproached a comrade for having gone to see a German film. Big indignation—then one couldn't play Beeethoven any longer etc. And then: no big deal about a few German movies, if one looks at all these Jewish Kraut refugees that we have to support. They don't miss one opportunity to disparage Jews. Eva [my cousin] supported me a little. But it does not touch her. She does not feel like a foreigner and who knows, maybe not as a Jew. She is quite a nice girl, but terribly full of herself.

Yesterday Mother insisted Father is surely in a moral depression. It is awful for me to believe that, it must not be. I hope Walter stayed in Australia. He now had his 20th birthday, how much, how awfully much do I hope that he did not feel alone. Perhaps he has nice friends who prepared a fun birthday for him.

April 14, 1941

Today the political news are so bad, one gets sick in one's stomach. In Egypt it is all about Suez. I then walk around with a rock on my chest, a huge rock which oppresses me. It would be so horribly terrible if the English lose that I cannot even imagine it. No, I won't and I can't image the Jewish destiny in that case. Why are they all running away from the Germans? I don't understand this at all. And why did the English ships not prevent the German troops from landing in Libya?

April 19, 1941

The Serbs have surrendered. I think it was crazy suicide for them to have fought at all. They were not strong enough, they had to crouch down. Of course it was good for the English. But so terribly much blood was shed in vain. I only think of the Serbish blood because I am no longer sorry for German blood. My heart has hardened itself and if I hear that the German army will die of thirst, I think: I hope so. Maybe England will win, I can't tell. But it is certain that it will all take a very long time and that we shall probably be in the United States by then. For better or for worse.

With Mother I am alternately on good and bad terms. She constantly has visitors which gets on my nerves. I am so angry that she sold all the gold coins. I told her not to. Now they would be worth a lot more. She is always committing such stupidities.

June 1, 1941

... Whitsunday. I keep postponing you, dear diary, until a moment in which I have a little more time. But it never arrives, this bienheureuse (happy) moment. I am accablée de travail (overwhelmed with work) but school lasts until end of July. If I had more time, this notebook would be full of lamentations. Is it overwork, the strange circumstances or I think above all *the lack of friends which often gets me so down. . . . I suppose we will sail away to America in one or two months, I don't care, I bow to my fate. At school I have now also found a friend, a level-headed one among all these idiotic hysterical girls. They are all for the Maréchal and chauvinists. . . .*

Until now I would not have cared if I had never been born. I tried to cheer Mother up for her birthday so she should not feel so abandoned. I bought her a little box in which one can put some sugar, and lovely white peonies mixed up with other flowers and made quite a funny poem.

Poem for my Mother's 1941 Birthday (45th birthday)
Unable to fashion a poem of worth
   Da ich nicht mehr dichten kann
For the one who gave me birth
   will ich's gar nicht erst versuchen
   Sondern meinen Kopf verfluchen
I shall not even try
   der nur trock'ne Worte findet
Just use a few words that are sadly dry.
   für die die mich hat erkindet
Only a little box I have for you as a gift
   Du kriegst nur diese kleine Schachtel
In these sad times where we live all adrift
   denn uns're Zeiten sind sehr Mist
in the air full of mists
   in den Lüften statt der Wachtel
Fly no birds but bombers and parachutists.
   fliegen die Parachutists
Just so you would not feel so blue
   Doch damit du dich nicht krånkst
And call me "you cruel daughter you"
   mich nicht Rabentochter nennst
I rushed in the early morning hours
   voller Eile heute Morgen
To buy for you a bunch of flowers.
   Ging ich Blumen dir besorgen.
Though nebbich shabby is the grass
   Dieses Gras ein bißchen schåbich
That I present you, alas, alas.
   schenk'ich Dir, ach nåbich, nåbich

Instead of a delicious roasted bird
    Au lieu d'úne gourmandise
A "backhendl," oh how absurd
    Backhendl, quel bêtise
Slippers or a hat smart and new
    pantoufle ou nouveau chapeau
It's a morbid gift I offer you
    te fais je un lugubre cadeau
Reminiscent of fruit jam too tart
    qui te rapelle les mauvaises confitures
And of our lives so hard so hard
    et nos temps si durs si durs
Made with ersatz sugar icky sweet
    où tout est fait au sucre de raisin
When we have not enough bread to eat.
    et où lón manque de pain
But a machine I will create
    Mais une machine je vais construire
That is certain to elate
    qui va beaucoup te rejouïr
It will be a clock with an alarm
    Einen Wecker will entdecken
To wake up the world to committed harm
    um die Völker aufzuwecken
To arise against the German nation
    der die Deutschen soll erschrecken
Sending Hitler to sure hell and damnation.
    durch die Hitler wird verrecken
I would so like to give you dear
    Schenkte gern Dir einen Sender
A radio so you can also hear
    damit du nicht nur hörst Engländer
Not only what our English sends
    sondern auch die Afrikaner
But also news from Mohammedans
    Buschneger, Mohamedaner
Africans, Zulus, and other places
    und die vielen anderen Erden

That we might have to visit all
> *die wir wohl besuchen werden*

Since our world has become too small
> *car la terre est trop petite*

In Europe they don't want us to stay
> *Dans l'Europe on nous veut pas*

So let us go to the USA
> *geh'n wir nach Amerika*

America has no more room
> *Amerika ist schon ganz voll*

To St. Paul with bikes we zoom
> *radel'n wir auf île St. Paul.*

For Jews no permit to stay to be had
> *Für Juden Aufenthalt verbot,*

The North Pole freezes us half dead
> *am Nordpol frier'n wir halbtot*

In Afghanistan tigers are ever bolder
> *Afghanistanens wilde Tieger*

Reminding too much of the Nazi soldier
> *erinnern trop an deutsche Krieger*

In the Congo no Prague ham to be found
> *Im Kongo fehlt uns Prager Schinken*

On the Nile by crocodiles we'll be drowned
> *am Nil uns Krokodile trinken*

Penguins, delicate but strong
> *Die Pengouine zart und schlank*

Tolerate us three years long
> *uns dulden ganz drei Jahre lang*

But after that they don't leave us in peace
> *Dann müde bald von unsern vices*

And return us back to Nice.
> *schicken zurück sie uns nach Nice.*

But a worldview so frightful and bad
> *Doch Weltbetrachtungen so schaurig*

Is for a birthday celebration too sad
> *sind für Geburtstage zu traurig*

Are you outraged at the omission
> *Auch vergaß ich, wie sichs gehört*

That I did not adhere to the tradition?
> *bist Du nicht schon sehr empört?*

And was so neglectful and should miss
> *nach althergebrachter Weise*

To gently touch your face with a kiss
> *Dir ganz leise, leise, leise*

And wish you a long life
> *ein dickes Pussi zu geben*

To be able to bicycle not using a hand
> *und zu wünschen langes Leben*

Your legs slim and beautifully tanned
> *Radfahrn können ganz ohne Hand*
> *Beine schlank und abgebrannt.*

Please do not compare
> *Ne pense pas à un Molière*

With Goethe, Schiller or Molière
> *Goethe ou à un Schiller*

When you are reading through
> *en lisant mes pauvres vers*

My poor verses dedicated to you.
> *tout de travers.*

The verses are quite sweet, but I think they appear to me better than they really are. They cost me quite a lot of effort. *I thank Edith Friedlander for help with the translation.*

There were lots of rumors about the course of the war. The French newspapers were censored and one could only read about German victories, which was depressing. On my little radio I listened to Churchill's famous "blood, sweat, and tears" speech. The Swiss weekly *Die Weltwoche* provided more accurate information. There were rumors that the Germans had attempted an invasion of England, that the Channel was set aflame, and burned corpses of soldiers were drifting ashore. In the summer of 1941, we heard on the radio that Hitler had started war with Russia. I prophesied correctly that, as it had happened to Napoleon, Hitler would choke on that bite. Unfortunately the final German defeat did not help those in the meantime who had died horrible deaths in concentration camps.

Meanwhile letters arrived from the United States, assuring us that we were not forgotten. Tante Lily touchingly continued to work on getting us an American visa.

I would not have expected that from her. Harry had taken it upon himself to become the family switchboard and sent us news from time to time. Worries about Grandmother Drucker and "the old aunts" were keenly felt.

GERMAN LETTER

> Boyko
> West 72nd Street, New York City
> June 2, 1941
> Dearest Esti,

We wrote you on May 21 that 5,000 French francs have been expedited to you, apart from the $50 sent to you in January, and the $25 in February—and hope that all these contributions are already in your hands. We also want to confirm the telegram of May 20 that we sent you: STATE DEPARTMENT GRANTED YOUR VISA CONTACT AMERICAN CONSUL NICE STOP GOLDMANN CABLED MONEY FOR YOUR TICKETS TO HIAS MARSEILLE BOYKO.

Meanwhile the World Jewish Congress has received a telegram from the HIAS in Marseille that your affidavits have not arrived. It was immediately cabled back that you don't need the affidavits, since the State Department in Washington had sent a telegram to the Consulate in Nice suggesting to give you visas for the voyage. We thus urgently hope that matters have meanwhile been arranged and are only very depressed that we are kept so little up to date by you.—

On May 29 we cabled you: IN CASE RECEPTION OF VISA AND MOTHER WITH YOU ASK AMERICAN CONSUL PERMISSION TO TAKE HER ALONG STOP SIMILAR CASES KNOWN HERE/CABLE SUCCESS SO MONEY FOR MOTHERS SHIP TICKET CAN BE SENT IMMEDITATELY. BOYKO.

Even if mother's case was not dealt with here, it could happen that the Consul, out of humanitarian consideration for an old lady as Mother and Grandmother, grants her the visa after granting you the same. Several of such cases are known here. Maybe you are lucky—asking the American Consul does not cost anything extra. But if things do not work out and Mother stays where she had been until now, you have to make arrangements, before leaving, that the mail gets forwarded to her.

[In ink written by Uncle Rudi] Lily was unfortunately ill in bed with the flu and a kidney infection. Now she is already feeling better and hopefully will be totally recovered in a few weeks.

Warmest greetings and wishes from all of us, Rudi and Lily.

Sophie's Diary

June 25, 1941

... *I go to one of the beaches where one does not have to pay but the swimming is equally great. Really wonderful. Sometimes I swim endless long distances. The events with Russia are really incredible. At the first moment I was dead happy and had the feeling, now everything will work out, the English united with the Russians will win. But now it no longer looks so great. But still I am happy that the English now get along with the Russians, as if two friends of mine had made peace with each other. ...*

The other day I saw Andromaque. *The pupils in my class with the best grades got free seats (otherwise they cost 25 francs). I had the best grades of the whole class and was very proud. It was like money that I had earned myself. The performance was very good, properly tragic and very well played. A propos earning money: My German teacher has promised me a private student, conversation lessons for a young man. Naturally I was in seventh heaven, flirted with my student, went to see a movie each week with G. [a girlfriend], bought myself some secondhand books, bought the book for art history, had my bicycle cleaned, bought mother a little wallet for her food card, went to play ping-pong, all that in thought. And now she no longer mentions that student. It is mean, although it is probably not her fault.*

It has gotten very hot. I go swimming every day. Evening I like to sit on the balcony. Tomorrow we have a test for a sports medal.

June 29, 1941

I got my sports medal. It was exhausting but easy. The Russians are in retreat, they will surely lose. It is horrible. Thomas Mann said today that the war will be endlessly drawn out, and I who had hoped it was the last stage. Mother thinks it will be the end of communism. Lately I have noticed that she has some very intelligent ideas. And often she predicts things correctly.

The other day I had my first new private English lesson. I am not sure if she is a good teacher—100 percent English, very reserved and stiff and she can't translate the things which I do not understand. I hope she gets used to me, otherwise it is very uncozy. But I have the intention of working very hard. At school they are playing the femmes savantes *by Molière. I would love to have a part but with my accent that is of course impossible.*

July 13, 1941

... Good Earth *is wonderful. I read more slowly because it is in English and I have to keep looking up words, but it is relatively easy. The other day my French essay on Brittanicus was read aloud in class. I was quite pleased.*

Yesterday the sea was so wild as never before. It was very beautiful. I have learned to swim even with very high waves.

The Germans keep advancing in Russia. It is unbearable. Yesterday we snapped a little hope because they stood still for a few days, but they only took a rest. The Germans will conquer all of Russia and then all is finally lost. With America things are not going so well either. Our visas have become invalid. And then France will declare war on England and we sit here.

July 23, 1941

This morning I was very glad because Tuesday is awards day. First it is a sign that school is ending, and second one gets book which is not to be spurned. I got the geography prize, and the honor list, and in principle the German prize, but there I am out of competition, and then I had once again, the felicitations du conseil de discipline *(congratulations of the faculty council) and I think for that I deserve something and in my inner heart I hope to get the* Prix d'excellence *although I have not really deserved it.*

I have held on, through the years, to the Carnet de Correspondance, LYCEE DE JEUNES FILLES DE NICE, *in which my achievements for the* Année Scolaire *1940–1941 are recorded. This is my first opportunity to display them with shameless pride. I had hoped, since starting this book, that I could somehow sneak them in as I am doing now—who knows, perhaps I am writing this whole book just for that purpose. I have been privileged with many recognitions in my academic life, but in my old eyes, I view these scholastic achievements in a relatively new language as the peak triumph of my life. I received the first prize in geography, the second prize in mathematics, a prize for German, but I was in all fairness* hors de concours *in that field, and an "accessory second prize" in history. I received for both semesters the* felicitations du conseil de discipline *as well as the* Tableau d"honneur.

SOPHIE'S DIARY

August 2, 1941

The award presentation was very boring. I received five books, more than I expected, but they are not beautiful books, not a single one is hardcover. But I have wonderful appreciations [Teachers' commentaries].

French: Intelligent and studious student, tenacious efforts, Considerable progress in French composition

Latin: Good work, succeeds well, especially in translations from Latin to French.

History: Distinguished mind, good work.

Geography: Excellent results, intelligent and regular work
Mathematics: Works with much interest and enthusiasm. Very good results
Physics and Chemistry: Student who understands and works. Satisfactory results
German: Excellent results. Very gifted student.
Admitted to the 12 grade

It is clear that these French teachers, whatever their political opinions may have been, treated their foreign Jewish pupil with benevolent fairness.

SOPHIE'S DIARY
September 9, 1941
School has started a week ago and with such stupid reforms that one can only shake one's head in desperation. Mornings are reserved for the brain, afternoons for gym and art, arts and crafts and singing. Mondays from 2 to 6 (!) National Education which means excursions into the city by good weather and care for our souls in bad weather. For that we have Miss Thomasie, the philosophy teacher. In gymnastics the method is Hebertism, a totally impossible method in which one has to run about all the time, two or four people have to carry others and one has to march in step. A girl noticed that I did not keep in step and when I answered: "I do that on purpose because I don't like it and I am not a soldier," she was of the opinion I had to obey, whether I liked it or not. Before and after the exercises we have to scream Prêtes *(Ready), but naturally I don't participate in the screaming. But the very best is the class on* action morale *(moral behavior). There we shall discuss the three new themes:* Famille, Travail, Patrie *(Family, Work, Fatherland). Our teacher explained that we used to discuss* Liberté, Egalité, Fraternité *which was beautiful, but the new themes are also beautiful. And for the first class she read us a speech from Carcoppino, the secretary of education to show us the sublime beauty in the themes. But then she did not have time for comments.*

He explains in his speech that the Lycées *will no longer be free and the reason for it. It was blithering drivel.* Pour délivrer les lycées de ses masses indésirables *(to liberate the lycées of its undesirable masses). But if he would know that even a single poor child would suffer from this new decree he would go along with all the injustice of the free system. And now there are scholarships, but to get them, one must be, I think, a general in the army, or have 20 siblings who are all on the edge of starvation. In brief, totally just. And all the girls listened with deathly earnest interest.*

Tomorrow Admiral Darlan is coming to Nice and all schools have to parade at 9:00 A.M. until the Masséna square. But I will suddenly get my menses and go swimming instead. What is too much is simply too much. I have a horror of all that patriotism and there is nobody in our class with whom one can complain. Today I wanted to talk to one of the girls and she instantly said: "cadenas devant la bouche" (a lock before your mouth). They are a cowardly riffraff.

The Latin-French teacher seems quite nice, except that she is probably a Petainist. But she is lively and interesting. In German I have once again the Krebbs which truly pleases me. She was so decent to lend me books again, even the wonderful poems by Heine, after I made a stain on the last book. . . .

Everyone is asking me when we shall finally steam off to America because they want to buy my bicycle. But first I shall try to take it along, and second I will certainly not sell it to someone who assaults me like a vulture and third certainly not to the porter of our hotel whom I can't stand or to my ex-student who left me in the cold after two sessions.

September 15, 1941

. . . I now give a German lesson. It is very agreeable to earn some money, but 20 francs a week is not very much. She has to take a make-up exam in German. But I have the disagreeable feeling that I don't teach her very much. One can accomplish very little in just one hour.

German letter

Boyko

New York, September 10, 1941

Dear Estilein,

Many thanks for you letter of August 17—you don't need to worry about money at the moment, but since Martin lives in a situation of severe money-export rules, he is at the moment not in a position to pay back anything. So we have to wait until the armistice which will hopefully happen soon. That he otherwise gives no sign of life is indeed very regrettable but is just like him. I sometimes hear from Harry that the whole family F. is faring well. Walter has returned to his father. He wrote Bea during the trip a very cheerful letter. He does not yet know what he will do, but promised Bea to write to her.

In terms of your visa, we are also very desperate that matters are not progressing. Perhaps it will when Grandmother gets her Cuba visa that we are in the process of obtaining. Rudi is considering going to Washington to see where the obstruction lies. Everything here takes forever and has become more difficult with the new law. Mother will shortly get notified by the Cuban Consulate and will receive her visa. However Cuba has a very hot climate and I am curious whether she will want to go there. We soon expect Marianne [Tante Janne] and family in Cuba, the trip [from Israel] will naturally last quite long since it is a very long distance that they have to traverse. I hope they will arrive in good health. And we are glad that we shall have at least a part of the family nearby. You will hopefully be the next. We are here in good spirits and hope that life will soon be normal once again. The main thing is that you retain your health. I am surprised that you don't write about packages, have you not received any? We never got Sophie's poem, it seems very much gets lost. The money that got sent to Grandmother was returned, because they could not find her. Write to us whether she needs anything, then we could transfer some money to the new address that you will cable to us. As long as it is possible.

The humid warmth here is hard to bear for me, and I don't leave the house for days. Bea is soon returning to her college and time with her was very enjoyable. I hope to write to you soon more favorable news and close my letter with many affectionate kisses for you and dear Ida. Your sister who loves you, Lily.

P.S. Do you have any idea what happened to our things? That we left in the flat?

P.S. Grandmother should burn useless things, but preserve photos and valuables.

Sophie's Diary

September 17, 1941

... At School there are endless new foolishnesses. At the salute of the flag on Monday morning there are five army guys and one of them gives the order "garde à vous," "préparez vous à monter les couleurs," "montez les couleurs" *("attention," "get ready to raise the colors," "raise the colors"). It is so horribly ridiculous. And during the refrain of the Marseillaise the girls make a Hitler greeting. Our two class representatives are super-Nazis and on top of that one of them is a class repeater.*

During the second moral education lecture the teacher talked about loyauté *[loyalty] (not to cheat) and* tenacité *[tenacity] (keeping our notebooks in good order and studying faithfully). She took herself very seriously yet I am still not interested in what she has to say, especially since she is not teaching me anything new. In gym I made the highest jump, 1 meter 20. I was quite proud. The teacher told me today that I have a horrible accent, which rather hurt my feelings. Then she preaches all the time that we should bear children and quickly get married. I can't stand that.*

September 19, 1941

Walter, my Walter has returned from the camp. Today we received a letter from Harry in which he explains that Walter had been freed for some time, but had no ship and now he finally did get one, with 15 comrades, and wrote Harry a letter from Panama and from Norfolk in Virginia. He was not allowed to go on land because he had no visa and he asked Harry to telegraph Father that he was on his way back. Whenever I think of Walter I feel incredibly anxious in my heart. I desperately want him to be happy and without worries. And I desperately want to see him again to see what has become of him and to be fond of him, once again. I am so horribly worried that the camp has damaged him morally. But perhaps it was the opposite.

The trip to America might come off after all. I am now remaining totally amorphous and let come what may, but since Walter is once again in England it has become even more difficult to leave.

When I told mother that Russia and England will fight another war after this one, she thought this was so stupid, she did not even answer. When I told her today that I would only marry a leftist and he must not be rich she responded right away: "Naturally he can be stupid, but left ... etc." She is a reactionary after all, and I will certainly let nobody interfere in my choice of husband.

September 28, 1941

... Today I heard that the schools no longer accept any Jewish immigrants. The shock that gave me has shown me once again how much I care to go to the Lycée. The Hausers [my Communist friends] in their idealism think if others of my kind are not allowed to attend the Lycée I should not be in such a favored position, but I am after all, not that big-hearted.

Sometimes I ask myself uneasily what we shall live on, in America. Mother asks herself the same thing but I don't want to talk to her about this. Besides Father will transfer us some money. Oh, I hope and so hope that I will get a scholarship.

September 31, 1941

Materialism in America. I am not worried about that for myself. I am now repelled by things that are superfashionable, and superficial and dancing-flirt-dolls. I intend to work hard, with all my strength, to surpass the others and to achieve something. If only I will get a scholarship to a university! And then I would like to have a close friend, intelligent, Communist, Jew, affectionate, cheerful, Viennese, to return with him to Vienna at the right moment. . . .

October 16, 1941

I am not looking at anything for school and am getting a very black conscience. As an excuse for myself I use my coming emigration to America and that I won't get to take the bac in any case. The emigration matter is actually not so quick. Mother was in Marseille and learned that the tickets for the ship are not entirely paid, only one, and even that one not totally, and that we won't get away before November, December. Therefore a million things could still intervene, for example a little declaration of war by America.

During the two days Mother was gone I practically ate only 8 pounds of grapes, nothing else, approximately. It was quite cozy. I also made myself pancakes and they came out quite well, only a bit hard. I was very proud the way I turned them around in the pan, with a Chinese-like gesture.

In Russia things are going very well. Leningrad is still holding tight. I now always read the Weltwoche, *quite interesting. The Lycée is no longer free which is disgusting.*

CHAPTER 33

Insanity Strikes

*M*other's dread of poverty, dread of becoming dependent on her "brothers-in-law," her conviction that they begrudged the possible need to help us financially or even with the money for the passage almost led to our staying in France and thus deathly deportation. My own obsession about getting a French baccalaureate added to the climate of insanity.

The apparently friendly exchanges of letters do not reveal this underlying issue.

GERMAN LETTER
> Boyko
> 269 West 72nd Street, New York City
> November 9, 1941
> Dear Esti,
> The joy was unspeakably great when we received your Telegram: "Passage alright. Many thanks HICEM fixed departure about 15 December."
> Marianne whom we cabled regarding your coming felt the same way. We suppose that you will be leaving Lisbon already around December 15 and we have to be kept informed in exact detail of the dates of your trip since we want to do everything to prepare your reception with strong publicity which is important for your further career. Marianne and we are very worried how we shall keep in touch with Mother after your departure. Please make careful arrangements in this matter. We greatly look forward to your coming and greet you affectionately, also Sopherl.
> Your Lily and Rudi

I received messages from my sister Lilly [*sic*] that her family had arrived safely, had obtained the immigration papers and were working on getting visas for Sophie and me. One of the problems was their payment of the boat passage to the Joint Distribution Committee. I think my brother-in-law was worried that I would not pay that amount back, which was ridiculous.

Our American visas arrived shortly before Pearl Harbor and the United States' entry into the war. Spain had closed its frontiers and no ships left her harbors to go to the United States. The boats had to be rerouted via Morocco. We were advised by the Joint that there would be a ship from Marseille to Casablanca where we would have to wait for another boat to the United States. It was winter. We had been in Nice nearly eighteen months. I had dispensed with my furniture by means of a moving company. The china and linen I owned were shipped to me. The magnificent silver flatware I had received as a wedding present from my grandmother and which I had deposited before the war in the Morgan Bank was included in that shipment. Miraculously it is still in my possession. I received the French permission to ship it since we had had it imported.

From time to time I traveled to Marseille to visit the American consul and offices of the Joint Distribution Committee, to find out about my visa application to the United States. These trips were most unpleasant since the trains were overcrowded and one had to fight to get into them.

LETTER FROM MOTHER IN MARSEILLE TO SOPHIE IN NICE

Marseille,
Wednesday, December 10, 1941
My darling Herzensschnäuzchen,
This morning arrived the photos, the telegram and the money that you sent me. I thank you many many times. Everything is as terrible as possible, I think I shall return to Nice with a damaged heart. Yesterday I got up at 6h in the morning and went to the Consulate. There they told me my visas had arrived, I should pay, give them two photos of mine and of yours and get the papers on Thursday. Two hours later I hear that all the visas are blocked, I could tear out my hair that I did not come earlier, all the other people had received them, my head felt hammered with a hatchet. This morning I returned and they said the blocking was only temporary and in a few days they will distribute visas again. Then I went to the HICEM who said I should wait a few days, they have telegraphed to Lisbon and they will distribute them again. In the afternoon, i.e., right now I went to extend my *sauf-conduit* [permission to travel] which I will only get Monday, so don't count any earlier

with me. I don't think that we will still get away, and given the new Jewish regulations, I am terribly desperate, do you think they will imprison us too? How is the atmosphere in Nice. Here it is horrible. I bought myself some stockings, mine are all torn. I am enclosing your meat ticket.

I was very pleased with Father's telegram. My dear, dear Herzens-schnäuzchen, this emigration surpasses my strength, I am totally shattered. And it is so unpleasantly cold here.

Many many thousand kisses, your Mother Esti.

Greet Lotte Kronheim most affectionately from me, I would need her urgently to comfort me.

SOPHIE'S DIARY

December 30, 1941

This last month was quite exciting and if the vacations had not finally arrived, I would have gone mad, C'est une façon de parler (In a manner of speaking) because one knows, people do not become mad so easily.

Mother went to Marseille to fetch money, Portuguese visas etc. While Mother was in Marseille I led a terrific life. I ate chestnuts for lunch, bread in the evening, sat down at noon on a bench in the sun until school started again, or usually until 3 h. I usually fell asleep on the bench with a book in my hand. Once I invited a friend for potatoes, but I got tired of that as well. Then I laid down on an easychair on the beach to study for my history exam. That was great, I mean the sun, not the history study.

On the morning of Mother's departure there was the long expected declaration of war from Japan to America. She left anyway, totally in vain because the Portuguese closed their frontier and instead of two days Mother stayed in Marseille for one week and collected the names of all the aid organizations where a terrible atmosphere prevailed (people get crying fits) which shatters one's nerves. Then she called me. I was not at home. I had waited for her call all afternoon in immeasurable excitement, thinking of the most impossible hypotheses and then she told me that Germany had declared war on America. . . .

The Nyassa, which was initially scheduled for December 15, was postponed until December 25, and then to January 1 and then to January 15. But those were only unpleasant trivia. At school I spread the word that I would be leaving after or still before Xmas and in general I took leave of my Nizza life without too much pain. Finally I had gotten so used to the idea of departure that I looked forward to the trip and to the change.

S*OPHIE'S* (N*EW*) D*IARY*

New Year's Eve, 1941

Today is new year's eve and I am at home, like last year and the year before. But I better continue where I left off in my last diary.

So Mother called me from Marseille to announce the declaration of war of Germany against America, or, much rather, to take comfort from my voice—She then returned after a week with vague news about a ship via Casablanca and from there one gets fetched, but that was only talk and neither of us had any desire to go to Casablanca to rot there in a camp. We comforted each other, looked at the bright side and prepared for staying put. I especially had looked forward to the Xmas vacations which now, alas, are about to end. Then, suddenly like lightening from the blue sky arrived a telegram: Portugal is granting visas once again. Because that had been the break-down of our trip plans, not that the Americans no longer wanted to let us in, as I had first thought, but because the Portuguese and Spaniards had closed their frontiers. Besides, the Nyassa has still not left.

January 1, 1941

We start to pack at greatneck speed, sell our china, stop sleeping, arrange things, stick photos into albums, take touching farewell from friends and I am horribly excited. Then, suddenly the news arrive: The Spaniards do not open their frontiers. Well, that means, everything is to be unpacked again, to prepare oneself to stay forever, to pay attention again to the neglected schoolwork; briefly, the mind is being totally turned around. But this time it was surely final. Or perhaps not, after all? Because today we get a telegram from the HICEM that we shall be fetched from Casablanca on January 15 and should present ourselves Sunday or Monday with all our stuff at the HICEM. Today is Thursday. I am so excited, I can hardly write. But I did not discuss this with Mother. Because she does not really want to leave. And yesterday when I reread Hausers' letter [my Communist friends] I understood why I was glad to stay here. Je veux être là. (I want to be HERE). Here, where we shall soon have won the victory, and I want to be part of the action—Mother does not want to leave for totally different reasons, but the end result is after all the same.

We sent Father a telegram (meaning Mother did), a sort of ultimatum, asking whether we should still leave and we shall take his answer as a verse from the bible. And if he answer NO, we shall stay, even if we are already on the ship. But he simply did not answer, which hurt me very deeply. No, this last sentence is not true, I wrote it mechanically, without thinking. I don't really care; I have totally stopped counting on Father, but still it is quite mean of him.

We reflect back and forth, and forth and back whether we should go to America or not and we cannot arrive at a satisfactory decision. FOR it is the journey, the adventure, the novelty of the enterprise. Mother thinks I should make a better marriage and perhaps she too, all of this being naturally nonsense. Well, I also did think of it, very secretly, but I really don't care any more whether I shall get married and above all I don't want to make a so-called gute partie *(favorable match). In this respect America is almost a danger for me. And with that Mother made known her intention, or rather her secret wish, to marry again. Not, she said, that she had a true desire for it, but she does not want to become a burden to her children when she is old and cannot work any longer. For the same reason she is also hoping for the inheritance, the two houses she still has in Vienna. I told her right away that if I will earn money some day, she will never be a burden and I also meant that very honestly although I don't quite see the earning of money at this moment. I am generally terribly scared of life, of the future. Everything seems so difficult and I have no confidence whatever in me and my strengths. But when I talked with a friend about that she found the answer: I expect too much from life. I think that is true, yet this knowledge is not helpful. For one, I would like to become famous, and it is almost an impossible thought that I might get submerged in the mass of people. But I don't know at all how I could become famous since I have no particular talents. Then I want to travel a lot, but have no money. and I don't want to marry a rich man.*

But I do have a special plan that Ms. Kronheim offered me. I shall have learned something, whatever, and then I can travel from city to city, start modestly everywhere, if only as a worker in a factory (factories attract me in general to see and experience the whole story with my own eyes) and when I get tired of that, I can move to another country. But not alone, only with a dear excellent life comrade.

So we decided not to leave. The FOR appear too small against giant AGAINST, at least in Mother's eyes. For: as I already said: novelty, adventurous, perhaps easier life, the somewhat insecure political situation. Against: finances, the same amount of pounds which are sufficient here will be much too small in America. Family: We shall be horribly dependent on the Boykos, precisely because of finances. War: over there they are losing the war for the moment, while meanwhile we are winning it over here. Profession: Mother fears that it will be very difficult. She looks forward to

a leftist Europe, me too, even if I imagine it differently. Briefly, we stay.
WE STAY.

A big decision, may we never regret it! I am sorry that I shall not see America, but I hope for a later time. Mother has made the decision and I am of her opinion. Hers is not without some regrets, my regrets are a somewhat greater, but that's already all. Now it means getting to work diligently, to pre- pare for the bac.

December 28, 1941

Thus, we are staying here. Well, so I thought an hour ago. Meanwhile a telegram from Father has arrived. I accused the poor man unfairly. "Still advise travel Amerika. Greetings [sic]." He could not decide, God forbid, to send kisses or love. With the word "greetings" I always see his grinning face, just as he said "kiss the hand" [instead of the German küss] because it is less intimate, he once explained to me. Mother said: " Donc (thus) he will send us money donc (thus) we leave."

LETTER FROM FATHER IN ENGLAND TO MOTHER IN AMERICA
ONE YEAR LATER (ENGLISH LETTER)

7.2.1943 (February 7, 1943)

Dear Esti,

You wrote to my brother Ernst concerning alimentation and I see from your letter that you have no idea what the situation really is. Therefore I have to explain.

1) There is no legal possibility of transfer.

2) Even if such a possibility were given I could not use it as I have no money to transfer; I have not inherited anything so far and I shall not as long as my mother lives. I could save my own money (it was never very much), but I spent from this small capital now for nearly four years and very little is left on my account. That what is left belongs to Sophie and to the Princess. I do not think I spent a big proportion of this money for myself, it went to Walter's studies and your and Sophie's support. I do not blame you for that, you were not in a position to earn your living and it was the only thing to be done.

For myself I always tried to live on my income. My income is now £3.18 a week with some meals and clothing provided and I feel that I am doing quite well on it. There is of course a real war on here and I could not spend much, even if I wished to do so. But the differences in prices and the rate of exchange makes it absolutely impossible for someone with a worker income in England to support dependants in the States.

3) In case my inheritance materialized I would still not be willing to spend it in a year or two by sending money to America. I would try not to touch it before the war is over and to try to build a new existence for the family. Otherwise there would be no hope left that the temporary poverty developed into a perpetual one.

I could of course find no work as a barrister, banker or publisher and as I wanted to earn my living I had to take over everything that was available. It was mostly very hard and very dirty work, carrying heavy burdens, cleaning, sweeping and mixing with people of a quite different class. I even worked in a mortuary; At present I like my work—in a surgical theatre—because it is really interesting, but I do not know how long it will last and the next job might be worse again. Even if I could find occasionally better paid work and could afford to send you £1 a week—it will never be more, as income tax is very high—as a help for you and Sophie 4 dollars will be absolutely ridiculous. There is only one solution, find work and support yourself till things are normal again.

I really do not know what else I could do. It does not sound encouraging, but these are the facts. Let us hope the whole misery will be over soon. I trust that Sophie is the right person to fight her way out and you have to do the same and not to rely on persons who for the moment are not able to help you. Forgive me if this letter sounds unfriendly.

Best regards

SOPHIE'S DIARY

January 2, 1942

I fought all evening to stay, even shed tears, painted a picture for Mother, how, after having drowned while she was saved, during the crossing, I shall appear to her as a water-ghost. In brief, all my arty tricks. And she really does not want to leave either. But on the other hand, it would be so unpleasant to cancel the HICEM by telephone, I can see that very well, and also inform the Boykos who made such an effort to help us. Nevertheless, we should rather stay here. Sometimes there appears something like a light in me and I see it clear as the sun: YOU HAVE TO STAY HERE, or, YOU MUST NOT LEAVE. Mother thinks only of herself and her profession. She does not waste any thoughts on my modest future. But the big hitch is, if not now, then never and for that reason we shall, after all, push off via Casablanca, Cuba. It is so absurd, we shall be hostile strangers, not a soul will accept me in a school, certainly not for free, one will be suspect and perhaps only due to the good name not outright imprisoned. It is disgusting, I stay.

January 4, 1942

Tomorrow we leave. First to Marseille with the evening train. Then, Thursday to Oran where we shall take the train to Casablanca and between the 15th and 17th from Casa to America, via Cuba. I look forward tremendously to the voyage. All my love of adventures can finally express itself. Good ship, bad ship, I don't care a bit. An outbreak of an epidemic would be unpleasant and so would capsizing, but I am not afraid of dying, honest. I have finished packing my suitcase which was properly stressful, due to the lack of space.

Yesterday I went to sleep at 4:30 A.M. and got up at 8:00 A.M. I am totally confused and exhausted. I shall wait to write about my books once on the ship. I would really enjoy with all my heart to flirt a little.

I bought myself a camera from Uncle Oli and am frightfully pleased with it. Unfortunately the weather is persistently cloudy and besides people are prophesying a huge storm, or confiscation of the camera. I feel a great impetus to take photos right and left and I can feel the beginning of a great expensive passion. I will especially have opportunities during my trip. Although supposedly taking photos is forbidden in Morocco. I think via Casa the voyage is even more interesting than via Lisbon.

Tomorrow morning I go to school to take leave. I look forward to that because I can make myself horribly important. But it would be embarrassing if we had to come back given that we have packed for days and definitely. And it is always unpleasant to return after good-byes.

I sit on my packed suitcase and cry. The voyage continues, France, I have to leave you. One tears me away. It is night time. I still have to write some letters of farewell. That is the most bitter part, taking leave.

January 11, 1942. Two days on the boat

On the last day I went everywhere in Nice to bid them good-bye and everyone was terribly nice to me. At school I took leave of Mademoiselle Crisostonia the math one, and Madame Krebs, the German one. To the German one I then said merci beaucoup *for all and everything, out of proper politeness, but she took it seriously and said, no, no, she had actually only done her duty (I never claimed the opposite) and that she had taken me especially into her heart (I had never noticed that) because she could understand my difficult situation so well, etc. etc. Then she also administered the famous French kiss next to both cheeks. Then I said good-bye to [four friends] and a few others. Not to the whole class, I had come too late during the break, and there was unfortunately not as much commotion as I had hoped. But enough to attract a supervisor's attention who asked me, as I stood there, to pay the new school tuition. But I protested most vigorously. Then I still looked up the Rosenbaum, my English teacher who was always exceptionally kind. She had overestimated me to some extent, who knows why, perhaps because I had written nice essays for her, and so she said she had been glad to get to know me, and tried to convey to me the whole time how intelligent I was and wished me much luck, that I should find my way because it would be such a pity if I didn't and it all came from her heart.*

CHAPTER 34

Mademoiselle Kronheim

Afin que quelque-unes de nous puissent survivre and raconter plus tard a un monde (So that some of us can survive and later tell the world)

*M*other does not mention Mlle. Kronheim in her biography. Yet, it was one of the few times when we shared an important friend. And, surprisingly, Mother did not quarrel with this particular friend and neither did I live in my former childhood fear that she would do so and it would spoil my relationship with this person. Actually, her relationship to Lotte Kronheim was warmer and more genuine than any other of her former friendships I had ever observed.

Mademoiselle Kronheim lived in the same Hotel Windsor as we did. Each of us occupied one room and we often visited each other. In my usual eagerness to recruit the interest of adult mother-figures—even at a time when Mother and I experienced considerable closeness—I reached out for her friendship and she responded in her measured, kind, semidistant way. We maintained the formal French VOUS and I never called her by her first name. She was then 40 years old, just a little younger than my mother and an academician from Danzig. Yet, in spite of our many talks, I do not remember her field of study, nor by what detours she happened to live in Nice, at the Hotel Windsor. I record our growing relationship in my diary.

Sophie's Diary

August 5, 1941

Tomorrow is my birthday, I already look forward to it. . . . Mrs. Kronheim, who is altogether terribly kind and intelligent, she also loaned me Lotte in Weimar *and evenings she comes to Mother's room to discuss politics, and then I stay there as well—she has given me* Les tentations de Lafontaine *von Girodoux (*The Temptations of LaFontaine*) That was terribly nice of her.*

September 19, 1941
—Miss Kronheim comes now to mother's room every evening and then I also stay there a long time and we gossip, and she tells stories and we discuss politics. She understands things much better than my mother and I learn a little from her, although not much. I am very drawn to her because she is so intelligent.

November 28, 1941
La guerre de Troie n'aura pas lieu (The Trojan war will not take place) by Girodoux is not deep enough for me, regardless of what Miss Kronheim may say. She praised the book up to the sky and allowed herself comments against my beloved Dostojewsky. Even if she is very nice and clever, still we don't share the same tastes. Besides she is quite cold and contemptuous of all ideas and basically, or not even basically, a convinced capitalist. But regardless, I am still very fond of her and when she visits Mother in the evening I like to stay there to listen to her.

New Year's Eve, 1941
. . . Communism or middle class society?
Sometimes I think, why get so upset, one dies one day and then nothing matters, whether one becomes famous or not, and in general. In a way I would like to avoid such thoughts and I keep them only for the dark depressed days. I torment myself very much these days with all these thoughts. I think my main worry is to make myself useful one day. We recently talked with Miss Kronheim about the future fate of Europe and I said, or expressed approximately that I wanted to return to Vienna if there will be, there, a communist regime. And why forever not ? I don't see why not. And she said quite sneeringly that they have been waiting there for me. That's true, but nowhere in the world are they waiting for me, and the least in America.
We consulted Miss Kronheim about emigrating to America, and she said, among other things, that if one is a convinced Communist, matters are quite simple. We stay here because Russia wins and we will change Europe and make a paradise on earth. Mother then responded that she was not a Communist, she did not believe in any doctrines because she had too much knowledge of people and rejects all doctrines and so on in general. Her words cut deep into my heart and I remained silent.

I have managed, over the many years, not to lose the four letters that I received from Miss Kronheim. But even without these letters I would never have forgotten her. Her disappearance has haunted me all my life. Now I am using—at the last *moment—the occasion of writing this book to carry out her request to tell the world about those dark days, and to mourn her death.*

During my stay in Nice I once made a two weeks' trip to my friends, the Hausers, who had managed, temporarily, to settle in the country. We had somehow found each other and they had invited me for a stay, spoiling me with milk and cheese and even eggs (!). I wrote Miss Kronheim a letter and she responded. Our whole correspondence was conducted in French.

Nice, August 27, 1941

Dear Mademoiselle,

Thank you infinitely for your kind letter and since your mother expects you back already next week I must hurry to respond in time. Don't think that I am usually so constrained—although my laziness is considerable—but after all, I have to make an effort and who likes that? Certainly not I. Your mother is as well as possible given the circumstances and that she misses you greatly, that's a given. I do my best to comfort her, for example, I have converted her to the *Weltwoche* [*an international newspaper from Switzerland*] and like all converts to a new religion, she practices it with zeal and enthusiasm. Besides we discuss from time to time the events, in fierce competition with the French totally nasty dirty tricks. Too bad that neither Churchill nor Roosevelt are apt to follow our advice.

As to myself, more or less humble and modest, I continue to do nothing, and frankly, that pleases me a great deal. Having worked all my life with a zeal that might have been devoted to worthier pursuits, I prefer an attitude of an interested but impartial spectator, of a spectator at the theater to that of an actor on the scene. It all means I work by taking things in, and if you were mean—which I am totally certain and sure you are not—you could think of "the fox with his sour grapes." Briefly, one waits (for visas and other things), one watches, one listens, one reads and one makes fun of everything. To strengthen myself I read the letters and anecdotes of Frederic the Great (which can be compared to those of the best French moral philosophers) and something specific to my field, an American proposal to establish a federation of the major democracies, written by a chief editor of the *New York Times*.

I hope you will be more reasonable and undertake even less than I. Vacations are good things and I would like to have some. On the other hand perpetual vacations are difficult to organize and I think I have almost succeeded in doing so but don't ask me at what price. Sometimes I am sick of it all. As to the political situation, let us not speak of it, mostly not in writing. Nice has not changed, the weather is rather bad, but that gives us pleasure when we draw conclusions about the weather in Russia.

So, I'll see you soon, I hope.

With my best greetings, etc. etc.

Your Lotte Kronheim

Farewell from Nice. We are leaving for America.

SOPHIE'S DIARY

January 11, 1942

The parting from Kronheim went very quickly. She came only at the last moment out of her room, said *adieu* and disappeared immediately. She probably dislikes such sentimental scenes or she herself felt wistful in her heart.

I surely underestimated how sad it had been for Lotte Kronheim to lose her relationship to us.

Our journey to America got delayed, and we had to wait in Casablanca for new visas. I wrote her regularly from Casablanca and here are her three responses, again all of them in French.

FIRST LETTER

Nice, April 8, 1942

Dear mademoiselle,

I was enchanted with your three letters and by the fact that you were not offended by my silence. It seems that you have a good life over there, even in spite of the blows from which we are also not protected. Keep writing to me and don't count on an answer, it is not out of indifference or laziness, that I don't write, it is rather my aversion to write more or less personal things in these kinds of times. I always show your letters to Ruth R., and she likes both them and you a lot. Give your grandmother's enclosed card to your mother, maybe she will find over there something edible to send her; here we have only greeneries. [*My Grandmother Drucker was stuck in Biarritz, from where she was sent to a nearby French camp and later released to live in Biarritz, before her final deportation.*]

You are totally right to recommend work, it is always the best pass-time, I think, better than to get drunk, but approximately at the same level. I liked your photo a great deal, but one of your Mr. Roger would give me equal pleasure, since I am curious to get to know your taste when it comes to men.

Here one is starting to assign more or less forced residences to persons who have come to France after 1936. One sends them to little villages in our *département* (State or region) which are sometimes good places with plenty of food, but at other times unable to lodge and feed no matter whom, and no matter how many; so one sends them back to Nice. In short, an unwanted change of air and formidable chaos.

But that might and will happen to all of us and naturally, it is not all that serious, especially for those who live in the hotel. In our hotel there are big changes....

You ask me what I do: I read, many of them English books, *Northwest Passage* by Kenneth Robert, very beautiful, a Bromfield: *The Farm* which I had not read and which is very interesting (development of the United States before the war of 1914, from the social point of view), and once again, *Zauberberg* (Magic Mountain).

As to the United States, let's not talk about it any more. But I do hope nevertheless, that you will go there. In the letters from over there one only reads about big receptions, silk dresses and weekend parties.

So, don't stop writing to me and you will always give me much pleasure.

Remember me warmly to your mother.

In much friendship, your Lotte Kronheim.

SECOND LETTER

Nice, June 1, 1942

Dear Sophie,

I am awfully glad with your letter and the beautiful photo; I find the young man very attractive, not bad at all. If he does not have many political ideas, all the better, you have enough of them, and nothing in the world is so tedious, not to say unproductive than being of the same opinion as one's partner. *Man hängt sich schon genügend selber zum Hals heraus* [sic] (one is sick enough of oneself), don't you think *und der sogenannte Gleichklang der Seelen führt zu einen Riesengähnen. Voraussetzung ist natürlich dass Verständigungsmöglichkeiten au fond vorhanden sind, aber wo sind die mühlos vorhanden?* [sic] (and the so-called harmony of souls leads to a giant yawn. The premise is, of course, that possibilities of basic understanding are present, but where is that the case without much effort?)

... Greet you mother from me and tell her a.) that the little Rosenbaum [Mother's patient] now speaks very well, but the whole family cries for your mother to correct her other speech defects b.) that her brother-in-law's store (your uncle) [Oliver Freud's photography store] was Aryanized [an administrative agent was installed who has apportioned the payment for the whole family at 1,500 francs per month, which is no joke, for three people].

As to us, nothing new, my brother was here on leave for 10 days, he is well, looks healthier than any of us. He is not at all dissatisfied with his work and he is asking to be used as agricultural worker in the village where he is currently located. If we cannot find any more or less favorable solutions for our financial questions we shall also retire to the countryside. But there is no hurry. As to the United States, let's not talk about it any longer. I think we could arrange a meeting in Paris rather than in New York. My friend from over there has written me that a governmental hearing will soon decide on our fate and that he will go to Washington, if the results are negative, to plead our case. So we shall see. But I think all that has only historical interest.

I read a lot, mostly English and American books, Bromfield, Cronin etc. and I see lots of people. The most serious folks (and not the emigrants who always confuse their wishes with reality) don't see an ending (naturally a happy ending) of the war before another 15 months.

I am glad that your grandmother is no longer in a camp. I had sent her two packages with little cakes, the first did not arrive (God knows who has eaten them, but they got eaten, no doubt about that) and the other is on the way. The food shortage has becomes easier thanks to cherries and strawberries that one finds in abundance. Tell your mother that my rooster-cabbage [no doubt a plant] has developed the most satisfying qualities, hers, in contrast, is increasingly shrinking and losing its color. No doubt that it misses her. The only things that we really miss is bread and potatoes. But we also miss spiritual bread and potatoes, because the *Weltwoche* has lost all interest and other newspapers are no better.

That is why I have taken a subscription to the *New Zür-Newspaper* [Zürich] we shall see. To compensate—you can buy all the German newspapers.

Well, surely you will excuse this (meaningless?) letter, the true, important and serious things do not get written at this moment. Forgive the handwriting, but I am writing in a coffee house.

I hope we shall see each other again, one day, and don't stop writing, it always gives me great pleasure.

With heartfelt greetings for your mother and you,

Your Lotte Kronheim

LAST LETTER

September 9, 1942

Dear Mademoiselle,

Your letter from the fourth certainly deserves a different answer. If I write you only a few words, you will understand the reason. I hope you will succeed to leave very soon so that some of us all can survive and tell to a world, let us hope a more normal world, what progress, what peak of progress had been attained in 1942. Let me know if and when you leave.

As to the new measures, unfortunately a good and big part of it all is true. It seems that there are about 7 to 8,000 persons that one has arrested here and sent God knows where, probably to Germany, to one of the occupied countries or to Occupied France. I am not telling you anything about the circumstances etc.

My brother had the same fate, he was called back from his service-job at Begiers and 16 days ago, he had to leave—with 1,200 men—direction East. Since that day I am without news from him and you can imagine our anxiety and our desolation.

Many of those one looks for, hide with friends, it seems that one aims at the moment for those less than 60 years old, who had arrived in France after 1936. But since many people hide, one also takes others and each time someone knocks at the door or one hears unknown steps, you think: that's it. In short, life is beautiful and each day could bring a radical change in one's residence.

My mother and aunt are spared, at the moment, because of their age, but the others, including French people—

As to myself, I am not hiding, I find that below my dignity. Besides, it is useless, there are already large holes among our common acquaintances.

So, if you arrive over there, explain to Miss Ko. the situation (her current address is 28 West 63 Street) and tell her to do the possible and the impossible to accelerate the proceedings. She had written to me that our hearing had taken place in the month of July or August. Because an American visa—even if one cannot make use of it, missing an exit visa—is the one and only effective protection that exists at the moment. Please inform also our attorney of the situation: Kurt Rosenberg c/o Weil, Gotshal and Manges, 60 East 42 Street, New York—that he should hurry. He is in charge of getting the visa and who went to Washington to plead our case at the hearing. I have written myself to these two persons, but who knows whether my letters arrive. Tell them about my brother, for him it will be too late! Our common friends Ruth and her whole family (her old mother included) are in great danger. I don't know where they are, and I hope nobody knows it.

You can imagine our despair, and the hazardous and unrealistic projects that one constructs to save oneself, too late, I believe. As to myself, I am quite fatalistic (not that I am not afraid) and my brother has written these precise words in his good-bye letter (I wish you, Mademoiselle, with all my heart, never to receive good-bye letters of the kind that we get every day!): There is no reason that our life should be less troubled than the lives of all the others.

Good luck to you and to your mother! LK

FROM: THE DEPORTATION OF GERMAN AND AUSTRIAN JEWS FROM FRANCE. BARBARA VORMEIER (*DIE DEPORTIERUNGEN DEUTSCHER UND ÖSTERREICHISCHER JUDEN AUS FRANKREICH. BARBARA VORMEIER*)

Starting September 8 1943, the Gestapo started to transfer the Jews from La Region Préfectorale de Nice to the Camp de Drancy, a transit camp outside of Paris. Charlotte Kronheim born April 4, 1902, in Danzig and living at the Hotel Windsor in Nice was among the list of people transported sometime after September 8, 1943, to *le camp de Drancy*.

FROM: MEMORIAL TO THE JEWS DEPORTED FROM FRANCE. 1942–1944. SERGE KLARSFELD.

On January 20, 1944, Convoy 66 was a transport from Camp de Drancy to Auschwitz. It included Charlotte Kronheim. "When they arrived in Auschwitz, 236 men were left alive and given numbers 172611 through 172846. Fifty-five women were assigned numbers 74783 through 74797 and 74835 through 74874. The rest of the convoy was immediately gassed. In 1945, there were 72 survivors. Thirty were women. But the name of Kronheim could not be found among the survivors.

Had she been among the survivors, we would have heard from her right away.

CHAPTER 35

From Marseille to Casablanca

We spent a night in a horrid hotel in Marseille and were eventually told by the Joint where to embark. The customs agent selected me for a body search. For this purpose we went to a stateroom where a woman customs employee searched me. It was strictly forbidden by French law to export any foreign currency. I had sewn a five-dollar bill into the seam of my shirt. The bill crackled and the woman found it. My heart stood still. All I could do was say, "keep it." We were permitted to continue the trip. During the night one of the terrible storms the Mediterranean was notorious for, arose. I am a good sailor and slipped out of my stateroom to go outside. To my astonishment a sailor with a drawn gun stood at the exit of the staircase. He told me that if panic broke out among the passengers he was under order to shoot. We arrived without further incident in the port and were taken to a refugee camp outside Casablanca.

SOPHIE'S DIARY

January 11, 1942 (continued)

Now I am already two days on the ship. And my fameux *journal du* bord? *(famous ship's diary?) Haha; until now I was constantly nauseous and should I accidentally feel five minutes in a normal state it is a true miracle that will not last long since writing will make me nauseous again. The sea is at the moment quite calm, which is why I can sit on the deck, at other times I lie groaning and squirming on the cabin bed. Seasickness is a terrible sickness, one wants to die, to jump into the ocean, everything to avoid the terrible nausea. Yesterday evening I vomited the entire lunch and for dinner I ate a pear and vomited it as well; this morning I went for breakfast, upstairs into*

Sophie on ship from Marseilles to Casablanca

the dining hall. Before I started I had to run back to the cabin to vomit again, but there was nothing left, only spittle. At least with this regimen I won't need to worry to arrive overweight in America.

Yesterday and this morning I lay the whole time with closed eyes in the cabin. That was not very amusing. But on deck it is also not amusing. I had hoped that some guy, a nice one, will address me, but I always remain alone. I am very disappointed. After all, I wanted to flirt and instead I am

Esti on ship to Casablanca

nauseous the whole time, and when I am not nauseous, nobody looks at me. Mother knows already all the nice men of the whole ship; I don't know how she does it.

January 12, 1942

I am writing on the deck in a deckchair. I feel no longer nauseous, it shakes much less and I have recovered again, a bit. A rather nasty guy courted me today. But let us return to Marseille.

We had a medium pleasant journey from Nice to Marseille, sort of as always, and in Marseille we found no room at first because the telegram had not arrived, which is by the way, pure sloppiness because I am sure to have sent it. First we telephoned all the hotels in Marseille, then Mother ran around for a search, it rained, and at 2:00 A.M.—we had arrived at midnight—we could lie down in a pretty room, after we had already counted on spending the night on a bench.

The next day in the morning the hunting around started and never finished for an instant. But actually only the first day was awful, otherwise it was quite amusing. In the morning a Jew came to fetch me, pretending to be a baggage *carrier but actually hiring one himself, to accompany me to the station—which I did not need—to make himself unpleasantly noticeable and made me pay 30 francs. Briefly, a conman. But on the way he talked all the time of vengeance. Of a 2,000-year-old people, of God with his justice, of being the chosen ones, etc. Briefly, a Jewish nationalist, besides that a conman and an ideal one to spread anti-Semitism.*

The afternoon was then quite terrible, almost as bad as the railway station in Paris. We had to get our passports from the police. There we waited for two hours sitting, two hours standing, in the worst crowding (while I also wrote letters) with all the other almost invariably shabby desperate Jews. The atmosphere was terrible and once again it broke my heart to think that we are such a seedy race, meaning most of us. What can one only do about this!!??

January 13, 1942

At the Messagerie Maritime *in Marseille we heard that the ship was only to part on the 11th. We worried that we might miss the* Serpapinto *[in Casablanca] but were otherwise quite pleased to be able to shop at leisure. We had planned to set aside the next day, in easy relaxation but luckily I still quickly bought myself a magnificent umbrella, the most beautiful, last, most expensive in all Marseille and a pair of leather gloves and a pair of wool gloves and Mother a magnificent scarf—I wanted to buy a similar one the next day—if only I had hurried more! The next day we went to the* Messagerie Maritime *because a rumor floated that one could get better ship tickets—we were to sail on the* Eridan. *That was true, but only on the* Providence *ship—on which we now find ourselves—that was to leave still the same afternoon at 2:00 P.M. and now the chase really began! Indescribable. Because everyone advised us to take the* Providence *since the* Eridan *probably would leave only with further delays and so we took it, paid the extra fare for second class. I raced to the hotel, packed the suitcases, accompanied the porter to the harbor. And in all this rush I lost the key to a suitcase, so that one had to blast it open—I had really lost my marbles—since the lock is now totally ruined and a new one will cost masses of money.*

At the harbor, at the customs, one had to queue up hours and hours in a sea of people and besides the air was so toxic that I had to cough up half of my lung. But after two-and-a-half hours a porter showed me a trick where one could get ahead of the line for 50 francs. But now the most exciting is coming. A woman customs officer looked very superficially through a suitcase—I already breathed a sigh of relief—when she talked about a bodily search. Mother flushed completely and I knew, çà y est, cela ira mal (that's it, it will go badly). We crawl into a cabin, she looks at the fur coat first— nothing. Then the jacket—Mother blushes more and more—something rustles—Mother tears the jacket open—gold? No, we had none, only led. She searches further, something rustles—dollars, two five-dollar pieces. First she wanted to denounce us, but after much persuasion she took one fiver, innerly beaming, an easily earned 500 francs and she was only a little concerned about troubles. But Mother was quite right, otherwise one would perhaps have examined us from head to foot, maybe imprisoned us, and God knows what unpleasantnesses. So things proceeded quickly and painlessly and one got away with a black eye and 500 francs less. She also fingered me. But it all happened only because Mother had only a scant quarter of an hour to hide things and she carried most her money in her purse, as I did with my pounds from Grandfather which nobody looked at.

January 15, 1942

Yesterday we left Oran, three days before we were in Algier. I had so looked forward to Africa and the new totally different cities. They comforted me for the loss of Spain. And then we stopped and all the immigrants to America, 85 of them are on board, were not allowed to go on land. That was bitter. All the other people joyfully walked down the planks—we spent one-and-a-half days in Oran and three hours in Algier. I stood on the deck and watched them sadly and malevolently. Ordre de la Préfecture. It is really such a filthy shame, it cries to heaven, unjustified, mean, sadistic, torturesome. I was so enraged, would have so much liked to look at Algiers, after all, we shall not return here very soon. And one has to stand there and ghost around on the ship and look for suitable corners from which to take photos and meanwhile one could climb about in Algiers. I took a few photos but they are surely all spoiled. Algier looked very beautiful from the distance, full of white four-cornered houses and palm trees and all that. Remains only Casablanca and I wanted to buy a briefcase and a pair of slippers in Casa but probably that will not work out either. Since we are in any case treated like prisoners, they will probably not even let us get out in Casa but they will lead us under police guard to the other boat—from the Providence *to the* Serpapinto.

Or, if not, we shall probably not have any time in Casa to look around to any extent. Because today is already the 15th day on which the Serpa was originally scheduled to leave Portugal and we have as yet not even passed Gibraltar, will only get there about tomorrow evening. Hopefully the Portuguese [the Serpapinto] *will get there before the 24th, the expiration day of our visas—otherwise there will be 1,000 difficulties.*

At the moment we pass paisiblement *(peacefully) along the coast of Africa where one sees quite close the naked mountains which please me greatly with their secrecy and blackness. We sail so peacefully because since Oran we are in a convoy which means several smaller ships are cruising next to us because we shall sail all together through Gibraltar. And a warship also accompanies us, pro forma. And since the small boats cannot go fast, we also are cruising slowly. At least it does not shake and since the sea is calm and we sail close to the coast I am in excellent health. Besides, perhaps I may have gotten used to ship travel and I experience again new hope that I might return to Europe as a stewardess on a ship.*

January 16, 1942

The day before yesterday French war airplanes exercised above us. They flew very low, just high enough not to touch the ship and made a deafening noise. It was quite exciting, we quickly ran to the highest deck. The next day an English airplane circled above us, which, according to the captain, was favorably disposed toward us.

The Rabbi of Bacherach of Heine is unfortunately only a fragment but very inspiring and even uncanny—Heine has remained after all a Jew in his heart; he was an unbeliever but the Jewish tradition and history attracted him. His heart probably looked similar to mine.

CHAPTER 36

The Delay of the *Serpapinto*

We arrived without further incident in the port and were taken to a refugee camp outside Casablanca. We were not allowed to go into the city. I have completely forgotten how we were fed. There was a big hall with mattresses spread on the floor where we were supposed to sleep. Sleeping was impossible with children crying all night long, people quarreling, and mosquitoes singing and stinging. In this situation it helped to have the name of Freud. The representative of the Joint in Casablanca and a Viennese Jew, was a neighbor of the Schrameks, my grandfather's family in the Novaragasse. He found me a private room where we were permitted to wash.

SOPHIE'S DIARY

January 23, 1942

So, 24 hours after Oran we arrived in Casablanca. The next morning we were disembarked—I had crazily looked forward to that moment. After hours of going through customs we all got loaded into buses ... and then I understood, no freedom for us. We were sent 8 km from Casa, to Beaulieu or Ain Sebaa. The first ride through Casa was very impressive. I opened up mouth and eyes. Palmtrees, veiled women, ragged men with hostile looks were passing by. White houses, cheerful, colorful nature.

January 24, 1942

Today our visas are expiring.

Finally we get there, 8 km from Casablanca. We stopped in front of a big glass pavilion located in a friendly garden. It was a sort of greenhouse. The floor was covered with strawsacks, one next to the other, without intervals and that was our flat, bed–dining–living room. I found it all hugely

259

enjoyable. All my life I had wanted to try out sleeping on strawsacks. For washing there were three or four washstands, in the middle of the garden, where everyone could watch. The toilet was unthinkable. That was actually unpleasant. They had made no preparations for our food and like hungry rats we stormed into the neighborhood restaurant and to the market. The restaurant fed us for two days as a big favor but then the manager threw us out and we ate "at home" which was also possible. The HICEM distributed bowls and then Arabs with carriages came to distribute the food and one queued up for it. It was always some thick stuff like beans or mashed peas. At the beginning I quite liked it but now I can hardly swallow it down.

The first night was a catastrophe. At least we were warm enough with our blankets, but most people had only their coats because the HICEM only distributed blankets on the second day. Eighty people in one hall are too many people. There was no question of changing for the night. With much effort I slipped off my skirt and blouse. The light stayed on all night, in case anyone needed to go out, which happened frequently. We were all stirred up and the whispering only stopped around 2 h. Then one has to count the people who snore like mad and cough and the little baby who screamed all night, and the hard strawsacks on which one could not turn around without waking Mother because they were so narrow. In sum, I did not close an eye all night. The most complicated thing was washing in the morning. We also went on a search for toilets. Finally we walked into a strange Arab villa and asked permission to use their toilet. The people were very friendly.

But in the morning, once one was finally dressed, it was great fun. I flirted with a Dutchman who had been born in Cracow and in the evening, before going to sleep, with a very friendly Hungarian. Also with a boy from Vienna and the evening was really totally enjoyable, with three men standing admiringly around me. But I was really only taken with the Hungarian. He was a member of an organized Zionist party and told extremely interesting things about Palestine and in general. I really enjoyed talking with him and I think I have fallen in love. But he looked at me as a little girl, he was indeed much older and he thought me very brave. In addition there was a Polish boy who wanted to flirt with me. Once we walked with the Dutchman to the sea. The scenery resembles the environs of Nice, but more southern and more lush. The gardens are all beautifully tended. Next to a most elegant villa we saw a tiny house built out of trash, with little pieces of iron and cardboard and such things. The sea was magnificent and if I had had a bathing suit and a big towel I would have gone swimming, the sea being warm with huge breakers.

We also went to inspect the other camp next to the sea. People had cab-ins there to change, and a very big hall and a big sunny porch and the beach in front of their noses. But I would not have changed because I had gotten to know our people. I think we were with especially nice people, almost no quarrels broke out (except here and there, for strawsacks) and the atmosphere was polite and friendly. The ship had been expected on January 23. Which was lucky because our visas expired the 24th. But I was not anx-ious because I assumed that one could fix such things through the HICEM. There were also a few French people among us. They carried on in a special way because they supposed themselves better than others.

The second night in our mousehole was much more pleasant, almost ideal. Because most people had gone on a feverish search for rooms and a few successfully so. Naturally they were incredibly exploited, 100 francs a day for a totally empty room with a washbasin. They even had to take along their strawsacks. Two hundred francs for a room with a bed. In Marseille we had paid 38 francs for a room with two beds. It is a truly disgusting how the misery of others is always exploited. That was also true during our flight from Paris, when they asked 20 francs for an omelet.

Finally we had permission to visit Casablanca. I had been terrified that we would not get it. So I traveled on the roof of a bus to Casa. We strolled around in the Arab quarter. One can hardly imagine such poverty. People are covered with a few rags, they lie about somewhere on the street, they seem to have no notion of cleanliness. Perhaps they feel comfortable in their misery. Quite diverse folks walk about—the women are usually covered up to their eyes with a white sheet. Those who are not covered are native Jewish women. One can recognize the Jews by the black caps that they wear but also by their intelli-gent and more finely chiseled faces. There are many Jews, they are as dirty as the others but they often wear black clothes. Many are blind.

In the Arab quarters there is a swarming and milling of crowds and noise but the stores are nothing special. Casablanca itself is not very un-usual. Big, white, bare houses and many broad streets. When the sun hides, everything looks dusty and wretched, but the sun embellishes everything. Everywhere one sells salted almonds. The most beautiful Arab stores are on the Boulevard de Zouaves. There they have magnificent rugs, blankets, slip-pers, pocketbooks, plates, big cups, and if one could spend three or four thousand francs, one could buy wonderful things.

January 25, 1942

And now I come to my bad luck story. A couple of days ago, in the morn-ing the news suddenly arrived that the Serpapinto will only get here on

Street children in rags in Casablanca

the 25th. Mother got instantly terribly excited, but not me, I did not believe that one would simply leave us here. Then Spaniel appeared, the highest chief of the whole French HICEM, a Russian Jew, big, fat, broad, with a mustache and totally repulsive. Mother started to bawl most awfully, he screamed at her like a wildman, he would fix things and to keep the matter silent, and since he screamed so loudly, we gained confidence. This Spaniel

Women in Casablanca

is altogether a disgusting screamer, as arrogant as one can possibly be, just barely that he does not spit down at you. He is full of himself, Mr. big shot. Perhaps he thinks he is dear God himself but we sure are by far as noble as he is. Everyone hates him because he has offended everyone in some way and in actuality he takes care of nobody, as it turned out for us. He too will end up with a bullet in his stomach, as did the HICEM man in Marseille, and he will have fully deserved it.

When we return from Casa in the evening the Commissaire announces we get moved into another building, into the Maternelle. *That was definitely a sharpening of punishment, given that we knew all the people upstairs. But Mother thought it had mysterious reasons and agreed. (She thought they wanted to embark us ahead of other people.) The Maternelle had the reputation of a prison by us upstairs and I started to cry, not so much, I must admit, because of the prison, but because of the Hungarian. But nothing could be done, we slept badly, but in the evening I still flirted with the Hungarian. Mother thought he was courting her, but I think he courted me, and I am almost sure of that. The move was really unnecessary, they did it, E. explained, because it was a much better place, and they wanted to improve our lives in some ways. Even though we both would have much preferred to stay upstairs. But it is not such a bad deal because I have found friends here as well, even if they are less interesting, because they are much younger. I can already predict I shall marry a much older man because they interest me much more.*

In sum, a bus arrived to pick up all those who preferred the Maternelle, like old women and mothers with tiny babies. The first impression of the Maternelle was horrible. We arrived about 11:00 A.M. and still saw all the parents sitting there waiting, downstairs, with their sick children. Because this is a hospital for young sick Jewish children. There is unimaginable poverty, only rags and the children's worst sickness is usually hunger.

So we had to wait downstairs for a few hours and meanwhile they told us that we could not be helped. I spent the entire day in tears. At 1:00 P.M. we could go upstairs and they served us a bit of cold inedible food. Behind the door stood two policemen, an Arab and a Frenchman who did not let you exit without permission, a regular prison. What an atmosphere, that first day, with all the strange people, the dark house, the heavy heart. In sum, I had to cry all day, apart from having to think about the Hungarian all the time. The day before we had seen the American consul, an icy Russian Jewish woman to whom we were as indifferent as mere flies. Cold and determined she explained to us that we should have gone on board on the 24th if the ship had arrived in time (we knew that it has only started its trip on the 24th). Now we should telegraph the State Department in Washington and first return to Nice to ask for an extension of our visas. There is a new law since the war that one was not allowed to extend the visas of all enemy aliens. And America was a democratic country that did not make exceptions, even for the name of Freud. (That was certainly exceptionally comforting.) And that we could also wait in Nice for the new permission and then return.

(Once in Nice I shall never undertake all these nightmares!) All that, because of 24 hours! And Cook transported all his clients in locked-up trains all through Spain.

We are really exceptionally unlucky! But I think the indifference of the HICEM and the consulate are much to blame. The HICEM which had rented the entire Serpapinto *surely could have gotten us on board with a bit of good will. I am enraged at Spaniel. And now we sit here, in Casablanca and wait for permission from Washington and meanwhile all the ships are departing. Everyone says we shall probably get into a camp since we do not have permission to stay in Morocco. A sad situation. Until the last moment I hoped for a miracle. The* Serpapinto *left Lisbon on the 24th and arrives on the 25th in the evening in Casablanca, Our Visas expires 24 hours or even fewer, too early. It is a misery.*

Time started to run out. If the boat from the United States did not arrive in four days our visas would expire and we would be stranded in Morocco. The boat did not arrive on time and the captain did not dare to let us embark with our expired visas. Knowing what I do now about the United States, we should have ventured it, since once arrived the immigration people would have let us in, even with expired visas. We had to prepare ourselves for a long stay in Casablanca until our visas renewed. The man from the Joint helped. At least we were a step further away from Hitler; although not too far from Rommel with his army in Africa.

Sᴏᴘʜɪᴇ's Dɪᴀʀʏ
    January 25, 1942
    So this evening the ship will arrive. I am not as unhappy, here in the Maternelle as I had expected at the first moment. Right away, the first evening, as I sat by myself so unhappy and wrote letters to everyone in the world, a boy from Vienna addressed me. He instantly wanted to be on DU terms, what I found a bit suspicious, and the next day he introduced me to all the other "Young People," everyone right away on DU terms and we played poker and in the evening writing games. His name is Harry and it was he who had organized the whole thing very effectively that we all got to know each other so quickly. Otherwise one remains alone, even if one would like to meet others. Harry is a big Communist, but not a Stalinist. He was always active in youth organizations and is generally very active, wants to convert everyone right away to his own opinion. When he noticed that I was also interested in politics and mentioned that he seemed to be a C.

[Communist] he blushed, but was very glad. Since then we discuss things for hours and even though I am much less well informed and educated than he is, I kept up with him. We could not agree on free love. Besides, that is a delicate subject. He is for it, but I am against it, since marriage is above all a protection for women, which they would be quite stupid to fight against. What would we do if men were not kept in line by a few legal restraints. After two years each woman with a child in her arms would be ditched and even if the state were to care for the child and she can work herself, it is not the right thing because her heart stays empty. But before a man dumps his legal wife for good he thinks about it twice and very frequently he returns from his mistress to his own wife. [I hear my mother's voice in all these worldly wisdoms.]

I much prefer another boy, Hans, to Harry. Because Harry is a bit the type of a Vienna lout, does not speak French after three years in France "because it did not interest him," is lazy and uneducated. Hans is politically less decent but he has better manner, has read books (which I wanted to discuss with him, but he could not remember the titles which I find quite neb-bich), is somehow better brought up more cultured. He was with the St. Louis, a ship that was returned from Cuba and whose passengers were divided among England, France, Belgium and Holland. They could express a preference for a country, but eventually they were divided up like cattle.

The fun I would have had on the Serpapinto, now that I know half the ship and would have had five admirers aged from 17 to 40 makes it even much more difficult to be left behind. But it cannot be changed. Maybe, with much luck, we will still catch the Nyassa. But she makes a horrible detour via Cuba, St. Domingo and Mexico. And what is the use of cruising around the whole world if one is never allowed to go on land.

January 28, 1942

The Serpapinto left on the 26th—without us. But now that she is gone, I have calmed down and I have become quite indifferent to what will happen to us. For example I felt hurt not to sail with the Serpapinto because I already had so many comrades there, like the Hungarian, his name is Eisynowitz and Klaus, and Hans and Harry etc. But now I no longer care about any of them, except the Hungarian. The Nyassa comes on the 30th and will leave without us, tant pis *(too bad). Meanwhile we have sent to the whole world, meaning to London and New York, totally desperate telegrams. Father has already telegrammed promising help, Aunt Lily responded that the intervention in Washington was difficult, but she could get us immediately a visa for Cuba. I am not at all happy about this. First, it costs terribly much money and who will pay for that? Father is not all that rich. One saves and saves and then one has to throw away money for such a stupidity. And then: what have we lost in Cuba? I have the feeling that once one is someplace, one never gets away from there. Maybe we will still get an extension of our visas. But I don't think so but just in case Mother will quickly get hold of a Cuban visa.*

The distribution of tickets for the Serpapinto *was terribly funny. Because the ship was overcrowded and there was almost no more room and everyone got a fourth class assignment except two or three people who paid a fortune. And most people were very angry, talking about their arthritic limbs, hearts etc. One person had a temper tantrum, in sum, it was funny. Some people got the choice between fourth class on the Serpapinot and first class on the* Nyassa. *Naturally they all chose the* Serpapinto *because one is only sure of departure after the ships begin to shake. And they were right, because all the HICEM people have to go fourth class on the* Nyassa *as well. I am only glad that one had not paid for us yet. Meanwhile we have to stay on at the Maternelle but with permission to leave almost every day.*

I had caught a mild case of conjunctivitis and Mother got terribly frightened because she thought right away of Trachoma, the illness that has blinded all the Arabs. But I was not scared myself, not sure why not. I did not care, although I did not want to get blind. And on the next day I also came down with a fever and was sick all night, with a cold and lumbago and a sore throat. It is possible that all this comes from my vaccination because I have a strong local reaction. Smallpox must be a fearsome illness if even such a little bit makes one quite ill. But now my eyes are already much better and it seems everyone who comes to Africa gets conjunctivitis. I woke up in the morning and I could hardly open my eyes, they were so glued together with stuff. Above all it would have been unpleasant for emigration because no country would admit me with sick eyes.

One hears and sees all the time so much misery here that I am terribly embarrassed to make much of our bad luck. The worst stories one hears are from the Legionnaires [men, mostly immigrants who had joined the French foreign legion to fight in the war against Germany but who were sent to build the Trans-Saharan Railroad]. They had to work by 70 degrees C [158 degrees F]. Mother knows a Mr. Oswald Singer, a student from her adult education classes in the Leopoldstadt. When he did not want to work on Rosh Hashanah his punishment was to spend eight days in a ditch with water and bread and the Arabs beat him. I think he has become a little crazy from the heat and the suffering he had to endure. I found it very decent how he said the worst was thinking of his comrades who are still stuck there and for whom there is no help. He could only get out through special protection. And there are also all the people here who have failed in some ways, their visa expired, they got sent back, they did not get a visa. Especially many have been sent back from Martinique.

CHAPTER 37

Waiting in Casablanca

The representative of the Joint recommended a halfway decent private room and also spread the word that Freud's granddaughter was a refugee in Casablanca. I had begun to evaluate our situation. There we were, two young women without male protection in a Mohammedan country, a country where women wore veils and were covered from head to toe by a kind of caftan and never seen on the street without the company of husbands or relatives. In the big cities, those customs were somewhat mitigated by French influence. Morocco was a French protectorate, conquered by Marshall Lyauty and subjected to French rule, although the French defeat in Europe had considerably loosened these bonds. I understood that the most awkward thing one could do was to sit in a coffee house on the main square. This problem was resolved by the Joint representative. He introduced us to a prominent Jewish Spanish family, who, so to speak, adopted us for the time of our stay. They had two daughters about the same age as Sophie and they became close friends. We had a permanent invitation to lunch. The Coriat family made an unbearable situation not only tolerable for us, but even pleasant. I still feel indebted to this family and am sorry I never was able to reciprocate their kindness.

God may not play dice with the world, according to Einstein, but her delegates, the Fates, surely do play dice with people. They sometimes grant us our wishes, which may not bring us the anticipated happiness, and at other times they spoil our plans with completely unexpected results. The disaster of missing our ship in Casablanca turned into one of the happiest years of my life, certainly of my adolescence, and perhaps strengthened me for the dark years ahead in the promised land. We see from

Sophie in a Morocco market with a camel

Mother's above account that the same was true for her. Our adoption by the Coriat family indeed made all the difference for me as well, because I became their quasi-foster child. How strange that Mother does not mention this detail. The Coriats had two daughters, Donna and her younger sister Flor, two years older than I. Donna, already pregnant, had just gotten married and I was invited to fill the empty bed she had left in the girls' common bedroom. Mother had a modest flat in the vicinity and we certainly met frequently, but it became thus a year when Mother and I lived somewhat separate lives, which was more of a relief to me than I would have antici-pated. Mother had allowed me to love Tante Janne when we moved to Paris, in spite of the painful jealousy she felt in that situation, and she allowed me to live with the Coriat family. Mother could be very generous.

In the middle of the war, in the now mythical city of Casablanca with hellfire burning across the narrow Mediterranean, I had 10 glorious months of normal ado-lescence with parties, beach picnics with fires in the dunes, excursions to a farm owned by one of our friends, where I learned horseback riding, and the usual boy/girl games. This happiness was all due to Flor who introduced me to her large circle of male and female friends, young men and women of all nationalities who had some-how landed, or lived for some time, in Casablanca.

Flor was and remains—because we are still in touch and still love each other, albeit at the distance from Boston to Paris—the most generous and kindhearted woman on this whole earth. After retiring from managing her dress-boutique, she started to paint and her pictures decorate my living room. In Casablanca, while always friendly and even-tempered, Flor was mourning the departure of a young man whom she had loved. The music of the record "Lover come back to me," which she played several times a day, is still in my ears. The lover came back, soon after my departure, and they will soon be celebrating their 60th wedding anniversary.

Flor's friends all accepted me instantly, without question and some of them, in addition to Flor, became dear friends. The Coriat household had open doors for refugees who drifted through Casablanca and we were never less than a dozen persons at the dinner table. I have tried, but have not been able to reproduce, the delicious cous cous made by the family's Arab cooks.

Although Jewish children had become barred from attending the Lyçée, they were allowed to present themselves for the baccalaureate examination. The Jewish parents in Morocco had organized a private school for their children, which I attended to prepare myself for the bac, but since I did not expect to stay very long in Casablanca, I could not muster the commitment I had shown at the French Lyçée and was desultory in my attendance. But, instead, I exchanged language lessons with a young English woman in our circle.

As one might have expected, I fell in love quite soon, and my diary has many uninteresting pages reviewing in retrospect my passionate love for Roger, from beginning to end. Roger was 33 years old, second maître mechanician on a war cruiser stationed in Casablanca. He was the only non-Jewish person in our friendship circle. He was stunningly handsome in his uniforms, blue in the winter and snow-white in the spring and summer, naturally a totally unsuitable "boyfriend" for me. Thanks partly to the watchful grown-ups around me, like dear Madame Coriat who forced herself to stay up as long as Roger's evening visits lasted, allied with my mother who flew into rages about a visit to the beach with Roger alone, my own attachment to my virginity fighting with my passion, and Roger's own sense of honor, I remained chaste. These were other times.

Sophie's Diary

July 17, 1942 [Casablanca!!]

What shall I start with? Above all not with the past, otherwise it will take me three months to get to what preoccupies me at the moment and by then I won't care about it any longer or I will have forgotten all the details. Why have I not written for so very long? At the beginning, approximately until March I really would have had time. But at that time I suddenly became totally inert. I neither wrote, nor read, nor drew pictures, did nothing at the beginning, and then I learned to type all day. Then I started to study for the baccalaureate and lost interest in the diary.

What preoccupies me today to such an extent? I am in love, for a long time already, approximately since March and properly so since April or May. Now it is actually approaching the end, not because my love has diminished, but he is leaving soon. Never would I have believed at the beginning that he would be the first to leave. Who could have predicted that we simply can't and can't get away from here. Did I not think initially that it would be a matter of 14 days, one month. And now we have been here for seven months. But I am not sorry, on the contrary, because I passed my baccalaureate, in quite the same way as if we had stayed in Nice, and that was the main thing, for me. The examination was in Rabat and Flor went with me to Rabat. I felt deathly sick at the time, no doubt out of excitement and Flor mothered me in such a tender way, never shall I forget this. [And indeed, I have not.]

Love starts with the first excursion:

It was the first time that I left the city. We left for Sidi Abdieraman. At that time everything seemed quaint and beautiful. Now I can no longer look at the bare desolate sand-landscape with the few monotone fields and want nothing as much as to look once again at big green forests and snow-covered mountains. In former days I never paid attention to such things, only to people, but it matters after all. True, we have the ocean, the Atlantic which is each time equally beautiful. But the surf is so strong that one cannot swim at all and even I who face the sea without any fear, do not dare to go in any further than up to my waist. The waves flood one, push you down and during one minute one feels intense anxiety and a life and death curiosity—will one come up again? The beach is very broad and very thick white sand, like in Grado, but even thicker and not so pleasantly clean, But I prefer the stony beach in Nice, there one could at least swim without danger as far out as the heart desired. In Nice I went to swim almost every day when I had two free hours. Here I go Saturday or Sunday, depending on Roger's leaves and if he has no time or inclination, I don't go either. One has to go by bicycle approximately 10 miles hilly county to get to Ain Diab, the first proper beach. And about two further miles until Sidi Abdierama because all the Philistines of Casa are in Ain Diab and they have tents that stand next to each other, like in a mass cemetery.

A few days later he invites me to a movie, a group outing.

We saw Hotel Imperial. On the way home Roger talked about my becoming famous one day and that I would write a book about my current experiences and he wanted a whole chapter. He attached great importance to that. And whenever we talk about meeting again some day, he talks of me as a grande dame who might perhaps look down at him. . . .

This is my mother's story and not the place to tell about the vicissitudes of my love for Roger, but since I apparently promised him a whole chapter and his prophecies have become partly true, I owe him at least my description of his beauty taken from my diary.

Sᴏᴘʜɪᴇ'ꜱ Dɪᴀʀʏ

July 17, 1942

Roger is as handsome as Walter and resembles Father a bit. He is very tall, over 6 feet, and has magnificent black hair with a natural wave in them. He has a beautiful small mouth, a Greek nose and eyes that tilt downwards, like mine. He is a mixture of Gary Cooper and Robert Taylor and every time Mother sees him she is stricken with his beauty and thinks he should absolutely become a film actor. He has a faultless body and attracts me like an irresistible magnet.

Casablanca's population is composed of several layers. Rabat was the government town, with large boulevards *à la Paris* where the big government offices stood and from where the colonial bureaucracy governed the country. King Hassan was just a figurehead, upon the sufferance of the French. We never had occasion to meet the wealthy or middle-class Arab population. One saw only poor people pursuing various trades on the streets of the Arab quarter, the Medina. The quarter where the poor native Jews lived was the Mellah. There the children played in the open sewers clad in rags and covered with sores. When they saw strangers all they could do was beg. I was told that these Jews had settled there when the Emperor Titus had destroyed the first temple. None of the Jewish women wore veils. There were also Spanish Jews who had immigrated in the fifteenth century when Isabella the Catholic chased them from Spain. The ones I met were very wealthy and lived in elegant villas in the fashionable outskirts. Some of them owned big estates in the countryside. Many were merchants and bankers. The Spanish Jews despised the Moroccan Jews and regarded them as not quite human. The servants in the home of the Spanish Jews were recruited exclusively from among the Moroccan Jews, who stole, as most servants all over the world do. If a Spanish Jew wanted to marry a Moroccan Jewish girl, it was regarded as a misalliance and a disgrace for the entire family.

Roger in uniform

For their professional education, the wealthy young men went to Paris and returned to practice in their own country. A group of Paris-educated physicians had organized a dispensary for the destitute Jewish population. Although it was built to be a hospital, it was used for ambulatory cases only. The majority of cases were trachoma and infantile diarrhea. Most of the time the women brought their sick infants in when it was too late and children were completely dehydrated and ostensibly moribund. They went first to the witch doctor and when they saw the futility of that move they came to the dispensary. The women knelt before the doctors imploring, *"donnez lui une piqûre, donnez lui une piqûre"* (give him an injection) believing that any kind of injection would save the life of the dying baby The doctors were furious but helpless in their fight against superstition and ignorance. Woe, if the new state of Israel has to do with this kind of population.

Soon in this forced stay in Casablanca, I learned about the dispensary. I immediately went to see its director and offered my services. Because I had worked two years with Professor Lemaître in Paris, there was no question about being accepted. In a short time I organized a school for deaf children. There was nothing like it in the entire country. Every morning I rode with my bike to the dispensary and taught speech, reading, and writing to 12 completely neglected deaf and hard-of-hearing children. My activity was soon known in the wealthier Jewish circles of Casa, and inquires streamed in requesting treatment for cases that would pay. Thus, in the afternoon, I rode with my bike to visit my private patients. I learned that the police in charge of refugees looked with benevolent eyes upon my activities and I understood that we were protected from unpleasant surprises.

Sophie was again enrolled in school, although not in the state-run Lycée. Jewish youngsters were no longer admitted to it. However, Jewish parents had organized a private equivalent of the Lycée and she could take her baccalaureate at the state school.

Among a number of cultural missions, the French state maintained a large library in Casablanca. I was asked by one of the physicians of the dispensary to do some technical translation of a manuscript about the workings of an electrical shock apparatus, which he had just received from Zurich. I needed some special reference books and thus met Monsieur Duprée, the director of the French library. He had moved to Morocco because his wife had suffered tuberculosis and wanted to live in a mild climate (she had, by this time, died of the disease). He was not only extremely helpful with the translation, but took a liking to me. So now we had a well-connected non-Jewish protector. He was a well-educated man, one of the few real gentlemen I have met in my life, who wanted nothing from me but my company. The Coriat family, my being able to work and earn money, and Monsieur Duprée are the three things that make Casablanca one of the more pleasant memories in our flight from Hitler.

One day Mother and Monsieur Duprée informed me that they had agreed that he would marry me, for protection, in case of a German invasion. I must shamefully admit it, in my complete stupidity, I started to cry. Monsieur Duprée then explained, as delicately as possible, that it would be only a pro forma marriage.

I was actually very pleased (and relieved) that Mother had found a man friend and was thus less lonely and more content. She told me that Monsieur Duprée had asked her to marry him. "Why don't you?" I said. She then angrily reproached me that I wanted to get rid of her. Perhaps she was right, although coming to America completely on my own would have been even harder. (I had never even considered staying on in Casablanca.) But in any case, Mother had no intention of marrying again—once had been bad enough—or, like me, of staying on in Casablanca.

One of the curious experiences we had during our sojourn in Casa was a lo-cust invasion. It was just as described in the Bible. Locusts were everywhere. They settled in your hair, they crunched under your feet, the grass in the park was brown with swarms of young locusts, and the branches of the trees were black, with no leaves left. We were told that the English, because of the war, had no crude oil to spare to put into Lake Chad, which is the insects' breeding ground, so the locusts were able to multiply.

During the period that we were in Africa, the war between Rommel and the English General Wavell was fought. It went back and forth several times. When the English were winning, the French colonial authorities were lenient with the Jewish refugees. When Rommel was the winner, I was certainly glad to have our protector.

SOPHIE'S DIARY

August 15, 1942

Heinrich Heine writes: "Let the Jews, those pariahs of modern society, ally themselves with all disinherited; because they are at present victims not so much of a religious prejudice, or a racial hatred, than of social injustice. Their enemies are the men who hold today's power, the same who pretend to hold all of Germany in tutelage, who try to suppress everywhere the free-dom to think and to speak. And indeed, in reality they have no other ene-mies. Because in the upper classes, the antipathy against Jews no longer has any religious roots, and in the lower classes it becomes from day to day more a social rage against the usurious power of capital, against the exploi-tation of the poor by the rich. Jews should finally understand that they will never be able to be truly emancipated until the emancipation of Christians themselves will be complete and definitive. The Jewish cause is similar to the cause of the German people and they should not desire, as Jews, what is due to them since a long time, as German citizens. In Europe, there are no longer any nations, but only political parties."

How wonderfully actual his words are. The first time that I see written in clear words the exact same standpoint which I share. I just read a biography of Heine; Henri Heine, penseur *(thinker) by Henri Lichtenberger and it confirmed and ordered the vague ideas I had about Heine. He mentions his private life, but only in passing, his ideas on religions (the same as mine, only unfortunately he believes in God), his politics (definitely leftist, but one would wish to see more* netteté *(clarity) in his positions. For example he often courted monarchs, or received pensions from them and he also does not like ordinary people and fears their taking power because he appreciates art more than social progress. He recognized exactly the importance of communism and regarded the revolution as a disagreeable but unavoidable event. He even associated with Marx for a time. He converted for material reasons.*

August 18, 1942

But he considered this all his life a disgrace and a personal humiliation. After his conversion he had a special rage against all gentiles and took all the more interest in Jews. He disliked his "racial brothers," often mocked them bitterly and was in favor of a complete emancipation. But he felt compassion for them and took their part because they were the oppressed and as a proper Jew he took the part of the weaker. But Mr. Lichtenberger may say what he wants, it was also an inborn pride that drew him to the Jews, as is the same situation with me. One can be ever so modern and unreligious, one feels oneself as Jew and is proud about that. One only needs to read the Rabbi of Bacharach *to see that Heine was not an enemy of Jews. When he later became so terribly sick, he turned toward God and consciously started to believe. . . .*

All his life Heine was awfully alone. He never belonged to a party but made fun of them all, never had a good friend, nor a female comrade in a wife. Why could I not have known him, I would so much have wanted to be his comrade, through thick and thin!

I found one of grandfather's books in the library, An Introduction to Psychoanalysis, *a written reproduction of two semester courses. It was naturally very interesting. The first part, about various slips in* The Psychopathology of Everyday Life *I could quite understand. It also reads very easily, like a novel, with all the amusing examples.*

Then I read Lenin's Le Stade supreme de l'Imperialism, *above all statistics with which he shows the impossible economy of capitalist countries. After that I read* La vie de Lenin (The Life of Lenin) *by his wife Kroupinskaïa. . . . Lenin was never married but he lived all his life with the same woman. Thus there is such a thing as* l'amour libre *(free love) but not all men are as special as Lenin and besides his love life had surely not played a big role for him. . . .*

I am not clear about the colonial question. When I talk to Dav for example [one young man in our friendship group, an Englishman] I am at a loss. And it is indeed true, the French have cut down on typhus in Morocco, instituted peace in the mountains among tribes, built cities and introduced running water and electricity. And if Morocco were independent it would not improve the condition of poor Arabs, on the contrary. And they need someone to pull them out of their squalor and humanize them. That is what Dav explained to me.

August 24, 1942

Today I am so tired, tired, my legs weigh 10 kg. Roger has left, I accompanied him to the station. . . .

I believe it took six months until our American visas were renewed. We now needed a Portuguese entrance visa, because Portugal was the only place in Europe from which ships still crossed the Atlantic to the States. I don't remember how often I went to the Portuguese Consul for this visa. I was afraid the same thing would happen again—that our visas would expire and we would be stranded for good in that godforsaken country. However, one day I finally succeeded. A man was waiting with me in the foyer. We started to talk and I told him our story. He seemed to have some pull with the consul and so we received our Portuguese visas. My responses were fast. I made sleeping car reservations for the night train to Tangiers from where we were to fly to Lisbon. We packed our few possessions and off we went. I believe it was a nice crowd that saw us off at the station. Monsieur Duprée cried when the train left. I gave the sleeping car conductor a considerable tip and our papers, telling him that I was recuperating from a serious illness and badly needed a night's sleep and to see if he could arrange it so that the passport control and the customs did not awake us. Although Tangiers is an international city we traveled from French-controlled territory to Spanish territory. I started to get very weary of the different kinds of control.

CHAPTER 38

From Casablanca to Lisbon

Sophie's Diary

October 22, 1942

Well, in the evening, after good-byes on all sides, to the station. My heart broke for Duprée because he seemed so miserable. We had a sleeping coach, second class to Tangier. Until the frontier I had terrible nightmares, probably expecting unconsciously to be sent back again. I dreamed of chantiers de jeuness (youth camps) where I was to be interned to teach me love of the fatherland and other similar things. But everything passed well. I love sleeping on trains, quite a different matter than on superstupid ships. On trains one can think of a 100 things, the fantasy becomes freer, horizons expand, one departs into a new life. The next day, arrival in Tangier. I only saw the beach a few seconds through the train window and never got back to it because our hotel was high up and it is an endless strenuous path to climb up. In Tangier one is terribly exploited. The Arabs at the station precipitated themselves on us like hungry vultures. The hotel was very expensive, at least for our means, perhaps not so bad for Tangier because life there is ruinous. But they had real mosquito nets which I greatly appreciate in every climate, country and circumstances.

We then went right away to the president of the Jewish community, a Mr. Laredo who was most charming with us, especially if one considers that he had to transfer the money for the airplane to us. He is a sales representative for Nestles and bestowed upon each of us a giant tablet of chocolate. I wanted to save mine to send to Mlle Kronheim, but Mother ate it away. Finally I didn't care, since anyway one was not allowed to send anything.

Tangier is a quaint old city, built entirely on a hill, with curving lively streets and a beautiful view from above on my dear fine old Mediterranean and on green gardens. The market place is huge and gay and teeming with people but there are no elegant objects in the store windows and everything is so crazily expensive that one can't believe it. One egg is 12 francs, one meter fabric 4,000 francs, two chocolates with one croissant for each, 50 francs. A very mediocre lunch is 60 francs etc.

On the next morning, at the airport, everything was very exciting because all the baggage got weighed and one had to pay 100 francs per kilo for any weight above 30 kg. And 200 francs per kilo for any weight above 60 kg. I was so worried that together we would have more than 60 kg that I tried to stuff as much as possible into my pockets. I was not sure whether they would weigh my briefcase and just in case I packed a few heavy books and bottles in it and since they did not weigh it I was only sorry that I had not stuffed it even more fully. One hour in the bus from the hotel to the airport. The politician who traveled with us naturally took a private car, he had a monocle, cigar in the corner of his mouth and looked exactly as stupid as little Moritz imagines the looks of a diplomat.

The flight from Tangiers to Lisbon in a small plane I remember to have been very beautiful. We were the only passengers [*Mother remembers this incorrectly*].

SOPHIE'S DIARY
October 22, 1942 (continued)
There were spaces for 12 persons, six single places on each side. It was quite a nice day. We started to roll and ascended slowly, first we flew right away over the sea. But my attention was directed to the sky. We flew through wooly cumulus clouds formed into mighty glaciers, strangely jagged, with wide infinite fields and deep blue glacier lakes—the sky that looked through the clouds. It was as I had imagined the Alaska of Jack London, like the Alaska that Supervielle sees with his artist's eyes. It put me into a poetic mood, I imagined lost souls that had to wander for eternity on these mighty snowfields, searching for things that cannot be found, perhaps for peace for their souls and for the world. In sum, I invented kitschy fairy tales stolen from all my recent literary memories. Then we flew over the South of Spain, I think the big delta was that of the Ebro. Towards Portugal the country looked more fertile and more densely settled. Everything is so ridiculously small from the airplane, like toys, and the roads that meander through the landscape also

look so very odd. We crossed once more the sea and then we saw from above the immense delta of the Tejo and Lisbon. I would have preferred to get to know the city first, and then fly over it, that profits you much more, because one recognizes things.

After we passed Lisbon, the shorter but more unpleasant part of the flight started, the landing which spoiled my positive memory of the flight. The airplane started jumps into the air and so did my stomach, it drew large circles and with hops and circles we approached the earth. At the end it flew so low that I was afraid one of the wings would brush against the ground and break. But everything turned out well, except at the landing and after we had already left the plane I got deathly nauseous. But only inside, thank God, I would have been embarrassed to throw up on the well kept grass of the air company. And then came the story with the police and Cintra.

In Lisbon, at the airport, the passport control people found something wrong with our visas and wanted to send us back immediately. I implored them to call the Joint and they were reassured that we already had our tickets to the United States of America and were staying in Portugal for a short time only. We were permitted to stay, but we had to take up residence in a small village [Cintra] with an old castle outside the capital.

SOPHIE'S DIARY

October 22, 1942

Cintra is a charming little town, totally buried in the woods and surrounded by rose-covered fairy tale castles, like in Tirol. The environs of Lisbon are generally teeming with royal castles where the aristocracy used to live. On top of the mountains there are even ruins that we climbed up to, since we spent, punitively, a few days in Cintra. Because, as we arrived with the airplane in Lisbon, the airport-border policewoman sniffed at our papers and as she read foreigners, Jews *etc. she instantly became frantically worried regarding her responsibility, as full of shit as she was and forbad us for one to enter the city. The HICEM had not telephoned the police to assure them that our ship tickets had already been paid. On the other hand this was obvious because without that we would not have received our American visas, but the Portuguese are so terrified that one might stay there. Briefly, we continued for a few minutes in the bus with the other flight passengers and got unloaded at the first police station, the other passengers being naturally very surprised and in retrospect a bit upset to have been together with such dangerous criminals. Especially the politician with his monocle, oxface and cigar in the corner of his mouth must surely have been very indignant that he was not being more adequately protected.*

So at 1:00 P.M. we installed ourselves in the police station, which was a little house inhabited by two policemen one of whom had a pregnant young wife, quite a friendly beautiful Spanish woman. Mother called the HICEM every 10 minutes, although the telephone was mostly busy and we sat on our few suitcases and sucked on candy to still our hunger. In terms of a triumphal reception it was rather nebbich. The Spanish woman then made us an omelet and gave us sausage and butter and bread and pears to devour and all three of us tried to converse, which was more an effort than pleasure if one considers that she only spoke Spanish and we did not have any Spanish knowledge.

As the answer of HICEM had not yet arrived toward evening and there was no motel far and wide (showing that Portugal is not prepared for tourism because in France there are several hotels in even smaller nests) the policeman decided to send us to Cintra for the night. There they put us into the nearest hotel (which, by the way, was also the most expensive, the poor Joint) which only had space in its satellite house, in a tiny mansard with one stonehard bed. There was infinitely much to eat, but I only take one meal a day, in order not to gain weight and although the environs were very charming, it was a bit desolate.

On the next day, Saturday, we had to return to the police station out of pure chicanery to convince the gentlemen that we had meanwhile not escaped, given that all our luggage was at the police station, but Saturday evening a telephone call came that we were free to do what we wanted. It was to Mother's great relief since, optimistic as always, she had already been sure that we would be sent back to Spain who would hand us over to the Germans. I could only prevent her with much effort to send telegrams into the whole world.

But we stayed until Tuesday, because Monday was Yom Kippur and the Joint was closed and we had to get money from them to pay the hotel bill. And that is how we came to stay in Cintra. It gave me a chance to almost finish reading the Pickwick Papers. . . .

CHAPTER 39

Lisbon

SOPHIE'S DIARY

> *October 1942*
>
> *When we first arrived in Lisbon I was totally enthusiastic, it seemed to me the most beautiful city in the world. Upon arrival one is strangely reminded of Paris. The station looks like the* Gâre St. Lazare, *but only on the inside. From the outside it looks like a distorted Venetian* Pallazzo *with the pretension, I fear, to think itself tasteful. Further on, one has the feeling from the outside of standing in front of the* Comédie Française, *but it is only a neb-bish* Theater *of Lisbon which is, on top of it, closed, and beyond that one has the illusion of coming upon the* Place de la Concord, *but unfortunately it was only an illusion. This part of the city is nevertheless the most beautiful, but nothing exists which can compare with Paris. Lisbon's most elegant street is the* Rua Garette *with really very beautiful stores.*
>
> *The best are the food stores where one can get everything. I got very excited at the beginning, all those stores without food tickets and in the morning as much sugar as one wishes and hours of whipped cream and, in general, totally everything. As we got money from Father (at the beginning we were so depleted that we had to save on food) Mother bought me a beautiful Scottish pleated skirt and a man's jacket with a zipper in front that I had wanted for a long time and dark blue shoes with a meter high heels which are so painful that I get exhausted to death after I wear them a little, but they are magnificently beautiful.*

Our funds were very low. My first visit was to the Joint. They were friendly and offered to lodge us in a boarding house with food (European pension) with all expenses paid. A sensible idea occurred to me. I said: "Why don't you give us the money this pension would cost and we can look for a private room and provide food for ourselves?" The Joint recommended decent lodgings and just gave us the keys. The room led into a huge court and at night all the cats of the neighborhood came to inspect us. During the day we went sightseeing with the money we had. We bought food in grocery stores and ate in a big park nearby. On occasions we drank milk and ate delicious pastry in one of the little *leitarias* the main boulevard of Lisbon is lined with. These were the only places women could go unescorted to have afternoon tea. Lisbon, when we were there, was one of the few neutral cities left and the center of espionage. It was flooded with German propaganda: German daily newspapers, illustrated magazines available on every news-stand, all of which flaunted the German victories. There was not a single American or British newspaper available.

SOPHIE'S DIARY

October 1942

So we spent one month in Lisbon. It was quite nice, but a bit lonesome. But if we had stayed another month that would have thoroughly changed because I made masses of conquests at the very last moment.

We had a rather big, not very bright but pleasantly furnished room. It went to a balcony which was connected to the back stairs and at night all the cats in the neighborhood came to sleep in our room. Usually there were one or two on my bed, a grey one which did not look very clean, and a white-black very old one, already terribly stiff and lazy. The old one usually slept on Mother's bed, the grey one on mine (she scratched herself all night and prevented me from sleeping) and then a very shy black dear one on the rug or in the easy chair on which it rocked all night. But they were very sweet and made it wonderfully cozy. In the first two weeks we ate in the boarding house where we were lodged, but Mother did not like the food (I don't care, am no longer spoiled and usually I like everything) and then we only ate when and where we liked. That worked very well because we had no money at all and I grabbed the opportunity to eat only coffee and two rolls for breakfast and in the evening only fruit and some small thing. As we arrived in Lisbon we had no money at all, because the few francs that we had still from Casa were nothing when exchanged and we had already spent them in Tangier. We were supported by the JOINT which granted us daily 50 escudos for both of us which was very generous. The room cost 20 escudos and then we still had Grandfather's 10 pounds which I had duly saved since my

15th birthday and been overlooked by customs. I gave it to Mother and she returned it as soon as we received money from Father after three weeks and that was our pocket money.

Sophie had caught an eye inflammation and we had to visit an ophthalmologist. I had the impression that medical treatment was very efficient in Lisbon. The physicians of many medical specialties had their offices together, a very convenient arrangement. If a patient needed an examination by another specialist he had just to walk through the waiting room.

Sᴏᴘʜɪᴇ's Dɪᴀʀʏ

October 1942

Our main expense was definitely doctors and medicine. Because Mother who was panicked lest I had trachoma, insisted all the time I had red eyes and dragged me to the doctor who prescribed expensive medicines. I also resented getting constantly creams and drops into my eyes. Then the doctor even postulated that I was anemic (how ridiculous!) and gave me a sort of liver extract to swallow, it was really too stupid. But the Portuguese doctor was extremely decent. Mother explained to him about immigration to America and so on. We had come to see him in a neighborhood clinic which is quite inexpensive and he asked me to come to his main clinic to examine me under a microscope. Before we left Lisbon he asked me back to have me examined by his chief. He smelled so much like Grandfather that I was very touched. It must have been the tobacco and he also found that I did not have trachoma which would indeed have annoyed me very much. But I was totally flabbergasted that he would make such an effort for an ordinary foreigner who had come to his consultation in a cheap setting.

Observing the clinic was quite interesting. There was a big waiting hall and one always admitted patients in groups of 10. They queued up in front of the doctor and one after the other sat in the chair and the doctor smeared or dribbled each one something into the eye. It was like a mass-soupkitchen for sick folks and not done very well, since one cannot imagine being cured with such à la chaîne (in rows) treatments, although it might be just as effective.

We spent our stay in Lisbon sightseeing, looking very conscientiously at all the tourist attractions, starting with those that had two stars in the guidebook. It was very beautiful and I love art much more than before although I already loved it in Venice, if only I got some explanations. Mother also does not know much about paintings and art and so I had to make do without explanations. I would like a husband who understands art and can make it come to life for me, but it is not an absolute condition. My future one, or let us say, my fairy tale prince should be young and sportive, enthusiastic, intelligent and affectionate. He should be modest in his tastes and we want to love each other crazily, terribly. He should also be poor but competent. He should not care about having to live in a mansard. For our honeymoon we want to drive through the country on bikes with a tent on our backs. He should not mind sailing fourth class if we want to look at the world without enough money. But I put less weight on this last point since I have been on ships. I would have to think thoroughly about going on a ship for mere pleasure. Sailing on ships is disagreeable, I confirm that once and for all.

The most beautiful building in Lisbon was the monastery of Jeronimus of which I have also taken a fine photo. Already from the outside with its many jagged towers it looks more like a fantasy made of spun sugar than out of stone. Just as I turned this and that way to get a good perspective of the cloister for my camera, Mother and the cloister guard precipitated themselves upon me, all excited, one is not allowed to take photos without a special permission from who knows what ministry. I quickly clicked the camera, closed it regretfully and said: quel dommage *(what a pity). I only would have liked to take the big entrance door from closer up.*

October 1942 (continued)

In the environs of Lisbon, in Queluz, there is a charming castle like a petit Trianon, *with a magnificent park, a little Versailles. I also took fine photos there, my first really artistic photos: a bridge under trees and I am so pleased that my filter was properly useful. Photographing is generally quite wonderful. If I am able, I shall buy myself in New York with the left over pounds (because I sent Miss Kronheim from Lisbon small packages of food, unfortunately one was only allowed canned fish and dried fruit) a little darkroom. First of all just to change negatives into positives, and then, should I earn some money, a more complete one. And then I want to exchange my little camera against a better one. In addition I shall save for a typewriter and a motorcycle. At least one cannot say that I am too modest in my wishes.*

I did arrange for a little darkroom in my first year in America, but the wish for a motorcycle had disappeared in my memory, it must have had little priority. But when I started my doctoral studies at the age of 43, at Brandeis University, only 6 miles from my home, I bought myself a motorcycle, well only a motorscooter, which became, for the next 30 years, my most practical vehicle of transportation, my favorite toy, and my stamp of identity.

CHAPTER 40

On the *Carvalho Arujo* to America

Finally, the day of our embarkation arrived. We were given a not too comfortable stateroom with two other women. One woman was taken off the ship because she had had an affair with a German officer. The passengers were a varied lot. There was a French priest who had escaped from a German prison camp. There were perhaps 20 former Polish soldiers (this human cargo endangered our ship which was supposed to be neutral). There were Americans who wanted to return home, and the rest were Jewish immigrants, who, like us, wanted to reach a safe shore, traveling into an otherwise unknown, insecure future. At night the ship was fully illuminated. At the same time that the *Carvalho Arujo* sailed to the United States—but we did not know this—a large American fleet traveled the opposite way to land in Morocco.

SOPHIE'S DIARY
    October 23, 1942
    Who would have thought it, we are sailing to America!! Just now I am sitting somewhere high up on the ship It seems impossible, fantastic and I could never have imagined this moment. The trip on this ship is only medium-great, at least until now. Tuesday, at 10:00 P.M. [October 20, 1942]— they might have wanted to save on dinner—we were sent on board. We are traveling third class, category two but our cabin and food are highly decent. We are four persons in the cabin, on one side Mother, and me on the upper berth, and on the other side two very friendly women, both of them married. We left Wednesday afternoon and today, Friday noon, we have thus been traveling for two days. The faster, the better, because since the evening of

the day before yesterday I am deathly seasick and starting at 5:00 P.M. my main occupation was to vomit, until 3:00 A.M. First all I had eaten for lunch, and then for dinner the evening before, and for that day's breakfast and finally, since nothing at all was left, just bile which was very bitter and the whole thing quite awful. Seasickness surely belongs to the worst sicknesses that exist in the world. One wants to die, anything, rather than being seasick. And yesterday I was so down that I could not get up all day and just tossed about from right to left, in the cabin. But today I got up again and had breakfast and lunch and if I continue to feel relatively well, I shall also have tea and dinner. Because they serve us four meals a day, all them fairytale-like. Our third-class cabins are bigger than the second class and the food is also considerably better. Well, for breakfast there is plum compote, as much as one wants, or as much as a normal person wants, because I can devour it by the kilo. And cold cuts, and magnificent white bread and butter and coffee and biscuits and since one might lose 1 or 2 kilos in one day of seasickness I don't need to watch my figure quite so carefully especially since I lost anyway almost 2 kg. in Lisbon. That was actually very difficult because they had such magnificent pastries and cocoa with whipped cream. I catch myself talking constantly about food. I have not yet made any conquests on the ship. Well, a few men wanted to make up to me, but they did not appeal to me. It is quite difficult to find attractive men around here because one man is more unappealing than the next.

I am always worried that people will have forgotten me. Such vanity not to want to be forgotten! I pretend that I don't care, as long as my friends fare well, but that is not really true, I am not that selfless and I always hope that people do not forget me, for example, Tante Janne, Walter, Father, my Vienna friends etc.

October 26

If only we did not have such a terrible storm. Already since Thursday. The first day I did not touch any food, just raced up to a deck after an agonizing morning toilet and stayed there until 11:00 P.M. without moving, except going to the loo twice each time a catastrophe. But then I got used to things and yesterday I went to eat, although without proper appetite. But I have never seen such a storm, the ship shook back and forth like a nutshell, the sea looked grey and mean and from time to time there was a cloudburst. This has now been going on for three days. The nuisance in the cabin is that we have to close our portholes during storms and then it becomes hot enough to die. I always sleep completely naked, totally without cover and in the morning I wake up with 2 inches of sweat on my whole body. The air in *the cabin is suffocating and one becomes immediately deathly nauseous if one stays there. Many people sleep on deck because they can't stand it. Once I went to the loo and got so sick that I almost had to lie down on the floor in the loo. But at that moment the bathroom became free and I threw myself next door into the bathtub.*

October 27, 1942

The last weeks in Lisbon I spent my time reading, as usual. Lisbon is full of beautiful parks; it is even one of its main beauties. They are all carefully cultivated, some to the extent of making them uncozy, like one park which is perhaps as big as the Bois de Boulogne *(a very big park in Paris) but does not have a single cozy place to sit down on, but only fenced-in grass and cleanly raked paths. Another park was full of quaint tropical plants and one felt underneath all these palms like in a cultivated rain forest. Half of my own park was not yet finished and therefore it was the only one which still had cozy places. It was very big, half of it* terrains vagues *and the other half a wood, in the middle a swan pond and next to it a wine arbor with a little library. This library, a chest with about 50 books stands in many parks with the same books everywhere. They are part of the* Bibliothek Municipale *and anyone can go there, fill out a form with name, address and profession and then one can read one's selected book, undisturbed and at no cost under the only condition to stay in the vicinity. The hook is that it is closed on Sundays when most people have time. But the whole arrangement is still very democratic. Equally useful are also the children's playgrounds that are set up in many parks, with swings, wading pools, jungle gyms and slides, very decent. In Paris this only exists in the* jardin d'acclimatation, *in Casa in the* Park Lyautey *and there is nothing like that in Vienna. It seems to be one of Portugal's few progressive institutions.*

SOPHIE'S DIARY

October 30, 1942

I had made an alphabetical list in Lisbon of all the writers whose books I had read. And each writer received a grade, 1 to 5, and then there were a few ones circled in gold and a few circled in blue. The gold circled were Heine, Freud, Buddenbrooks *by Thomas Mann,* Thibaults *by Roger Martin du Gars, Traven, Dostojewesky and Malraux, a great Communist French writer. He has written two magnificent books,* La Condition Humaine *the story of the Chinese revolution and* L' Éspoir *about the Spanish civil war which was almost even superior to the one about China. He describes the incredible self-sacrifices by the masses, bravery above any description and afterwards one is totally downcast and ashamed about one's own mediocre person.*

The guardian of the books with whom I sometimes exchanged a few words and once gave a little lesson in French pronunciation gave me a most charming good-bye greeting. Then there were also some students in the park. I had seen them from a distance but had not given them any opportunity to approach me. But on the last day they placed themselves all around me and threw German, French and English words at me, until I finally started to laugh and initiated a conversation. One of the young men was terribly nice and I really regret not to have gotten to know him more closely. They attended industrial and commercial study programs and with one of them, a 20-year-old totally attractive young man, I had quite a serious interesting discussion. He was a sort of anarchist with ideals about liberty but not at all practical. I wanted to show him that he will not get far with his passive ideals. (He was, for example, indifferent to forms of governments.) But I had too much of an advantage because although while he could speak French quite acceptably, he could not squeeze out his ideas as he wanted. Then I bid them all good-bye, and they all wished me a good trip and that I should return to Portugal and I was almost sorry to be leaving, and they felt the same way. They probably thought first it took us so long to tame her and now she is leaving right away. This was actually my only true contact with Portuguese folks. But I am glad at least not to have been driven to great sorrows at the departure from Portugal. . . . I have had to bid adieu to sufficient people, am sick of it.

In Lisbon I still got a letter from Father. It was the first written news since June 1941 and I had not the faintest idea what had become of him. I also got terribly upset after this first longingly awaited letter. It is a pleasant letter, nothing to be said against it, but not a loving one, nor affectionate. It is the same kind of letter that Father wrote me four years ago, to a little girl. And he always remains on the surface and never leaves his magazine style for a minute. I sensed it immediately the first time I read through the letter and a total lack of interest in me, my future and past. In sum, it was an empty, insincere letter.

ENGLISH LETTER

    1 Holly Terrace
    Highgate West Hill
    London, N6, 4.10.42
    (October 10, 1942)
    Dear Sophlein,
    I was very glad indeed when I received the news that you and mother had escaped and I liked your nice long letter describing the voyage and all

your adventures. Of course I got the photos and I did show them to everybody, being very proud of my daughter to have been photographed together with a camel.

I did send 20 pounds to Mother and you, you must understand that it is rather complicated to send money out of the country, I need a license each time and amounts are limited. I am not supposed to mention financial transactions at all. I am in contact with the Princess, doing some work for her in the British Museum.

Now I report how everybody is going on. My mother looks much older lately, but has so far been well. Anna is very busy with homes for poor children, so is Dorothy Burlingham, who stays with her and supported our interventions in U.S.A. in a very helpful way. Mathilde and Ernst are in business. I am so far the only member of the family that could not settle down. After a good start—a novel published by a good publisher—and some experiments as a small manufacturer, I had nothing but the most humble jobs, I was a private in the army mostly on kitchen and scullery duty, a mechanic in some docks in a big port, a fitters mate in a great food factory and, in Civil Defence, a stretcher-bearer in a University Hospital. The last job is, or better was, Air Raid Warden, as I expect to leave this job within the very next days, end of this week already! There was, as you certainly will know, nothing to do for us Wardens for over a year but to warn people to draw their blackout curtains and to sit and wait for raids which—fortunately—don't come.

I am certain I shall find something else very soon and I know it will, whatever it is, be rather simple and humble, but connected with the war. I earn what I need for my living, except the rent, which I pay from my savings account, that will of course not last forever. My life is nearly proletarian, I cook my own food and make my own bed and in case I do not feel like it, everything gets untidy. Yesterday I cooked: oxliver with bacon, potatoes and cabage [sic] and 1 kukurruz (corn on the cob). I ate it out of the frying pan and it was absolutely wonderful. Fancy that some years ago I lived on *Suppenhuhn und gekochten Kalbfleisch*! (boiled fowl and boiled veal). We had a bad and cool summer and I went swimming only twice, once for 3 1/2 minutes and the other time for 2. But on the other hand I have a bycicle [sic] and do quite a lot of cycling in my free time.

It is about seven weeks since I have seen Walter. He came on leave armed with rifle and bayonet and changed immediately into shorts and sandals. He looks fine, but very thin, and is in great spirits. His girl, the same one for the last four years, claims him as her private property and is not willing to lend him to me during his leaves for more than a few hours.

Now this has become a long letter and I hope it gives you some idea about our life here. I hope you write to me now very regularly. Tell Mother that I shall write to Lily about sending money to Grandmother, but she really should write to her herself.

I close with kisses

Your father

I no longer know why I was so disappointed in this letter although I must admit, I still have an uneasy feeling about it.

SOPHIE'S DIARY

October 30, 1942 (continued)

But when I read the letter, I thought above all that father is not doing especially well, My proud, prince-like arrogant father a common soldier in the army, doing kitchen duty, being stretcher bearer in a hospital, worker in a factory for conserves, air raid warden, one's heart must break. I was so proud of him, his intelligence, talents, humor, charm, and I love him so much and the thought that he is being humiliated breaks my heart. I would so terribly much like to see him again, am sure we would, one two three, greatly love each other, it is not so hard for me to gain someone's love. He writes he makes his own bed and cooks for himself (a quarter of the letter deals with yesterday's menu which seems a bit silly after three years). If I lived with him I would try to make a home for him. Maybe it is all comedy, but if all he writes is true, he is very alone. Maybe I can hop over for a summer, he writes nothing of a reunion.

October 31, 1942

Today is already Saturday and Monday evening, or the day after in the morning, we shall get there. Thank God, finally firm earth under our feet once again, have more than enough of the constant wobbling. Otherwise it is not unpleasant on the ship. The first days I surrounded myself with solitude and lay down to sleep on all the decks I could find. I thus got to know the sea officers all of whom distinguish themselves by being well nourished. (If I think of Roger in comparison!) One of them courted me right away, I had played a few games of ping-pong with him and once went for a walk with him in the evening, up and down the deck. The conversation was sufficiently boring and exhausting since it took him much effort to squeeze out a bit of French. He was medium tall, well nourished, glasses and looked like Fräulein's admirer, the dentist. The second day we ping-ponged again and he begged me urgently to come up again on deck in the evening, parce que je suis gentille et jolie et qu'il aime converser avec moi *(because I was so sweet and pretty and he loves talking with me). But I was right away on my guard because he had put his arm on mine. But I quickly withdrew it, finding his contact repellent. And right after lunch I had a ping-ponging rendezvous with him. But I only came up around 4 h because I was more than tired of him. He showed me the rooms with the machines, I am surely the only passenger who has seen it, and then he led me to the highest place, to a tiny circumscribed deck and offered to put a chair there, and I could sun myself and write etc. But that was so to say the price and I started to be uncomfortable up there, all alone with him, and when he asked me whether I would come I said no, and he wanted to draw me to him to kiss me. I tore myself away and went down. Who does this guy think he is? Then he said to his comrades, I liked it up there, but I did not want to come back, he did not know why. And then he showed me the captain's quarters and made another shy attempt but I left never to be seen again. Because since then I make a large, large detour around him. Because he repelled me physically and in general he was barely good enough to play, not too often, ping-pong with him. Then I stayed all day with the others. But that was also not much fun, feeling quite strange to always be with the grown-ups. And then I discovered a perfect deck on the back corner of the ship and settled there from then on. For a few days I surrounded myself with solitude until I got to know the Poles whose habitual place it was as well. I am very pleased to have gotten to know them, I think it was the first time that I talked to Aryan Poles. Until then I only knew that they were awful anti-Semites. But those that I got to know are not at all anti-Semites, but all of them friendly young guys. There are six or seven of them, all of them going to Canada where they already have a job in some factory, because they are all skilled workers, airplane or mechanical engineers and one, a very gay one, even a professional soldier. He comes from Lemberg and looks like a vassal from the 30 Years' War. He is from the motorized division, limps and jokes around all day, sings and engages in acrobatics. He does speak very poor German but is a very expressive story teller, one only needs to look at his hands. He had a 20-year-old daughter who was shot by the Russians because she had participated in an anti-Russian-German conspiracy. (The Russians shot 3,000 Poles, how cruel— I am totally confused and in turmoil, thought the Russians are our friends—to shoot a 20-year-old girl, that is the limit.) And his 24-year-old son is in the R.A.F. in England. He and his comrades do not want to stay in Canada, but wander over Alaska, Siberia to Persia where the first Polish corps is situated.*

They all want to fight, not work. In the evening I joined them and they sang Slavic folk songs. I was really sad not to have understood them, the melodies were so lively and gay, all different, that I had a truly splendid time even without understanding the words. . . . He participated in the French-Polish part of the Polish legion and is enraged against the French who always did this: (and he raises his hands), casting off their guns and thinking only of their bottles of wine. And the other man tells how he arrived at Marseille

Sophie's Polish friends who made the trip to America enjoyable

and, when he saw all the soldiers with open jackets and extruding bellies, he got disgusted. Another one is a magnificent guy, tall, slender, broad, with goldblond curls and a proud beautiful face and a sweet, magical smile with wonderful teeth. I lost my eyes over him but he was awfully reserved. But one evening, when he, the soldier, and I were alone, he started to talk, announced to me that he is already married with a 13-year-old daughter and a 9-year-old son in Poland. He looks like 23, but is already 35. He is a fervent Polish patriot, worries about his family and is a serious decent fellow. For example, he said he loved to dance but not at the moment because how could he dance when he thinks of all the misery in Poland and that they are starving. In France he was chauffeur of the Polish Generalissimo. He comes from Posen and speaks beautiful German, not fluent, but without errors. The third Pole is an athlete, very tall and broad and kindhearted, helplessly child-ish as such giants often are. This soldier and another one were one year in a Stalag and so he could tell me a bit about it. They got 200 g bread to eat and watercoffee for breakfast, potato soup for lunch, and potato soup in the evening and they were hungry enough that they could have eaten their boots. He was in a camp in Bavaria, mixed in with Poles and Frenchmen. And every time when Poles and the French got together there were huge fights because the Poles accused the French pourquoi faire comme cela, *and he lifts his hands. And they had to work, building highways. In the French barracks there was supposedly damn much filth and lice but the Polish bar-racks were clean. And the Austrian guards were very friendly and they said for example: "Come, you are a Pole. You were on our side during the last war," and they secretly got them some whiskey and cigarettes. The Prussians were revolting. And Russian prisoners were there as well, but one could not talk with them, they were surrounded with barbed wire and beaten and when they refused to work, they shot a few of them. These Russians are damn courageous and who does not conclude that they are satisfied with their regime does not admit facts.*

The Poles are very gallant, yesterday evening they declared as a group that I had beautiful eyes.

CHAPTER 41

Arrival in America

On November 3, the day of the American landing in Anfa, the port of Casablanca, Sophie and I landed in Baltimore. We were not permitted to go ashore. The FBI staff came aboard ship and every passenger who was not an American citizen was interrogated. I was questioned for two days. They wanted to make sure I was the person I seemed to be. When we were eventually permitted to disembark we had to go through customs once again, which was a cumbersome affair. The customs official took Sophie's camera, which he had no right to do. As Austrians we were not regarded as enemy aliens, but who was I to protest? The HIAS people, who were at the port in order to help the Jewish immigrants, wanted us to wait until they had assembled a group going to New York. I was able to persuade them to let us take the next train by arguing that we had gone alone from Paris to Nice to Marseille to Casablanca to Tangiers to Lisbon and so we might be able to take the train from Baltimore to New York City.

SOPHIE'S DIARY

November 4, 1942

We have arrived in Baltimore. I am writing this as if it were some ordinary event, but these last days were really very exciting—starting with the moment we spied some land, until the arrival, and until the disembarkment which, however, remains in the future. Every seagull, every airplane and every ship was initially an event. Then one got used to it, because so many boats came our way. They lined up with us and officers and sailors came on board, control of documents. We got through the first one. One is astounded and almost embarrassed about the friendliness of the American officials, we had become accustomed to different behavior in France. But here one is approximately treated like a human being. The sailors are all young guys between 20 and 22, all very straight-grown and sweet fellows. In any case, very gallant. Their way of starting a conversation is to call to one: "you are a pretty girl" and it goes from there. I talked to a few, they were all very friendly and gave me courage and painted the future in the most glowing colors. They all complimented my English, perhaps to say something pleasant. It does not slide out with as much difficulty as I had feared and I also understand quite well, except if someone speaks too much into his beard. All in all I have enormous success with the American sailors whose fathers all come from different countries. That is very funny.

Monday morning we arrived in Baltimore. That was yesterday, a terrible day. The baggage was unloaded in the morning, into the harbor. And then one waits all day on the ship, up on the second deck without permission to come down until one gets called for customs of one's baggage. Then, starting at 6:30 A.M. we waited three hours in the harbor until we were assigned a customs inspector. It was really hellish punishment and reminded me vividly of our departure from Marseille, only even more unpleasant, except that we are effectively now in America. I think if they had employed four or eight additional inspectors it would have had no ill effect, but we might not have had to wait for three hours. At least our inspector was very friendly. One looked very carefully through every suitcase, a few letters were held back but we will receive them today. It was only unpleasant to close the suitcases again. And they kept my not-yet-developed film (photos from Lisbon and the ship, which I care about a lot, because I would like to have a souvenir of the Poles). We had to pay for the development and they will forward them to us later on. I do hope they develop them properly and that they won't get lost. They took away my camera which naturally upset me greatly.

The confiscation of my beloved camera of which I naturally never heard again, threw a dark shadow over the friendliness of American authorities, the reception in the United States, and being approximately treated like human beings.

SOPHIE'S DIARY

November 5, 1942

Now we are waiting once again for a whole day, it is enough to drive you crazy, to climb the walls, and perhaps this will continue another two days. I comfort myself remembering that everything has an end, even a 50 hours' day.

All of us sit since morning on the first deck, it is cold and we wait, wait, wait. One calls up one person after another for cross-examinations which last up to five hours. Naturally this is not a quick process, well well, the famous American tempo. If I did not have, right now, my Polish friends, I would be totally lost. Because I had not kept back books, and I can only motivate myself to write with much effort, one loses one's courage and hope. But we talk to each other. We stand together all day on the deck and he talks to me. He is the soldier, my favorite guy, a totally distinguished intelligent wild fellow. He looks exactly like a Russian partisan fighter. All the adventures he has had! Once during the war, he cut through barbed wire and a comrade next to him stepped on a bomb and he flew upwards, into the sky, thinking he was flying straight into heaven, but then he flew back down, onto the barbed wire. And he has scars everywhere. The poor guy has a damaged heart and he limps on his injured leg, making him look like Mephisto. His rage against the French is undescribable. He says they have no honneur (if a Frenchman heard that!) and no culture and have to disappear from the earth. And then he told me, when it came to bayonet fights, the Germans withdrew but they were a treat for the Poles. Well, I think it is more humane to dislike such fights. But he said Poles fight without heart and love with all their heart. His comrade, the big and proud one with the blond curls, also greatly appeals to me. He is very reserved and talks little but yesterday he too explained to me that he surely would have fallen in love with me if he were not married.

November 5, 1942

Today I had my cross-examination and it lasted for hours and they kept wanting to know what was going on between me and the Poles. Since how long do I know them, what do we do together, is one of them or several of them my lover? Always the same questions. I had nothing to hide, stuck to the truth but they were dissatisfied and I did not know what they wanted from me. It was really disagreeable. Mother explained to me afterwards that the authorities must have taken me for a prostitute and she laughed.

AMERICA

Part VIII

U.S.A.

CHAPTER 42

The New Country

W hen we arrived at Pennsylvania Station, my sisters found us and there was a sad welcome, sad because our mother was not with us.

At the end of the war, Mother informed me one day that her mother had been trans-
ported from Biarritz to Theresienstadt and had died there. We never again talked
about this tragedy, nor did I discuss it with Tante Janne or Tante Lily. I had hoped
that Grandmother Drucker may have died of a natural death there. It was a startling
discovery, when I learned, in connection with research for this memoir, that she had
been transported from Biarritz to Auschwitz via the French transit camp Drancy
near Paris, on November 11, 1942, in transport #45, nine days after our ship
reached the safety of the Baltimore harbor. It was an early deportation.

Since Mother writes, at the beginning of her biography, that her mother "died
in one of Germany's concentration camps" I assume that she was not sure whether
it was indeed Theresienstadt or some other camp. She writes to Walter:

March 1946

Of my mother it was found out that she died in Theresienstadt due to weakness from DYSENTERY—she is said to have cried a lot and I am only glad that she was not sent to Poland and gassed there.

But her name and birthdate appear on the French Deportation List compiled by
S. Klarsfeld, in the International Tracing Service records of the Red Cross in Arolsen,
Germany, as well as in the lists of the Auschwitz-Birkenau archives at Auschwitz.
I could not find out whether she died during the transport or was gassed upon arrival.

They found us a room in the Masters Hotel on 103rd Street, still a decent neighborhood but too far away from everything. Since we had no money left I had to discuss that problem with them. They were in possession of father's entire inheritance and all the considerable jewelry of my mother, which they were able to take out of Vienna. As long as I had money, I did not ask them for an accounting. Marianne said that for the time being they would give us 25 dollars a week, which was not enough since the rent we had was nearly as much. I did not feel like fighting for the money. What they should have done was give me my share of the inheritance and not behave as if they were giving me charity. My brothers-in-law were terribly afraid that I wouldn't be able to support myself. Fortunately Freud's nephew Edward Bernays, the son of his sister Anna, had managed to get Sophie accepted at Radcliffe, the best woman's college in the United States, and paid her tuition.

The first few months in America, in New York City, living with Mother, who was naturally desperate and in a constant high state of starvation anxiety, were hard. "Do you love America?" I was asked by everyone I met, perhaps 20 times a week and, while I naturally answered in the affirmative, I disliked everything about this new country, this haven of salvation from the savage slaughter across the Atlantic. My job search, with my broken English, was also not very successful and I spent the rest of this school semester in a secretarial school learning shorthand and speed-typing to the tune of "Praise the Lord and pass the ammunition." Mother and I went to see many "important people," no doubt in her hope of finding support in getting professionally established.

I also met again a young man I had known in France. He was a German emigrant and had come to New York City half a year before us, after escaping from the French internment camp, Le Mille. He and his family had been hiding in their summer house in the Haute Savoie until their American visas arrived. Paul Loewenstein had, unbeknownst to me, fallen in love with me in France and announced to his family that, if we ever met again, he hoped to marry me. He asked me to do so within a week after we met again, but I was not ready to commit myself at that time.

CHAPTER 43

Neither the Family Nor Papa Have the Slightest Intention of Sending Money

I applied at Hunter College but was refused admission because Mother had not yet established legal residence in the city. Then a miracle happened once again—like getting accepted at the Lycée in Paris—it was surely in my karma to get an education—and my father's cousin, Uncle Edward Bernays (who was among the important people we visited) enrolled me at Radcliffe College and paid the first semester tuition. An anonymous donor paid all my college tuition through the three years, and I only found out many years later that Uncle Edward had continued to pay it.

I had not heard of Radcliffe College, nor of Harvard University, for that matter—the two schools merged during my stay there—but was elated at the prospect of continuing my education wherever I could. Radcliffe, in deference to wartime conditions, had just changed to a three-semester schedule, enabling students to complete their undergraduate program in three years—which I did—and for the first time admitted students at the beginning of any of the three semesters, which was of course very lucky for me, albeit also more difficult. The School placed me in The International Student House, which accepted students in the middle of the school year. It would have been, and actually was, a very suitable placement, except that the Mead family in charge had been Chinese missionaries and fervent adherents of Chang Kai Chek, clashing with my nonreligious pro-Mao leanings. But I contained my politics.

Another difficulty was that I had quietly assumed that I would eventually become a psychoanalyst and was therefore in need of a medical degree. I thus enrolled in physics and biology courses, for which I had neither sufficient preparation, nor much talent.

Aunt Doris (Fleischman) Bernays had given me $10 pocket money and off I went to Cambridge, Massachusetts.

Within a year, Mother's and my ways would separate more sharply, each dedicated to pursuing her own life. But in the first half year in the new country our connection is vividly alive, much more so than I had remembered. She had kept many of the letters I wrote her at that time, most of them in German, as I have kept many of her letters, actually mostly twice weekly postcards from that period, written for some unknown reason in gobbledygook French. I am thus able to turn to these letters, replacing my former diary, which I had discontinued, to call up those months of the beginning of our American life.

My memory was jolted by the nature of my letters. While it is difficult, for me at least, when reviewing a long life to pinpoint what the hardest times had been, I always thought the first months at Radcliffe had a high priority as the blackest period, even worse than coming to Paris from Vienna. A review of my letters now raises questions about this assumption. While I obviously struggle with the new language, the difficult course material, and the lack of money, I also find friends, report on a number of enjoyable activities, and find myself ready to strike out on my own. Within a few months, I come to fully appreciate the enormous privilege that had come my way. I write to Mother:

The longer I am here, the more do I become conscious of how lucky I am to be able to be here, simply, one two three, to attend the best College in America (April 5, 1943).

LETTER FROM SOPHIE IN CAMBRIDGE TO MOTHER IN NEW YORK
February 1, 1943
Dear Mother,
Excuse this piece of paper, I am just at School and have nothing better on hand. Life is grey and ugly. If only I had started College right away in November. This is most people's second semester and I am in the middle of the year, totally lost. Especially chemistry makes me quite miserable. Sciences are here much more rigorously taught than in France and everyone else knows much more and I don't even know what the prof. talks about. In chemistry he looked at my French lab. notebook and declared he did not think I would be able to follow the class, because what I had done so far was totally elementary. And the worst is that the course had already started in September. About the other subjects I am still uncertain but I only understand the teachers with difficulty. In any case, chemistry is supposed to be my main subject. On top of that there is so much work that I am struggling up to my head. In psychology we learned today about Grandfather. But I think the prof. is an ass. I have failed the English anticipatory examination.

Sunday evening we had a gathering of international students in our house. I met a girl who is being psychoanalyzed by Felix Deutsch. She says he has helped her a lot. He also lives in Cambridge, but I won't call him, I don't feel like continuing the active social life we had in New York City.

But after Father had written me that Felix Deutsch had been his intimate friend, I did call him, with greetings from Father and mentioned that I had met one of his analysands. This last bit interested him, but nothing else. It was a short, awkward telephone conversation that he ended as soon as possible. Five years later, already married and quite well established as a social work student, I met him for the first time. I reminded him of our earlier contact. "You sounded so anxious and forlorn," he explained, "I did not want to have anything to do with you."

LETTER TO MOTHER
February 3, 1943
Dear Mother,
If you could send me $2, I would be very grateful. It is not my fault, but books, boots, and copybooks have devoured all my money. I am really very sorry, but it is not my fault, I really bought nothing else for myself, and the boots I wear day and night, I really needed them.

Oh, yes, I had not mentioned them before. I ran in vain into 20 stores and in the 21st I caught the last pair, the last in Boston. They could be a little bigger, I cannot wear them with very thick wool socks, but they are awfully pretty and very good, $3.45 (not so bad for boots), black, and dainty. The books I bought secondhand except for one new edition. But I can sell those

Books	2.75
	3.00
Notebooks	2.00
Boots	3.45
Postage	0.25
Oranges	0.20
Paper	0.75
Laundry soap	0.20
Subway	0.30
	15.60
Baggage	1.45
	17.05

at the end of the year. I still owe Mrs. Mead the money for the baggage, and I have 20 cents left. I am so sorry that I spent so much, but this was because of the beginning. After that I shall certainly not need more than $1 a week.

Yesterday I was so upset about my money affairs that I went to the students employment office and they gave me a crazy job. I went with Ba (Mrs. Mead's daughter) to a guy [a psychologist, A. A. Roback] who gave us questionnaires and we went from house to house in the prescribed streets and posed these questions. It was for some kind of psychological research and the guy then showed me letters he had gotten from Grandfather. I don't know why he was so proud, they all said that he was an idiot. For each interview, 15 cents. But Mrs. Mead does not want us to continue because of going alone in the evening into people's houses, and I am rather glad that she is forbidding it because it is quite disagreeable and at the moment I can only take jobs during which I can study because I have to get used to things. The girls are all very nice, at home and at school. The baggage has arrived and I arranged my room in an especially sweet way, if I have time I shall make a picture for you.

I just got a very dear letter from Walter. He will not marry Jean after all, she does not know how to bake poppyseed strudel and does not like to wash dishes. And letters from Paul, I am so happy he is here, otherwise I would feel much worse.—

I had an examination by a doctor, which one has to get because of gym. She is a German immigrant (Dr. Nauen) and was very nice and I am of course totally healthy, but she only looked me over superficially. I also told her that since a month I bleed like a slaughtered pig, every day as I brush my teeth, and she found out that my gums are a bit inflamed and that I need vitamin C. Thus I bought a dozen oranges because we have fruit only for breakfast. But the food is very adequate and I do my best to eat the money's worth and I keep gaining weight. But one can't just go into the kitchen and pour oneself a glass of milk, for example.

Later

Today I had swimming for the first time in gym. I am learning crawling and the teacher said I would learn it very fast. It is quite strenuous and one's hair gets wet. But there are hair dryers available. Naturally I now look like a witch.

I went to my job-man. He gave me $1.25 more than he had promised and was actually very friendly. He is a Jew and has enormous respect for me. And Saturday from 2:30 to 4:30 I go there to do typing jobs, for which one gets 50 cents an hour. I am to type the letters that Grandfather had sent him. Because he noticed that I can read them and he could never quite *decipher them. So I was able to pay my debts (the baggage cost to Mrs. Mead) and on Saturday I shall even have masses of money left over. So you don't need to send me any. At most next week, one dollar. But not more. Evenings I put on the electric heater in my room. It makes it cozily warm,* tant pis *[too bad] for the family's electric heating bill. Did I tell you that they were missionaries in China?*

—Sunday I went with them to their Congregational Church. The minister only begged for money during the entire sermon. Today they have a dance downstairs, but I am too busy and I would not enjoy it in any case. My letter is anything but a literary masterpiece, but I hope you don't care. I only wanted to tell you the most important news as quickly as possible. Many kisses, your Sophie

The story of the wounded gums took a dramatic turn. The bleeding continued and Dr. Nauen started to insist that I visit a dentist. I found out that this would cost $25 and explained to Dr. Nauen that I could simply not afford it. She then suggested that Radcliffe might be too expensive a college for me to attend. Panicked about possible expulsion, I wrote to Father (in vain) and sent Mother an SOS letter. Tante Janne immediately sent me the needed money within days. I now wonder whether Mother, out of her rageful pride, never told Tante Janne of my almost desperate financial situation, neither felt I free to do so myself.

GERMAN LETTER

February 9, 1943

Dearest good little Mäu,

Your letters are rather desperate, but console, console, in three months you will have gotten your bearings, just don't lose courage until then. I am only glad that I sent you $5, because I had a premonition that you may be out of money.

With me all is also failing at the moment. The Lipshütz [private patient] have canceled me for February. The School of the Deaf, Lexington Avenue invited me to come and introduce myself, to tell me they do not need me. My voice case has already canceled twice because she did not have time, announced herself for today, 2:00 P.M. and it is already later and she has still not arrived, besides she promised to pay today. Yesterday, Friday, I had guests and cooked them a terribly elegant meal, too bad you were not here: Tomato soup with rice, mushrooms with egg, jellied fish with potato salad, cheese, compote, and coffee. On this occasion I broke my Silex coffee maker. An hour later I was still washing dishes.

The patient did arrive after all, but did not pay, instead she got sick. Then Janne brought me her carpet. In one room I have paper curtains. The custodian is not as nice as he looks, one cannot ask him for anything. What do you hear from Walterl? Does he mention Father? The flat is not yet cozy.

Many kisses Mother Esti

FRENCH POSTCARD
February 16
Dear Mäu ... today I am sending you $2, buy yourself a warm undershirt, because it is very very cold. I am okay, earning a bit of money but not enough.... I am in treatment with a dentist. That will cost a pretty penny.

Write me soon. I am very touched by your Valentine.

Kiss, kiss, kiss, Mother

FRENCH POSTCARD
February 19
Dear Sophie,
Thank you for your letter. With the money I sent you, buy yourself some warm things. This evening I have a conference. My student has loaned me two blankets, if you want I can send you one. I am quite disheartened due to the political news. My radio does not yet work. Evenings I sometimes feel very lonely. Today I bought myself some rubber gloves because my hands are in quite a state from cleaning filth, you can't imagine how much soot there is everywhere. Everything goes very slowly. I am for hours and hours at home without the telephone ringing a single time. Have you started to work yourself in a bit? Kisses from your mother.

MARCH 6, 1943
Dearest Mother,
Thank you for your nice card.... Today I earned $4. For that I typed three hours, during the week one or two hours at home (I get up at 6:00 A.M. and type from 6 to 7) and this evening I have a job for three hours serving at table and doing the dishes. It ruined my Saturday, but $4 are not to be sneered at. I wanted to save for a pair of shoes, but today I received a bill for health fees: $5. As I was clearing the table a man asked me about Grandfather etc. etc. As time passes, I can hardly stand it any longer and only introduce myself with reluctance lest someone asks whether I am related.... After 10 times I get bored, after the 20th time I start to hate everyone who asks things and after the 30th time I become insane.

In the kitchen it was very amusing, the cook told me the whole time how the family lets her starve and the governess will quit tomorrow. I buy myself a big bottle of milk for my lunch. I have tried to manage without lunch but then I am deathly exhausted by 3:00 P.M. and have to find a bed in some building, to lie down.

I shall come to New York around March 27. Easter is only at the end of April and we have no vacations. . . . But the semester already ends at the end of May. Then there is one month vacation and after that the summer semester starts. This is a totally new change, because of the war there are three semesters per year, instead of two, but one does not have to attend all of them. It makes it possible to finish college in two years and eight months. It is quite strenuous, only one-month vacation all year, especially if one works so terribly hard.

A boy just called me to invite me to go skiing. I met him once, for two minutes and since then he calls me twice every week. Was that not a quick conquest? And two others have also repeatedly asked me for a date. But I have never gone out yet. I don't have time and I don't care about it. In no case will I go out with American boys, only with emigrants—why should I go out with complete strangers? It is only for my self-respect since I don't have other successes to report, I mean, I would care more about good grades.

My English teacher told me that my writing is very interesting. Even the language is not bad. But up to now we had easy essays: An autobiography. I wrote a good piece (I think) about our flight from and also about "my hometown." I wrote about the Viennese workers with their adult education school and public housing, about the Turkish siege, the Habsburg monarchs, the Burgtheater *and our* Wienerwald *[the woods around Vienna]. I was quite hit with nostalgia. But I shall certainly never return to Vienna, Paul would never want to live in Vienna, he would like to stay here,*

After my physics exam, the day before yesterday I had suicidal thoughts.

FRENCH POSTCARDS
March 8
Dear Sopherel,
I just got a letter from Ernst Freud where he writes that neither the family, nor papa, have the least intention to send us money, we can just work. Your money from the Freud books they will give you only when you are a Major. The only thing you can do is to write to Walter about our financial circumstances and that you too have the right to go to school and get an education. But I will no longer write to anybody.
Many kisses, your mother Esti

MARCH 17

Dear Mäu,

I am already very impatient to see you again. Next Wednesday I talk at a conference in the ward of Dr. Bender, but only honorary. With money it is very *nebbich*. I got a gift of curtains and two chairs. Now I have already five chairs. I work a lot but no results.... Why don't you write? I count the days until your arrival.

Many kisses from your mother E.F.

MAY 19, 1943

Dearest Mother,

I did feel very sorry for you this morning, but I still don't feel especially guilty, because I could not have foreseen that you would receive me like a prodigal son. The feeling that there is so much turmoil about my coming "home" is definitely very uncomfortable. Besides the telephone call was not worth the money, for $1.25 I have to wash dishes for 2 1/2 hours. You have to admit that I purposefully wrote that I would only come with 50 percent certainty.

Monday I have a physics exam, next Saturday biology. This Monday I had psychology, and Tuesday bio lab. You can see I am rather busy. Which is why I did not come after all. I would have had to bring too many books along.

Don't send me any more money, I can manage and I don't spend anything, except for stamps.

Mother was so upset about my not visiting her—when I had (50 percent) promised— and seemed so lonely all around, I appealed to Tante Janne for advice. Below is her answer, including advice for a personal psychoanalysis that I would often receive in the future from different adults around me, but never followed.

LETTER FROM TANTE JANNE

My very dear Zäpfelchen,

Please remember once and for all that you are not responsible that your Mother is alone, nor for her unhappy way to push away all people and to hurt those who are close to her. To free yourself of these problems I would much like to see you being psychoanalyzed as soon as possible because it is for you the only possibility to come to peace with these problems in a humane and reasonable way and to find a solution. It is not possible that the conflicts between Esti and Martin have not affected you—Probably Esti has at the moment a depressive period because she can't claim that she is starving since she is earning quite well so the depression is oriented toward you. Meanwhile it is probably all settled and don't take it so tragically. It has almost nothing to do with you! I have meanwhile learned that in my analysis. Please don't let this get you down. Write her a very friendly letter but don't visit her if you have made other plans.

Your Janne

FRENCH POSTCARD
   March 25
   Dear Mau,
   Through the intervention of Dr. Sachs we have received $100 from the psychoanalytic society. I am sending you $13 from this money. Buy yourself if you want some shoes and a skirt and if there is anything left over a slip. With the rest I shall pay the rent and the dentist and a few small purchases, a tea-kettle, a teapot, and some flowers. I will write Dr. Sachs a long thank you letter.
   Kisses, kisses, from your mother Esti

MARCH 27, 1943
   Dearest Mother,
   I am writing from a babysitting job, the babies are already sleeping peacefully. Today I had my exam. In bio. I failed it catastrophically and totally. Nothing to be done, I suspected that this would be the result. Listen, Mother, I have decided not to become a physician, I hate biology and chemistry and all that stuff. Why on earth should I learn things that I hate when there are very beautiful subjects? I don't care what the whole family will say, I am changing to languages and this summer I shall take Russian, Spanish, mathematics, and maybe English and psychology.
   Thank you a whole lot for the $13. I did not know what had gotten into you and whether you had accidentally won the big prize in the lottery. I will save the $13 check. The two other $2 checks which I did not need, but are just enough to finish paying the board for Mrs. Mead. So my whole school year only costs Uncle Rudi $35, I earned $4.50 this week. Are you impressed? If I did not have to pay for the stupid milk, I would already have saved $8. But whenever I save some money a stupid bill snows into the house. Because I had a dishwashing job this week, and two watching children jobs and a typing job. And all of them did not take too much time because I can work while the children sleep and the typing was today from 12:00 noon to 2:30 P.M., a time

in which I usually only sit about. I have become this guy's real secretary, write bills for him and the funniest letters, it is quite entertaining. Washing dishes was also quite pleasant. I was already the second time with the same lady and she asked especially for me. I think she enjoys telling at table that "the grandchild" is serving at her table and then all sorts of people come into the kitchen and want to get to know me, or they claim that they know Tante Anna etc. But the cook there has taken me into her heart and she does not even let me wash dishes, at most dry them, and the other day my main occupation was to eat ice cream and cake and drink coffee. For that I got $1.50.

Listen, big problem, shall I buy a pair of summer or winter shoes? ... It is already deliciously warm and that is wonderful. The other day at school I lay on the meadow and took a sun bath. All the buds are already starting to burst. Or shall I buy myself a cotton dress. ... Monday I am starting crew, my gym for the spring term. Is that not wonderful, on the Charles River.

In two weeks I come to New York.

APRIL 5 [1943]

Dearest Mu,

Thank you for your dear card. I will have the evening gown that I got as a gift dry-cleaned, but it costs $1.25. That is bitter. I saved $8 but the trip [to New York] will swallow up everything. Unfortunately my psychologist is leaving for New York during April, making me unemployed. Imagine, I typed a letter the other day about publishing Tante Anna's books in America. Is that not too funny. If she knew that. ... I am very grateful to the Bernays to have brought me here. The longer I am here, the more I realize how fortunate I am to suddenly, without any preparation, attend the best college in America. I accepted the summer job. The woman seems friendly, cleaned her house last Sunday.

Above all don't send me any more money, I now have more than necessary and I will not be using the $5 you sent me. But perhaps I will buy some shoes. In any case, I have no more need of money, I am earning quite well with my babysitting.

What I wanted to tell you, please don't be so vengeful and forget unpleasantnesses as quickly as possible. We have wars only because people are so vengeful. Being full of grudges never improves a situation.

FRENCH LETTER

April 10 [after a visit to Mother]

... You know, I was very happy to see you again, I embrace you tightly.

FRENCH POSTCARDS

April 21

Dear Mau,

Imagine, I had a letter from Duprée. All is going well and he is sad that we left. I hope you got the $3 check. It is a long time since I have not had any news from you. I think in a few days I can send you a larger sum, I have almost $30 owed to me. Perhaps I will be able to pay my rent this month and I still have Rudi's [Boyko] check he gave me in March, with that, I will have enough for June and July and after that we shall see.

APRIL 25

Dear Mau,

Write to Doris Bernays, perhaps they will offer you the money for the school again. The best would be if the lady at the school office to whom the Bernays have paid the first time, will write to them again. I think, if necessary, I can find the $100 for you.... In any case, I will send you all my extra money, you can believe me. At the moment I am poor but I am owed $20.

Kisses, Mother

GERMAN LETTER

Saturday, April 25

Dear Heartmäu,

Imagine, I am sitting at the East river down below, in the close vicinity of our house, on a bench in the sun and am looking at the boats and it is almost cozy.

I hope you got the little package with the tea and the white fabric....

Tante Lily need not make a fuss, the check that they have given me mid-March is still untouched, and if we have a bit of luck I can manage through the summer. When I get the $20 that are owed to me, I shall send you money again. I also have to put up with a lot, you can believe me, and I will remember everything precisely but at the moment I clench my teeth....

Kisses, Mother

FRENCH POSTCARD

N.Y., May 14

Dear Mau,

Already three days without news from you, I hope you are not sick. My catarrh is much better.... I work enormously much but the results are still very thin. My dentist wants another $30 from me. These are hard times. It is really shameful that I am not sending you money. But I still do not have the rent for this month. . . .

Kisses mother Esti

GERMAN LETTER

May 18

Dear Heartmäuli,

Please don't care so much because of Dick, there are masses of nice young men in this world, who will find you wonderful and vice versa, one has all the time such experiences and finally it is boring to always walk around with a broken heart, it is not much fun in the long run. . . .

Kisses, kisses, kisses Mother

It had been very hard to pay Mrs. Mead her room and board fee and there was no question that we could continue this. I therefore applied for an au pair position, which was then an exchange of three hours of household and/or childcare work per day, for room and board. Miss Almy, the student employment officer who had become almost a friend, given that I was her best customer, acted with more kindness than wisdom. Thinking I would feel more "at home" in a family in which the mother of the house spoke German she placed me in a household with a non-Jewish authentically German woman who was worrying about her German family—presumably engaged in killing my European family—and her poor brother in the German army. She specified, moreover, that she appreciated her private meals with her husband, which relegated me to the kitchen. I decided to accept the placement and also take the offer to work there as a full-time maid during the three weeks of vacations between the spring term and the summer term. This would prepare me for the part-time work during the summer term.

GERMAN LETTER

Saturday, May 22, 1943

Much loved Mutterpitz,

This morning I have started to work. I learned to bathe the baby, feed him, prepare the baby food, diaper him. It is a cute good-natured baby who only cries when he is uncomfortable. For the work here the woman gives me cotton dresses and smocks for housecleaning and dishwashing. This saves my clothes, because with a baby everything is a mess. . . . Otherwise I am naturally very downhearted, above all I feel very alone and besides washing dishes and cleaning rooms brings on melancholia. I repeat for myself all the time that I am not an idiot, and that I attend college on the side, otherwise I *get horrible inferiority feelings. Too bad I can't go on Monday to our school dance.*

I have meanwhile managed to strike Dick out of my head. For a while I dreamed every night about him, which has never happened with a boy. But I have told you, I am only able to love people who do not love me back or who treat me badly, I already know that for sure.

The people here have a pure wonderful German Shepard, big as a lamb. I keep worrying that he will swallow the baby by mistake.

Pussi, Pussi, Pussi, Sophie

I had sent Mother for her birthday on May 21 another poem in which I thank her for bringing me safely to America. Unfortunately it got lost.

FRENCH POSTCARD

May 21, 1943

Dear Mau,

This morning I got your birthday congratulations with the beautiful poem, I cried a lot, as always. Yesterday I had a terrific success. They sent me an old man, father of a doctor in New York, with total aphasia, he could only whisper. After six minutes with my treatment he had his normal voice. This treatment will earn me $30 which I will ask (after consultation with the doctor who had sent me the case) and a great reputation.... If my practice continues to go well I shall come to see you!!

Kisses, kisses Mother Esti

GERMAN LETTER

May 26, 1943

Dearest Mu,

Thank you for your card. Too bad you did not have a nice birthday, but see to it that you get along with your sister. After all, they are the only ones who have helped us to come here. And the malicious things you only imagine, they don't mean to be malicious.

I got a very dear letter from Father, the first really solid letter. The letter took eight days. He has found a government job in which he can use his knowledge as banker and lawyer, travel around the whole country and is quite well paid. He is enormously pleased and proud, and says he is slowly getting fat because he spends all his time strutting around with his briefcase with impressive letters. Walter is well. I am very happy that Father has finally found something. It is also important for Walter's future.

There are no other agreeable events to report. It is not easy to earn $20 a week, this you can believe me. I work terribly hard and the woman gives me too much work. Until now I never worked less than 12 hours and yesterday she had guests and I worked from 7:00 A.M. to 11 at night. If you ever have a choice between being a maid (I mean as main occupation for all one's life) and suicide, then better choose the latter. But I can stand it for one month—a matter of principle. I hate the woman who is a Nazi in her heart because her brother serves in the German army. But yesterday I was so wild at her that she gave me much less work today.

I don't get time to read at all. I am usually too tired in the evening to take my clothes off. The Werfel book about the Armenians [The 40 Days of Musa Dagh] is horrifying and reminds me too much of Jewish persecutions and upsets me.

Today I baked cookies. It is very easy and they turned out very well. I will certainly not learn to cook here, rather teach, she asks me all the time for advice. Could you please write me how you prepare the turnips so well and how you make Goulash and vanilla crescents.

The baby is only seven months old, it cannot yet sit on a pot. But I don't have to wash. The last week I will certainly come to N.Y. In this way I can look forward to something. I am very alone. The whole thing might do me good. My feet are damned painful. My room is very nice, I arranged it prettily. Tomorrow afternoon I have free time, once a week. Pussi, Sophie

The woman is pregnant (four months). She is a German Aryan from Munich who came here through her marriage. Her husband is American and works for the labor department. Her whole family is in Germany.

French letter

June 4, 1943

Dearest Mu,

Thank you very much for the package. The cookbook was not really needed. You can imagine that I could not care less whether these folks eat well or badly. Let them kick the bucket if they want. A maid never likes her mistress, it would not be different with another. (Don't imagine that our maids liked you.) If I did not come to New York for these vacations, it was not for lack of wanting, you can believe me but 1.) I would have lost about three days ($9). 2.) I could not have found for three weeks a job that would have paid me more than $20 per week. So you would have had to pay for the food and you have said yourself that you spend more than double when we are two people than when you are alone. And I don't know why I should not *muddle through for once by myself, and not always you for me. After all, I must leave one day my protective glass shell, why not now. I did not want you to come because I don't see why you should spend a day in a stranger's kitchen. It is unpleasant enough when I am on my own. It would embarrass me if you saw me at work, you more than anyone else. Okay, that is all on this subject.*

I hope you will get the job in the summer camp. That would get you out of the city in the worst heat. I am holding both my thumbs for you. You can't expect many patients during the summer. You know that everyone a little well off leaves. Thus, don't get upset if the practice goes less well at the moment. It will do you good to gain a bit of weight, you look better with rounder cheeks. . . .

I have bought, no, not shoes, nor a blouse, neither a dress, nor a camera. Well, what??

—— ? —— ? —— ? ——

!! a man's bicycle!!!!!!! For $5. I thought it was such a bargain (it was left behind by a student at one of the Harvard dorms and the caretaker wanted $5). The bike, although far from being perfect, was certainly worth $5 and I made the decision in two minutes. I have always secretly mourned my bike and I am very pleased to have another one. It needs little things, altogether for $3, but even $8 is not much for a bike. Above all because I live a good 10 minutes from the school and a bike will make my life much easier. What do you think about this, mother?

I have Thursday afternoon and evening free, and Sunday or Saturday evening from 7:30 or 8:00, which is not too soon.

And when I have my free day, she leaves all the dishes for the next day because she is too lazy to move her little finger herself.

Last Sunday I was at a little party at M.I.T. and the boy who invited me does not particularly appeal to me. Immer gefällt man den Falschen (One always attracts the wrong people). He has no sense of humor and he seemed terribly nervous. And, what is worse, he stutters the m and the n. Do you think I should go out with him from time to time until I have found a better one, or should I get rid of him right away? I wanted to tell you a lot of things, but I am tired and now I forgot. It will keep for the next time.

Kisses, kisses, kisses, Sophie

CHAPTER 44

Radcliffe Summer 1943

GERMAN LETTER

July 11, 1943

Dearest Pitz,

Thank you for your unfortunately very depressed letter. First of all I am sending quickly my grades:

English C+

Biology C−

Physics C

Psychology B−

The worst one is allowed to get and still pass are three C's and 1 D. Thus, I did not fail, not even almost—To get a scholarship one has to have at least all B's. As you see I am still very far from that. Do you now understand?

You did not mention my bike. Did you think it was frivolous? Yesterday I went to Boston which is 4 miles. It runs very nicely although it is quite heavy. With repair, light, bell, baggage rack, license etc. it cost me $9. But I was already offered $15 or even more for it. But I won't sell it.

Don't be so upset because of your patients. Don't forget that summer is a dead season. In the fall it will start again in a big way. Don't always say such hateful things about my family. The Oli Freuds probably have their heads full of worries, you must remember how it is when one just arrives. The family has nothing whatever to do with it. . . .

GERMAN LETTER

July 12, 1943 (during mathematics)

Much loved Pitz,

Am very angry that you have not yet let me know how you are doing.

Next time I too will have an operation and not let you know for weeks how I am feeling.

Dynamic Psychology is a very interesting course in which one learns a lot about Freud, but unfortunately our teacher is deadly dull. He reads his lectures, or rather he drones them out tonelessly. When I mentioned my name the whole class (Radcliffe and Harvard) started to scream and the teacher said: "Could you spell that please!"

The unpleasant part is that we have to write an autobiography for Friday. About one's whole life, background, inner life, sex-life (typical questions of the outline that we are supposed to follow: When did you begin to masturbate? Did you ever watch sexual relations between your parents? Do you experience affection, worshipness, disgust, loss of self-respect in sexual relations, etc. etc.).

The whole thing is very disgusting and I will give a very reserved picture of my inner life, you can be dead sure of that, especially since he knows my name. . . . Two boys (quite nice) accompanied me home and asked me whether they could meet me again next Sunday, and a third whom I quite liked, a new physics instructor at Harvard, asked me whether he could sometimes call me for a date.

In math we have a young man with blond locks but the course looks very unpromising. . . . Fine Arts, I think, is going to be super. It is an art appreciation course and next time I come to New York I take you to a museum and explain all about the pictures.

Kisses, kisses, kisses, Sophie

JULY 12

In English we have a poet, we even had to buy an anthology in which it is said that he is a genius. First I thought he would spend all his time making cynical comments. But then he turned out to be quite friendly and interesting. He is said to be very interested in psychology and stutters a bit and emits every five minutes a tomblike sigh. I explained to him right away, the first hour that I did not care about poetry and afterwards I learned that he was a poet.

JULY 28

The most alluring of all is my English teacher. I would love to conquer him, he is so intelligent. But I never have any luck with teachers.

I would only learn many years later, when I read a biography of Delmore Schwartz, that I had indeed a very exceptional English teacher.

During the summer of 1943, my second term at Radciffe, I was assigned to the introductory English A course (not offered during the winter term, my first term). I had been absorbed in books since early adolescence, starting with Schiller and Goethe, submerged myself in the French classics that summer in Castillonès, almost swallowed up most of the library in Nice, fallen in love with the characters of Heine, Dostoevsky, and Tolstoy, but I could not master The Education of Henry Adams, *which was this course's main reading assignment.* The Education *was completely out of my reach, given that I was overwhelmed by the mass of the book, uncomprehending of much of its sophisticated vocabulary, ignorant of the American political system, as well as incapable of grasping, or finding the slightest interest in, the subtleties of the intellectual development of a Boston Brahmin at home and abroad. Later, in an assignment of our choice, I would write a tortuous paper on Heinrich Heine for that same class, naturally in bad English, for which Professor Schwartz showed interest and great indulgence.*

Had Professor Schwartz not been extremely charitable and given me a passing grade, knowing that I had been unable to complete this central assignment—not to mention my inadequate mastery of the English language—I might have become a college dropout, a disheartening beginning for a new American, and my entire life might have taken a different turn.

I was totally surprised, many years later, when I found that my engaging professor had twice mentioned my name in his correspondence. Had I thus not been as invisible as I then assumed myself to be? Teaching an introductory English course at Radcliffe was not Delmore Schwartz's idea of an interesting pursuit, but the prospect of having at least one interesting student seems to have cheered him a little.

The Navy is here and I must teach two Radcliffe classes, to justify the deferment the University gave me. This means teaching on every day but Sunday and Monday for the next 16 weeks, beginning in the middle of next week.... The one note of promise is that Morrison told me that the granddaughter of Sigmund Freud is to be one of the students. She is probably neurotic (p. 180).

In a second letter he revises his assumption about me.

I went with zest to my new Radcliffe class, having been told that Sophie Freud, granddaughter of the Viennese was to be one of my students. She is probably neurotic I said to myself, but on the contrary she turned out to be a veritable butterball, full of assurance, and when the class read *The Turn of the Screw* and I asked Sophie what she thought of it, she said: "A clear case of paranoia" (p. 187).

Given that I was feeling totally lost and overwhelmed, Professor Schwartz cannot be given credit for a correct perception of my state of mind. But he can be given credit for his generosity. Delmore Schwartz went on to have a dark life and an early death. I wish I had had the opportunity to thank him for his understanding, kind-ness, and the difference he had made to my life. At least I did find him very compel-ling at the time as indicated above, in letters to my mother.

JULY 24

The physicist will surely fall in love with me but although he is incredibly competent and intelligent etc. and of course an emigrant, he is even from Vienna, he leaves me cold. He resembles Paul, but seems an even more absolute scientist. I do have bad luck, always falling on scientists who take everything so seriously.

You are dreadfully touching but also frivolous. The most beautiful um-brella of the 20th century has arrived and I was terribly pleased. It rains in any case all the time. I was all excited when a long tube arrived, a bit early for a birthday present. Hopefully I will not forget it somewhere. And then I could not blame you for it. Thank you for the nice card. I am very glad that you are again earning a bit of money. I am very happy at the Wyatts.

I am dead tired and overwhelmed with work. Don't worry about my fall-ing in love, my heart is as cold as an icicle.—

Pussi, Pussi, Dein Sophilein

Toward the end of the three weeks as maid in the Northey family, we had some nasty conflicts and I vigorously declined to continue there as an au pair student and Miss Almy found me another family, indeed a Viennese family who knew my mother. Although I quickly realized that the mother of the household had been among my mother's enemies in Vienna, I did not care.

Sophie had to work for her room and board. Something strange happened in this regard. The Radcliffe administration placed Sophie as a maid in order to earn her room and board, at the family of a woman, Mrs. Gertrud Lasch, who had been my serious competitor in Vienna. (She had also been trained at the Fröschels Clinic and had a private practice.) Why Mrs. Lasch came to the United States is still a riddle for me. She was a Catholic, married to a Catholic physician. She eloped with a much younger man, a psychologist called Fritz Weiss, who was Jewish, went with him to England, married him and came to the States. She had a little girl with him. It was in this house-hold that Sophie was placed. I was worried about her. Would she be able to manage, not being able to speak English in a totally strange environment? Mrs. Lasch asked too many services of her, although she did not have to pay her a penny. Sophie could take it. After two terms, Sophie received a scholar-ship that included not only tuition but also room and board and hence did not need to be a servant in a house where life was made especially difficult for her. One of the youngsters who was a member of her Paris dancing class had previously arrived in New York City and now served in the Navy. He found her since an interview with Sophie as Freud's granddaughter had appeared in *The New Yorker*. The auguries for her future became more favorable.

This is to be almost the last mention of my name in my mother's autobiography. She could foresee a suitable marriage, my education eventually completed, and feel the satisfaction of having fulfilled her maternal obligations toward me. Few readers will notice, or care about, Mother's apparently insignificant lapse of memory, con-fusing my unpleasant maid-service with the German woman's family and my satis-factory stay with the Wyatts. And yet, reading how Mother projects her own past hostile competition with Gertrude Lasch-Weiss awoke too many unhappy childhood memories of Mother's endless quarrels and made me very angry. "With the Wyatts (the changed family name from Weiss) I am very happy," I wrote to her in July 1943.

Both Mr. and Mrs. Wyatt treated me indeed as a grown-up daughter, which did mean that the hours of work were not exactly counted, but they were also sup-portive of my studies, my interests, and included me fully into their social life, which included some of the academic and psychoanalytic community in Cambridge. I grew deeply fond of the dear baby girl in the family whose main care always remained in Mrs. Wyatt's hands, and they forgave me for regularly burning their rice and my generally poor cooking skills. I stayed with the Wyatts for one year, but the place-ment isolated me from a regular student life and for my last year I moved to Edmonds House, a cooperative students' house, in which the students did their own cooking and housekeeping and thus paid a much lower fee, supporting myself with a part-time job at the Widener library. The Wyatts and I remained friends for many years.

Yes, and I did marry Paul Loewenstein, a very handsome young man with beautiful blue eyes. He was a Jewish immigrant like myself; we had both lived and known each other in France. He offered me a permanent link with the Europe I had sadly left behind. I was extremely happy to be no longer alone, and I looked forward to founding a new family with him in this foreign country. He was kind, extremely conscientious, considerate, and devoted to me. He was in every respect a contrast to my selfish, ungenerous father, and I knew that he would treat me better than my father had treated my mother and that he would be a caring father to our children. My expectation proved correct; we had three children, two of whom have their voices in this book, and had a relatively peaceful marriage for 40 years. But when he broke that unspoken contract, the marriage ended, or maybe the other way around.

CHAPTER 45

It Was Very Difficult at the Beginning

I too had some lucky breaks. I was soon asked to lecture about the adventures we had in Europe trying to escape from Hitler. My main occupation for the first few months, however, was running around looking for a job in my field, speech pathology. I had numerous introductions. I visited psychoanalysts I had known in Vienna and Paris. I visited and visited—if only my English had been better! One of the visits was made to Mrs. Catherine Hirsch, a German woman who was trained in England by Mrs. Lasch in speech pathology. She was in New York for quite some time and as a relative of the famous wealthy Baron de Hirsch had excellent connections and spoke fluent English, having lived in England before coming to the United States. Mrs. de Hirsch was a speech pathologist when I visited her. She had a volunteer job in the profession at Manhattan Eyes, Ear, Nose, and Throat Hospital and asked me if I wanted to take over for her. She introduced me to Dr. Daniel Cunning, the head of the hospital's throat department and I was permitted to work there.

It was very difficult at the beginning.

Mother had been able to resume contact, at least for a time, with her son who was then serving in the English army, and we can thus follow her description of her life. Most of her correspondence was in German.

GERMAN LETTER

February 1943, 444 East 58 Street New York City
Dearest Herzensmuckerl,
I was very pleased with your dear letter although it was strange for me and made it sound foreign that you wrote in English. In spite of the many

countries and languages that I traversed with Sopherl, I still speak German with her.

I think I have not changed much in appearance, a few wrinkles more but not too bad, and many white hairs. Sometimes I continue to be very cheerful and although we are currently having a very bad time and I live for days on only bread and coffee with milk because I simply have no money, still I think that in about a year things will go quite well, unfortunately I don't have the money for English lessons, which would naturally help me a lot since my English is after all still quite miserable. I now took a small flat and furnished it with an old couch and two old chairs and a little table because living in a hotel is too expensive. I hope not too many bedbugs will crawl out of the couch. Neither Sophie nor I hear anything from Father. He does not seem to find it worth while to write to us since he assumes that we shall, in any case, soon have starved to death. Believe me, it is no pleasure to have to live off the charity of relatives and you can imagine how much I run around to put an end to this situation, for me alone it would not be so hard but to be able to also support Sopherl should take a pretty piece of time.

Up to now I am working in two hospitals and in one school. The best prospects are for voice problems which is not done here.

Basically I still feel it very strange to be in America. New York is terribly big but in part quite pretty, I really like the skyscrapers, and Downtown, in Wall Street one feels like in a great Canyon. I now live close to my hospitals because the hours in the subway and bus exhausted me.

In the English Consulate here I was told that Father would certainly get permission to send us money if he applied for it and that even you could apply for support money at the military, which would be sent directly to me without any deduction for you. I think you could try that. Neither Sophie nor I have any clothes (no warm things) our baggage which I had to forward—we flew from Tangier to Lisbon—got stuck in Bermuda. I assume that Schnapserl has told you in detail about our travel adventures.

Sopherl is a big success, everyone likes her and tries to help her as much as they can. She also has terribly many admirers. Edward Bernays arranged the school for her—it is the best college for girls in the United States. It is very hard to get accepted there.

Dear Puckerl, I hope to see you again some day, everyone says how handsome you are/what else—my son. After the war you could finish your school here, I think it might be easier to get ahead; how come Father could not get on his feet after such a long time? I have heard that Mathilde and Ernst are doing very well, and Anna has become terribly famous. By the way, the analysts here do not move a finger for us, even though there are many of them, and the name of Freud is mentioned every five minutes by somebody. Did Father get our birthday telegram?

I hope next time I can already report more positive things about me. Many many kisses, your Mother

Even finding an empty room where I could see my patients proved to be a problem with mountains of obstacles. First I worked in the bronchoscope

Esti as a professional woman

room, then in a big meeting room, and finally the dental room was permanently assigned to me since the dentist worked only in the morning and my clinic was in the afternoon. I was especially successful with esophageal voice training and I believe I was also the first in New York City to introduce such training. Except for Dr. Green's National Hospital for Speech Disorders, no such services existed in New York. The clinic was written up in the *New York Times* and as an aftermath I received a number of crank calls.

Mother was very upset about these crank calls. She called me to tell me how upset she was. It was hard to hear about them.

I worked there for approximately 17 years twice a week without salary. My only rewards were a few referrals of private patients.

After I left, the hospital organized a speech and hearing clinic with a well-paid staff. Fortunately some other opportunities were soon available to me. One of the psychoanalysts I visited referred me to Dr. Ernest Kulka, a Viennese gynecologist who sent me to an E.N.T. specialist on the staff of New York Hospital-Cornell Medical College. The attending E.N.T. was Dr. Arthur Palmer, who accepted me on a volunteer basis. Two afternoons a week were dedicated to building up a speech clinic in New York Hospital. I encountered less hostility there than in the Manhattan EENT Hospital thanks to the head nurse, Evelyn Clark. I started there in June 1943 and stayed until 1971. My path there was also far from smooth.

Now I had plenty of work but still not enough money to make a living. I lived for weeks on bread and coffee and this was pretty hard to do.

CHAPTER 46

Lectures for the United Jewish Appeal

An idea came to my help. I went to the office of the United Jewish Appeal (U.J.A.), the agency which collected money to finance HIAS and the JOINT in Europe. As a Freud I was received by the director, Mr. Blitz, to whom I told my story about how helpful the JOINT and HIAS had been in bringing us to the States. I asked if I could do something for the United Jewish Appeal in order to pay them back for those services. Mr. Blitz asked me if I wouldn't lecture for various Jewish groups organized to collect money for U.J.A. He suggested that I tell my own story. I could not speak English, so I dictated in German what I had to say and a man recommended by my cousin wrote it for me in English. I memorized the lecture word for word. I received a $10 fee for each speaking engagement.

It was not an easy job. Because of the war, most of the trains were late and frequently, after having traveled all night long, I had to go to a meeting without being able to freshen up. When I arrived at my destination, two ladies from the committee were already waiting. Often I had to give a radio interview in the morning (fortunately in the forties television had not yet been invented), then speak at a luncheon meeting and follow this with a cocktail party and a lecture at dinner at night. I was paid for one lecture only. I believe the pay was $25 and an amount per diem for my expenses. With the exception of California, Washington State, Oregon, Idaho, Wyoming, Utah, and New Mexico, I was sent to every State in the Union. I was also sent to Canada. I did this for three years, traveling around the country. I remember it as strenuous, but rather smooth going. Nothing really unpleasant happened to me, at least as I remember it 30 years later. Once in Kansas City, when I spoke at the temple, the day of the meeting coincided with

Esti lecturing for the United Jewish Appeal

workmen repairing the roof. I do not think that with the constant hammering many people understood what I was saying.

Once after a meeting I started crying. It was a luncheon meeting arranged in the mansion of a rich plate glass manufacturer in Pittsburgh. The house stood on top of a hill with a magnificent view of the river and surrounding hills. One of the members of the plate glass family, the mother-in-law of one of them, sat there in her fatness, with an enormous bosom, condescending and speaking down to me. She made me feel so miserable, forlorn, and beaten by fate that after the meeting was over and the U.J.A. representative came for me, I began to cry my heart out.

Mother called me about this upsetting incident. It was hard to hear about it.

I was always introduced as being a speech pathologist and once a woman asked me if I had practiced this profession in Europe as well. I was upset by this question which implied I was a fraud and couldn't help but answer, "No, when I came to the United States the Holy Ghost came over me!" My U.J.A. engagements had to be carefully planned so that they did not conflict with my clinical work. Looking back 30 years, how I managed all this is a riddle to me.

Although Mother's backward look at these trips has a negative flavor, they were not only an important source of income, but also gave her opportunity to travel throughout the country. The following letters to Walter suggest that she rather enjoyed them at the time, as tiring as they were. And her energy is indeed unbelievable.

JULY 23, 1944

. . . I am earning money with private patients and—you will laugh—with lectures. This spring, in May, I traveled all over the country and talked for the United Jewish Appeal, the famous JOINT. I "invented" a nice talk. Some days very tiring, thus for ex. I would have already traveled two nights, and the next day have two newspaper interviews, one radio broadcast and three lectures, the last one at 11:00 P.M. But it is quite well paid, so that I saved enough to come to see you in the summer, a time when one does not earn anything.

NOVEMBER 16, 1944

. . . I am well, I do work very hard, but most of the time it is quite fun and very interesting. Two weeks ago I was for a week in the South, in the Mississippi delta where the cotton grows and I talked in four places. Last Sunday I was in Boston and received $100 for my lecture, what do you say to your mother! English is still not quite inside my head—but perhaps with time.

MAY 2, 1945

. . . I get around a bit once again to give lectures, on which occasion I get to know the country and people. I am saving to visit Europe after the war once again and bid a definite good-bye to the country of my fathers.

MRS. FREUD TELLS OF ESCAPE HERE

The Jersey Journal, February 17, 1944

By telling a Spanish Moroccan immigration official that he looked like Douglas Fairbanks and later by leaving her daughter as a deposit for a hotel bill outside Lisbon, Mrs. Esti Freud, daughter-in-law of the late Sigmund Freud, world-famous exponent of psycho-analysis, was able to make her way from Austria, through France and finally North Africa to this country.

Mrs. Freud, now is living in New York and her 19-year-old daughter is a student at Radcliffe College. She was in Chester Monday night to speak to the Youth and Women's Divisions of the United Jewish Appeal for Refugees, Overseas Needs and Palestine.

A slight energetic woman, Mrs. Freud has an outstanding reputation of her own, having been a professor at the University of Vienna. Mentioning the famous psychoanalyst only when directly questioned about him, she told how "Pa-pa" (with the accent on the last syllable) fled with the family to France. He remained there only one day, continuing to England where he died after writing his last book on Moses. She remained in Paris "because I was able to secure a good job and when you are a refugee from whom the Nazis have taken everything you are glad for any security you can find."

Having been in this country only a short time, she apologized for her difficulty in expressing herself clearly in English, but her slow and careful enunciation, the European flavor of her accent ... conjured pictures of Vienna, street waltzes and the Danube. She studied philosophy and speech therapy at the University of Vienna and acquired her knowledge of elocution in highly specialized training with actors of the world-famous Austrian Burgtheater. In 1932 she became assistant professor of Phonetics, Speech Therapy and Elocution at the University of Vienna. In May 1938, two months after the occupation of Austria by the Germans, she and her daughter were able to go to Paris. Here she worked as a specialist for speech and voice defects at the Lariboisière Hospital, Paris.

In June 1940, two days before Hitler entered the city, she and her daughter left Paris to the accompaniment of cannons, riding on bicycles with all their belongings in knapsacks on their backs....

THE DAILY OKLAHOMAN
   Sunday, October 26, 1947
   By Osborne Beeney
   ... The daughter-in-law of the famous old Viennese psychiatrist has more dynamic personality packed into her five foot two frame than you can find in a dozen Freudian libraries.
   She undoubtedly wowed the young Viennese gallants of about 30 years ago, and something about her indicates that Papa Freud must have executed a few approving whistles himself when his son brought Ernestine home to meet the family.
   If she cared to camouflage the gray now creeping into her once coal-black tresses, Ernestine, or Mrs. Esti D. Freud, as she is better known, could still evoke the whistles from the most discriminate whistlers.
   The diminutive bundle of Austrian-German-French-American exuberance paid Oklahoma City a visit on her way to Hot Springs, Ark. where she will speak for the United Jewish Appeal.
   Ernestine Freud lived a happy life in Vienna until the Nazis came. She was a speech teacher there and specialized in training footlight aspirants. Among them was Hedy Lamarr.

"Ooooo! What a beauty she was!" exclaimed Mrs. Freud.

But what about Sigmund Freud? What was he really like? Sigmund Freud could look at a person and know whether he was good or bad, she said, which made it a little tough on the family acquaintances sometimes.

"The only regret I have about marrying into the Freud family is that Papa had to be such an intellectual wonder. People always are more interested in him than in me," she said.

CHAPTER 47

Getting Settled in New York City

Meanwhile my clinic at the Manhattan EENT hospital provided me with connections I could use to help some of my Viennese friends. Dr. Vermes, an ENT resident from the Viennese Neumann Clinic where I had done my internship had arrived in New York and was looking for a hospital connection. I arranged a party in my shabby apartment on Sutton Place and invited one of the more influential physicians of EENT who knew and liked me. Dr. Vermes was appointed to the staff of this highly regarded specialized hospital. Although 30 years have passed, I am still proud of my success.

I am also proud of an incident in which I obtained the opposite result. I learned that Dr. Arnold, the Nazi of the Neumann Clinic who had succeeded Fröschels and had thrown me out of the outpatient department, had arrived in New York and was appointed at Bellevue Hospital. In Austria, after the breakdown of the thousand-year Reich, the Christian Socialist Party took over the government and all the prominent Nazis were fired from their jobs. Many came to the United States where they could get work. Fröschels wanted me to be quiet about Dr. Arnold. Nevertheless, I went ahead and thus forced Dr. Fröschels' hand. We reported Dr. Arnold's former activity to the authorities. I was investigated from all sides to determine if I were telling the truth. Anyway, to make a long story short, Dr. Arnold could not stay at Bellevue Hospital or even in New York City. At present, he is professor at the University of Jackson in Mississippi. I am sure that by this action I made myself a great number of enemies. *Tant pis* (too bad).

In 1946, at the end of the war, many changes were taking place at New York Hospital. I learned that Dr. Herbert Conway was made head of plastic surgery. I sent word through the pediatric social worker that I would be

interested in doing speech rehabilitation with children afflicted with con-
genital cleft palate after correction of this defect by surgery. To my astonishment, the social worker returned with the message that Dr. Conway wanted
to talk to me. Dr. Conway told me that he had received a grant and that if
I wanted to work for him once a week I would get a weekly salary of $25.

This was the first time that someone offered me a regular paid job.
Before I could accept I had to ask Dr. Palmer's permission. This was granted.
Now I had to work two afternoons and one morning at New York Hospital.
Dr. Conway may have been a good plastic surgeon, but he was a peculiar
boss, to say the least. In the early days of my appointment I greeted him
with, "Good morning, Dr. Conway." He answered, "How are you?" to which
I replied, "thank you," whereupon Conway repeated with an angry intona-
tion, "good morning, how are you, did you hear me?" Eventually it dawned
on me that in America etiquette the correct greeting is, "Good morning, how
are you?" The way I learned it, in Europe, to ask the professor *"comment allez
vous?"* or *"Wie geht es Ihnen?"* after the greeting would have been regarded
as much too intimate.

I was well acquainted with cleft palate speech rehabilitation. At the
Vienna clinic, Dr. Fröschels had done a lot of research with a dentist, Dr.
Schallitt. At the Lariboisière Hospital and in Nice, I had to handle a few complicated cases. In order to make a really good progress with my cleft palate
patients, I saw them also on days I worked at the ENT clinic. That too was a
mistake in etiquette, but I did not know it.

In 1948, I finally became an American citizen. Around this time the Vet-
eran's Administration was reorganized and large health centers were created
for American veterans on their way to being discharged from the army. Personnel was needed. Dr. Conway suggested I see someone downtown who
seemed to be doing the hiring for the VA. This man told me that the New
York City VA clinics were already staffed with speech pathologists, but if I
wanted to I could go to the VA outpatient clinic in Newark, New Jersey,
where they were looking for one. I did this and was accepted by the chief
psychologist, Dr. Sam Kutash. I did not want full-time employment and suggested a 20-hour two-day workweek, with evening hours so that veterans
who worked during the day could be treated. I had in mind the hard-of-
hearing, stutterers, and the educationally handicapped.

I filled out oodles of forms and started working in September 1948 on
the master's degree level with a rather modest salary. I was part of the psychology department and the chief psychologist was my supervisor. There
were two women psychologists on the staff who tried to make life miserable

for me, but I did not let them. I just did not care. The department had its own building, a former men's club, which during the depression had lost its members. One day it was decided that my office should be in the basement of that building. I could never find out why this decision was made. It disturbed me that I should be alone in the basement of the building with the seriously disturbed veterans newly discharged from the armed forces coming to the clinic. Some of them were quite destructive. I thought the least they could do for me was give me a telephone line so that I could call for help if necessary. What did you do when you wanted a phone? You went to the supply office situated on the other side of the street from the central office on Washington Place. That is what I did, putting on the charm as thickly as possible.

About half an hour later, Dr. Kutash requested my presence in his office. "You asked for a telephone," he said in an ominous voice, as if he had just found out that I was stealing money from briefcases. My answer was, "Yes, I'm scared of being alone in the basement with all those disturbed veterans coming to the clinic."

"Don't you know that you have to go through channels to obtain anything?" he said. "If you do this once more that will be just that." My explanation was that where I came from one did not go to the head of a department for minor supplies, but to the office where, one assumes, those things were available. I was very upset about this open hostility and never forgave Kutash his behavior toward me.

Mother telephoned me about this, in a state of desperation. It was hard to hear about it.

CHAPTER 48

It Took Me Seven Years to Finish
My Ph.D.

I realized that without a Ph.D. I could not pursue much of a career at the VA. I decided to study for it. I had to find a college where one could take all the needed courses in the evening. At the time, the only school with night courses was the New School for Social Research, a university created to employ European scholars who had to flee Hitler. I was told I had to take 60 credits and then write a Ph.D. thesis. It took me seven years to finish. I was 59 years old at graduation. I joked, "Some Ph.D. candidates invite their grandmothers to the graduation ceremonies. I invited my grandchildren." During those seven years, besides earning a living, I had to use every minute of my free time for studying for my courses, writing term papers, and preparing a seminar. At first I worried about being able to pay for my courses. It took me an entire year to write my Ph.D. thesis.

Again, in her (mostly German) letters to her son, we can follow, over the years, the arduous details of this quite awesome, truly heroic undertaking, with never a doubt, from her or from us, that she will pursue it to the end. Curiously, in contrast to people in her jobs, she does not complain about chicanery or unfair treatment by any of her teachers, not even when her thesis advisor demands extensive changes.

LETTERS TO WALTER
    November 6, 1949
    . . . I am okay, so far, have to work horribly much for the doctorate with no pleasure whatsoever. In addition it is very expensive. I procrastinated all day over a "paper" by J. S. Mills.

MARCH 25, 1950

... Besides, I am now studying for a Ph.D. If I am lucky and can bear it, I can get it in about two years. They gave me credit for quite a bit of my European studies. In a government job [The Veterans Administration], I get a much higher salary and nobody can order me around any longer.

MAY 31, 1950

... I could not answer your letter earlier because I worked too terribly much, many nights until 2:00 A.M., I was already in a complete state of exhaustion. My three hospitals, the praxis, and these studies, for a woman of my age. This semester I took three courses, all of them in the evening, so that some days, each Monday, for example, I got up at 6:30 A.M. because I have to be at 9:00 A.M. at the Veterans Administration Clinic in Newark, and came home at 11:30 at night; I am then always totally exhausted. I wrote three papers, about 5,000 words each, and had to prepare myself for a written exam. I am not sure yet how I made out.

JANUARY 1, 1951

... I am extremely busy, the praxis going quite well, and my three clinics. No way can you imagine how I rush around. I only keep being surprised that I can stand it.

FEBRUARY 18, 1951

... I failed my statistics exam. I was very aggrieved. I had very expensive and in return bad tutoring, now I have a much better one. Doing this doctorate is very stressful for me since I don't have much time. In a way I work without interruption, very exhausting.

JUNE 3, 1951

... I survived my first course in statistics but have to repeat the second course. It is truly a miracle that I got that far, since I never, in all my life learned anything like that. Correlations and factor analysis, but I think I shall manage it. I am not taking any vacations and will absorb myself in studies all summer because I want to take my qualifying exam. This exam in this school is notoriously difficult, they ask Talmudic questions. This school has been founded by Jewish professors from Berlin and one teaches about Gestalt psychology, something I had never heard about. Very tricky and Talmudic, besides it is very expensive and the whole enterprise costs me masses of money, probably more than it is worth. It might have been a better plan to use the time to make friends and connections, but one never knows what one should do, or rather what would be more advantageous.

OCTOBER 14, 1951

... I am very depressed, at the moment, have failed my qualifying exam, it really disheartens me. God knows whether I shall ever succeed in these doctorate studies!!

JANUARY 25, 1952

... I am already very sick of the school, since I failed the main exam, I have to take three more semesters, very exhausting to still go to school after a 10-hour working day.

ENGLISH LETTER

May 17, 1952

I am still going to school, it will take me another two terms until I have taken all my courses for my Ph.D. Then I have to write my thesis. I will be a great-great-grandmother, until I will be finished with my studies. My health is good and as Walter said the last time I saw him, I am a tough old woman.

JUNE 1, 1952

A little [professional] paper of mine has been published. Unfortunately I have little time to publish since I have to go to school and write papers for school. Just now I am writing about the Primal Crime, father murder, as Freud deals with it in his various works, starting with Totem and Taboo etc. until Moses. It was much work, but it gave me great pleasure. All my free time goes into that. I have two more semesters, then I am finished. I shall attend school in July, awful.

ENGLISH LETTER

August 10, 1952

... The July was so terrible in New York that I expected not to survive; it took certainly months out of my life, if not years.... I went twice a week to school and once I fell the stairs down—in that damned school, and hurt my two legs quite nicely, but nothing was broken fortunately, but I was blue and very swollen.

FEBRUARY 28, 1953

... I am horribly overworked and have no time for anything. I think that is my last semester in the school, although I fear I might need to take one more course. But I have not finished my papers for this semester. I only have Saturday afternoon and Sunday for writing and such an afternoon passes in a flash. The school is also very expensive, about $200 for one semester, without books. I just discussed my thesis with my advisor. Once I am finished with everything I shall quickly die. (I shall not go to Europe this summer. I want to finish writing my thesis. I am fed up to my neck with going to school. I will only come [to visit them] when I can put my doctoral hat on my blue hair.)

MARCH 29, 1953

... My advisor did not accept anything I have written so far for my thesis, and I have to do everything once again. I shall never finish. I shall be able to invite not only my grandchildren to my graduation, but also my great-grandchildren.

DECEMBER 6, 1953

... I finished about two-thirds of my thesis. It tires me a great deal and I have the feeling I shall still have to be working on it on my deathbed.

NOVEMBER 14, 1954

I turned in to my advisor my corrected thesis at the beginning of the week and hope it will now be in good order. The first chapter that I wrote anew and the last one he had already okayed a week ago. After my thesis is accepted I then have to pass the orals to get my doctorate. It is very important that I do this, with an American doctorate I can always maintain myself here and I would not like at all to die in a poorhouse.

DECEMBER 25, 1954

My thesis has been accepted by the Committee and is being typed. That will cost me, nebbich $200. Luckily $155 have arrived from Vienna. My part of the sale of the house in the Novaragasse—remember, this is the house where the Schramek family had lived. I was already going to ask Sophie to lend me the money. End of January I have my orals.

ESTI D. FREUD, PH.D.
SPEECH AND VOICE THERAPIST
444 East 58th Street
New York 22, N.Y.
Plaza 8 0675
March 9, 1955
Starting today there is once again a Dr. Freud, since I received my Dr. title this afternoon and passed my last exam. The last exam was rather fun. I expect your news every day. Kisses, Mother Dr. Freud. Esti Ph.D.

CHAPTER 49

Neither of My Children Invited Me to Their Weddings

In those seven years a lot of things happened to me that had nothing to do with my studies. Both of my children got married, neither of them inviting me to their weddings. In 1949 and 1950, my first grandchildren were born, my son had a son and my daughter a daughter.

This one sober and critical sentence on her children's marriages might imply limited interest on Mother's part and this would be a false assumption. The subject of marriages, his and mine, was of enormous concern to Mother as testified by her letters to Walter. Interestingly, given her critical outlook on many people, she was extremely satisfied with our choices of partners and through all the letters there is not a critical sentence against them.

My husband was probably not overly fond of his mother-in-law, but he treated her unfailingly with respect and consideration. But I believe that was not the main reason for her satisfaction with him. Rather she viewed him, and rightly so, as a safe, conscientious man—a reliable "breadbasket," according to my brother's report.

Prior to his eventual engagement and marriage, my brother had been temporarily engaged to an English girl and my mother voices her disappointment in a letter to him.

LETTER TO WALTER
November 16, 1944

... I cannot say anything to your engagement, a pity that you did not wait, with your name, looks and charm you could have married a very rich American, and then be able to study medicine. The American girls are very pretty and pleasant. America is generally a wonderful country, so big and rich, one cannot really imagine that in Europe.

In the same letter, Mother mentions my own quasi-engagement to my future husband, naturally not without exaggerating the presumed fame of Paul's father, who had indeed been in Germany, and in New York City, a competent well-earning head of an engineering department.

LETTER TO WALTER
November 16, 1944
... About Schnapperl you know that she is as good as engaged. Paul is an especially handsome and friendly guy, very talented and from a very good family, the father is a famous engineer and inventor. Hopefully nothing will intervene, but please be sure not to write to her how much I approve, otherwise she will instantly love him less.

I married my husband in August 1945, almost immediately after the armistice. He was then serving in the Navy, stationed in Washington, D.C., at an electronic Navy school. We married alone at a Justice of the Peace during one of his eight-hour leaves. I thus spared my mother—and deprived her—of making a fuss. She did send, without consulting me, knowing I would have vetoed it, a formal announcement of my marriage in both her own and my father's name, causing him the consternation expressed in a letter to me.

FATHER TO SOPHIE (GERMAN LETTER)
December 2, 1945
It took quite a long time until I recovered from the shock; caused not by the fact of your marriage, but by the formal announcement *in August nineteen hundred and forty-five London-New York by Mr. and Mrs. Jean Martin Freud,* an announcement that somehow found its way to me and totally surprised me.

MOTHER TO WALTER (ENGLISH LETTER)
September 28, 1945
... The biggest news for me is still Zapferls marriage and I am very happy about it. I believe she has a very, very nice husband and hope that she will be happy with him. You know how fond and proud I always was of Sophie and that even my ambitions for her are satisfied.

Mr. and Mrs. Jean Martin Freud

announce the marriage of their daughter

Sophie Miriam

to

Mr. Paul Loewenstein, M. E.

August, Nineteen hundred and forty-five

London - New York

Announcement of Sophie's marriage, which shocks Martin and annoys Sophie

The following letters from Walter, one in English and one in German, are addressed to me rather than to Mother, but I believe they belong in our story of family survival.

> Lt. A. W. Freud
> 1 Holly Terrace
> Highgate, London, N.W.
> (Father's address)
> 3 August 1945
> Mein bestes Zafferl,

Many happy returns *und das Allerbeste* wünscht Dir Dein favourite brother (and the very best wishes from your favorite brother). You have my permission now to stay out until ten past ten and be taken to the picture by an approved boyfriend (approved by me).

Thank you very much for your sweet letter. They have not forwarded the other one yet. I am still on leave, nearly three months now. However, I cannot go away from London because I might be recalled any day and have to be available. It is getting a bit boring to have nothing to do for such a long time, last week I took a job with Uncle Ernst, surveying bomb-damaged houses. I still have not got a clue when and to what they are going to recall me, anything from managing Prisoners of War to The Allied Control Commission might creep up. My postwar plans are all but definite. I hope to go back to college after my release from the Army (another year), I am even toying with the idea of an army career. (How would you like this?)

Here are a few tales from the Heimat.

Well stuffed with money and every other conceivable article (yes, THIS too) our American pilot dropped us 20 miles off our dropping zone and I landed not on the intended *Bergwiese* (mountain meadow), but right in a small and picturesque town in the valley of the Mur. You will remember, I am sure, that I am a good sprinter; and this my quality came in very handy. Most of our luggage landed on the market square, however, I did not call at the lost property office next morning. I was alone, i.e., we had been more, but we never found each other in the Heimat. All the farmers gave me food and not away to the police, my H.Q. was a comfortable *Almhütte* (mountain hut). The weather was very bad, it snowed a lot so I had difficulty in moving about. On the first of May I thought it is time for me to appear openly, the first thing I did was to get a car (Styr 50), from the Bürgermeister (mayor) of S. then I took over the greatest aerodrome in Austria (*Herr Kommandant, ich bin der Oberleutnant Freud von der 8. britischen Armee und ich bin gekommen um Ihr Flugfeld zu übernehmen*) (Mr. commander, I am the first lieutenant of the 8th British army and I have come to take over your airfield). He was very surprised. Then I went to the German High Command (in Linz) to arrange for the surrender, then I ran into some Austrian troops mutinying against the Germans, and had lots of other adventures. Eventually I joined the Americans in Styr, and via Passau, Regensburg, Nürnberg, from there by private plane to Paris and by air to London. There are lots of interesting details to the story, like the one of the Vicegauleiter of Steiermark professing to know grandfather to get on good terms with me; and the weeping S.S. officer etc. etc. but I keep those to tell you personally.

Now something very secret, don't tell it to anyone. Father does not know either. I am still meeting Chris secretly. Her parents must not know, of course. (If you should write, don't put your name on the envelope.) For the present I am not going to marry her, but she is very nice as a girlfriend.

The whole family is getting on fine, it was grandmother's birthday on the 26th. Father speaks of nothing but food, food and food all day long and he usually thinks he has *Magenkrebs* (stomach cancer) when he has overeaten. He has shaved off his beard which suited him very well.

Have you heard anything from grandmother Drucker? That's all for today, I hope you will have a nice birthday and a good holiday. I let you know as soon as I get a new job.

Allerherzlichst, with a big *Geburtstagspussi* (birthday kiss), Dein Walter

German letter

> Hazlerigg Hall
> Ashby Road Loughborough, Leics.
> January 5, 1947
> Very best, long-neglected Zafferl,
> No, nobody could claim that I suffered from a writing addiction, but I started at least 10 letters to you without finishing them for some reason.
> You are naturally "extremely interested" in what your brother is up to, and I am just finding myself in the right mood to give you a detailed autobiographical account of my adventures.
> At the moment I am back at Loughborough College studying "Chemical Engineering." If everything works out, I will have finished the studies July 1949. Chemical engineer is a very interesting occupation and Mother always said that I am a good cook.

I lucked out to have been discharged from the army just at the beginning of school. At the moment we have Xmas vacations, but I returned earlier to make up some things (the typical honor student).

The studies are very difficult, I have forgotten everything in these seven years and returned to too high a class level.

Now I have to start my congratulations: For all the birthdays and for the "summa cum laude" I wish you the very best, dear Zafferl. [*I assume Mother must have changed a modest "cum laude" into a "summa."*] I always kept thinking of you and started a letter. I also still have a gift for you and as soon as I find someone who goes to America I will send it along.

Since I saw you last a few days after your 15th birthday, I cannot very vividly imagine you as a married woman, when shall I become an uncle? Besides, each brother naturally thinks his sister is much too good for every man.

To return to my biography: After I liberated Austria (I admit, a few American, Russian and British troops helped along)—they gave me a long furlough to fatten me up a bit. (I could not find Rosa, thus food was scarce.) My affair with Christine totally dissolved itself during that time. Her parents are anti-Semitic junk dealers and she too behaved poorly (not a lady). I was then sent to "Bad Oeynhausen" in Germany, first in the "war crimes executive team" (as Captain).... I was part of the team that investigated Gustav Krupp von Bohlen & Haltech, you know that he was finally not accused. (He was, by the way, not a real Nazi and protected the Jews in his firm up to the end.) After ending the Krupp matter, I got to the "Judge Advocat general's war crimes team" and we indicted somewhat minor war criminals. (In the British Zone, such as for example Belsen, the man who manufactured the prussic acid for Auschwitz, Ravensbrück etc.) I was very successful and got a lot of death verdicts. (The sentence depended on how well one had prepared the case against the criminal, one had to find the right witnesses and documentary evidence.) I was promoted to major in February 1946 and had my own team. I got around a lot in Europe, the most beautiful trip was to Prague. I had a look at Theresienstadt, was in Karlsbad and Marienbad, but did not get to Vienna. A pity. The Jewish cemetery in Prague is one of the most interesting sights in Europe. The oldest tomb dates from 606 (Golem, etc.) During one of my visits to Denmark I met a very nice girl. (You will hear more about her, her name is Annette.)

In Germany I had a grand time and led a really "bad" life. Went out every evening. Came home every night with a different one. (English girls, not German etc.) I had my own house, three servants, a very fine car and

I lived like a high status God in France (before the war). In Germany, I tell you, what's happening there is really something. Persecuting Jews has turned against them.

In July I had my accident which, thank God, got me a bit down to earth. (I am quite o.k. again, only a little, very little, hard of hearing.) [*It was an accident with a jeep and left my brother with a lifelong quite serious hearing deficit.*]

... They took excellent care of me, at the hospital, and I then went directly without a furlough, to the school.

Meanwhile I had a lively correspondence with Annette and she has decided to follow me here (it sounds romantic, doesn't it) and has found a position at the Danish embassy in London. She is a *real lady*, comes from a very high status Danish family (related to the Danish king), and has very nice parents who live in a big estate, one hour from Copenhagen. And—you don't say—we shall get unofficially engaged in the next weeks. Engagement in Denmark is a big deal (not like in England where a friend said to me: "damn, I have to break up the engagement with Jane, she wants to marry me." Annette is a most special personable and refined girl, I think the whole family liked her a lot. Very intelligent, very competent, in other words *Eine Ausgezeichnete Partie* (a very favorable match).

Our family is in excellent shape. Anna [Freud] has recently bought a country house and everyone is thriving and blossoming. (Touch wood.)

In the next days I shall become a British Citizen, meaning I can travel once again. I would terribly much like to visit you, If I could *work my way to America* I could come in the summer. But I am not sure what the travel possibilities are. How is Paul and Mother? Details about the latter please.

Old friends ...

Now I almost forgot to thank you for the wonderful packages. Unfortunately, Zafferl, few of them arrived, I only got one with newspapers and one with honey.

Now it got to be very late and thus I better wish you good night. I hope—and will do my best—that our correspondence will become a bit more lively. Should I write to Paul?

Most affectionately your brother, still the old Walter

I answered Walter's letter and asked him many questions, which he answers in telegram style:

Jewish: No, of course not, but as Tante Anna rightly states, we do not want to bow to Hitler's racial principles.

School: I have now quite caught up; I only returned early from the Xmas vacations to catch up with laboratory work (I was a bit awkward). My fellow students are most particularly friendly, there are several ex-service men here, also some who were here with me in 1939.

Subject: It is very interesting and I also hope to work in the atomic energy field. (From the chemical engineer's point of view.) Atomic energy in England is almost exclusively staffed by Austrians and Germans; I applied there for a summer job.

Life: I live in a very nice single room with flowing water, central heating and a desk. Every two weeks I go to London. It is only 100 miles, but in the current railroad conditions it can last four hours. (Normally two hours.)

State help: Ex-service men get a grant; not much, but enough. In my case, I have, after all the bills are paid, 40 pounds per year pocket money. If I did not live in such a good hostel, I could naturally save more.

Accent: Naturally, to the great enthusiasm of English females. Every English girl succumbs immediately, as soon as she hears an Austrian accent; many English men therefore try to imitate it on purpose. One does not get asked here, where one is from that would be too personal.

Visit: This summer, I think Zafferl, it will not work out. I do have already a passport and could come over any time. I am not above "working my passage" either. We shall discuss this in more detail. . . .

Working with children would not be a job for me. I would have thrashed them all to death on the second day! . . .

Horrible idea to solve other people's emotional or practical problems. [*I was then in my first year of social work school, working with children and their families.*]

Will you be writing a book about your experiences? I hope you keep a diary about your more interesting cases so that you can refer to them, like grandfather did. "Patient A.B., 16 years old, from an impoverished family. Complains about pain in the left second toe. When asked he responds that he dreams of naked girls" . . . etc. . . .

Congratulations to your apartment. Here too, there is a severe housing shortage, but rents are more or less fixed. (Father, for example still pays his £185 a year for our lovely flat in Highgate. . . .)

Mother: A problem. She sends me letters from time to time (which I answer but they are an "undiluted pleasure to read"). They always contain something unpleasant, ugly or malicious. I am afraid, for example, to mention Annette's last name, lest she then writes her disagreeable letters. For sure. And that is of course not a relation that one should have to one's mother. By the way, she sent me a very good photo of hers, if she really looks like that, I would not recognize her in the street. (But don't tell her that.)

Father: I get along very well with Father, he continues to be hypochondriacal, but his health is actually in very good shape. His housekeeper is an especially nice English girl (about 30), he could really not have done any better. She takes very good care of him and I personally would have no objections if he were to marry her. She is a fine girl from a typically middle class family and loves him very deeply.

Whatever you think of it, it works. He dreads our Mother but he longs terribly for you two. Mother seems to be sending from time to time anonymous letters to his family and friends. He does not have a very good but also not a bad job, is always planning something new, which, thank God, he cannot quite put into place. At the moment he wants to open an optical business. He travels a lot and I see him about every two to three months. Grandmother is getting ever smarter and Tante Anna is horribly busy.

Your letter is now answered.

No doubt my brother had a real Danish wedding in Denmark in which my father must have been present. My Mother sends several loving wishes but she also repeatedly expresses the hope to be a guest at his wedding.

JUNE 8, 1945

. . . Will you marry soon? Or only after the war has ended? I will be very hurt if I will not be able to come to your wedding.

MAY 29, 1947

I am especially pleased with the news that you are getting married. . . . I would have loved to come to your wedding but have unfortunately not sufficient money for such an expensive journey. That is very hurtful.

JULY 29, 1947

I wish you with all my heart every good thing for your marriage, I hope you will be a good and loving husband.

Eventually Mother sends a telegram (found among her papers):

TELEGRAM TO WALTER

Wish to attend your wedding. Made application for English entrance permit. Could family lend additional $250 for round trip transportation. Expect cable answer. Love Mother.

The money did not come forth and Mother sent the couple a telegram wishing them mazel tov, a Yiddish expression for good luck, which my mother seldom used. It was her way to express her dissatisfaction with getting a non-Jewish daughter-in-law. But when she eventually met her daughter-in-law, she was very enthusiastic about her as she conveys in her autobiography.

I liked my daughter-in-law immediately. What a nice attractive young woman! I wondered why she took my son! Although now I see, in hindsight, that she did not do so badly at all.

My mother's reflections regarding why her own mother had married her father, or why Annette had been willing to marry her beloved and apparently highly admired son are intriguing to me, all the more so because she had the opposite reaction when it came to me, her daughter. She wrote to my brother in June 1960,

I am very proud that Sophie, who is rather very unattractive and was at that time quite poor without dowry, given that I was at that time quite badly off, made such a good match. I never said Paul was a good breadbasket. He is an asset even for the arrogant Freud family.

She thus thought both of her children had made "lucky catches." Mother must be congratulated for hiding perhaps her true feelings so well. Indeed, she had showered my brother with flattering comments and had never made me feel unattractive. Thank you, Mother.

CHAPTER 50

At the New York Hospital

At the New York Hospital clinic, Dr. Conway suddenly asked me if I would work twice a week for him. Our original agreement had been once a week. It had been a short time earlier that I had accepted employment at the VA clinic and there were just no morning or afternoons left for additional work. I very politely pointed this out to Dr. Conway, telling him that I saw his patients twice a week anyway since I scheduled them for days I was at the Ear, Nose, and Throat Department. "Ho," exclaimed Conway, "You are just contributing to Dr. Palmer's statistics." Thus, I learned that statistics were more important than the progress that my cleft palate patients made. Again I had broken some rule of etiquette without knowing it. One of the residents told me that Dr. Conway had hired another speech pathologist to work for him and that I should expect to be fired in the near future. I went to Dr. Palmer the ENT attending who had, so to speak, hired me originally. That again was a mistake.

Mother was very upset about these developments, resulting in many painful telephone calls.

During a very short span of time something had happened about which I knew nothing. Dr. Palmer, who was only 64, was asked to resign, and Dr. James A. Moore was appointed head of the department. Dr. Moore never forgave me my not going to him with the problem. In any case, I was not fired, but it was worked out that I should be at the ENT clinic three times a week. In a relatively short time, patients were referred to the speech clinic from all departments of the New York Hospital. In the fifties it became

"SPEECH TRAINING"

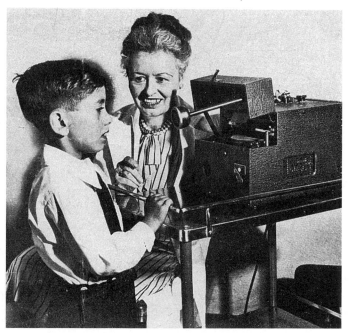

Esti working with a boy at her speech clinic

officially the Speech and Hearing Clinic. That is again another story, one having to do with me indirectly. The speech clinic became a speech and hearing clinic. It was the hearing testing that soon became the dominant field in the profession. The "hearing technician," P.S., became the director of the Speech and Hearing Clinic and worked full time. From the beginning P.S. was hostile to me and remained hostile until I retired in June 1971. For my last six months, in order to make me really unhappy, she did not refer a single patient to my clinic and I had to sit around doing nothing.

Mother telephoned me many times about these developments, always in a state of desperation. It was hard to hear.

Slowly I had built a private practice which, on occasion, was very good, but frequently very poor. Most of my cases were referred to me by physicians. The connections I had made in Vienna proved valuable.

CHAPTER 51

A Case of False Memory

WALTER'S *ERNESTINE*

Another way of showing her displeasure was by demonstrating a complete lack of interest in my family, though I do not know if this lack of curiosity also extended to the family of my sister. My son, her oldest grandson, was born in June 1950. Soon afterwards she told me that she was flying from New York, where she lived, to Vienna, in order to buy there a new dress. (As if there weren't enough dress-shops within walking distance of East 85th Street.) I suggested to her that this excursion might be a good opportunity for making a stopover in England for the admiration of the new baby grandson. A cold "No" was her reply.

Here we have a case of false memory in which the actual facts can be proven without a doubt. Mother mentions her visit to admire his baby son, his first-born child, in her autobiography.

In 1950, for the first time, I traveled by boat to the continent to admire my newborn grandchild David, and meet my Danish daughter-in-law and my son whom I hadn't seen since the summer of 1939, shortly before the outbreak of the war. I was unconsciously hoping that perhaps my husband would make an attempt to see me. 1950 was the beginning of the Korean War and people told me I should not go to Europe because I would not be able to come back. I went anyway. I stayed in England. When I arrived by boat and train at what I believed was the Victoria station and stepped on the platform, I immediately saw Walter, but he passed me by without recognizing me and I had to run after him.

Walter claims that when they first met at Victoria station, she looked at him and said, "Your teeth have not improved."

Did Mother's memory fail her perhaps, rather than Walter's? Not so. Here are the (mostly German) letters around that first visit and two subsequent visits.

May 30, 1950

My ship (*Parthia*) leaves New York on July 21.... You can't imagine my joy to see you again. I am not yet sure how long I will stay since I want to go to Vienna, we have some money there and besides I want to visit the tomb of Grandfather [Drucker] ... and a few friends on the continent, I don't think that I will be able to afford to return to Europe since I had to go into debt for this trip.

Did I write you that I will give a talk at the Congress for Speech Therapy in Amsterdam? There is the possibility that I can be sent there as delegate of the USA Governments, Veterans Administration. Still very uncertain, but it would be great, if yes, because of the money. The Congress takes place August 21 to 26 and my ship returns on the second (naturally September).

I have become quite a restless spirit, want to go to Paris as well, visit friends, perhaps even consult on one or two patients. I feel generally very grand, with a grandchild of the name of David.

July 18, 1950

I am already very excited. Tomorrow will be the day after tomorrow of my departure and I still have so much to accomplish.... Many people have tried to spoil things, thinking that one does not leave the country in these times. Last time we met a world war broke out as well, do you remember?

You know that I will be giving a talk in Amsterdam about *Language Rehabilitation of the USA Veterans Administration*. I will have to write the talk on the ship because I had no other time. It is possible that the VA will compensate the money, but everything always lasts so long.

Thus, this is my last letter. According to schedule I arrive on July 29 and then take the next train I can catch to London. Where shall I find you? ... If it does not tire you and you feel like it, come to Liverpool, the ship arrives in the morning and since I know nothing about distances and so on, I am not sure of the most reasonable plan.

German card

August 9, 1950

Dear Walter, dear Annette,

I want to thank you for your extraordinarily dear and affectionate hospitality. I had much pleasure with all of you and can only congratulate you both for the especially sweet baby.

GERMAN LETTER

> September 2, 1950
> Cunard Line—Cunard White Star *"Parthia"*
> Dear Children,
> I am already on board. Have a very fine cabin.... The best part of the trip was to be together with you and to admire the marvelous baby. I think if Annette and I were together for longer she would very soon become a very dear daughter and she could probably also get used to me. She should spoil David a lot. Grandfather says over and over that the surest capital for a son is to be loved by his mother. The father should be rather severe. Read it yourself in Freud's autobiography!!
> Otherwise I am very glad to get home. Although everything was very interesting, one learns by comparison more and more what a wonderful country the USA is.
> My dear children, as a good-bye I still want to tell you, love each other and be happy with each other, all else is unimportant. Life is a very hard school and if one loves each other everything is easier to bear.
> Many kisses to the three of you, Mother Esti
> I shall send coffee to Annette's parents as soon as I arrive.

I saw my husband, but it was a very peculiar meeting. I came out of the British Museum, and passed a tobacconist's shop, with a display of foreign newspapers, such as the *Figaro*, the *Tribune*, and the *New York Times*. I was just wondering about the foreign papers—I did not remember having seen French and American papers sold at other tobacconists' shops, when I saw Martin crossing the street. He stopped walking as soon as he reached the sidewalk and stood there looking at me. I stood there looking at him, unable to move or open my mouth. After a few minutes of standing there motionless, Martin turned around and entered his store. And that was that—I never saw him again. When Walter asked his father why he did not speak to me that time, Martin denied having seen me.

"I loved your father all my life," Mother told me on her deathbed.

> *This was surely true, in some ways and Mother never seemed to take serious interest in another man, as far as I know, and certainly never wanted to be married again. But she also never forgave him—what else—their conflicts about money. "Your father will be furious that he cannot rob me of that as well" (May 25, 1963), she writes to Walter when she receives $3,000 from Vienna, her part of the sale of her father's house.*

Martin in front of tobacco shop

Father visited the United States in 1958, in order to promote his book about his father, Glory Reflected, in this country. He stayed with us for about a week, during which he required very many cups of tea. Neither Walter nor I mentioned Father's visit to Mother and she expressed her anger to Walter:

DECEMBER 21, 1958

I am very offended that neither you nor Sophie informed me of Father's stay. I heard about it from strangers, which was very embarrassing. Why did you make a secret out of it? I have never bitten Father and will also not do it presently. He did not find it worth his while to pay me a visit.

Naturally, there were other secrets as well. Already in 1947, in an above letter, Walter had informed me of Father's new partner. Thus Father was now asking for a divorce, but Mother had no intention to grant him that wish. It was her vengeance against the man she loved all her life. Well, people kill each other out of love. Father then adopted his partner, so she could carry his name—Margaret Freud—and inherit the very little property he left.

In 1950, England was still in the postwar doldrums. The city around St. Paul's Cathedral was in shambles. Bombed houses were in the main thoroughfare and many items such as fruit juices and nylon stockings were difficult to obtain. The gifts I brought from the United States were more than welcome. I did not want to impose myself on my family for too long a time, but did not want to travel to the continent either, so I went for a week to an English resort town. It was a dreary place. The chambermaid accused me of having stolen the bedcover. While I was packing she came to my room, asking, "Where is the bedcover?"

"I don't know," was my answer, "actually I was wondering why you did not cover my bed."

"The bedcover is not here," she said menacingly.

"Let's look around," I said, and sure enough, there it was, having slipped itself between the end of the bed and the mattress. It was such an unpleasant incident I cannot forget it! With the stupid public relations coverage the United States received in foreign boulevard newspapers, the maid must have taken me for an American gangster absconding with dirty moth-eaten bedcovers.

Mother has only a few sentences in her autobiography about this memorable first visit to her son and his family after so many years. She expresses approval of her daughter-in-law, but "... the grandson, David, was six weeks old, so there was not much one could tell about him." Yet she writes effusively about him in her letters.

JUNE 3, 1951

I am totally sure that your baby will grow up to be very special. The way one knew that about Grandfather Freud from the beginning, the same way one will know about your baby.

JULY 8, 1951

He is the sweetest baby I ever have seen in my life.

Walter and Annette seem more welcoming and generous toward my mother's visits than I would have expected and than I was myself. Did they really tell her she could come and live with them as suggested by her reply below?

JANUARY 25, 1952

... I am not sure when I can come for a visit. As long as I have to attend school, I cannot save anything. I also thank you for your dear invitation, as long as I am able to work, I can scrape by on my own reasonably well, but I will make use of your invitation when I am old and frail.

Her next visits were in 1954 and in 1960, for the first time by plane, and were preceded by the usual worry that she will not have enough money to visit them. The visits must have proceeded well given the very warm thank you notes she writes after every visit, praising the children, or at least one of them, and hoping that she had not caused too much work for Annette.

NOVEMBER 14, 1953

... Given the current state of my finances, I can not even afford an inexpensive summer vacation, let alone a trip to England. I have definite money worries because my praxis is in such bad shape.

DECEMBER 6, 1953

... Hopefully I will be able to visit you around August 20. I can then stay for one week with you. I hope that this will not be too long for you, but you have to expect that I will then not be able to come again for many years. Sophie can never stand me for more than 24 hours. I keep my fingers crossed that I can save enough money until August.

GERMAN LETTER

January 13, 1961

I want to thank you most heartily for your hospitality ... Ida especially found a place in my heart. I also thank you many times for bringing me to the airport. I hope your electricity bill was not too high due to my visit. I will send you a check for it. Many kisses for everyone, especially Ida

Mutter Esti.

Perhaps my brother was hurt by instances of invitations that my mother did not accept, and in later years, her preference to go to Vienna, rather than to London, and this hurt interfered with memories of her earlier visits.

SEPTEMBER 7, 1958

... Thank you for your invitation to London. At the moment I have no money. I have a bill of $500 from my dentist, ... already paid $425, although I think he did not do a good job. I am also afraid of London, so many family members whom I don't want to see. It would be much nicer if we could meet somewhere. If you rent a house in Spain, I will pay half of it. But first I must earn a lot of money.

APRIL 28, 1963

... I have little desire to go to England. Then the *comble* (the peak) of my stay is permission to visit—Mathilde—brrr.

I understand, dear dead brother, that you did not like Mother, at times you were even repelled by her, yet also offended that she did not visit you frequently enough. But how could you, no matter how old or sick—you did not have Alzheimer's after all—forget her intense interest in you and your family, her numerous letters, her curiosity about your doings. Your children sent me all the letters that they found carefully preserved among your papers, along with all the other letters you ever received. There were 67 letters between 1945 and 1949, 38 letters from 1950 to 1954, 56 letters from 1955 to 1959, and 45 letters from 1960 to 1964. She thus wrote you about once or twice a month, faithfully through the years.

Besides the 200 letters, there were numerous constant gifts and constant follow-up inquiries whether you received these gifts, since you seem to have been negligent about acknowledging them. You could not have forgotten all these things.

ENGLISH LETTER TO ANNETTE

January 10, 1949

I recently sent *the Freuds* [my emphasis] and to you and Walter lots of very good candy (*Pischingerschnitten*), a cake Walter was very fond of as a young boy.... Nobody has yet confirmed the parcel and I begin to worry, if it was not lost. It would be a pity.

English letter
>June 5, 1949
>This is to tell you that I forwarded three pairs of nylons to Annette.

September 25, 1949
>I sent your wife per airmail a pair of nylons and will send some again as soon as she acknowledges them.

January 1, 1951
>Besides, I will send off a package of candy tomorrow. Party candy. Please look carefully inside the bottom of the gingerbread tin can, a surprise for your wife, only a trifle.

February 18, 1951
>Yesterday, I arranged a meat package for you. I hope it gets to you in time for your birthday.

English letter
>June 21, 1951
>I am writing to you because this morning I sent you by airmail a cookie jar with chocolates. Be careful about the bottom of the jar, and please do write immediately if the cookies arrived well, and if you liked them. I thought you will be able to use the chocolate for your vacation, therefore I mailed it airmail so that you would get the cookies in time.

October 14, 1951
>Annette should write how she likes the flowered dress. As soon as I earn more money I shall send you more things.

May 10, 1953
>I sent you two shirts on Thursday. I hope they arrive well and fit you. One does not get all sizes.

January 7, 1957
>I sent your wife a very pretty hand-embroidered silk blouse with the morning mail. Annette should write me right away when she gets the blouse and whether she likes it.

JULY 5, 1957
Did David get the book I sent him a few weeks ago?

NOVEMBER 29, 1957
I sent you the day before yesterday a lovely shawl—by mail. I hope it will arrive. I also sent you several *National Geographics* which you never acknowledged.

OCTOBER 4, 1958
. . . I shall send Annette $25 soon again.

SEPTEMBER 7, 1959
. . . I sent your wife a pretty elegant white jersey blouse. I hope the blouse arrived, she has not acknowledged it.

SEPTEMBER 9, 1959
. . . Did Annette get the slip and the handkerchiefs?

JANUARY 1, 1962
Dear Herzenskind, I have not heard from you for a very long time. I hope you are all well. I have sent your three children in three different letters three checks of $6. I don't know if you have received them.

JUNE 9, 1962
. . . Enclosed $10 check as a birthday gift for David.

JULY 15, 1962
I have not heard from you for already a very long time. I wrote you a letter in which I enclosed $10 for David. Please write whether you have received the check. Kisses for everyone. Mother Esti.

ENGLISH LETTER
April 20, 1963
Dear David:
I was just informed by your father that you are the best pupil in your class. Such an achievement deserves certainly a reward. I enclose a check of $10 (a little more than three pounds) and I hope that you will make good use of the money. Tell your parents that I have not made summer plans. A

trip to Europe will probably be beyond my means. With love from your Grandmother Esti Freud

NOVEMBER 17, 1963
... I sent your wife an evening dress for Xmas. I earn very decently but need a lot of money. Xmas will cost me a fortune.

Annette, who, so writes mother, has a special place in her heart, gets the most gifts, and all her letters seem to get answered although one asks oneself to whom the letters are really addressed.

ENGLISH LETTER
May 22, 1955
Dear Annette:
I thank you very much for your birthday wishes and the sweet pictures of the children. I think David is especially cute on them. Ida looks as if she were crying. Don't worry too much about her speech, play with her choo-choo train, with the emphasis on the CH*CH*CH* so that she will learn the sound in this way and read her every evening a little story or a poem for children and let her repeat it, two or three words at the time. She is still very young and she will learn it. The important thing is that she started to speak.

I hear from all sides that your husband and my son is so smart and efficient. I heard that he discovered a new process in his field. I think you can be very proud of him and I imagine that his success will soon be expressed in monetary values and position. Let's keep our fingers crossed.

It might interest you that one of my patients is Mrs. Vanderbilt, a member of one of the richest families of the U.S.A. Let's hope she will stay a long time with me and recommend me to all her rich friends. Since I have the Ph.D., I ask higher fees for my services in the office. Beside Mrs. V. the private praxis is not too good, and I have still debts to pay. I don't know what I will do during vacation. Anyway I bought myself two very pretty hats. I look very distinguished in them.

Tell your husband that I just finished two articles, one has already been accepted by a very good medical journal, and the other will be sent to a publisher as soon as it is okayed by Washington, because I want to have it published coming from the Veterans Administration. It gives prestige to my clinic when articles appear from there. But I think this will not interest you too much, but maybe Walter. I am now writing an article on the education of the deaf where I want to describe my invention and the effects it has on the improvement of speech of the born deaf.

Otherwise I don't know what might interest you. I heard that your father-in-law [Martin!] wants to come on a lecture tour to the States and wants to lecture on occasion of the 100th anniversary of his father. Maybe he will succeed.

That is all for today. Once again many thanks for the birthday wishes. Many kisses to all of you, Mother Esti

I am still preoccupied with my brother's false memory. Above examples are only a few examples of the mentioning of gifts sent (and not acknowledged) not to mention the never-neglected birthday wishes and birthday gifts for every member of the family.

Through all the years, from 1944 to 1964 and then again from 1977 until her death, Mother wrote Walter one or sometimes even two birthday letters.

MARCH 25, 1951

Dear Herzenskind,

I am writing to you because I want to congratulate you for your birthday. I wish you the very best. A very good job with a big salary, stay healthy, that is actually the most important.

I recently sent you two packages with canned meats and I hope they will arrive safely. Everything is in surplus here; only very expensive, especially if one's income is restricted to a fixed salary.

Unfortunately I had an accident, fell down with a chair at school while trying to open the window and broke several ribs. It hurts horribly. One cannot breathe properly, nor cough, and above all not sneeze. Each movement hurts a lot, especially if one has to run around and has to keep working. I am totally upset. The doctor, bandages, etc. were all very expensive and I could not earn as much. You must therefore excuse me if I will send something for your birthday a bit late.

Dear Herzenskind, do write me soon. again. I miss you so. I hope you had a very fine enjoyable birthday. Once again many good wishes, and many kisses, Mother Esti.

MARCH 21, 1952

I congratulate you most warmly to your birthday and wish you all the best. Stay healthy and continue to be as successful as you have been.... There is little to tell about myself, except that the bus, I was inside, threw me down on my back and head as it suddenly stopped. I thought I had broken my spinal cord and had a head concussion but it was only a bump on the head and bruises in the back.

My office is in very bad shape, I am depressed and worry a lot. I have big expenses, have to be well dressed and everything gets more and more expensive. I am never fully rested, twice a week I have to get up at 6:30, return home at 11:00 at night. It is very tiring.

Surely there can be no question of Mother's love and interest in her English family. But I find the juxtaposition of wishes for a happy life, good vacations, etc. with personal news about frightening accidents truly bizarre and disturbing. Did the English family really enjoy a stream of gifts from someone who complained of chronic financial distress? Did they appreciate the good wishes for happy times when desperate worries, loneliness, or scary accidents are mentioned within the next line of the same letter. This may be the reason why neither my brother nor I appreciated Mother's devotion to us.

I am sure she never realized how upsetting I found her constant despairing telephone calls. She must have thought that we were not affected by her suffering.

SEPTEMBER 28, 1952
    . . . Why does Annette never write to me?

DECEMBER 6, 1953
    . . . Please, please, write me soon, my heart is torn apart that my children take so little notice of me.

MARCH 26, 1954
    . . . I hear very little from Sophie. If I did not call her now and then, I would hear nothing at all. She hardly ever writes.

DECEMBER 27, 1959
    I have not heard from you already for a long time. You two write very seldom.

APRIL 28, 1963
    Nobody can claim that you write much or diligently.

While Mother has an intense desire for him to know how she lives, sometimes in excruciating detail ("I would so much want you to have a sense of how I live,"

January 25, 1952), frequently repeated, she also constantly expresses her equally detailed interest in him, his wife, and children. Did he alone get a salary increase, or did everyone else get one as well? Has David gotten his teeth? Has he started to speak? And, if not, immediately a bit of anxiety ("I am a bit worried. Both you and Sopherl talked very early," June 1, 1952).

JANUARY 1, 1958

Dear Herzenskind,

... I am taut like a bow (Quotation from Walter Freud when he was still young), to hear how the move went, how you like the new house and above all about your new job. I have meanwhile heard you are employed by the Anglo-Iranian Oil Co. Not in research. What is your position? Are you getting a raise? How did you find the job? I so much would like to know all that?? How is the new house? Did you sell the old one?? Rented? Sold well or with a loss? How far is Walter's job from his office? Could you answer all these questions for me?

All of you be embraced, most affectionately Mother Esti.

P.S. What school will David attend? Are the children unhappy about the move? What has actually happened with your invention?? You never write any details. Apparently you think I am too stupid to understand things. Please write soon.

A few times Mother is apprised of some little accident or trouble with a child, certainly only by Annette still ignorant of Mother's tendency to dramatize small mishaps. I shudder at Mother's exaggerated responses. "Mother'" I want to scream at her "just write a few reassuring words and explain to her these are the normal expected ups and downs of raising children." But Mother is dead, Annette is dead, and besides, except for Mother, we did not scream at each other in our family. We hurt each other by silence and cutoffs.

MOTHER TO ANNETTE (ENGLISH LETTER)

July 8, 1951

... I was very upset about the scalding of David. The poor baby, what a terrible shock for him! He is the sweetest baby I ever have seen in my life, and I prophesize he will be as smart as Grandfather Freud, but for goodness sake, be careful with him. Don't let him into the kitchen at all!! Your kitchen is too small. Tell his grandfather to give him for his birthday, a little table, which can be highered and put down, with the seat fixed with it, so that he has a place where he can sit and play and eat. Sopherl too has this for her baby.

MAY 10, 1953

... I am a bit worried that you want to send the children with total strangers to Denmark. I mean total strangers for the children, the trip will frighten the little one to death. Send along the little babysitter that you have, otherwise the children could get a mental shock, which could damage them for the rest of their lives.

When Annette wrote about worries with Ida, Mother responds:

OCTOBER 24, 1959

... If Ida is so fully of anxieties, I advise you to ask Anna Freud about it. This should *not* be *neglected*!!

DECEMBER 5, 1959

Please ask your wife to take Ida to Tante Anna. Sodium Penthathol is a devilish medication. An ordinary practitioner does not understand anything about emotional difficulties, and after all, your Aunt is the best psychologist in the world.

When I told Mother that Andrea had come down with the measles, she instantly mentioned the possibility of meningitis as an aftermath. Actually, I had understood early not to burden Mother with my worries, but must have slipped up. Her responses to Annette seem highly inappropriate, but I have started to realize, in the course of this book, to what extent my poor Mother was haunted by constant anxieties of every kind.

Mother is also tormented by terrible loneliness, which finds expression in most of her letters. Although realistic in her life situation, it also connotes lifelong suffering, since mention of it is also made in the bridal letters to her fiancé. Highlighting a few examples from letters to her son must suffice.

LETTERS TO WALTER

June 1, 1952

I am so lonely for you. At times I miss you so much that it is hard to bear, and I am sometimes so sad that I have to grow old without my children.

MAY 10, 1953

It is too sad that you are not here, I am too much alone. I have not a soul with whom I could talk, and who is interested in my goings-on.

JULY 5, 1959

It is so terrible that I have none of you with me. I am quite depressed. Many kisses for everyone, Your mother Esti who loves you very much wishes you an especially lovely vacation.

NOVEMBER 17, 1963

I miss you all so very very much.

Mother's letters to her son, apart from seeking a somewhat illusory human connection, are also simply a testimony of her successful attempt to survive in a world she experienced predominantly as dangerous and hostile. The main emphasis was on her financial survival, or rather, on her anxiety about her financial survival. If there are a few letters in which money is not mentioned in one manner or another, I did not notice them. Even the one letter to her grandson David mentions her lack of money. It is possible that the anxiety about money toward the end, in Europe, or even more, the threat of extreme poverty in her early days in the United States traumatized her. Yet conflicts about money had characterized her marriage and perhaps helped to break it up. Her mood rises when her private praxis prospers and inevitably falls when it lags. And here, again, there is a strange continuity, because even in Vienna she (and I) worried intensely about the state of her private speech disorder praxis.

Here are some thoughts on her private practice, in one of her birthday letters.

MARCH 24, 1948

. . . I have no psychoanalytic connections. It would have been good initially and even now for my private praxis to have recommendations and friends in that circle and I did try very hard, but they all showed me a very cold shoulder.

Most Viennese here are psychoanalysts. If they sold grandmother toilet paper and hairpins, they call themselves personal pupils of Dr. Freud, if they only delivered packages to the maid, then they are of the Freudian school. They persecute me with their hatred since I know right away that they are horrible liars. The psychoanalysts have a very good business, they don't need to know anything, just have an elegant office on Park Avenue and they shovel money. I have it here very difficult, no secretary, no KlimBim no money, with speech defects one has to know all about it, and one cannot ask for the fees that psychoanalysts get. In sum, I am horribly worried.

One is here nothing but dirty rubbish if one is poor. For the rich New York Jews, I would need a very elegant apartment on Park Avenue, with a blond secretary and elegant furniture, but one would need, at least for a while, to have money to invest.

CHAPTER 52

Mrs. Sigmund Freud

I was invited to see my mother-in-law, a visit that upset me considerably. *[Mother visited Martha Freud during this first London visit in 1950.]* Mama was 90 years old. Although she looked frail, she was intelligent and as clear in her head as when I had last seen her in June 1938. She died in her sleep two years later.

Mother's relationship to her mother-in-law remains a puzzle to me. Martha Freud certainly seems to have kept an eye on Mother and was in charge of selecting household help for her. Sometimes this was a disaster ("the baby nurse was an old dragon") and a signal that Mother herself was considered incompetent. But at other times, such as when she went to work, she experienced Martha's assistance as helpful. She even thought Grandmother might have been fond of her (June 15, 1946). Then there is a mention in a letter to Annette about having visited her mother-in-law.

JANUARY 10, 1949

. . . I believe, that you are a lucky girl, having a mother-in-law who lives 4,000 miles away across the Atlantic ocean. Imagine, if I were to live round the corner, and you had to pay me a visit twice a week, as I did for 20 years with my mother-in-law, Walter's grandmother.

This was most certainly a total invention. Mother never accompanied us to the gathering of Grandfather's sisters on Sunday mornings, but sent Fräulein to accompany us. If they had been on friendly terms, would it not have been natural for Mother to pay this weekly visit with us, at least occasionally? I suspect these two women saw each other infrequently. There was actually considerable silent hostility between them. Martha Freud's birthday gifts to my mother were never well received, either being the wrong gifts or insufficient amounts of money. I think she yearned for her love and respect and the anger was caused by her hurt about what she sensed as rejection "by the whole family." Eventually she settled on Tante Janne's affair with Uncle Ernst as the cause of that rejection.

I assume Martha Freud indeed did not like Esti who had such a radically different style from her own. Besides, it is difficult for a mother to accept a daughter-in-law so profoundly disliked by her own son. When my father needed special care after a kidney stone operation, he was well taken care of, by both his own family and his wife. Martha acknowledges Esti's good care of him in a letter to her son Ernst adding, "... only he cannot stand her." Probably my own feelings that Grandmother Freud was cool and distant were caused by my impression that fondness between us might be a disloyalty to my mother. This was not the case for my brother who thought of her with great affection, which was apparently reciprocated.

LETTER FROM MARTHA IN VIENNA TO SON ERNST IN BERLIN

April 3, 1925

... Today our little Anton Walter became four years old, had a lovely birthday. He usually visits me Sunday afternoons to play together. This time he had a new suit and showed it to me proudly, whereupon I asked him: you probably wear this only on Sunday? And he, with his high little voice: No, also on Wednesday! Indeed, he does not yet know the sequence of days and just arbitrarily picked out Wednesday. Very sweet, don't you think?

Walter remembers with special pleasure their yearly fall excursion to buy new school clothing and he repeated that treat with his own nine grandchildren. I, on the other hand, do not remember any joint activities with my Grandmother Freud. I think, by the time I came along, relationships had further deteriorated and mother subtly discouraged any relationship between me and my grandmother.

Given this history of unspoken hostility, I was thus quite startled when my mother wrote and published a eulogy to my still-living grandmother.

Mother writes to her son in 1948, "I have written an article about Grandmother, got $50 for it, will send it to you as soon as it appears in the next few days."

MRS. SIGMUND FREUD

"Frau Professor! Frau Professor!—"Yes?" The frail distinguished old lady at the Chippendale desk raised her eyes from a letter in surprise as the door of her living-room was opened suddenly, without even a knock. "Why are you so excited, Paula?" "Thirty Nazis armed with guns are storming our entrance door!" The frail lady's eyes returned to her letter. "Surely Paula, you did not expect the Nazis to come with flowers."

The Nazi gangsters ransacked her home so thoroughly that there was not enough money left to buy food for the next day. This outrage was neither the first nor the last of her trials; but to keep perfectly calm amidst the most turbulent situations was one of the remarkable qualities of Mrs. Sigmund Freud.

As her daughter-in-law, I had the pleasure of living in close proximity to her for twenty years; and during those years, through war and revolution, through sickness and death, again and again I was able to observe her self-control and equanimity.

I was told that her greatest attraction for the young Sigmund Freud had been not her slender grace or charming features but her inner peace and serenity. She radiated calmness; and he sensed instinctively how wonderful it would be to have her near him after a day of hard work.

When they became engaged Freud was not yet established as a psychiatrist. He did scientific research at the Physiological Institute in Vienna, a poorly paid job in the old Austrian Empire. Consequently, Mrs. Freud's family tried to discourage her from marrying a man whose prospects seemed so poor.

She is now eighty-six and lives in London. In her most recent letter to me commenting on the pending marriage of my son—her grandson—she wrote: "Do you remember the prediction the family made for my future? It turned out differently than they expected! We were obliged to wait four years to be wed. It was such a torture. Today youth is more courageous; they marry and go to college, and somehow it works out. How shocked everybody was when the first rent of Dr. Freud's office and apartment was paid with the little sum I brought with me as my dowry."

How was Pappá when he was young?" I once asked. Her face lit up with a smile; she was eighteen again. "Oh, he was the most charming and fascinating man I ever met. Everybody who came to know him wanted to do something nice for him."

For me, the newest member of the family, the most striking impression of the Freud household in 1919 was its unchangeable, rhythmic regularity— so compulsory that everyone who lived there was caught up in it. At five minutes before the hour my mother-in-law, Mammá would look at the clock and say: "In five minutes Pappá will be through with his patient; I hope he is not tired." If a visitor was with her whom she knew Dr. Freud liked, she would say: "You stay! The professor will be glad to meet you." But if it happened to be somebody who might be bothersome, she said: "You had better go now. I am sorry the Professor will be in a hurry and can't see you."

At the stroke of the hour the door of Dr. Freud's office, which was connected with his private apartment, opened and Dr. Freud came out. My recollection of his walking through all the rooms is still vivid, just as if it happened yesterday. He was a tall, slim, slightly bent man; his blue searching eyes and a tremendous forehead dominated his face. A small well-trimmed beard was the only concession he made to the typical "Viennese professor."

Dr. Freud would greet the children and their friends with a cheerful grunt, smile at his wife, and, leaving in his wake the smoke of his inevitable cigar, return to his office. When the door closed behind him, my mother-in-law sometimes said with a sigh: "It is too bad Pappá has a headache; maybe his office is overheated. I had better check on it." Mrs. Freud needed neither words nor complaints to know how her husband felt. The performance of this hourly cycle was something like a holy ritual. It seemed to me that Dr. Freud walked through the apartment on a visit to his family once every hour to gather new energy for his difficult task, just as the giant Atreus must have needed to go down and touch Mother Earth to regain strength before he could go on fighting.

Dr. Freud had to lead a most carefully planned life to be able to accomplish his tremendous amount of work. From nine to one he saw his patients. At one o'clock sharp he was served lunch. From two until seven he again had office hours. At seven he dined, and then until midnight he wrote the books in which he proved to be the Columbus of the human mind. Observing him I learned that to be a genius it is not enough to have the creative spark; one must also have the courage and physical energy to persevere.

In the choice of his wife Freud was guided by his lucky star. She knew how to remove from his path all the common annoyances of everyday life. He was not permitted even to take a tie or a handkerchief from his drawer: everything was prepared for him. Mrs. Freud understood how to imbue the household—children, family, guests, servants—with such love, admiration and respect for the great man who was her husband that all of them submitted with pleasure all the circumstances of their lives to Freud's work and well-being. (My mother-in-law's attitude contrasted sharply with what I had been accustomed to see at my own home where my father, in worshipful adoration of my mother, adjusted his life to all her wishes.)

Mrs. Freud's task was not an easy one. She had six children to rear, three boys and three girls. In addition, the family nephews and nieces were left in her care. "I had enough trouble with all those children," she admitted. "They had the measles and scarlet fever at the same time, and I had to watch out that those with the measles did not catch the scarlet fever. We were twelve at the dinner table during these years."

But whatever happened, nothing was permitted to disturb Dr. Freud's work and schedule. During all the fifty years the Freuds lived in Vienna there was never a day when the soup was not on the table exactly on the minute. At each meal Mrs. Freud had a pitcher of hot water and a special napkin at her place, so that if anybody made a spot on the table cloth she could hurry to remove it. Only her husband was permitted to make as many spots as he wished.

Although Mrs. Freud did not directly cooperate in Freud's work, she was to a great extent his Egeria. Readers of the *Interpretation of Dreams*, which appeared in 1900, may remember that some of Freud's fundamental discoveries were made by observing his own children. Mrs. Freud was his assistant in helping to transform the nursery into a psychological laboratory. But the children were not to know they were being used as guinea pigs. "Above all, the family must be normal," she said.

For many years the world would not admit the validity of Freud's discoveries. He thus shared the hard unjust fate of many scientific explorers. He stood alone amidst a sea of hostility. It was Mrs. Freud's unshakable admiration and unfaltering belief in her husband which made the isolation easier to bear.

If God has favorite children, Mrs. Freud is one of them. Nevertheless she was not spared the cruel strokes of a merciless destiny. Her beloved young married daughter Sophie died suddenly in February 1920 from an attack of Spanish influenza. Four years later Dr. Freud underwent his first palate operation, from the effects of which he never completely recovered; it was followed by a series of painful surgeries throughout the rest of his life.

About that time, however, Dr. Freud suddenly became world-famous. Patients, pupils and celebrities from all over the world flocked to see him. These guests brought many new responsibilities for his wife, since Viennese hospitality required that they be entertained. Moreover, she had to help many of them find their way around Vienna since they could not speak German. She helped them find apartments and buy tickets for the opera. She went with the ladies to the dressmaker and to the beauty parlor; she gave them advice on how to transform themselves into seductive and chic femmes fatales—sometimes a rather strenuous job.

At Christmas and other holidays, as a sign of grateful appreciation, Dr. Freud's admirers deluged the house with flowers, mostly orchids, as they were known to be Freud's favorite. The apartment looked like an exotic tropical garden. "If they would only send their flowers on the installment plan," Mrs. Freud remarked wistfully, "we could enjoy them all the year round."

People with vivid imaginations, averse to bringing "commonplace" flowers, thought of more personal gifts. Princess Bonaparte, for instance, surprised the Freuds with two precious chow puppies. My father-in-law loved to play with them and enjoyed them very much; hence, to keep them in good health became a constant concern of Mrs. Freud. Nevertheless she held the opinion that somehow Pappá spoiled them too much.

Every day she went to the most exclusive delicatessen shop in the city to get fresh tender ham for Dr. Freud. But when, during the meal, he fed the chow dogs with Vienna's best ham instead of eating it himself, she was justified in remarking that the ham from the neighborhood store would have been good enough for the dogs, and anyway their favorite desert was the edge of the antique Persian rug in the dining room. So when an eccentric patient brought an exotic viper from a South American snake farm, she categorically refused the gift with the excuse: "I don't know a thing about the diet for reptiles."

Freud's last birthday in Vienna was overshadowed by the threat of Nazi persecution and by impending emigration. Books were packed, furniture moved; the beautiful home built up with so much work, love and artistic understanding was in a state of disarray. Everyone was depressed. My birthday present was intended to cheer them up a bit. I brought a huge cake on which was cleverly painted in icing a map of the "Western world." This world was populated with readers of Freud's books. A tiny sugar Eskimo sat on the North Pole reading *Totem and Taboo*. On the South Pole a penguin lingered over *The Interpretation of Dreams*. In South America an Indian labored over *Civilization and Its Discontent*; while Uncle Sam studied a volume of *Psychopathology of Everyday Life*. When, after much hesitation Mrs. Freud cut the cake, she reasoned: "This is a nice present Esti; at least it is something I don't need to pack."

In June 1938 they departed for England, where Freud became the recipient of various, international honors. Mrs. Freud never accompanied her husband to receptions at which these honors were bestowed upon him; she always sent her daughter in her place. Once, when pressed to appear she argued: "I shun any kind of publicity. I believe in the proverb that the best wife is the one about whom the least is said."

She certainly was the "best wife." In one of her latest letters to her granddaughter she wrote: "I wish for you to be as fortunate in your marriage as I have been in mine. For during the fifty-three years I was married to your grandfather, there was never an unfriendly look or a harsh word between us." This letter is truly a document of a successful life. To be loved and cherished a lifetime by one's husband is indeed an accomplishment of which any woman may be proud. If the husband happened to be Sigmund Freud, this accomplishment made Mrs. Freud *par excellence* "a grand woman."

Let it be admitted, I find my mother's sanctimonious and deceitful fairy-tale repellent. There are, of course, the usual historical inventions. But at least we reencounter the detail of the dog being fed delicatessen ham, and with two independent witnesses the story approaches historical truth.

Mother sent Martha her article. Was my grandmother pleased with so much adulation? By no means, yet, being indeed a gracious lady, she was not as angry as might be expected and even adds at the end some conciliatory words about Walter and Annette.

GERMAN LETTER

20 MARESFIELD GARDENS
LONDON, N.W.3
April 2, 1948
My dear Esti,

The manuscript you sent me was for me an unwelcome, veritably embarrassing surprise, which will hardly astonish you, since you are well acquainted with my horror of every kind of publicity. To view my modest person moved into the public eye is all too repugnant to me. Since it happened without my knowledge and without my consent I have to put on a brave face, which I find hard. That you sing my praise in such an exaggerated manner should render me pleased, but in no way do I deserve it, I can only state with Hans Sachs (Mastersingers) "You give my poor person too much honor." I am exactly conscious of not having accomplished more than an average person, only lucky life circumstances, like my connection to an outstanding personality have lifted me up. This is why your description oppresses me and puts me to shame. I hope I have not hurt you too much with my protests, dear Est. I can besides not deny you my admiration for your literary talents. Only at the end let me express regrets that your reader will not get a better impression of me than conveyed by that terrible photo.

I sometimes see your children with pleasure at the house. Your daughter-in-law is not only charming but also intelligent and competent. You would have your joy with her.

Good-bye for today, with greetings from your old mother-in-law.

My mother did not include this episode in her autobiography, nor did she mention it to me and we thus don't know her feelings about this response.

Martha Freud and her grandson, Martin, as an English Major

CHAPTER 53

Grandmother Freud's Letters
to Sophie and Paul

A few years before this exchange, a correspondence had started between Grand-mother and myself. Suddenly this woman I had viewed as formal and reserved revealed herself as warmly affectionate. There was also sadness about my passed missed relationship with her. (Our following correspondence was in German.)

LONDON, OCTOBER 10, 1945
  20 Maresfield Gardens, N.W.3
  My dearest Sopherl,
  Your dear radiant letter which I received yesterday, filled my heart with joy. Now I know everything that the dry printed announcement still owed me [*Grandmother is referring here to the regrettable marital announcement that Mother had sent to everyone*] but I still did send you a few wishes (to your d. mother's address). But now when I can see from every line of your letter that you have found such full and rich happiness, now I am really happy with all my heart and have the vivid wish to see both of you, face to face, once more in my life!
  The picture of Your Dearest has so far been withheld, but I will claim it as soon as your father or brother come by again. I am very sorry for both of you that you now have to separate again for an extended time but it is certainly the right thing to finish college and then to start dreaming [*I got married to my husband, who was stationed at the Navel Research Laboratory in Washington, D.C., the summer before my last semester at Radcliffe, and then returned to college in Cambridge in the fall to finish my studies*]. You young people of today are so much better off and how much more sensible the whole attitude to important questions of living have become! When I think of the

endless years of my own engagement! Because you must know, my dear child, at that time no man had the courage to decide on a marriage before a safe sufficient income gave him the possibility to maintain, next to his wife also a servant, as well as the obligatory four room flat! And waiting for all this, one lost the best years of one's youth. A woman's helping with her work was out of the question since she was not prepared for anything but running a household. That was "the world of yesterday"! (By the way, have you read the wonderful book by Zweig?)

[end of existing letter]

LONDON, MARCH 15, 1946

My dear Sopherl,

I enjoyed your dear letter of February 9 with all my heart. Most of all about the news of your glorious graduation. Getting "distinctions" is a family tradition, nevertheless one also needs some luck. Good that this stress is now behind you and you can rest for a while on your laurels. And I was very amused that the string of pearls motivated you to acquire a black silk dress. [*The Princess Bonaparte had brought with her to the USA my Aunt Minna's pearl necklace for me, a precious piece of jewelry at the time. My husband had gone to pick it up in New York City.*] Imagine, in olden days the dowry of every young girl always had to include not only a black silk dress but also a bonnet with strings, something that even today's grandmothers would reject as too old-fashioned. But I can only congratulate you to the silk dress which is always elegant without being conspicuous, and if one is as freshly youthful as you are, one can allow oneself something serious.

You can refute doubts about the pearls genuineness in clean conscience!

I am saddened that you have to move again. The general scarcity of apartments all over the world is practically adventurous: to have these days a roof over your head is like a gift of mercy by fate. And so I wish both of you that some day Your dear Paul will build you a nice little house, absolutely with a guest room to be able to make others happy, now and then! Besides also to be used as a future-room since I strongly count on great-grandchildren.

I think I have written you about Annerl's [Anna Freud] illness on a card. She is now, thank God, improved enough that she can spend a few days at the sea. Unfortunately we have still wintry cold and we infinitely long for spring.

For today, my dear Sopherl I bid you adieu and hope to hear from You soon again. To You and Your dear husband the warmest greetings from Your old Grannie.

LONDON, NOVEMBER 9, 1949

My dear Paul, although I only know you through pictures, I don't want to fail to wish you all possible earthly joy to the birth of your little daughter! May the loved child grow up to fill you with pride and happiness and joy. I received Sopherl's dear words yesterday, with an enclosed photo and joined in her happy anticipation of the coming event. And now it has happily happened!!

My niece Judith Heller, sister of Edward Bernays will soon bring you or send you a few trifles to complete your daughter's wardrobe. She was here this summer and has now gone back.

Be well, both of you, my dear children, with most affectionate greetings from you old grandmother.

Chapter 54

Disaster at Valløe

German letter

May 23, 1964

Dear Herzenskind,

I thank you many times for all your birthday gifts. All the books are very fine but you are really T.M. [totally *meschugge*] to send me a whole library. Please never do that again; otherwise I get annoyed. You are the only one who congratulated me on time, gave me a gift on time. Otherwise I did not receive anything.

But now for the big news. I have decided to attend the audiology congress in Copenhagen. The Congress starts Tuesday, August 25, and lasts until September first. I shall get to Europe beginning August, by boat, to take a rest. Will perhaps take the hot baths at Gastein. For my bad arthritis with the sciatica. True, I have not yet assembled the money, but there are prospects that I shall get it together.

I work terribly hard at the moment.

I hope to see all of you a lot and for a long time. I forgot when you are in Copenhagen. What should I bring for Annette's parents—mother? I will probably have to ask for many favors.

I think all of that is very exciting.

Enclosed again a check. Use it for a birthday gift for David.

June 14, 1964

... Here are my plans. I leave with the New Amsterdam on July 24....

Want to stay two nights in Rotterdam, want to visit someone on business. Then go on to Brussels. Two days in Brussels. And then I will go to Spa to take hot baths.... The best would be if you, you and Annette also, would come to Spa and we are together there. You have to return, nebbich, already so soon.

Yesterday I gave for a resident of the clinic in New York Hospital, who is leaving, a party buffet dinner for 20 persons. I am so tired today that I feel like dying. All I can think of is rest, rest, rest. On the ship I shall have a very good chance for a good rest.

I have not yet made hotel reservations for the spa. I would like to live privately and invite you for the week. That is what I would certainly like to do.

Many many kisses from your

very tired Mother Esti

The office is already much weaker again and some people have not paid me from the good times. Kisses for Annette and the children.

ENGLISH LETTER

June 20, 1964

Mr. and Mrs. John Krarup

Valløe, Denmark

My dear John and Vibeke:

I thank you very much indeed for your friendly letter and invitation. I am very much looking forward to seeing you again and meeting Annette's family.

JUNE 27, 1964

Dear Walter,

I wrote you a few days ago about my travel plans but have not received an answer from you. I have never been in Brussels and want to look at it and also at Ghent, Antwerpen und Brügge. Could we not do this together, I mean Annette, you and I. I would invite you.... I am enclosing a check of $15, give Ida $10 for her birthday and the rest for David. Please answer otherwise I will lose the way....

This was the last letter before the painful quarrel regarding the visit in Denmark, which resulted in 12 years of silence. After their reconciliation in New York City, in October 1975, the correspondence started off again, not so different from before.

WALTER'S *ERNESTINE*

Her ability to embarrass and scandalize me did not end with my youth. Indeed she seemed to enjoy her hateful behavior and did it on purpose, like in the typical example I shall quote below. I must give the social background of my in-laws. My father-in-law was the keeper and administrator of a Royal Danish Castle, called Valløe; his father was the Chief Judge of Denmark. My in-laws, who lived in a big house on the grounds of the castle, naturally wanted to see their daughter and grandchildren and my family spent most summer-holidays at Valløe. One year, in the early sixties, Esti turned up at Valløe, she must have been invited. Instead of coming soberly dressed, as befitting a visit to a castle and her son's in-laws, she wore an Austrian dirndl with white ankle socks. It would have looked charming on a 17-year-old waitress but rather less so on a 65-year-old stout American woman with bright blue hair and a face-lift. In fact, she looked like a mixture of a witch and a clown. Had she shown herself in this outfit in Salem three-hundred years earlier, she would not have lasted five minutes. [My brother naturally refers here to the Salem witch trials.] The white ankle socks used to be well-known unofficial uniform of the prohibited Austrian Nazi party. Luckily my in-laws were ignorant of this Teutonic preening.

My brother informed me, around that time, that he had discontinued his correspondence with Mother because she had behaved in an unforgivable manner. It seems that she could not sleep at his in-laws' house. The next morning, my brother claimed, she accused her son's parents-in-law of assigning her purposefully to a bed with a mattress filled with corncobs. As to my brother, the offense was all that more serious because, as he explained to me, the Danes have a very keen sense of hospitality and they were thus very hurt by my mother's accusations. I think one of the reasons why this was so upsetting to Walter was because he had always felt extremely proud and privileged that he, as a homeless Jew, had been accepted by this Danish aristocratic family. Mother could have done nothing worse than humiliate him in this particular way. But had Mother really behaved that rudely to her son's in-laws? She herself never mentioned the incident, Walter, in his old age had forgotten the crucial corncob mattress while still remembering her apparently unseemly attire. We have only Walter's explanation from that time. But he could have exaggerated the matter and used it as a pretext to break relations with his burdensome mother. Another painful episode that Ida, his daughter, remembers from that summer was that Mother had wanted to take her on a trip to Sweden, which her mother vetoed. She does remember a rather joyless day trip with Mother to Copenhagen. I too had vetoed trips my mother wanted to take with any of my children.

A few weeks after I wrote the above disclaimer, my extremely kind younger English niece Caroline announced (per e-mail, of course) that she did remember that fateful night. Hurrah for objective witnesses!

CAROLINE'S VOICE

To get back to my memories of Grandmother's visit to Denmark. I was very young. Probably 9 or 10 I can't remember the exact year of the visit. I can remember the atmosphere. Dad was excruciatingly embarrassed by her. She wore socks inside sandals when she arrived (God knows why I remember that) and looked very stereotypically American in Bermuda checked shorts. [*What about the Dirndl?*] I could feel that she was being disapproved of. She became paranoid, thinking that my other grandparents, Bedemor and Bedefar, had given her a straw mattress so that she could not sleep.

She woke me up one night and asked me to help her carry the mattress to another bedroom that was empty and change the mattresses around. We spent the night carrying mattresses around the top floor of the house in silence because Esti did not want to wake anyone else up. Ida also helped. We were not to tell Bedemor. However, Bedemor did find out the next day and was very insulted.

One other Memory is going to Copenhagen with Esti and she said she would buy me something. I really fell in love with some Russian dolls (the one that have ever-decreasing dolls inside). Esti said I was much to old to have that and I was very disappointed!!

Mother thus clearly did not complain to her hosts about the bed and may never have known that they had found out about that night's activities. I thus believe she had no idea of what she might have done wrong and why her son punished her so severely. Given the intensity of her fantasy relationship with him, this cutoff must have wounded her very deeply. It is one wound, however, that she did not choose to discuss with me.

WALTER'S *ERNESTINE*

In contrast to my parents and maternal grandparents, I married a very solid Danish girl, with no trace of hysteria and no family history of forced emigration. Naturally my mother disapproved, but luckily she was 3,000 miles away. By this marriage I broke the taint of the Schrameks. There is a saying: No cloud without a silver lining. The cloud of my emigration had not just a silver but indeed a golden lining.

A. W. Freud, Oxted, November 2002

With this last paragraph the false memory has ended. In this book full of uncertainties, we have now come upon three incontrovertible truths. One is that Mother beat my brother for not calling her the Best Mother, next that Grandfather fed his dog delicatessen ham, and the third is that my brother won the jackpot in the lottery of marriages.

Not a single voice is raised against that last certainty. Being my mother's daughter I question whether this was true for Annette. Walter, with his hypersensitivity to any slights—a family trait—and his difficult struggles and disappointments in his working life, could not have been an easy husband. He explained to me that he expected dinner to be ready for him within minutes after he came home, and it always was. He saw himself as the head of the family and made their major decisions. Just once, just once, Annette said to me, "I don't know what got into me to leave my own beloved Denmark, but it was wartime, and your brother was so dashing." It was the most intimate thing she ever said to me. But when Annette had a number of serious health problems in her later years, she experienced my brother as unfailingly supportive to her.

Unlike myself, Annette did not pursue any personal ambitions except the creation and cultivation of an astounding rose garden, a jewel in the whole region. Oh those lucky husbands who find unambitious wives! She devoted herself to her family, to moderating my brother's angry responses to perceived slights, when necessary, to protecting her children against his more irrational moods, when necessary, and to creating altogether a beautiful, peaceful, and welcoming home for her grateful children and any guests. My mother's "thank you for your hospitality" letters were not fake, Annette was an accomplished gracious hostess in every way. Annette's death preceded Walter's by three years. Here is the last sentence in the obituary their son David wrote for his father:

Above all Anton Freud's happiness was his wife, a woman of poise and beauty, from whose death in February 2000 he never recovered in spirit. (February 11, 2004)

CHAPTER 55

Those Honorable Brothers-in-Law

In the fifties my second sister, the one who had helped me get to the States, died a miserable death of multiple sclerosis. I, involved in my work and Ph.D. studies, could not visit her as frequently as I should have. A few months after her death, her husband remarried.

I remember Tante Lily's already fragile health when we came to America. She probably already had early MS symptoms, but I did not know about it, and do not even know when she was diagnosed. In her birthday letter to Walter, Mother mentions, among other worries, her sister's grave illness.

MARCH 26, 1954

You will be interested that Aunt Lilly [*sic*] was close to death, she was already in a coma and the doctors said she would not live through the night and one telegraphed Bea to Madrid, she should come so she could attend the funeral. But she then recovered quite well, will be brought home today from the hospital. She has, thank God such a good man who does everything possible in the world for her. The best doctors, three nurses, a full-time maid. He also earns very well, which is of course the most important in such a case.

Unfortunately, I cannot say the same for myself. I have my two jobs, in which I work horribly hard, but which bring in only enough to pay for the ongoing expenses. With food expenses I already have to be careful. Since January 15 my office has completely stopped. That worries me a lot. . . .

Although I have already reserved the ship tickets I am not yet sure whether I shall be able to travel, because I won't have any money.

Everyone is scared of me because I am "the poor relation." Thank God I don't need anything from anybody. But they all worry that I might perhaps. So they are all cool and unfriendly *including* your sister.

Once again, all good wishes for your birthday.

Bea, two years older than I, had been very supportive of me when I came to Paris, and then again when I came to New York. We were friends, but our life paths led us in very different directions and we lost touch until a few years ago. Unfortunately, our renewed relationship would be of short duration. She also died during the years I wrote this book. Unlike Tante Janne, Tante Lily was a stern woman, with whom I had not formed a close relationship, but I do remember her also as kind and well meaning.

We have met Tante Lily throughout this book—she was in Paris—her family having fled there from Prague—when we went to Paris, and later we went to Biarritz together. We have seen in all her letters from New York to Nice and Casablanca her untiring efforts to rescue us and help us to get American visas. Both Mother and I agree that we probably owe her our very lives. Mother's repeated hateful comments against her "brothers-in-law," which might also be an indirect accusation of her sisters, her conviction that they had tried to cheat her out of money, her often repeated assertion that they mistreated her when she came to this country and continued to mistreat her lest she needed money from them ("the family here was so worried that they would need to help me, they preferred to give up any relations with me," March 9, 1947) are painful in light of this history. Hateful comments against "her family" are sprinkled throughout the letter to Walter.

AUGUST 1946

I think Zafferl and I have happily left the worst time in America behind us. Believe me it was no joke at the beginning and my family, especially those two honorable brothers-in-law, trembled lest I might need something from them and cleaned their shoes on me.

JANUARY 1, 1951

You ask after my sisters. Tante Lilly [*sic*] is very sick, I brought her some medicine, but nobody can help her at the moment.... I am not rich enough for my family to make the effort to associate with me, they only know me if they need a favor from me.

Tante Lily dies and Mother's grief about her sister's death is quite temperate, as we learn from her letters to Walter.

POSTCARD

October 28, 1954

I have to inform you that my sister Lilly [*sic*] died Saturday, October 23. The funeral was on Monday. She was horribly sick for already many months. Bea will soon have a baby.

I sent you a long time ago some ink and magazines. Did you get the things? I also wrote you a letter you never answered. I hope you are all well. I am horribly tired, overworked and stressed.

Kisses for all, Mother Esti

NOVEMBER 14, 1954

My very dear child,

I thank you for your condolence letter. I did not feel close to Lilly [*sic*]. She was very strange in the last few years. I think the illness had gone to her head. It is true she helped me to immigrate and without her help I and Sophie would probably have been killed. Since I have been here, especially at the beginning when things were so hard for me, neither she nor her husband nor the Zittaus were in any way humane toward me. They gave me very many wise lectures but nobody asked me do you have enough to eat? Do you have a warm coat or adequate shoes? I did not have them.

The suspicions and accusations continue after Tante Lily's death.

LETTERS TO WALTER

JUNE 22, 1958

Dear Herzenskind,

I have to ask your advice. Zittau and Boyko want to swindle me out of my fatherly inheritance. One likes to do that sort of thing with single women. They want to sell the house and give me only a ridiculous part of the money.... Please, what should I do? It is, after all, your money, I don't need it since I can maintain myself quite decently, thank God. But you have three children to raise.... Please look into the affair. You are, after all, of the age in which one should know something about business, I would much rather for you to inherit it, or I give it to you right away, than allow them to cheat me out of everything. My parents' cash money disappeared in any way, in their hands. Please find out the worth of a house in Vienna. I owe my dentist still $300.

Many many kisses, Mother Esti

At the time we came to the United States, both the Zittau and the Boyko families were also in the process of establishing themselves in the new country and were surely anxious about their own survival. It is quite possible that they initially feared my mother's demands for money and that my mother's accusations are not completely irrational. The idea that they kept her at bay, later on, because she might make financial demands at some point is however absurd.

It is also true, in my experience, that money issues hover nearby in most family crises, such as at times of divorce, marriages and remarriages, illness, old age, and death. It is possible that Uncle Rudi and Uncle Henry were not scrupulous in their financial dealings with Mother. When Tante Lily was so desperately ill, Tante Janne, who took an active part in supervising her care, felt that not enough was done for her. Tante Janne became extremely upset and begged her to sell her jewels to pay for extra care, which Tante Lily refused to do. It became a bitter matter between Tante Janne and the Boyko family. Much later, when Rudolf Boyko died in very old age, his daughter Bea had to sue his second wife for the legal part of her inheritance. I am thus, after all, making a case that my poor mother's dark accusations may not be as crazy as they seem.

CHAPTER 56

Let Me Complain

I was a negligent and unloving daughter. Mother had taken the best care she could of me, somehow gotten me out of Europe alive, seen to it that I could continue my studies. She did not deserve my emotional abandonment of her. Even after writing this whole book about Mother, I am still not sure why I felt that, unless I distanced myself, Mother's negative karma would invade and destroy the little household I was trying to create and maintain. So I must take refuge in knowing that at least I gave her no cause to worry about me, which could be viewed as a not inconsiderable offering from child to parent. Moreover, it is not only in retrospect that I recognize this particular filial duty. Few words of dissatisfaction with my life did I ever voice, and I probably would not have divorced my husband, had she still been alive, given her ongoing 100 percent endorsement of him and the chagrin this would have caused her. Moreover, I think Mother recognized this gift. I believe it was the reason why I had remained "a good girl," all though life, from birth on. Mother was especially proud that she had done such a fine job finding me a good husband.

"It is so lucky if one has managed a favorable marriage for one's daughter," she wrote to Walter in 1956.

MAY 27, 1954

... I telephoned with Sopherl a few days ago. Thank God, she is doing very well. She has much pleasure with her children and is very fond of her husband. I think he is very competent and hardworking and decent and will have a good career.

"Your mother and I had a lifelong unclouded, harmonious, loving relationship," she told my children when they came to bid her good-bye, a few weeks before her death. "I hope you will have a similar relationship to your mother," she added.

Walter gets regular reports on her contacts with me.

MARCH 1, 1947
I miss Sopherl most horribly.

JUNE 3, 1951
It is truly sad that I have no advantage of my children and grandchildren, since they are the only pleasure one has when one gets older.

AUGUST 10, 1952
Sophy is fine and looks well. Very slim and smart. Her children are sweet, especially the second one, who is gold blond, very pretty, and very cute. The big one is rather naughty, very spoiled, but intelligent and speaks like a book. I hope she will become more obedient with time.

I remember Mother looking at the 10-month-old baby and saying in admiration, eine Blondine *(a blond child)* eine Blondine. *Everyone in our family had pitch-black hair, father, mother, brother, and myself. The blond streak came from the Loewenstein side. I am told that Father wanted a blond daughter, so from infancy on my mother tinted my incoming hair with peroxide for quite a long time, because I have a picture in which I may already be three years old and still have blond hair.*

GEORGE'S GRANDMOTHER
When I was young, I always dreaded visits from "Grandmother" as we called Esti. When she came, I was forced to give up my room to her, and, when I came to retrieve clothes or toys from the room, there was always a tall glass of foul-smelling prune juice on the bureau. Though I was forced to give up my room to her, I never got any sense that I was expected to be nice to her. The very name by which she was called—the somewhat formal "grandmother," as opposed to the much warmer "Oma" that we called my paternal grandmother—was probably chosen by my mother (who clearly detested her mother) to deliberately establish distance.

Given her notable lack of charm, and the lack of external pressure to treat her warmly, she cannot have felt particularly welcomed. Maybe that's why she would bribe me to spend time with her. She would slip me $5 or $10 to have a conversation with her, and I don't recall feeling particularly guilty about accepting the money. Beyond these few details, my memory of her visits is vague, perhaps because they became ever-rarer as I grew up, and finally ceased altogether by the time I was in my early teens.

I must contradict my son on two points. I explained earlier that grandmother (or grandfather) was the name generally used is in our family and the name that I use for myself, with my grandchildren—Grandmother, was simply a family tradition.

Second, as we have heard, Mother was always sending the English children money, so that her giving George money cannot be viewed as a bribe, but simply the way she related to her grandchildren. My daughter, the blond one, explained to me that Mother gave each child money after every chat they had together.

But my son is right, I did not enjoy my mother's visits and she knew it. We remember her words to Walter, "Sophie can never stand me longer than 24 hours."

"I visit with her about every six to nine months. Have not seen her or the children since last April but she does not make a peep that I should come to visit again" (December 6, 1953).

NOVEMBER 14, 1953

... I quite enjoy working, and it will certainly not make me sick. If I get sick it is only that I feel so hurt that Sophie treats me so badly. She was now for several days in New York and came to see me for half an hour. Neither she nor the children look particularly well, the only one who looks well is Sophie's husband.

DECEMBER 16, 1954

Sophie made it several times very clear that I am a great burden for her when I visit and so I have stopped doing it. I have never asked for anything without pay, and always brought at least $20 worth of gifts, which should, after all, be more than sufficient for a 24-hour visit, But I guess it was too little after all. They are full of fear that I could become a burden to them. Of all the many hurts that I have had to endure in my life, Sopherl's attitude is perhaps the one that has affected me most deeply.

From time to time I visited Mother in New York City where I also saw my parents-in-law and some friends. But no visit was long enough. If I stayed overnight, she wanted me to stay two days, if I planned a morning visit, she was hurt that I did not stay the whole day, and every visit ended thus in disappointment and reproach. She then insisted on calling a taxi to take me to the airport, of course at her expense, although she had just described her anxieties about lack of money and I prefer public transportation, never taking taxis if I can avoid it.

But the visits were quite manageable compared with the many years of frequent telephone calls. Mother called me whenever she felt her praxis went downhill, and whenever she experienced any other emotional or physical distress, perhaps once a week. The calls were frequent enough so that I started to dread answering the telephone. My son thinks I detested my mother, but it was her unhappy desperations that I could not bear.

MARCH 24, 1948

Sometimes I call her in Boston, otherwise I would never hear from her at all.

AUGUST 6, 1955

I telephone with Sopherl from time to time. I hope my ribs will heal soon, coughing and sneezing and certain movements hurt a lot.

APRIL 5, 1957

I have much annoyance and insults at New York Hospital. The chief took in his niece and she gets all the private referrals, so that I have practically no more private practice and do not earn enough. All is for naught, the parties, the gifts, the many friends, the publications, I cannot make any headway. I am very depressed. I am generally depressed most of the time. I just telephoned with Sophie. She is very well. The baby talks already.

Sophie visits Esti in New York City

As the years went by, my husband started to earn well, I started an academic career, and we felt financially secure. When Mother called next, starting with her predictions that she would end up in the poorhouse, I interrupted her. I cheerfully explained that we were in good shape and she no longer needed to worry about her financial security in her old age. She replied curtly, "Let me complain."

Part IX

Recent Years

CHAPTER 57

I Like to Remember the Good Days in the Freud Household

In 1954, I returned to Europe again, and this time visited Vienna, the city where I was born. I was curious to see my own reaction to the home I was chased from. There was nothing. It was just a place where I was able to find my way around.

The city looked sad to me. Part of it was still occupied by the Russians, many buildings still in ruins. I went to the Central Cemetery, to the grave of my father and grandfather, the latter of whom had a grave of honor. I tried to reclaim some of the stolen property belonging to my family but just did not have the strength and courage to follow through. The only thing I got from my father's beautiful collection was a little picture, the head of a peasant girl. Everywhere inaccessible walls were erected. I was under the impression that if I pursued the matter an attempt on my life would be made. I saw some friends, who, not being Jewish, were saved from persecution and death. I even met Erich Bruckner whose marriage to a Catholic saved him from extermination. Erich Bruckner, the millionaire I was supposed to have married, was as poor as a beggar. I went to Berggasse 19 and wanted to see the former home of the Freuds, but the people who had some sort of business there, just slammed the door in my face. In spite of all the disappointments I came back to Vienna, but not every time I visited Europe.

I am constantly amazed about what Mother remembers, or rather, decides to include in her life story, and what is left out. Her ongoing relationship with Fräulein, who had been, either in spite of or because of their mistress-servant relationship, Mother's closest, most intimate friend and probably her only confidant in Vienna, is, apart

394

from a few sentences, mostly left out, both in the accounts of early and later years during the Vienna visits.

But Fräulein certainly deserves to be fully remembered in my mother's saga not that I plan to tell my Fräulein's life story, which I do not know. I only know the little piece of her life that intersects with the life of our family.

Good natured, gentle Rosa, our cook, I was sad to hear years later, died during the war, her death being possibly related to a violent boyfriend who may or may not have been our useful Nazi protection, and so I never saw her again. In contrast, my own relationship with Fräulein, Amalia Seitz, ended up stretching over 60 years.

"Don't forget," she said, as I bid her good-bye in 1992, after her small 90th birthday celebration, "I came to the Family Freud in 1931 and stayed with you until 1938." Not that I would have forgotten it, but she surely wanted to nail down the dates once and for all, since by then she tended to forget this and that. She may not have known, for example, from what distant land I kept coming back for visits, but such details are not very important when one has reached 90 years. Still, she always knew exactly who I was, and, as just mentioned, she never forgot that she had been Fräulein in the Freud family for seven years.

The psychological literature suggests that one should help old people to remember their childhood. "Tell me about your childhood," I invited her encouragingly. "Oh, you were such a dear obedient child," she responded. But afterward she remembered that her mother had loved flowers, just as she did herself. "But don't bring me cut flowers, they don't keep" and so she got little and big flower pots that accumulated in her flat during my yearly visits to Vienna.

Fräulein must have been a tactful and discreet woman in her younger years, to maintain her place as mediator in our troubled family. "Your mother was really a moody and difficult woman," she once explained to me during one visit, "but with all the children on the farm, I had not been spoiled as a child, and was used to harder circumstances than your difficult mother. Besides she was often very unhappy with her unfaithful husband," she added.

After the Nazi takeover, my Fräulein had carried compromising financial documents from my father's private quarters to her own flat, and I believe hidden them there for a while. She had taken considerable risks to help our family. "Your grandmother gave me a very nice brooch to thank me for that," she once mentioned, and I was much relieved that Grandmother Freud had thought of that. In the summer of 1986, I was very happy to arrange, with Dr. Leopold Loewenthal, then director of the Freud Museum, for Fräulein to receive a medal for her faithful assistance to the Freud family, at a time when such loyalty was not only discouraged, but positively dangerous. He arranged for a festive little party with all the museum staff in attendance, flowers on the table, and a shiny medal for Fräulein. I had the opportunity to make a short speech in which I could, for the very first time, officially express the extent of my gratitude. I was particularly happy at that time because Fräulein had become cold and hard toward everyone in those years, dissatisfaction engraved in her often angry face. But at the occasion of the festivity in the Freud Museum (i.e., the old Berggasse), she pressed me to her heart and seemed to enjoy life once again, for a few hours.

"Sophilein, do you still remember the lovely party in the Berggasse," she asked a few years later, but then she sighed because her husband, her beloved Karli, had died and she could not grasp how this could have happened. "Karli told me," she said, "when Sophie comes you must . . ." but she had forgotten the rest.

A few years after the war Fräulein had become well established in a modest middle-class lifestyle. She lived in a tastefully furnished comfortable flat that was situated directly opposite our former house, on the other side of the Donaukanal. "Look Sophilein, over there is the house in which we lived together for so many years," she said to me, as we both stood on her balcony and she pointed to our old house clearly visible on the other side of the Augartenbrücke. Sometimes, she explained, when she felt too sad about her husband's death, she stepped out on her balcony to look at our old house, while thinking of the happy years in the Freud family. "Those were good times," she said, and sighed, but then reconsidered and added that sometimes not everything had been so easy. Walter, she said had referred to himself as a naughty boy in his letter, but really, he had not been all that naughty, just a difficult household.

You were not at all naughty as a child, only alert and very lively, just the way a regular boy should be. (Fräulein to Walter, February 22, 1948)

"Do you remember when we went to the country together so you could recover from your whooping cough?" she then asked. It was her favorite question, and must have been among her happiest experiences, being a guest in a small resort hotel. She then mentioned "the children's visit," of my son George and Walter's daughter Caroline who had, during their short stay in Vienna, once spent overnight in her flat, my son George sleeping on the floor. But Fräuli's favorite topics of conversation were our weekly visits to the Berggasse, or to my grandparents' beautiful summer homes. "Do you remember how grandfather always gave you pocket money and he always gave me money too?" she often asked me.

"They killed the Old Aunts whom we always saw at the Berggasse," I said to Fräulein, but she looked away and said each time when such talk came up, "What do I know what happened, I was not there."

But now I want to start this story at the beginning, or rather in the middle. We have seen that Mother mentions that Fräulein and cook had been loyal. Then Grandmother Drucker writes that Fräulein got married and wanted to buy a rug from her. Later again, Mother accuses Fräulein of having stolen things from her, after her departure, a mean and unfair accusation because Fräulein was scrupulously honest. Subsequently, we learn that Mother sends Fräulein old clothes and that Fräulein appreciates them. In other words, they had resumed contact as I would do soon as well.

From Fräulein to Walter
February 22, 1948
From your dear mother I received the first mail in April 1947, and since then Sopherl has also already written and sent photos, her letters are full of happiness and satisfaction. She is very happy with her husband. I am truly pleased that the whole big Freud family is faring so well. Please send them all my best regards.

From Mother to Walter
July 1, 1952
I sometimes get letters from Fräulein. If Annette cannot find anyone to take care of her after her consignment, get Fräulein to come for a month.

Fräulein being married and perhaps having other obligations is not part of Mother's mindset.

The war years separated our destinies. For us, they were the years on the road, and at the end, the devastating news of the slaughter of millions of Jews. Fräulein had to survive the Allied bombings and then the Russian invasion of Vienna. But Mother and I and Walter and Fräulein had survived the war, and her husband, Mr. Karl Seitz, had survived his military service. We had all regained the privilege of living normal lives. Although in many parts of today's world, war and devastation have become the "normal" everyday life. I was pleased to find two of Fräulein's letters to Walter among his correspondence.

Her answer to Walter's letter gives us a small hint about her life during and after the war.

German letter
Wolfsberg [the name of Fräulein's home village], February 22, 1948
Dear Walter,
It was really a great surprise for me when I got your dear letter. I had already heard from Sopherl that you had been a major and participated in the entire war. You even jumped into Austria with a parachute, showing a whole lot of courage. You were not exactly fearful as a boy either. I am very pleased with your photo, you look terrific.

I wish you the very best for the future. You are now ending your studies, what do you want to become? Do you perhaps have the intention of returning occasionally to Vienna? Once upon a time Vienna was wonderful but now absolutely no more. I am very pleased that you and your family have survived the war so well, it was lucky that you got away at the right time. I still remember the day of your departure so vividly. ["Fräulein accompanied us to the station."]

I like to think back to the good days in the Freud household, since then all the years have been so bleak. I married in 1940, my husband then got drafted right away and was always on the Eastern front, just before the invasion he was sent to France, and on June 27, 1944, at Cherbourg he became an English prisoner of war, which was wonderful luck, had he remained on the Eastern front he might today perhaps still be in Russia, came home healthy from England on July 26. We had a lovely apartment in Vienna, on the Obere Donaustraße, directly opposite Kai 65, but unfortunately it got totally destroyed at the beginning of 45, I had nothing stored away and therefore lost everything. Right now I commute back and forth between Wolfsberg and Vienna, so far we have not gotten a new flat.

You might anyway be aware of life in Vienna right now, simply desolate. I was just there for a fortnight, which is as long as I can hardly bear it there. It is now very cold with much snow and we have no heating fuel, I suffer in these last year from a nasty case of arthritis. Perhaps we will manage to get a flat in the spring, I would then move immediately. My husband is an employee of an insurance agency, he is related to Jo. Krisps, conductor of the Vienna Philharmonic (Krisps conducted a few months ago in London). . . .

[*She has heard from mother.*]

I was most especially pleased dear Walter that you have written to me as well. I often thought of you during the war years and assumed that you were in the army . . . and I also want to wish you much success and happiness for your further journey.

Warm greetings as well for your lady spouse and if you could sometimes send me a photo from both of you I would be very happy with it.

Affectionate greetings, Seitz

After her first few visits to England, Mother preferred to spend her vacations in Vienna and other places in Austria. Fräulein was actually one of the few people in Vienna with whom she was still connected.

LETTER TO WALTER
1975
... Frau Dr. E. Freud comes every year to Vienna. Last year she came at Easter and in August. We get along quite well, I say nothing that could annoy her, my husband is courteous and we make excursions and thus she likes to come. Your dear letter gave me much pleasure, I like to remember the Freud house, even if it was not always so peaceful.

"We always picked up your mother at the airport. She always stayed at the Hotel Regina, and afternoons we took walks in the Inner City and of course your mother always enjoyed buying things," Fräulein told me.

I returned to Vienna in 1960 for the first time, eager to show my husband my home city. Walter and Annette were willing to take care of my three children for a week, which was kind of them, although unfortunately my brother took the opportunity to teach my son no doubt badly needed better manners.

Half my joy consisted in seeing Vienna again, and the other half was the reunion with Fräulein. She was the only person whom I still knew from before the war, all others having left Vienna or been killed. There were many tears of joy, and invitations to her delicious homemade meals, and walks through the Inner City, and accompanying our husbands to the Heurigen *(the famous Viennese wine bars in the suburbs of the city). Together we went to Baden (a popular tourist town near Vienna) where my grandparents Drucker had owned a house and where Fräulein and Karl often spent their weekends. I visited the tomb of Grandfather Drucker, which Mother had found on her first return. Naturally we went by the Berggasse, not yet the later museum, but already with a plaque stating that Grandfather had lived there. We looked at my old school,* die Schwarzwaldschule, *from the outside because it had become a civil service building that one was not allowed to enter without special permission. Arm in arm, Fräulein and I went along the old way to school that we had taken so many years, from the Donaukanal, up the Schottenring, by the* Börse *(stockmarket building), across the Freyung, through the Herrengasse, and passing by the old* Hochhaus *(high house) that we as students had watched being built opposite our School. One could not have predicted such a return to Vienna, any more than one could have predicted the prior expulsion. Has life become so unpredictable in our century or has life always been like that?*

Both Mother and I found Mr. Karl most engaging, and we were exceedingly pleased that Fräulein had found such a good-natured and hardworking man. He always treated us with special courteous cordiality. He was a respected insurance agent, a jolly warmhearted jokester, a former swimming champion, a faithful devoted husband, and even freely dispensed old Viennese charm: küss die Hand, gnädige Frau *(kiss your hand, gracious lady).*

I still cannot quite imagine what feelings Fräulein nurtured in her heart toward her former mistress. Probably she felt a good deal of hatred but also mixed with some affection, given the important years they had spent together. Mother and Fräulein surely never discussed their respective war experiences. I certainly did not, given that my conversations with Fräulein, all through the years remained strictly superficial. Neither of us really knew how the other spent her days, what the other did throughout the years, what the other thought or felt.

But sometimes words fell that hinted at Fräulein's hard experiences during the war.

"Fräuli," I said to her, "I heard Bruno Kreisky speak, it was very interesting" (B. Kreisky had been Austria's chancellor some years after the war, having spent the war years in Sweden). "It's easy for him to talk, he ran away when we were having such a horrible time."

"But Fräuli, they would have killed him if he had stayed here."

"What do I know, but in those dreadful times, he was not with us. The way the Russians raged around here, nobody knows that any longer."

After 1960, I made a few further visits to Vienna alternating with Mother. And I spent half of my sabbatical year in Vienna, 1987 to 1988, the year of the 50th memorial of the Anschluss. Subsequently, I went to Vienna every summer to continue the important friendships I had made during that half year.

Fräuli and Mr. Karl continued to have a quiet life in their spotless flat, Karl growing ever more heavy-set thanks to his wife's ample delicious Viennese cuisine. She was a faithful, undemanding, reliable woman who never developed any personal interests, and hardly even cultivated any friendships, apart from the few other couples with whom they occasionally got together. For a few years, Fräulein and Karl fostered the two daughters of one of her nieces who had fallen ill, Hexlein (little witch) and Zwerglein (little dwarf) as Herr Kurt called them with fervent affection. This gave Fräulein a second opportunity to play a mother role. It appeared that these were the couple's happiest years.

A few times, Freud biographers came to interview Fräulein in the hope of learning more about "the family," but as a discreet woman, she had—unlike myself—no wish to spread gossip about the Freud family.

I stayed twice with Fräulein in her flat, sleeping on her living room couch. The first time Karl was at the hospital for a few days with a cataract operation, a happening of great worry and turmoil for her. He relied on her to bring him and take back telephone messages of his insurance clients—in these times before cell phones—and I noticed how anxious and stressed she was lest she made a mistake. We visited him together at the hospital and we had a cozy sisterly time, living alone in her apartment. I usually went out to see my old Burgtheater plays in the evening—the same as in my youth, but no longer as arresting—and, although she had no wish to accompany me, she would still be awake when I returned. I seated myself next to her bed and told her about the play. I don't think she listened to me very closely, but frequently she smiled and took my hand. All through the plays I always looked forward to "coming home."

But my second stay at her flat took a most unfortunate turn. It happened toward the end of the seventies, when a shadow had started to spread over my Fräulein's soul. "I am no longer visiting Fräulein," my mother declared at that time, "I can no longer stand her constant bickering against her husband." Mother herself had not exactly been a model loving wife, and neither was I, but she was right. I, too, had found it more and more difficult to visit Fräulein and Karl. His well-known anecdotes about Hexlein *and* Zwerglein *had yellowed with age, and his usual jokes had lost their appeal. He must have grated on Fräulein's nerves. "Shut your stupid mouth," "for heaven's sakes, stop babbling," "don't keep going on with all that brainless nonsense" were the phrases with which Fräulein regularly interrupted her husband's attempts at entertaining his visitors. He never responded angrily, but turned to me and asked in a submissive, little-boy voice, "Was she always so strict? Was she always so strict?"*

I knew from the beginning that my second stay at her house was unwise and more than she could manage because it quickly became clear that my presence had become a terrible burden for her. I was about to move to a hotel, but unfortunately I came down with a vertigo attack, which descended on me about two or three times a year in those days, making me unable to move for about 24 hours while constantly retching. Fräulein hardly entered my room in all this time.

The life of this couple had become sad and lonely. Although Mr. Karl never retired, the old man could no longer drive and they missed the distraction of their former little excursions. The few couples with whom they had exchanged visits seemed to disappear with the years. My own visits became more and more infrequent. I had gained the impression that Fräulein no longer enjoyed my visits and besides they offered too many opportunities for conflicts. Should I take the U4 or U2 (Vienna's underground subways) to visit a certain place, should they serve me tea or orange juice, was yesterday's TV program enjoyable or dull? All these questions were reasons for Fräulein's attacks against her husband's stupid opinions. Fräulein often did not feel well and complained that Karl completely lacked empathy with her pains. She sat in her chair with a bitter dissatisfied look and voiced anti-Semitic opinions: "Do you want to know why the Jews hate Waldheim so much?"

"Oh?

"We paid them millions of Schillings in Wiedergutmachung *(restitution). But the Jews are so greedy, they want to blackmail us Austrians for every penny they can squeeze out of us, and he opposes that."*

Then Fräulein complained about what she called Bronfman's atrocity propaganda. "But Fräuli, you must know that this is not mere propaganda."

"Why, I was not present, one does not need to believe all one hears."

I tried to squelch feelings of rage against this ignorant stupid woman who shared the opinions of the Austrian tabloids, while also holding on to a Fräulein who had been a true and loyal friend in times of dire need. Thus I merely said, "But Fräuli, how can you say that?" And she answered, "I know they killed some old people, but your Grandmother Drucker was in any case already very sick."

The exploitation of the housekeepers in the Freud family also frequently came up. Fräulein would simply not believe me that Tante Anna had left her housekeeper Paula enough money to be adequately cared for over her old years. She would bring up how she had to put up with my mother's terrible moodiness, her attacks of rage, and her self-centered demandingness, and how she had been exploited in our household. I believe that she was clearly hurt when my mother had stopped her visits, which is what fueled her anger. And then she mentioned with contempt how my mother had left her a mere thousand schillings ($100) in her will. I had had to remind Fräulein that mother had left her $1,000, which I had personally brought to her in cash. No doubt her sense of feeling misused and unappreciated by my mother outweighed the reality of certain sums of money. Besides, she was basically correct, because Mother had indeed not left her any money in her will, and I had simply rectified that situation with my own money. She also was not entirely in error about poor Paula who had emigrated from Vienna to London with "her family" in 1938 and continued to serve them there. Naturally, Anna Freud had left enough money for her care, but had made no other provisions for her, by then, somewhat demented old servant. Paula, unlike Fräulein, did not have a loving family. They had to practically extract her forcefully from her urine-smelling maid's room in Maresfield Gardens to ship her from London to a nursing home near Salzburg. She received there the icy impersonal care of indifferent nuns who, moreover, discouraged any communications among patients. But Paula's frightening isolation and despair in her old age, which I observed during several visits, is the last chapter of a different book.

The conversations about Mother and money with Fräulein were astonishing given that Fräulein never wanted to accept any significant gifts and generally was never willing to express any wishes. Then, as I left she would say in a worried voice, "Sophilein, you are not warmly enough dressed, be careful that you don't catch cold."

It was thus with uncertainty that I telephoned her in the summer of 1991 to ask permission to visit her. Perhaps she no longer wanted to see me? "Oh Sophilein, how wonderful to hear from you, naturally, come by at any time." It was a new, warm voice I had not heard for a long time. As soon as I entered her apartment she embraced me over and over, tearfully. "My darling Sophilein, I am so happy to see you again, imagine, my beloved Karli died. Oh, thank you for the beautiful flowers, I always loved you most in the world and then Karli, but now Karli died." She told me how Karl had suddenly collapsed and their doctor, who had come immediately had turned to her and said, "You must be strong and brave because your husband just died of a heart attack."

Fräulein, then 88 years old, told me Karl had been a few years younger, possibly only 84, but she was no longer very good on dates. Why did her beloved Karli have to die? Why, oh, why did he have to die, when she had loved him so much? There was a great deal of sorrow and crying, but her face had lost its hateful bitterness, as had her manners.

Fräulein wanted to continue to live alone, although her relatives in Kärnten (Carynthia) would have liked for her to move close to them. But she wanted to stay in her flat and could still shop on her own. "You know I am not tired of living," she explained to me.

But in the year of Fräulein's 90th birthday, 1992, she appeared quite frail. I understood her relatives' increasing reluctance to let her live alone. She had become quiet and withdrawn. "Yes, such is life," she would murmur, "I don't know why Karli had to die, but such is life." And then she sighed. Her aunt and nephew and the children whom she had fostered so lovingly all took turns to visit her regularly. Soon they did help her to move to a nursing home in their vicinity, where I visited a few times and noticed with satisfaction the caring and dignified care she received, until her death in her late nineties.

The last time I saw her still at home, it was an afternoon. I found her alone, getting out of bed in her nightgown to open the door with some difficulty. The flat smelled of urine and was in disarray. I seated myself next to her bed, as I had done at my first stay in her home. "Should I read you a few poems from your book," I asked her, noticing a little booklet on her table. "Yes, by all means." I read her a few amusing poems and we laughed. Then we tried, without much success, to solve a crossword puzzle. "Ach Sophilein, it is so cozy to have you sit here," Fräulein said, and grasped my hand to press it ever so tightly.

Sophie visits Fräulein in her nursing home

CHAPTER 58

After My Ph.D., My Life Took a Much Smoother Course

I always attended the International Logopedic Congress, which was held in Amsterdam, Madrid, Barcelona, Copenhagen, and Paris. On three occasions, I presented a paper. If one attends a convention, one has the advantage of deducting the expenses from one's income tax.

The most adventurous vacation trips I ever took were two sojourns to Mexico and one to Guatemala. All three times I became sick. That convinced me that I should confine my vacations to more civilized places. I explored the Rocky Mountains and part of California. Eventually I returned to the haunts of my youth, the Austrian Alps. I could not help it, but it was there that I felt most comfortable.

Vacation in the Austrian Alp must have reminded Mother of her youthful happy hiking trips. Her two vacation letters to Walter from that time sound almost happy about life, a mood I hasten to record:

ENGLISH LETTER

July 19, 1977

I am here since Sunday evening and I am very pleased with my choice. This place is outside the Village. My window and balcony faces the pine woods and two mountain lifts. I have already made an excursion by bus to Stallersattle, a mountain pass at 2050 meters on a little lake.... in the near future I will try whether I still have the stamina to walk up to one of the "alms."

404

July 27, 1977

In spite of the cold and lots of rain I enjoy my vacations. If it does not pour I am hiking and still do quite well, much better than before my operation. I return August 10 to Vienna where I stay at the Hotel Parkring. On August 9 I intend to travel from Lienz the Dolomite road.

Walter and Annette came to the United States in October 1975 and stayed with us in Boston for a time. They then went on to visit New York City where Walter had a number of childhood friends. He did not plan to visit Mother, but his friends, most of whom were in contact with her, insisted that he do so. He reported that they had a very thorough discussion of different train schedules. I presume no words were lost about the 12 years of silence between them. They thus resumed their contact and once again a relatively lively correspondence, albeit at a somewhat slower rate and with reduced intensity of feelings, resumed, with 31 letters between April 1976 and her death in October 1980. Liebstes Herzenkind *became mostly* Lieber Walter *or* Liebe Kinder. *Her English grandchildren came by for visits and got royal treatment from Mother.*

Letter to Walter

April 24, 1976

I much look forward to Caroline's visit. Apart from the $50 birthday gift for you, I will give Caroline $100, as much as David and Ida received when they were here.

After receiving my Ph.D., my life took a much smoother course. The VA immediately advanced my position. I received a considerably higher salary and worked many years in the newly built VA hospital in East Orange. Again I organized a speech and hearing department since the hospital had no such services. Commuting was not easy. I took the 7:22 train to Newark and then a cab to the hospital. Cabs were often not available in the winter and I would be late for my job, which made life even more difficult. I was so busy that every minute counted. I kept this complicated assignment for a number of years, when suddenly the hospital received money from the federal government to establish an official Speech and Hearing Clinic and had to hire additional personnel. I expected to become director of the new clinic. My last serious disappointment came when a man became director. When I inquired about why I was passed by, I was told they needed a full-time employee for the supervision of the Clinic. I was so furious I reduced my hours to 10 a week at the outpatient clinic. Not getting up at six in the morning twice a week in order to arrive at work at eight made my life much easier. I started to think about ending my career instead of advancing it, but I wondered whether I would have enough income for independent living when I was no longer employable or became incapacitated by illness. Private practice was the best solution and I tried to build it up. My European physician friends have by now all passed away. When one is over 80, as I am at present, one finds one's friends at the cemetery.

CHAPTER 59

Friends at the Cemetery

*T*ante Janne and Father were two people to be found at the cemetery, but their
T deaths are not mentioned in Mother's own story. Father died in April 1968 in
Hove, England, in a little house to which he and Margaret had retired. Father, born in
1989, thus died at 79. Our correspondence had somehow stopped some years before
that and I did not know of his illness or mourn his death, at least not at that time.
Tante Anna told me that father had been ill for several years and without Margaret's
devoted care he would have ended up in a nursing home. Walter and Annette claimed
that Father was demented, had perhaps Alzheimer's disease, and no longer recognized
them. Margaret, with whom I also took up contact during my year in London, dis-
puted that vehemently. Years later I wanted to know more about my genetic inheri-
tance and wrote to his doctor for information, getting a prompt and courteous answer.

MARCH 16, 2001

Your father died of the toxic effects due to a paralytic ileus resulting in a
sudden collapse associated with a cardiac arrhythmia. The intestinal obstruction was due to a neuro-muscular dysfunction which can be intermittent and
has the same effect as a mechanical bowel obstruction. The fluid and electro-
lyte balance is upset so the patient may become confused and disorientated . . .
but this is not any primary cerebral pathology. He did not have any evidence
of Alzheimer's disease. He was a charming erudite person with a delightful
wry sense of humor.

Kindest regards, Yours sincerely Stuart Weir

WALTER'S *ERNESTINE*

The final insult occurred at the death of my father who was legally still
her husband although they had not seen each other for 30 years. Father died

in April 1968. Soon afterwards I had a particularly rude and unpleasant letter from her lawyer, Frank Parker (Franz Pollak), the older brother of my
schoolmate George. In this letter, that was obviously inspired by Esti, Frank
accused me of usurping the inheritance due to her from her "husband." I
told Frank, whom I knew from childhood, to stop being a repulsive idiot, he
must have known the mental state of his client Esti. She was called T.M.
meaning total meschugge [totally crazy] as long as I remember, in her
Vienna days. Fortunately Frank did not pursue his correspondence but our
friendly relationship was finished. As a matter of fact, my father was virtu-
ally broke by the time he died; he had sold all the letters from his father and
his gold watch. I was the recipient of a negative inheritance; the solicitor's
fee was larger than the value of what was inherited.

*My heart cramps up when I think of Father dying in poverty. Margaret inherited
their little house, exchanged it for a flat in Brighton where she worked in a pharmacy
and maintained herself on a very modest footing. I visited Margaret several times
and maintained my contact with her, a friendly and unassuming woman of my age.
Tante Anna had sent her occasional small money gifts to thank her for her devotion
to her brother during his long illness and I took over that tradition.*

*Margaret had come to London from the country to look for a job in London and
had found my father's ad for a helper in his tobacco shop. Sometimes later she had
also become his housekeeper and his life partner and, as we have heard, eventually
his nurse. One day, she told me quite proudly, he had told her he would be home
late, a former (woman) friend of his was coming through London. Margaret had
made it clear, he was either coming home on time, or he would return to an empty
house. Father apparently thought it over and decided he could no longer afford to be
a "ladies man" and returned home on time.*

Margaret's last years seem to have been truly tragic.

*Here is the letter I received from the same doctor who had treated my father and
had been her friend, but was traveling during her last illness.*

March 16, 2001

Margaret became almost housebound due to her knee joint wearing out
and getting angulated. She was always such an active independent person
that her impaired mobility made her depressed. This was not surprising as
her flat was on the third floor and was reached by climbing about 70 stairs
from the pavement. Prior to her death she fell downstairs injuring her head
and leg. She died as a result of pneumonia. Her last days were characterized
by medical neglect, I am sorry to say, until she was admitted to hospital.

I did lodge an official complaint but did not pursue the matter as nothing could be gained.

Yours sincerely Stuart Weir

Margaret had nursed my father, but nobody was there for her in her own time of illness and need, a not uncommon fate for widows and single women.

CHAPTER 60

Tante Janne's Tragedy

Tante Janne died of emphysema in 1972 at the early age of 71. In my diaries, I had repeatedly expressed the hope that Tante Janne would help me once again with the transition to a new country. ("It is only the idea that I shall find Tante Janne there, which reconciles me with going to America," I had written in my diary.)

The Zittaus, as mentioned earlier, had fled from Paris several months before we did, in good time, leaving for Israel, emigrating from there to Cuba, where they had waited for their visas to the United States. Thus, indeed, Tante Janne was in New York City, was there for me, welcomed me with open arms in her old affectionate way. Tante Janne tried her hand at various jobs, once again, but unlike my mother, in spite of her many talents, she was never able to earn money on her own.

Herbert graduated from Columbia University, survived his army service, and went to a midwest graduate school—where he had a psychotic breakdown. Tante Janne's life turned to ashes. His illness broke Tante Janne's heart and spirits.

Before Herbert became ill, his mother had viewed him, correctly it seems, as brilliant, but emotionally vulnerable. She once confessed to me, much later, that she had hoped we would get married, counting on my sturdy nature to maintain his equilibrium—as she thought herself to have done with her husband. Herbert and I had indeed become good friends in New York City and I was thankful for his friendship in the new country. Unfortunately, Herbert then made sexual advances to me, but I thought of him as a brother, not a lover, and made this quite clear. Tante Janne mentioned once, albeit without seeming reproachfulness, that some doctors had viewed my rejection of Herbert as one of the precipitating events of his illness.

After Herbert had fallen ill, Tante Janne would still sometimes visit my young family, coming from New York to Boston, but after a few hours become restless, decide that Herbert needed her, and return home on the same day. Eventually, she stopped any visits and I only saw her during my rare visits to New York City when she talked to me of her despair and her attempts to help him.

Mother's comments in her letters to Walter chronicle some of the steps of the disaster and even Mother, with all her mixed feelings toward her sister, clearly felt increasing pity for her sister's tragedy.

LETTERS TO WALTER

May 17, 1952

... Herbert is still very sick, and the Zittaus have to spend a terrific amount of money for Doctors. They are taking it very much to heart.

AUGUST 25, 1953

Herbert Zittau is still schizophrenic, his parents have to spend all their money for psychiatrists. But it does not seem to help. I saw him the other day. He is heavy and fat and stuffed with food and flees into being crazy because he does not want to work. He expects his old father to get up and get him a match for his pipe.

MAY 27, 1954

Herbert Zittau is still mentally ill. Marianne has engaged the most expensive doctors in New York. I think $50 for one sitting. His father earns a lot of money. He is Director of an enterprise that rents movies for television. It is big business. That is now lasting three years. Nothing helps. He absolute refuses to work and sits and broods and gets ever fatter. It is a great misfortune. Tante Janne is also half crazy she is so deeply hurt.

MAY 15, 1955

My sister Marianne has let herself be run over. Her foot is broken. Some bones in her head and probably a rib. She looked awful. Now she is better again. She is already back at home.

JULY 1, 1955

Imagine, poor Herbert became totally insane. He started to become raving mad and one had to hospitalize him instantly. Now he is catatonic. My sister Marianne is also half crazy with grief and excitement. Don't write Sopherl about this, I did not inform her either. She is after all pregnant and not supposed to get upset.

August 21, 1955

Herbert is improving somewhat. He is getting thorazine, the new medication for psychosis. He is still at the hospital. It is such a great misfortune.

February 25, 1956

Herbert might be a bit better. He is back home since a few weeks. The new medication, thorazine, invented by the French is helping him a great deal. Janne spent $30,000 for a psychoanalyst who supposedly treats schizophrenia with persuasion and achieves cures. At the end Herbert fell into a rage, as a result of the treatment. The doctor is called Rosen and treats only millionaires, the Rockfellers etc.

Tante Janne, totally indifferent to financial considerations, did not leave a stone unturned to seek help for her son in the whole Western world, from psychoanalysis in New York City, to insulin therapy in Vienna and shock therapy in Switzerland. They eventually got into the clutches of Philadelphia-based infamous Dr. John Rosen who was believed to have found a magic method for curing mentally ill people. Dr. Rosen, Tante Janne, explained to me, first invested himself 100 percent in Herbert, made great promises, apparently took him into his house, spent many hours with him, and then suddenly when Herbert did not improve, "he dropped him overnight." Dr. John Rosen was condemned for unethical, abusive treatment of his patients—and deprived of his medical license in 1983. (For the rise and fall of infamous Dr. John Rosen, see Jeffrey Masson's chapter on him in Against Therapy.)*

Eventually, the new medication helped Herbert's condition. Again, we can follow the fate of the Zittau family through Mother's reports to Walter.

June 1959

. . . My sister Marianne joined her son in Vienna. He is improving and they will go for the summer to St. Gilgen on the Wolfgangsee.

September 1959

. . . Herbert is in Vienna in a clinic for mental illness, but he is better.

May 19, 1962

As you know Uncle Heinrich Zittau is very seriously ill. He has had two cardiac infarcts. He will stop working and they will move to Vienna since they don't have enough money to live here. Herbert does not want to move to Vienna, but does not earn a penny. He imagines himself to be a great writer. Marianne is horribly upset. The way she looks, she will be the first to die.

OCTOBER 6, 1962

I have to inform you that my brother-in-law Heinrich Zittau suddenly died yesterday evening. I had told you before, he had had a coronary in May, but he had already felt much better. His death was very quick and sudden. My sister is totally besides herself. Herbert is quite awful and she has absolutely no support in him.... It is now my generation's turn to die.

I am still glad that, in defiance of my mother's wishes, who insisted that a telephone call was quite sufficient, I went to stay with Tante Janne for a few days after Uncle Henry died, because she was in extreme distress. Uncle Henry had died of a bad case of flu, so said Tante Janne, completely sure he would not have died if she had sent him to see a doctor earlier in his illness. While widows often profess similar self-reproaches, hers were boundless. Thirty years of guilt over not having been a loving wife to this emotionally stunted man crashed down on her and kept her in agonized sobs for three days and three nights.

JANUARY 6, 1963

Marianne has dissolved her apartment and will be flying to Vienna on Wednesday and probably live there or in Spain. Herbert stays in New York without working at anything. He has the illusion of being a great writer. I only saw him at the funeral of his father, where he made not at good impression on me AT ALL. It is very sad.

Uncle Henri's funeral was indeed a grim affair. There had been a painful conflict with Herbert who did not want to wear a hat—which was de rigueur in a Jewish funeral—the rabbi mouthed some sham clichés about Uncle Henri's good life and Tante Janne cried without interruption. Soon after, she departed for Europe while Herbert stayed behind in New York.

MAY 25, 1963

My sister nebbich fell down and hurt her spine. If you go to Austria, visit her, she is nebbich very alone, and supports it less well than I do.

DECEMBER 22, 1963

Marianne has now returned from Vienna. She is getting from United Artists where her husband had worked, $1,000 a month for the next three years. She has taken a very nice flat in my vicinity. She wants to earn money with photography. Herbert is unable to earn anything. Very "hostile." She is now back for about three months and he has never come to see her. Wrote her a very crazy letter. It is such a misfortune.

Tante Janne lived another 10 years after her husband's death. She actually showed great talents as a photographer and took some beautiful photos of my children during one of her rare visits. But I fear her old years were joyless and terribly burdened by the worries about Herbert's mental health. One of her important distractions during those years was playing bridge, which reminds one of Freud's famous poor Dora who also spent her old years in emigration earning a little money by giving bridge lessons. But at least Tante Janne was relatively economically secure.

After a lifetime of addiction to chain-smoking, Tante Janne choked to death; she called me from the hospital to whisper a good-bye. She made me one of the executors of her will, which was drawn up to provide protection for her vulnerable son. This meant she trusted me and that our long relationship had remained meaningful to her as well. I was also glad that I could return, in some small way, the immense kindness Tante Janne had always shown toward me.

Despite Uncle Henry's long years of good earnings, Herbert was provided with only a modest safety net. I believe much of their savings must have been spent on his illness.

In retrospect, I am no longer sure whether Tante Janne or my mother had a better life, and who had the worse marriage. Uncle Henry was adept at earning money, but he had no other discernible social skills, to an extreme degree, and I now feel sure he had an Asperger's condition. It is uncertain whether disgust, contempt, or pity had been my aunt's predominant emotion toward him, referring to him alternately as the imbecile, the fool, the insane one, yet willing over a lifetime to sustain him in her own fashion. Whether this Professor Unrath knew of his wife's love affairs or not, he was content to live devotedly in the periphery of his Blue Angel. Indeed, he might have gone under without her. Why did you marry such a man, had been my puzzled question to Tante Janne, way back when we lived together in Biarritz. "Well," she responded,

I had been flattered as a young woman to be courted by this important established banker. I had hated growing up, with my discontented mother and my secretly gambling father and was very eager to leave home. When I discovered Henri's emotional deficits during my disastrous honeymoon, and knew that I had made a fatal mistake, it was already too late, I was pregnant.

She then stayed with her husband, she explained, to assure her son a stable upbringing, sacrificing any hope for marital happiness. And, I must add, Uncle Henry did have an excellent talent for making money and Tante Janne an equally well-developed talent to spend it generously and rapidly. The Drucker household had not prepared their daughters for a humble life.

Herbert moved to La Jolla and found a considerably older woman partner who remained devoted to him into his old age. They founded a satisfying household, including a beloved cat and a lovely garden, judging by the photos. Although he never took a regular job, he wrote very abstract poems that were published in sophisticated poetry journals. We remained in friendly contact, but we never met again after he moved to La Jolla. He, too, like our cousin Bea and my brother Walter, died during the writing of this book.

Chapter 61

Martin's Ghost

"*It was eerie,*" *Mother told me,* "*there stood young Martin at my door and I thought I was seeing a ghost.*" *The resemblance was real. I once could pass, to his sisters, a photo of my father as a young man for a photo of their brother, they looked so much alike.* "*Why is George wearing such a funny hat?*" *they asked.*

Mother was startled when I announced joyfully that I was pregnant with a third child. "*Don't you remember,*" *she asked reproachfully,* "*that I had only two children?*" *Mother was ahead of her time. Two children were enough for one family. When she heard that Walter was expecting a third child, she also wrote critically:*

LETTERS TO WALTER

January 7, 1956

I congratulate you for the coming addition to the family. It seems as if you and Annette have decided to make up single-handedly for the population losses of the second world war. Is that not too exhausting for Annette? First, all that giving birth and second raising so many little children all at once? Besides, do you have enough money?

But once George was born, he became her favorite grandchild in my family, starting with his babyhood, even though, as a mother she had preferred her daughter over her son. Here are her reports to Walter after her visits:

NOVEMBER 6, 1954

Last Sunday I visited Sophie to have a look at the new baby. He is very cute and well behaved, gains proper weight, and if one talks to him, he tries to respond in the same tone of voice, which is very very precocious.

MAY 1956

Sopherl has great pleasure with her sonnyboy, he is very intelligent and handsome.

MAY 26, 1957

The children are very sweet, the little boy is especially friendly and did not scream at all when I carried him around. He is big and strong and still talks very little.

MAY 23, 1964

As you know I went to see Sopherl. All the children are healthy and on the whole they are okay. George appealed to me the most. His development is proceeding very well. A very friendly, charming, intelligent child. Also well behaved and obedient.

GEORGE'S GRANDMOTHER (CONTINUED)

There was therefore not much of a foundation for a close relationship with Esti when, after graduating from college I moved to Manhattan, only a short subway ride to her apartment on East 85th Street. But, probably motivated largely by curiosity (possibly tinged with some small degree of family sentiment, though family values were never very prominent in my upbringing), I decided to make an effort to befriend Esti.

When I reconnected with her in my early adulthood, Esti was a lonely, embittered woman in her seventies who assumed the worst, and, as a consequence, generally brought out the worst, in everyone she interacted with. She was, however, completely unaware of her role in this vicious cycle; to her the world seemed populated by rude, hostile people. In an encounter typical of those she often related to me to illustrate the rudeness of her fellow New Yorkers, Esti recounted to me how, as a speech therapist, she noticed the coarse voice of a woman engaged in a conversation behind her in a line at the bank. Perhaps intrigued by how the woman's voice had acquired such a rough edge, she turned around and inquired: "Vy do you haf such a throaty voice? Do you smoke cigarettes?" (She, herself, had not only a strong German accent, but what sounded to me like an extremely "throaty" voice, though she didn't herself smoke. I could never understand how she could function as a speech therapist.) Needless to say, the woman didn't respond by enquiring about whether Esti could help to salvage her ailing voice, but instead reacted angrily to what Esti had viewed as a perfectly natural, polite inquiry. Esti was mystified by the woman's hostility, but it fit into her general perception that New Yorkers were unfriendly.

Life had not been good to her; she had married into the Freud family, but been rejected from it as decisively as it is possible to be rejected. And she had been forced to relocate and start from scratch in a new country, not once but twice. As a speech therapist, changing languages twice must have been especially trying. But, seemingly far worse than her experiences during the war were the injustices she recalls having experienced in childhood and later wrote about in the memoir she wrote for her grandchildren. Whether it was due to unlucky genes, or not having been loved as a child, Esti was her own worst enemy; she was, as I came to see her, a *victim of her own personality*. She desperately needed love and companionship, but she couldn't escape her own character flaws and the way they made her behave toward other people.

Despite having been rejected by the Freud family, she was obsessed by Freud and her connection to him. Her apartment was full of Freud paraphernalia, and she brought up her connection to Freud at the drop of a hat. At my sister's wedding, she repeatedly reminded my brother-in-law's mother about how lucky her son was to be marrying into the Freud family until she (and she had her own personality issues) finally blurted out that she couldn't give a shit about the Freud connection.

On one of my many visits to Esti, I brought along a woman I was seeing. I don't remember the woman's name now, but I do remember that I was more attached to her body than her mind, that she had the bad habit of leaving the television on all night, even when we were sleeping (and would resist any effort to turn it off), and that the dinner she once invited me to share in her apartment consisted of a single huge smoked fish head. It seemed strange to me, but I wasn't going to raise the issue if she wasn't, so we ate the fish head without comment. The woman worked as a care-taker for the elderly and made the mistake of assuming that my grandmother was like the other old people she took care of. Her first mistake was to call Esti "Ernestine." It was bad enough to use the informal first name, rather than the more proper "Dr. Freud," but Ernestine was Esti's hated name from childhood. The visit went downhill from there, with Esti barraging the poor woman with questions whose obvious intent was to plumb the depths of her inferior social class. The next time I saw Esti after the visit, she inquired hopefully that I was not serious about the woman, referring to her with a mischievous cackle as a "silly goose."

My visits to Esti rapidly fell into an established routine. I would get to her apartment, we would talk over a glass of Dubonnet, then we would move on to one of the many Italian restaurants in her neighborhood. I wish I had a better memory of our dinner-time conversations, and I wish that I had asked her more questions about her life, but my main memory of these dinners is of the way they almost inevitably ended. If it was on the menu, Esti would always order the Zabayone (a kind of custard made with egg whites and some kind of liquor) for dessert. When it arrived at the table, she would dip her spoon into it, take a tiny taste, and then petulantly announce "Nicht zabayone! Nicht zabayone!" and have the waiter return it to the kitchen. One evening, when my sister, who was visiting New York, joined me for one of these dinners, and I had given her a preview of what to expect, the two of us had a terrible case of the giggles, as my grandmother looked on suspiciously, when the script unfolded as I had led my sister to expect.

One other memory is of a dinner party she arranged for two relatives who, as she recounted bitterly when she invited me to the dinner, had slighted her in some way that she hadn't forgiven. Because she didn't really like these guests (a couple about my parents' age, from Vienna), she took special pains to impress them, dressing her cleaning lady up in prim uniform to serve dinner. It was downhill from the first course, which was tomato soup, served with a dollop of sour cream. When the man in the couple told Esti that he liked the soup, she responded with an obvious tone of superiority, "Really? It's Campbell's."

The negative quality of these stories is as much a function of inherited traits of the stories' author as it is about negative interactions with Esti. In fact, we had quite a warm relationship, and talked in a candid fashion about subjects that most young men probably don't talk to their grandmothers about; we connected at some real level. Looking back, I have the impression that Esti desperately wanted to be loved but mistakenly believed that she wanted to be respected, or perhaps thought that that was the best she could hope for. Her bid for respect began even before you entered her apartment; the "welcome" mat just outside of her door was embossed with the title "Dr. Esti Freud, Ph.D." But Esti put these defensive pretensions aside in her interactions with me. I believe that I was the last person that she connected to at a personal level, and I'm glad that I'm able to remember her as more than the old lady who drank prune juice.

MAY 30, 1980

George will go next year to Yale. He is very pleased but I shall miss him a lot. It was so pleasant having somebody of the close family living in N.Y. He is a very sweet boy and has inherited from his grandfather Freud, to be a great ladies friend.

My son and I are relieved about these friendly words, suggesting that the separation was not as unfriendly as we both remembered. Mother was in the hospital with her first operation, as I recall, and constantly asked her grandson for various services, to bring her this and that from her flat. It was too much for him and he started to withdraw. But fortunately Mother seems to have experienced this differently, at least in retrospect.

CHAPTER 62

Working until Her Last Breath

*M*other referred, in her old age, to her excellent lifelong prior health, and it is *true that she had no chronic conditions and practically never missed work. But as I remember our telephone calls and we peruse her letters, we find constant accounts of illnesses, one bad cold after another causing her almost as much distress as her personal and professional upsets. It is possible that she caught these illnesses from her patients at the hospital clinics, because I do not recall many illnesses while we were still in Europe. She complains in almost every letter of extreme fatigue, specifically her two long days at the Newark Veterans Administration, and it is also possible that this job, and her truly exhausting schedule in general, resulted in diminished resistance. Following excerpts are all from (German) letters to Walter.*

LETTERS TO WALTER

October 9, 1955

Once again I had a nasty catarrh with fever and feel again very tired. I drag myself to everything and everything stresses me horribly. Especially the Veterans Administration. With the 16-hour-long working day. To get up at 6.30 A.M. and get home at 9:30 P.M. But I don't have the courage to give it up. I know I have the security of the check.... Lately I generally come down all the time with something. I am getting old.

JANUARY 17, 1958

I now had twice in a row disgusting catarrhs. One was not yet gone a second and started again. The second has still not subsided. Here it is once again inhumanly hot and working gets to be very hard. I would wish one of you, you or Sopherl were rich and I could retire. It is so exhausting, especially the two days when I have to get up at 6:00 A.M. and come home at half past nine. I don't feel especially well and I am always afraid I will get seriously sick and not be able to work. It is so awful that I have none of you with me.

I am quite depressed. Many kisses for everyone, Your mother Esti who loves you very much wishes you an especially lovely vacation.

In addition, we have a series of strange accidents some of which we have already heard about, but there were others. In 1952, she fell down the stairs at her university. In 1953, a man in the street ran into her and she fell on the back of her head; in August 1955, she broke a rib; a few months later she fell on the newly washed floor in the lobby of her apartment house. In 1961, a child moved the chair under her and she fell on the floor and was badly hurt and frightened. She herself could not understand all these accidents and eventually took out a very high accident insurance. I wonder whether Mother's inner chaos, which she could keep under control in many ways, burst out at intervals into accidents.

The physical discomforts of illnesses were only one aspect of Mother's distress. The other, possibly worse suffering, was her terrible ever-present anxiety that illnesses would prevent her from working and earning the money she needed for her survival. Moreover, whenever she was ill, or even just contemplated illnesses, she felt especially lonely and abandoned by the world all faithfully reported to Walter.

Letters to Walter

April 24, 1954

It is really such a misery that thanks to Mr. Hitler the family is scattered over the earth. All of us are very alone. When I am not well, I have nobody who offers me only a glass of water. It is also very sad that we can never see each other and that I do not profit from my grandchildren. I am not getting any younger, am working very hard, and cannot save anything.

March 4, 1962 (a "Happy Birthday" letter)

Dear Herzenskind:

Thank you for your letter. Two weeks ago, already 16 days, I was vaccinated and since then I am ill and cannot recover. I feel terrible and working stresses me most horribly. I am already quite desperate.... Being ill is not at all pleasant if one is all alone and nobody even to give you a glass of water. Not a soul came to see me. Not even my sister found it worth her while, even though I managed to get Herbert on a platter a very good job.

Many many kisses. I miss you all so much. Kisses, Mother Esti

MAY 19, 1962
   I also work myself to the bone and am afraid that I cannot go on for long to work that way. What will then happen with me, I don't know.

But when Mother had colon cancer, she complained almost less than she did about much minor ailments and recovered remarkably quickly and well.

In spring of 1974, I suddenly became seriously ill. It started when I was working with a little girl, correcting a speech problem. I began to shiver and could not stop it. After my session with the child, I took my temperature and it was 41 C. I called Dr. W. Barnes who had treated me on several previous occasions and with whom I was on very friendly terms. The secretary answered the phone, "Dr. Barnes is not here." I said that I had a high fever and needed a doctor badly and that Dr. Barnes had treated me before. Her answer was "you know very well that Dr. Barnes is a surgeon" and hung up. I was desperate. I called Dr. Berglass, who I knew from Vienna, and he recommended Dr. Hauser, who came to examine me and diagnosed a tumor of the colon and admitted me to Mount Sinai Hospital. There for six days I underwent endless tests, one more horrible than the other, until eventually I was operated on for a malignant tumor of the colon. I was convinced that I would not survive, since I had just reached the age of my father when he died. However, I recovered promptly.

   Five weeks following my discharge from the hospital I flew to Interlaken to attend a logopedic convention. I traveled in the company of a woman of my profession from Denver. After the convention, we went to Montreux where she proved to be rather restless. Every day we had to take another trip and I, recovering from my operation, had an enormous need to rest, to lie in the sun and look at the beautiful countryside. We ended up in Geneva with its countless opportunities for sightseeing. Nevertheless, back in New York, I felt very well and resumed all my former activities.

Indeed, Mother made even one more visit to the London family in August 1977, in connection with another logopedic convention in Copenhagen, and judging from her enthusiastic thank you letter—I have not been that spoiled since 1938—all had gone smoothly. The gifts resumed as well.

   In 1977, Mother opened a saving account for Walter, which contained $274.16 by April 1979.

ENGLISH LETTER
   February 18, 1978
   Approximately four weeks ago, I bought a light blue evening dress for

your wife, to wear on her cruise. I had it mailed airmail by the store, directly. Please let me know whether it arrived and how much you had to pay custom duty, so I can mail you a check for the amount.

Naturally, there are wedding gifts for her English grandchildren and even for the new spouses, also up to the last moment.

MARCH 28, 1980
I sent Cilla [David's new wife] a package, let me know whether it arrived.

Once in a while, among all the effusiveness a more authentic comment slips out.

NOVEMBER 15, 1978
Ida's wedding looks very grand. A "real society" wedding. The journey from the Pazmaniten temple to St. John's Church took only three generations, approximately 80 years!

She had, however, not really surmounted her cancer, on the contrary.

Although I was pensioned off from New York Hospital, I had started to work at the Lee Strassberg Theater Institute and continued my employment at the VA Newark outpatient clinic. To my regret, I had to resign there because of renewed illness in December 1978. In the summer of 1978, coming back from a strenuous hike (I spent that summer in East Tyrol, in the Defregger Valley), I started to cough. This cough did not subside but became worse. Suddenly I had trouble breathing. Returning home I found breathing more and more difficult. Dr. Hauser admitted me to the hospital, where, following a direct bronchoscopy, a metastatic adenoidal tumor in my left lung was discovered. I refused surgery but accepted X-ray treatment. I received 13 weekly X-ray sessions, altogether 4,800 rads. My breathing, as Dr. Boland, Head of Radiotherapy at Mount Sinai Hospital predicted, became much easier. Side effects were peculiar dreams, poor appetite, and great tiredness.

Nevertheless, I could resume work in private practice and in March was able to resume teaching until the end of June at the theater institute.

I am truly awed by mother's determination to work until her last breath with no apparent slowing down with age and illnesses. This had also been true of Tante Anna and now I have to step into these women's shoes by writing a book in my own old age!

November 27, 1976

Thank God, I am still able to work and earn money. I ended last week a two months' long twice a week course on Speech and Voice Technique in Sarah Lawrence College, which is a very noble exclusive onetime girl college here and they were very satisfied with me. Besides I am consultant to a big medical insurance company in New York (HIP, Health Insurance Plan of Greater New York) where I also always get cases referred to me, although one always has to wait very long for the money. I feel for an 80-year-old lady I am still in good shape. I also still have my Veterans Adm. job, but I am not sure for how much longer.

MARCH 21, 1977

Thank God I can still earn money.

While Mother was a godless Jew, she surely evokes God almost constantly. Both her satisfaction with and her distress about earning or not earning enough money continue into old age and determine her mood, even at a time when she surely could have managed to live on her pensions, albeit perhaps without making so many gifts.

MARCH 19, 1979

I am at the moment not in a position to earn any money and am short on funds, David thus has to wait for his wedding gift. It is steadily going downhill with me, I can hardly earn anything.

DECEMBER 4, 1979

My practice is very poor and I don't know what to do to improve it.

Perhaps it was at that point of discouragement when Mother said to me in that bitter croaking voice used for such statements, "They treat you like dirt in this country when you get old. My ashes should get buried in Vienna, next to my father."

I don't know why Mother, at the end of her life, cursed this country when we had read many admiring comments about this country in her earlier letters. It had, after all, been a haven of rescue, and where she had been able to lead a dignified professional life. And why return to Austria, a country that had cruelly expelled her? We Austrian Jews have that curious nostalgia for our homeland.

But when Walter seems to inquire whether she can still get around, perhaps assuming she might be housebound with her illness, she reports indignantly, contradicting the above condemnation.

April 6, 1979

Naturally, I go out and about. I still have four private patients, am still consultant to the HIP, and since end of March I have taken a one evening a week job at the theater school.

I left New York City for six weeks and spent them in good hotels in New Hampshire and Maine. I gained five pounds during the summer.

I visited Mother in that summer resort in 1980, and she seemed unusually content. She reported with pride that she was still able to take long walks and wondered whether they had perhaps misdiagnosed her. In April of that last year, we find an incredible landmark. In this last year of her life, half a year before her death, Mother declares for the first time that she is not worried about money.

APRIL 29, 1980

Usually I am very tired and sleepy. It is very unpleasant when one is sick and all alone. Thank God I have no money worries since I have lived very thriftily.

Since I am back in the city I have the impression that my breathing is slowly deteriorating. I wheeze and rattle and on some days it hurts very badly. On other days my breathing impediment is minimal and I have the illusion I am improving. I am still teaching one class, but it seems more effort than it was in the spring. My tiredness is aggravated by arthritis pain in the left hip.

For the time being, without the bad coughing spells at night, I have no need for medication. When I do things that interest me and keep my mind away from my illness, I feel much, much better. Unfortunately, my thoughts return all too quickly to my breathing. I can only hope that the end will not be too terrible and that Dr. Hauser will help me.

CHAPTER 63

Mother's Death without Daughter and without Son

I visited Mother a few times during those days, both at home and in the hospital, and I think she did not quite believe in her own death. Perhaps nobody does. "I am not dead yet," she responded angrily to any attempts to discuss her approaching death. But she did specify that she wanted her body to be cremated and, if possible, have the ashes close to her father's grave in Vienna. She once took me to her bank to show me the silver that the grandchildren would inherit. "This silver flatware is for Andrea's wedding gift," she said. "Andrea has become a lesbian woman, and may not have a regular wedding," I replied, choosing this odd moment in the vault of a bank to share an important piece of information. Mother made a grimace of horror, hissed "don't say such things," and turned back to her silverware. "Perhaps she would prefer a silver platter," she asked in her former voice.

I hope, when my time of serious illness arrives, I can make the admirable decisions that Mother made. Dr. Hauser had hoped, he told me, to remove her cancerous lung, but Mother felt it would make her into a helpless invalid and opted only for radiation treatment. For similar reasons, she also refused chemotherapy.

LETTER TO WALTER
March 28, 1980
I don't want to live if one has to vomit and suffer all the time from diarrhea. Side effects of the medication. A few months less or more is not of the essence.

And third, she had apparently an agreement with Dr. Hauser to let her die in peace without last-minute extraordinary measures ("Dr. Hauser will help me"). She made these decisions even though she was not ready to die. She wrote, for example, several *desperate letters to her grandchild Ida, who had become a physician, begging her for interferon and other hopeful medications. We have the last two letters that she wrote to Walter from the hospital.*

LETTERS TO WALTER (ENGLISH LETTERS)

September 21, 1980

Dear children,

I don't know that you know that for the last 10 days I am in the Mt. Sinai Hospital with great pain and unable to walk! I feel very sick and have had numerous tests, until they found at least what they said to me, a metastatic tumor of the right pelvis. So far I have received two X-ray treatments and will receive three more. According to the doctors, that will relieve the pain. I am not too optimistic about it. It is too bad that your two daughters, Caroline and Ida, live in another country. I do hope that you and Annette had a nice vacation in Crete.

A friend is kind enough to write this letter for me as I am unable to do so. Love Mother Esti [signed by herself]

SEPTEMBER 29, 1980

Dear children,

Much luck to Caroline and her future husband. For the time being, I cannot send a wedding gift. It is too bad that I cannot meet Caroline's husband and the little Anne. [Ida's child, Walter's first grandchild.] Why don't you mail me a few snapshots.

I am still with great pain laying in the Hospital. Walking the steps to the toilet is hell. So far all treatments (X-rays) were for naught. On Monday they will give me a nerve block injection. Then the physicians are at their end with their Latin.

I *implore* you Walter when you travel in France buy a container or two of Veronal and pack it in *another* container, bottle of medicine or box and mail it as a sample *échentillon sans valeur* (sample without value) to me. The doctors give me nothing to assuage my constant *Schmerzen* (pains).

I love you both very much

Mother Esti

Inc. $20 for expenses.

This is the last extant letter, although Mother would live for another month.

Mother's need to pay her way, to constantly send gifts to the English family, including paying for the customs fee or for the alteration of the dress or fur coat she sent Annette, to bring along $20 of gifts for her 24-hour stay in Boston (!), to *constantly give everyone she dealt with, such as the nurses she worked with at her hospitals, small gifts of perfume or candy, not to mention the onerous large Xmas gifts she gave everyone who had done her, or might do her, a favor, eventually took on a runaway quality. Including $5 in her letter for the additional expenses when asking that five more people be sent announcements of Ida's wedding or sending $30 to reimburse the London family when they call her at the arrival of their first grandchild, are just a few more bizarre examples. But the inclusion of $20 for some medication with which she may or may not plan to commit suicide truly approaches a form of madness.*

I don't know why Mother made that request for Veronal of Walter. I don't think she wanted to kill herself with the Veronal, because I found some Veronal in her possession after her death and Walter certainly did not send any. She had, moreover, refused stronger pain medication, her doctor told me, in order not to impair the clarity of her mind of which she was justly proud. This was a poor decision. She did not need 100 percent of her mind any longer and she should not have had to bear so much pain. The day I spent sitting next to her hospital bed is now only a faint memory, so I must turn to the epitaph I wrote within a few days of her death.

A few weeks ago I sat near her bed while she held my hand and screamed in pain my childhood name, over and over all through that day. "Sopherle, Sopherle." She was the only person who used that particular diminutive of my name. It is now gone from my life.

I did not gladly hold her old hand. I could not find the words of comfort that I might have found in my heart for many others. I sat next to her bed with an icy and armored heart and waited for the day to pass to return to Boston, to my family, friends, and work, waited until I could flee in terror lest her spirit invade me and defeat my lifelong struggle to be separate and different.... The screaming of my name on that last day when I saw her fully conscious was her last complaint to me, yet once more the last time that she asked me to take away some unbearable pain, arousing my familiar defensive rage to ward off overwhelming feelings of pity, guilt and helplessness. (*My Three Mothers and Other Passions*, p. 328)

For the coming bitter account I have only my own voice, and perhaps my brother would have told this story very differently. I went back to Boston, called my brother to tell him that our mother was dying and that he needed to come immediately if he still wanted to see her. He said he was going off for a vacation in France. She had not been a good mother to him and he did not want to see her one last time. I said I understood and did not blame him, but I wanted to be on record for having warned him in good time. Had I known at the time of the intense correspondence they had had over so many years I might have tried to persuade him to come and see her anyway. He called her at the hospital, and called me back within a short time to say that Mother had been very reproachful that he was going on vacation, rather than coming to say good-bye to her and she had then hung up on him. I explained that Mother was at a huge hospital in which telephone calls get interrupted. But he could not be convinced and was very upset.

Soon after, Mother was discharged from the hospital and sent home to be under the care of a home health aide and her long-time faithful cleaning woman. The home health aide got sick and I was called to come to New York in an emergency situation. I found Mother alone, an oxygen tank helping her to breathe. She still recognized me as I entered the apartment, but then fell into a coma. She called for her cleaning woman "Johanna" in her coma. Eventually Johanna came and we arranged to have her moved within a few hours, to a hospital with private nursing care. Naturally, I should have stayed and helped my Mother die at the hospital, and I wish I had done this, but I did not and it troubles me to confess that. I have never canceled a class at the last moment in my 30 years of teaching and I could not do it then. I am my mother's daughter.

I called my brother again, to tell him that she was in a coma, and would die within a few days. He called me back within a short time and complained that Mother had not wanted to talk to him. The cleaning woman had held the telephone to her ear, as he requested, but she would not talk to him. I explained that she was in a coma, but he was convinced that this had been her last rejection of him and was very upset.

Mother died on October 29, 1980, at the age of 84 years.

I wrote a letter to Walter and Annette, to each of his three children, and to Tante Anna. In my eyes there was no longer any hurry about the matter. His son, who lived in London while Walter lived in a suburb, received the news one day before he did, which made him extremely angry. He also wanted to know about the funeral—would he perhaps have come over for the funeral?—but Mother did not have a funeral.

Well, she did in some odd way. The Nazis forgot, in one of their very few negligences, to wreck the tombstones of the Vienna Jewish community in the huge Zentralfriedhof (central cemetery). These old tombstones, many of them still from the turn of the century, are among the sparse authentic souvenirs left of the prewar Jewish life and death in Vienna. Mother thus found the tombstone of her father and his brother, Leopold and Julius Drucker, standing there—an upright, quite large, simple stone, relatively untouched. A few years later, Tante Janne bought the plot and had her murdered mother's name, Ida Drucker, engraved on the stone in golden letters.

I waited until next summer, packed the urn in my suitcase, and went to Vienna. I had invited my brother to meet me in Vienna so we could bury Mother's ashes together, but he was much too angry at me and, unfortunately for both of us, not interested in the enterprise. At the Zentralfriedhof, *I searched for the location of the grave that she had described to me in detail:*

You have to enter Gate 1 and go straight down the alley until you come to a tiny chapel, which is the most important signpost. The chapel has a green copper roof and a sign like a club above the door. There is only one such chapel. Immediately after the chapel one turns sharply to the right, don't confuse it with less sharp a turn. And then one takes the first little path to the left. Our tomb is the third tomb on the right side.

Full tombstone, with insert showing (false) imprinting of Esti's year of death

Suddenly there was the grave, overgrown with weeds, yet intact, with the right family names. I dug a deep hole right next to the tombstone, lowered the urn into it, covered it over with earth, grass, and fresh flowers. I did all that secretly because it was surely against the rules: for one, against the rules of the Jewish religion, which does not allow cremation, and surely also against the rules of the cemetery. And that is how Mother, or at least her ashes, came to be buried just the way she wanted, right next to her father. I then arranged to add her name to the engravings, underneath her mother's name, in gold letters. The engravings were badly supervised by Fräulein and contains an error, which disturbs me in my almost yearly visits. Yet these visits do not evoke special feelings in me. Mother's spirit does not reside somewhere under the earth. It resides in my head, in my character, and perhaps I have finally given it a proper rest in this book. Naturally, I wonder whether this would be a good place for my ashes as well, but I don't think so.

My apparently inexcusable behavior around Mother's death—although I truly never understood what had made my brother so angry—led to several years of silence between Walter and me. It was neither the first, nor the last, time that our relationship was broken by several years of silence. But Caroline called me in 2001 to report that her father had asbestos on his lungs and was given only a few more months to live. I felt a deep pang in my heart and called him immediately. I am very happy that we resumed friendly contact. He lived three more years and wrote his

Walter and Sophie meeting in old age in Velden am Wörthersee, in Austria

Ernestine *as a gift for me. We were able to meet a last time in Austria where he took a vacation in Velden am Wörthersee, a place where we had been with our mother and that evoked happy memories in him. I was fortuitously in Vienna at the same time and took the four-hour train ride to visit him. We had a quiet warm good-bye. Our last exchange is recorded earlier in this book. My brother's death by cancer is very sad. I had hoped that he might read this book one day, although he would not have liked it. He never liked what I wrote.*

OBITUARY WRITTEN BY WALTER'S SON DAVID FREUD
The Times Register, February 25, 2004
ANTON FREUD, Grandson of Sigmund, who captured a German air-base and became a respected chemist.

A grandson of Sigmund Freud, Anton Freud fled Nazi-occupied Vienna in 1938, later recalling that Freud's fame meant that no Jewish family had an easier escape.

During the war he served with the Special Operations Executive, and in April 1945 he was parachuted into Austria and single-handedly took command of a German-held airfield. Tall, dark, handsome and superbly fit, he briefly became the stuff of legend, and the details of that night-time parachute drop never deserted him.

Landing far from any visible colleague because of an unexpected wind, he set off, first alone on foot, later in a commandeered fire-engine with the local mayor, for the Zeltweg airfield. "I am Lieutenant Freud of the British 8th Army and I have come to take over this aerodrome," he announced to the compliant Germans who promptly threw a banquet in his honour, at which each officer came separately to whisper that personally he had never had anything against Jews.

It was, however difficult for Anton Freud—who was never a member of the 8th Army—to make radio contact with his SOE masters in London and register his achievements. As a result, after a hazardous journey over the Alps, he arrived at the British Embassy in Paris to a cool welcome. Though he left the army with rank of major, nothing was ever said of his capture of Zeltweg, which he resented.

Anton Walter Freud was born in Vienna in 1921, the first child of Sigmund Freud's eldest son Jean-Martin (Martin) and his wife Ernestine (Esti) Drucker. Just as his father was named after the eminent physician Jean-Martin Charcot, so under grandfatherly pressure he was named after Anton von Freund, a Hungarian sponsor of psychoanalysis recently deceased. To his wife and English friends Anton became Tony, though he preferred A.W.

Growing up in daily contact with the orderly intellectual household at 19 Berggasse—Martin's family lived just around the corner on Franz-Josef Kai—was an asset to be set against Martin and Esti's stormy marriage.

The 1938 political crisis gave Anton Walter's parents the chance to go their separate ways: Sophie and her mother to Paris, Martin and Anton Walter to London. Family loyalties remained divided that way, and Anton always defended his father on charges that he strayed from the marriage.

Anton was 18 and a student at Loughborough College when he was interned as an enemy alien in the summer of 1940, when British panic soared after the Germans conquered France. Shortly afterwards he was deported to Australia on the notorious SS *Dunera*. On that punitive nine-week journey the internees were treated as criminals and enemies, though Freud himself was not mistreated and mostly remembers playing bridge. As the true loyalties of the deportees were discovered, he was among the first to be sent back to England, once again thanks to his name.

He joined the Pioneer Corps, the army division for non-citizens fighting on the Allied side, and after a frustrating 18 months confined to menial jobs he was selected to train as an officer with the SOE.

Immediately after the war he served with a war crimes investigation unit and was responsible for bringing to justice the manufacturers and suppliers of the Zyklon-B gas used in the death camps. But he ached to marry and begin a normal life. After being demobilized in September 1946 he married Annette Krarup, a Danish aristocrat whom he had met in Copenhagen while investigating the Krupp armaments family.

Becoming a British citizen, and feeling that he had to prove himself independently of his name, he embarked upon a solid career as an industrial chemist. Resuming his studies at Loughborough, he graduated with a degree in chemical engineering and worked for British Oxygen Corporation, then for British Nylon Spinners in Pontypool.

In 1957 British Hydrocarbons recruited him back to London, where through a series of mergers his job was quickly absorbed into BP Chemicals. Plans he had drawn up to produce nylon, then much sought-after, were reversed, and he was left in a frustrating secondary role for the rest of his career, although he remained with BP until his retirement at the age of 55 in 1977.

Having been disappointed by the official reception of his military adventures in 1945, he salvaged his pride by writing his autobiography for home consumption. In his last decade German and Austrian journalists sought him out for the details of his adventure.

With his sister Sophie he was also in demand as the last remaining witness to the marriage of Sigmund and Martha Freud. He especially loved and admired his grandmother, whom he remembered as a civilising influence in a demanding family, and when in the 1980s a BBC drama raised the possibility that Freud had had a sexual relationship with his sister-in-law Minna, he publicly repudiated the idea. Most recently he told a journalist for the *Times Literary Supplement* that if such an affair took place it must have been with Martha's permission.

While respecting his grandfather's name, he was an eminently practical man who cherished family life. The partly medieval home in Surrey, with the towering rose gardens and the staircase plastered from floor to ceiling with family photographs, was his abiding pleasure.

Above all Anton Freud's happiness was his wife, a woman of poise and beauty, from whose death in February 2000 he never recovered in spirit.

He is survived by his son and two daughters.

Anton Freud, chemist and SOE officer, was born on April 3, 1921. He died on February 8, 2004, aged 82.

Unlike my father, Mother was not impoverished when she died and did not have to sell her letters from her father-in-law to survive. Her professional and financial success far surpassed his. Indeed, she left $24,000 (I think) to her four granddaughters.

I had asked her to leave her money to her grandchildren, rather than her children, and she followed my advice, but excluded her two grandsons, which was strange, given that George was the only grandchild with whom she had established a warm personal relationship. He was the recipient of a big silver platter, which I fear he may not appreciate. She explained her decisions by pointing out that women had harder lives than men. Fortunately, my mother's inheritance did not create bad feelings; the English nieces shared the money with their brother and my son did not appear perturbed.

Mother had been lonely much of her later life, perhaps even much of her whole life, and she thus died alone, without her daughter and without her son. But she was well cared for. It was not a terrible death, not like her mother's death in a gas chamber in Auschwitz. I myself, also hope to die in a bed, a great privilege for a European twentieth-century Jew. I am not sure who will be standing around that hoped-for bed. My children seem to care about me each in her or his inimitable ways but, as Andrea points out at the beginning of this story, history has such a fatal way of repeating itself. In any case, I promise not to call out anyone's name in desperation. Instead, I will turn my head to the wall and I will think of global warming, the rising oceans, the felling of forests for quick profits, the drilling of oil in beautiful wildlands, the plagues that will invade our countries, with an occasional atom bomb explosion. I shall think of the sorrow of my children for their children and of the sorrow of my grandchildren for their children in this harsh new world, and I will leave the world with relief thinking of all that will have been spared me.

But it is not I, but Mother, who should have the last words in her own story.

I am stopping with what has become a sort of biography. I do not believe anything interesting worth recording will happen to me now. I wrote down these memories because I wanted my descendants to be aware of where they came from. And perhaps it can teach them something about what life is going to be. In my own life, I was not guided by any philosophy. I attempted to live and especially to act according to what Freud called "the reality principle." I tried to select or plan my actions in such a way that in the long run—as much as circumstances made it possible—they would be advantageous to the future course of my life. I am sure that I made many serious mistakes in my planning and selecting. My equipment for living was favorable. I was born into a well-to-do family and reared in a culturally rich environment. I was very pretty, fairly intelligent, and had an inborn charm. Whether I have used these endowments wisely may be assessed by my present offspring and future descendants. It is to those that this work is dedicated.

November 1979 (Mother)
Spring 2006 (Sophie)

Acknowledgments

My sincere thanks extend to the many people who have helped me to write and launch this book. My special appreciation goes out to Professor Stein Bråten whose invitation to the Institute for Higher Studies in Oslo, Norway, started me on this writing project. I am also very grateful and much indebted to my German editor and dear friend Krista Maria Schädlich who encouraged me for years to write this book and then helped to cut it down to readable size.

Esti Freud's article, *Mrs. Sigmund Freud,* was published a first time in *The Menorah Journal,* 1948, and a second time in *The Jewish Spectator,* 1980, Vol. 45(1): 29–31. *The Jewish Spectator* gave permission for the reproduction.

Part of the chapter on my Fräulein appeared first under the title "Das Fräuli und die Familie Freud," in *Die Frauen Wiens,* ed. E. Geber, S. Rotter, and M. Schneider Herausgeber (Vienna: Verlag der Apfel, 1992).

The quote from Father is taken from his book: *Glory Reflected: Sigmund Freud—Man and Father by His Eldest Son* (London: Angus and Robertson, 1957).

References

Breger, Louis. *Darkness in the Midst of Vision.* New York: John Wiley and Sons, 2000.

Freud, Ernestine. "Mrs. Sigmund Freud." *The Jewish Spectator,* 1980, Vol. 45(1): 29–31.

Freud, Martin. *Glory Reflected: Sigmund Freud—Man and Father by His Eldest Son.* London: Angus and Robertson, 1957.

Freud, Sigmund. *The Diary of Sigmund Freud.* Annotated and edited by Michael Molnar. London: Freud Museum Publications, 1992.

Freud, Sophie. *My Three Mothers and Other Passions.* New York: New York University Press, 1988.

———. "Das Fräuli und die Familie Freud." In *Die Frauen Wiens,* edited by Eva Geber, Sonja Rotter, and Marietta Schneider. Vienna: Verlag der Apfel, 1992.

Jones, Ernest. *The Life and Work of Sigmund Freud,* vol. 1. New York: Basic Books, 1953.

Klang, Marcel, ed. *The Intellectual Elite of Austria: A Handbook for the Leaders in Culture and Commerce* [in German]. Vienna: Eduard Castle, 1936.

Krüll, Marianne. *Freud and His Father.* New York: W. W. Norton, 1986.

Masson, J. Moussaieff. *Against Therapy.* Monroe, ME: Common Courage Press, 1994.

Phillips, Robert, ed. *Letters of Delmore Schwartz.* Princeton, NJ: Ontario Review Press, 1984.

Index

Page numbers in italics refer to photographs.

About the Author

SOPHIE FREUD is a distinguished and internationally known Professor Emeritus of Social Work at Simmons College. Also previously a practicing Clinical Social Worker and Supervisor, she was born in Vienna and lived near her famed grandfather, psychologist Sigmund Freud, until she emigrated with her mother, first to France then to the United States. Sophie Freud attended Harvard College and the Simmons School of Social Work. She continues teaching and writing in her retirement.